SHIKI TSUKAI

4

Story by To-ru Zekuu

Art by Yuna Takanagi

Translated and adapted by Mayumi Kobayashi

Lettered by North Market Street Graphics

Ballantine Books · New York

P9-AOC-025

Shiki Tsukai volume 4 is a work of fiction. Names, characters, places, and incidents are the products of the author's imagination or are used fictitiously. Any resemblance to actual events, locales, or persons, living or dead, is entirely coincidental.

A Del Rey Manga/Kodansha Trade Paperback Original

Shiki Tsukai volume 4 copyright © 2007 by To-ru Zekuu and Yuna Takanagi
English translation copyright © 2008 by To-ru Zekuu and Yuna Takanagi

All rights reserved.

Published in the United States by Del Rey Books, an imprint of The Random House Publishing Group, a division of Random House, Inc., New York.

DEL REY is a registered trademark and the Del Rey colophon is a trademark of Random House, Inc.

Publication rights arranged through Kodansha Ltd.

First published in Japan in 2007 by Kodansha Ltd., Tokyo

ISBN 978-0-345-50665-8

Printed in the United States of America

www.delreymanga.com

9 8 7 6 5 4 3 2 1

Translator and adaptor: Mayumi Kobayashi
Lettering: NMSG

Contents

Introductory Note

Since *Shiki Tsukai* is about the seasons, calendars are very important to the story. Two types of calendars are referenced throughout this series. One is the Gregorian calendar, the familiar 12-month January-through-December system that is commonly used throughout the West and in many other parts of the world. But the lunisolar calendar—the one that was used in Japan until 1873, when Japan adopted the Gregorian calendar—is also referred to often. A lunisolar calendar is one that indicates both the moon phase and the time of the solar year.

Under the Gregorian calendar, in Japanese the months are literally called "first month (January)," "second month (February)," "third month (March)," etc.

But under the lunisolar calendar, each month has a name specifically tied to the seasons. They are as follows, with the names literally translated, and where the name is derived from.

January = *Mutsuki*, affection month. Family and friends get together to celebrate the New Year.

February = *Kisaragi*, layering clothes month. This month, wear layers for protection from the cold.

March = *Yayoi*, new life month. Derived from Spring.

April = *Uzuki*, Deutzias flower month. This month is when the Deutzias flowers bloom.

May = *Satsuki*, crop month. This is the best month to plant crops.

June = *Minazuki*, water month. End of the rainy season.

July = *Fumizuki*, letter month. Derived from the *Tanabata* holiday where you write a wish or a song on a piece of paper and hang it on bamboo.

August = *Hazuki*, leaf month. Month when the leaves fall.

September = *Nagazuki*, long month. The time of year when nights grow longer.

October = *Kannazuki*, God month. Gods gather in October for an annual meeting at the Izumo shrine.

November = *Shimotsuki*, frost month. The first frost of the Winter.

December = *Shiwasu*, priest month. Priests are busy making end-of-year prayers and blessings.

The lunisolar calendar is also divided into 24 *sekki*. The 24 *sekki* are days that divide the lunisolar calendar into 24 equal sections and have special names to mark the change in seasons. The dates below are approximate and shift due to the differences in the lunisolar and Gregorian calendars.

Rishhun. February 4. First day of Spring.

Usui. February 19.

Keichitsu. March 5.

Shunbun. March 20. Vernal equinox. Middle of Spring.

Seimei. April 5.

Kokuu. April 20.

Rikka. May 5. First day of Summer.

Shouman. May 21.

Boushu. June 6.

Geshi. June 21. Summer solstice. Middle of Summer.

Shousho. July 7.

Taisho. July 23.

Rishuu. August 7. First day of Autumn.

Shouho. August 23.

Hakuro. September 7.

Shuubun. September 23. Autumnal equinox. Middle of Autumn.

Kanro. October 8.

Shoukou. October 23.

Rittou. November 7. First day of Winter.

Shousetsu. November 22.

Taisetsu. December 7.

Touji. December 22. Winter solstice. Middle of Winter.

Shoukan. January 5.

Daikan. January 20.

Honorifics Explained

Throughout the Del Rey Manga books, you will find Japanese honorifics left intact in the translations. For those not familiar with how the Japanese use honorifics and, more important, how they differ from American honorifics, we present this brief overview.

Politeness has always been a critical facet of Japanese culture. Ever since the feudal era, when Japan was a highly stratified society, use of honorifics—which can be defined as polite speech that indicates relationship or status—has played an essential role in the Japanese language. When addressing someone in Japanese, an honorific usually takes the form of a suffix attached to one's name (example: "Asuna-san"), is used as a title at the end of one's name, or appears in place of the name itself (example: "Negi-sensei," or simply "Sensei!").

Honorifics can be expressions of respect or endearment. In the context of manga and anime, honorifics give insight into the nature of the relationship between characters. Many English translations leave out these important honorifics, and therefore distort the feel of the original Japanese. Because Japanese honorifics contain nuances that English honorifics lack, it is our policy at Del Rey not to translate them. Here, instead, is a guide to some of the honorifics you may encounter in Del Rey Manga.

-san: This is the most common honorific, and is equivalent to Mr., Miss, Ms., or Mrs. It is the all-purpose honorific and can be used in any situation where politeness is required.

-sama: This is one level higher than "-san" and is used to confer great respect.

-dono: This comes from the word "tono," which means "lord." It is an even higher level than "-sama" and confers utmost respect.

-kun: This suffix is used at the end of boys' names to express familiarity or endearment. It is also sometimes used by men among friends, or when addressing someone younger or of a lower station.

-chan: This is used to express endearment, mostly toward girls. It is also used for little boys, pets, and even among lovers. It gives a sense of childish cuteness.

Bozu: This is an informal way to refer to a boy, similar to the English terms "kid" and "squirt."

Sempai/Senpai: This title suggests that the addressee is one's senior in a group or organization. It is most often used in a school setting, where underclassmen refer to their upperclassmen as "sempai." It can also be used in the workplace, such as when a newer employee addresses an employee who has seniority in the company.

Kohai: This is the opposite of "sempai" and is used toward underclassmen in school or newcomers in the workplace. It connotes that the addressee is of a lower station.

Sensei: Literally meaning "one who has come before," this title is used for teachers, doctors, or masters of any profession or art.

[blank]: This is usually forgotten in these lists, but it is perhaps the most significant difference between Japanese and English. The lack of honorific means that the speaker has permission to address the person in a very intimate way. Usually, only family, spouses, or very close friends have this kind of permission. Known as *yobisute*, it can be gratifying when someone who has earned the intimacy starts to call one by one's name without an honorific. But when that intimacy hasn't been earned, it can be very insulting.

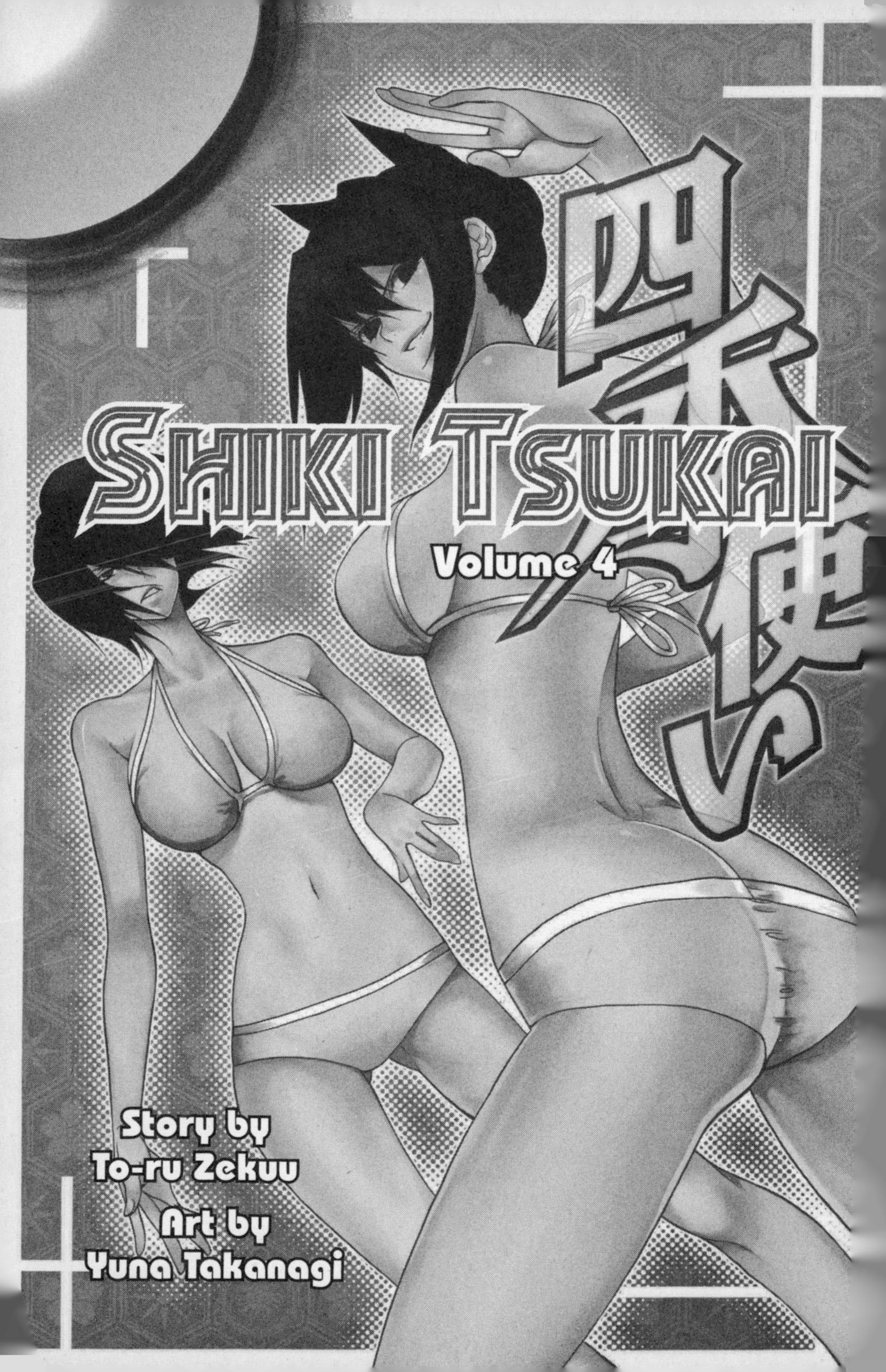
SHIKI TSUKAI
Volume 4
Story by
To-ru Zekuu
Art by
Yuna Takanagi

Table of Contents

SHIKI TSUKAI

Synopsis

Akira Kizuki, a kindhearted boy, lived a peaceful life as an ordinary middle school student—until he met Koyomi Sakuragi, a Shiki Tsukai. With Koyomi's guidance, Akira became a Shiki Tsukai.

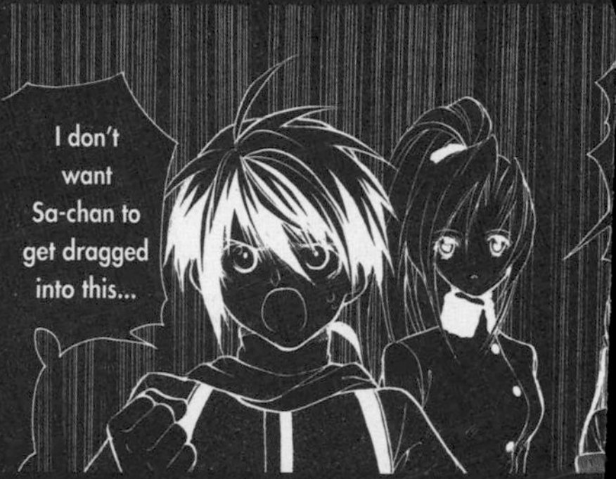
I don't want Sa-chan to get dragged into this...

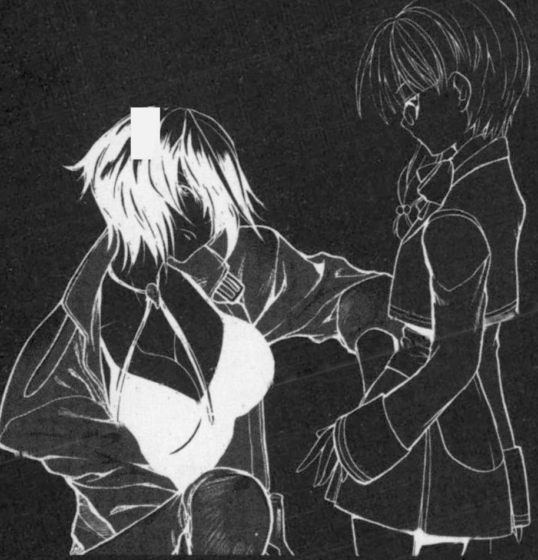

A Shiki Tsukai wields the seasons using a Shikifu. As the Shiki Tsukai of March, Koyomi's mission is to protect Akira (the boy who has the possibility of becoming the Shinra who can wield all the seasons) from the Shiki Tsukai of Summer.

The Shiki Tsukai of Summer (Rinsho, Ryuka, and Nanayo Rangetsu) unleashed their attack. Koyomi was injured after falling into the Shiki Tsukai of Summer's trap. Thanks to Rei, the Shiki Tsukai of February, and Moe, the Shiki Tsukai of January, they were able to hold t[redacted]hiki Tsukai of Summer back. From this battle, Akira learned that he doesn't stand a chance against Nanayo.

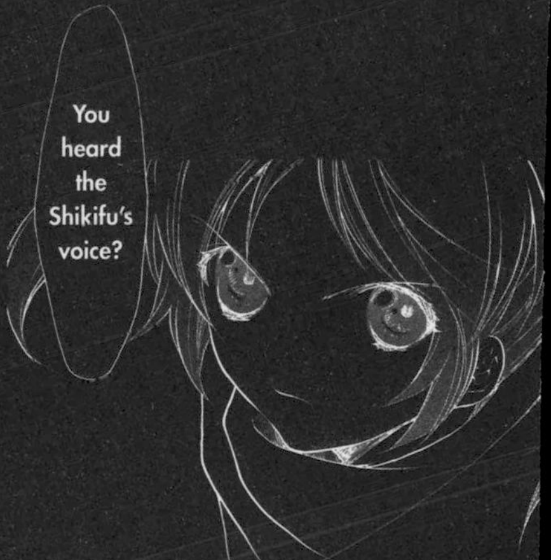
You heard the Shikifu's voice?

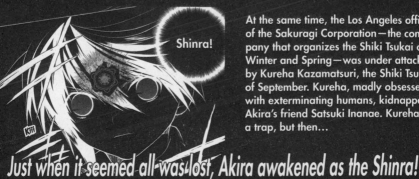

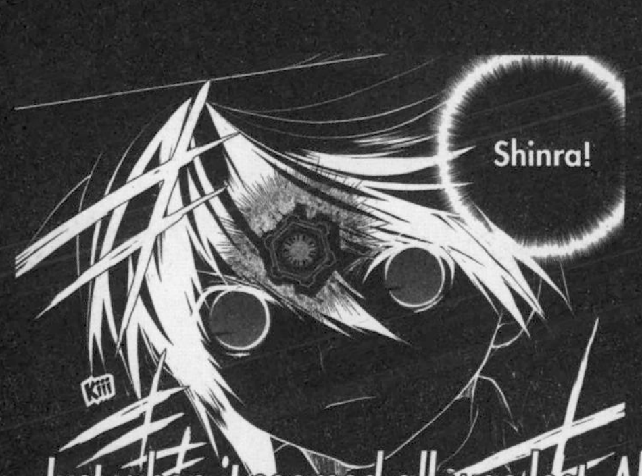
Shinra!
Kiii

At the same time, the Los Angeles office of the Sakuragi Corporation—the company that organizes the Shiki Tsukai of Winter and Spring—was under attack by Kureha Kazamatsuri, the Shiki Tsukai of September. Kureha, madly obsessed with exterminating humans, kidnapped Akira's friend Satsuki Inanae. Kureha set a trap, but then...

Just when it seemed all was lost, Akira awakened as the Shinra!

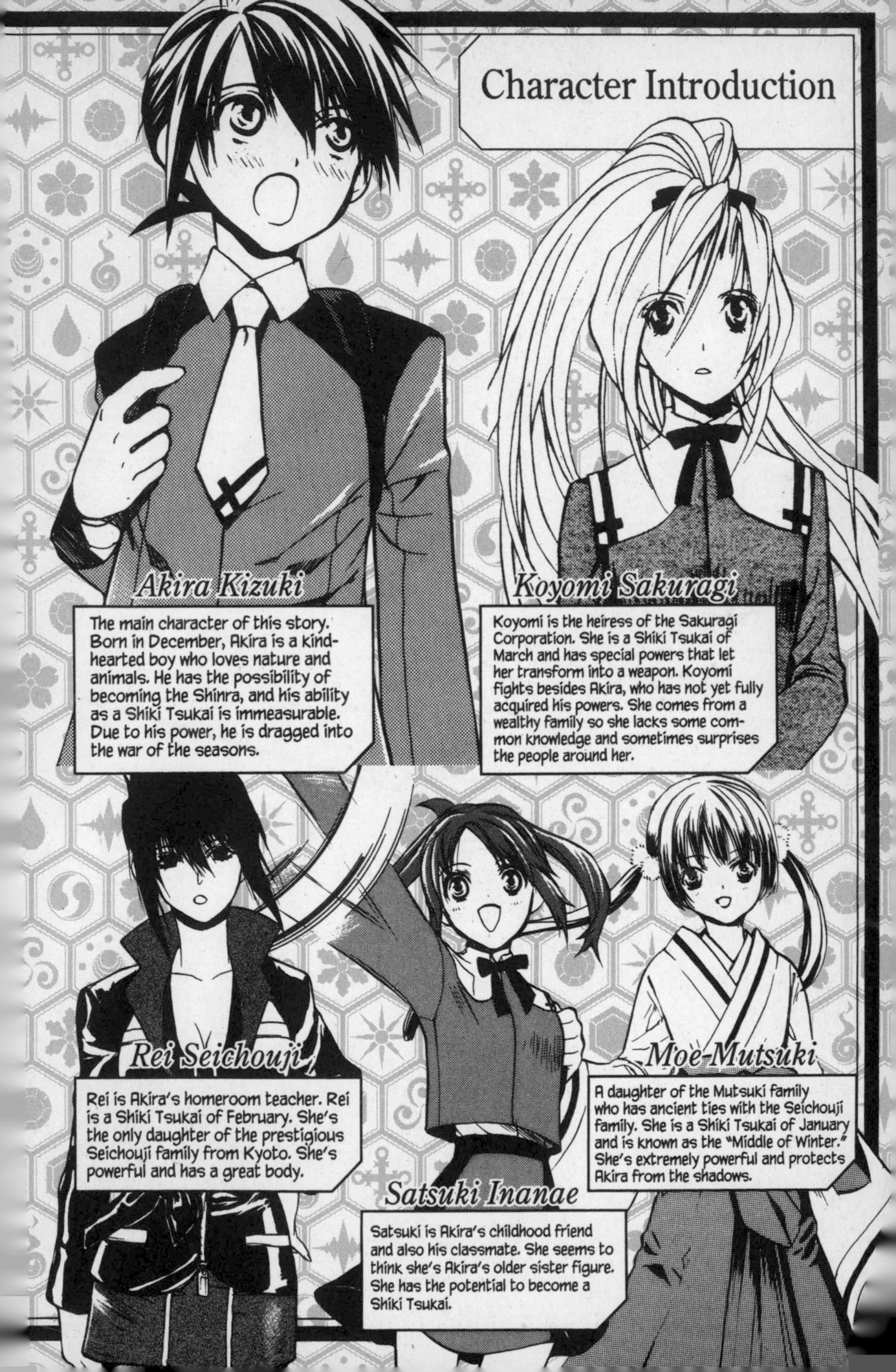
Character Introduction
Akira Kizuki
The main character of this story. Born in December, Akira is a kind-hearted boy who loves nature and animals. He has the possibility of becoming the Shinra, and his ability as a Shiki Tsukai is immeasurable. Due to his power, he is dragged into the war of the seasons.
Koyomi Sakuragi
Koyomi is the heiress of the Sakuragi Corporation. She is a Shiki Tsukai of March and has special powers that let her transform into a weapon. Koyomi fights besides Akira, who has not yet fully acquired his powers. She comes from a wealthy family so she lacks some common knowledge and sometimes surprises the people around her.
Rei Seichouji
Rei is Akira's homeroom teacher. Rei is a Shiki Tsukai of February. She's the only daughter of the prestigious Seichouji family from Kyoto. She's powerful and has a great body.
Moe Mutsuki
A daughter of the Mutsuki family who has ancient ties with the Seichouji family. She is a Shiki Tsukai of January and is known as the "Middle of Winter." She's extremely powerful and protects Akira from the shadows.
Satsuki Inanae
Satsuki is Akira's childhood friend and also his classmate. She seems to think she's Akira's older sister figure. She has the potential to become a Shiki Tsukai.

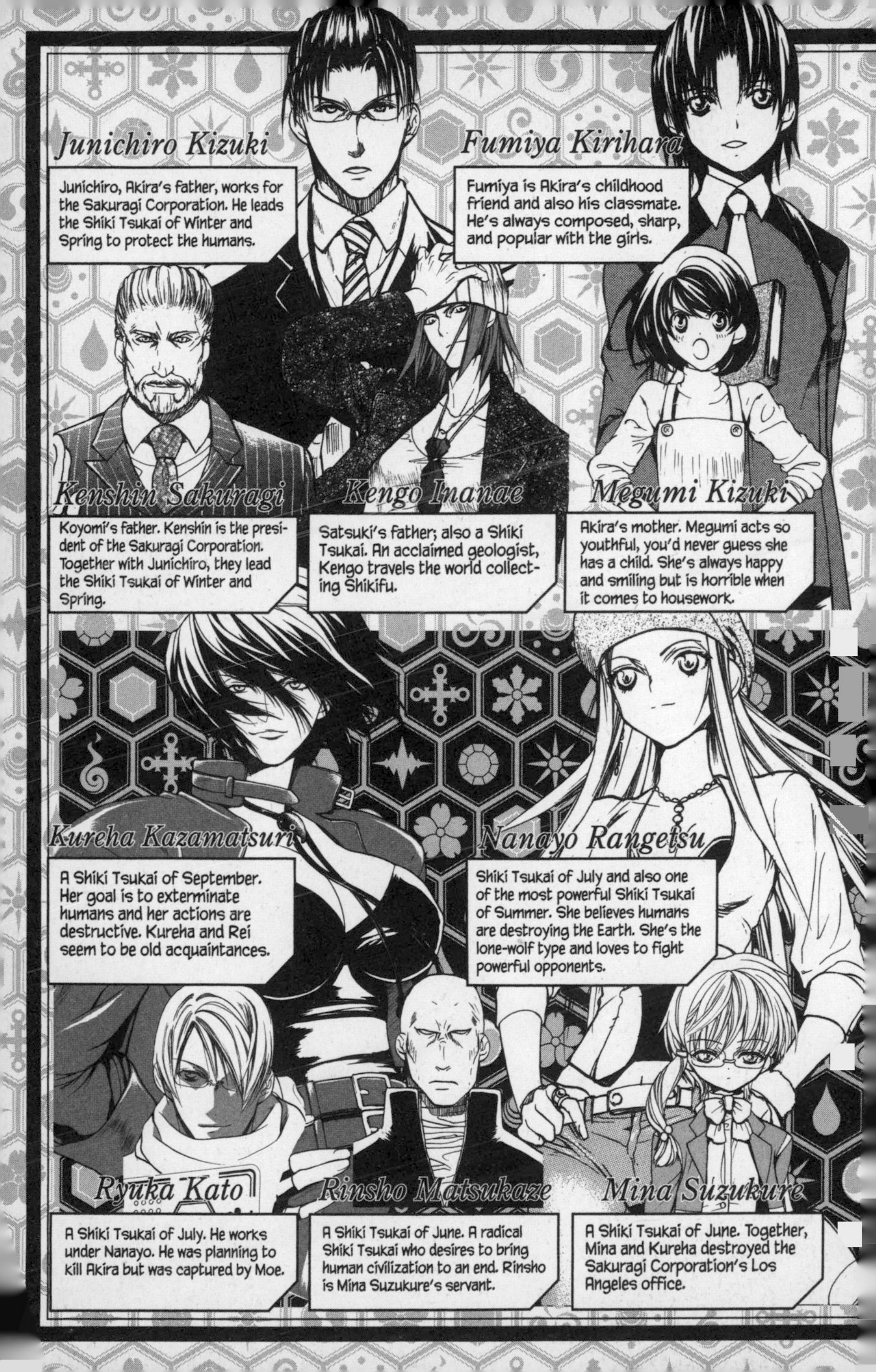
Fumiya Kirihara
Fumiya is Akira's childhood friend and also his classmate. He's always composed, sharp, and popular with the girls.
Junichiro Kizuki
Junichiro, Akira's father, works for the Sakuragi Corporation. He leads the Shiki Tsukai of Winter and Spring to protect the humans.
Megumi Kizuki
Akira's mother. Megumi acts so youthful, you'd never guess she has a child. She's always happy and smiling but is horrible when it comes to housework.
Kengo Inanae
Satsuki's father; also a Shiki Tsukai. An acclaimed geologist, Kengo travels the world collecting Shikifu.
Kenshin Sakuragi
Koyomi's father. Kenshin is the president of the Sakuragi Corporation. Together with Junichiro, they lead the Shiki Tsukai of Winter and Spring.
Nanayo Rangetsu
Shiki Tsukai of July and also one of the most powerful Shiki Tsukai of Summer. She believes humans are destroying the Earth. She's the lone-wolf type and loves to fight powerful opponents.
Kureha Kazamatsuri
A Shiki Tsukai of September. Her goal is to exterminate humans and her actions are destructive. Kureha and Rei seem to be old acquaintances.
Mina Suzukure
A Shiki Tsukai of June. Together, Mina and Kureha destroyed the Sakuragi Corporation's Los Angeles office.
Rinsho Matsukaze
A Shiki Tsukai of June. A radical Shiki Tsukai who desires to bring human civilization to an end. Rinsho is Mina Suzukure's servant.
Ryuka Kato
A Shiki Tsukai of July. He works under Nanayo. He was planning to kill Akira but was captured by Moe.

Seventeenth Season

Fantasia of the Shinra

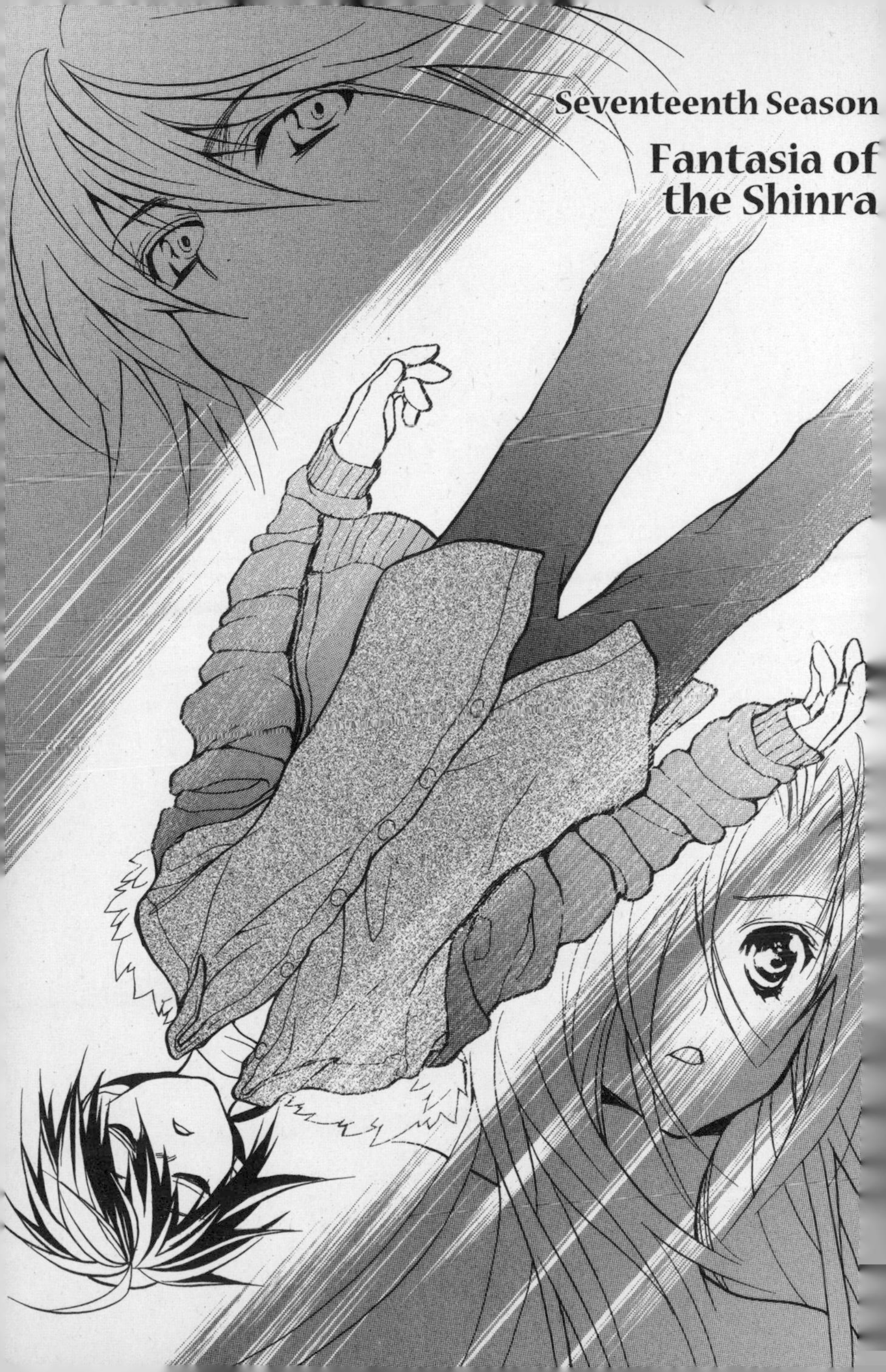

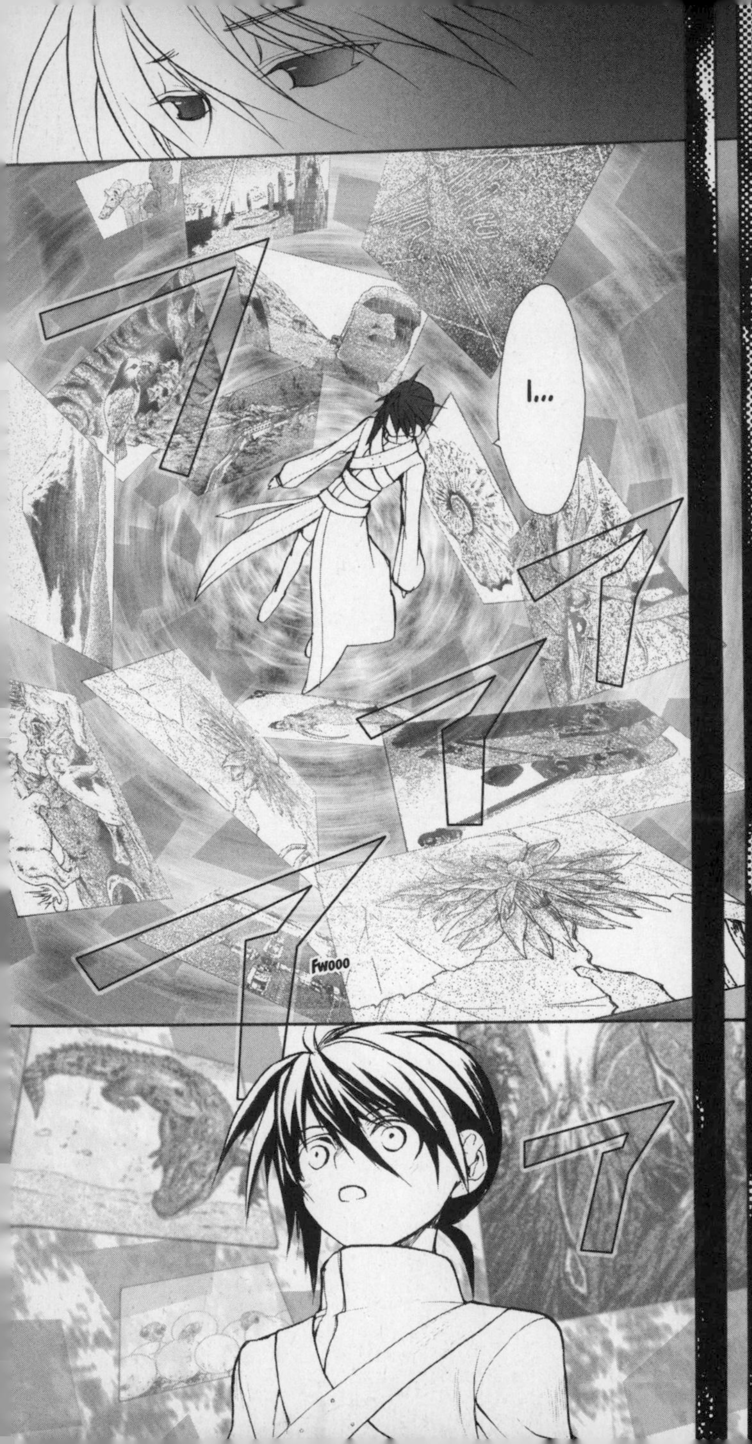
I...
Fwooo

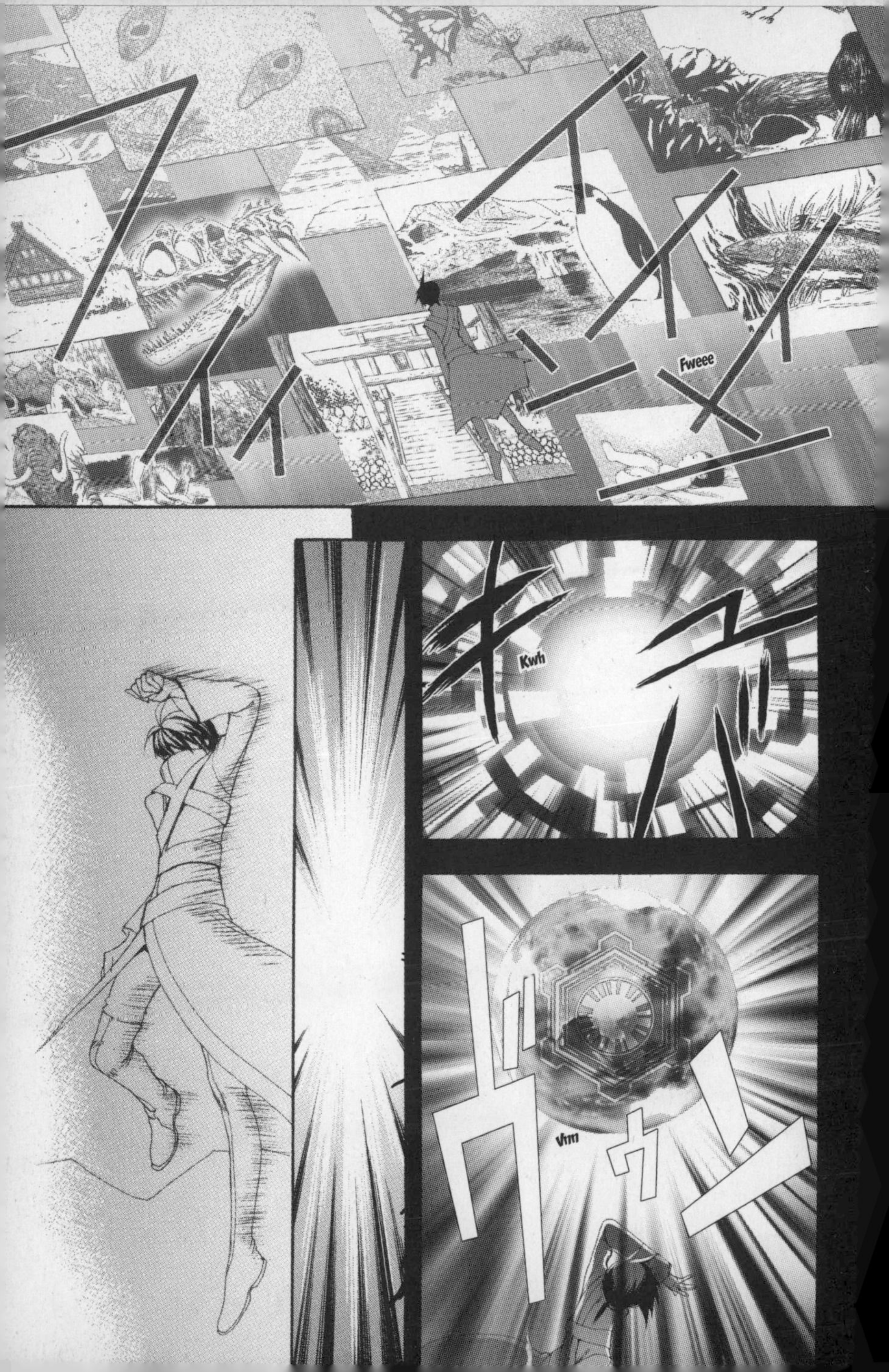

Fweee
Kwh
Vmn

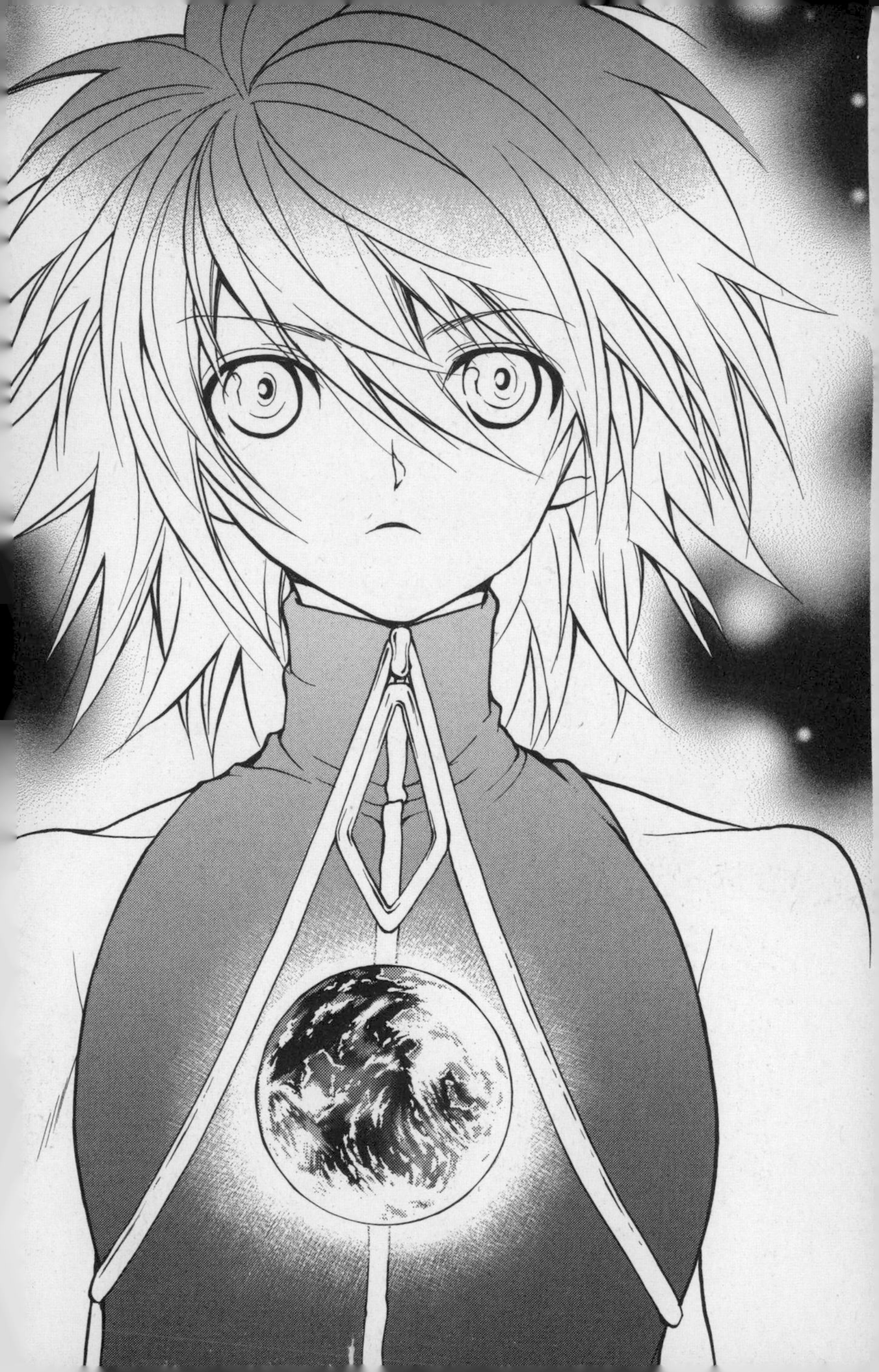

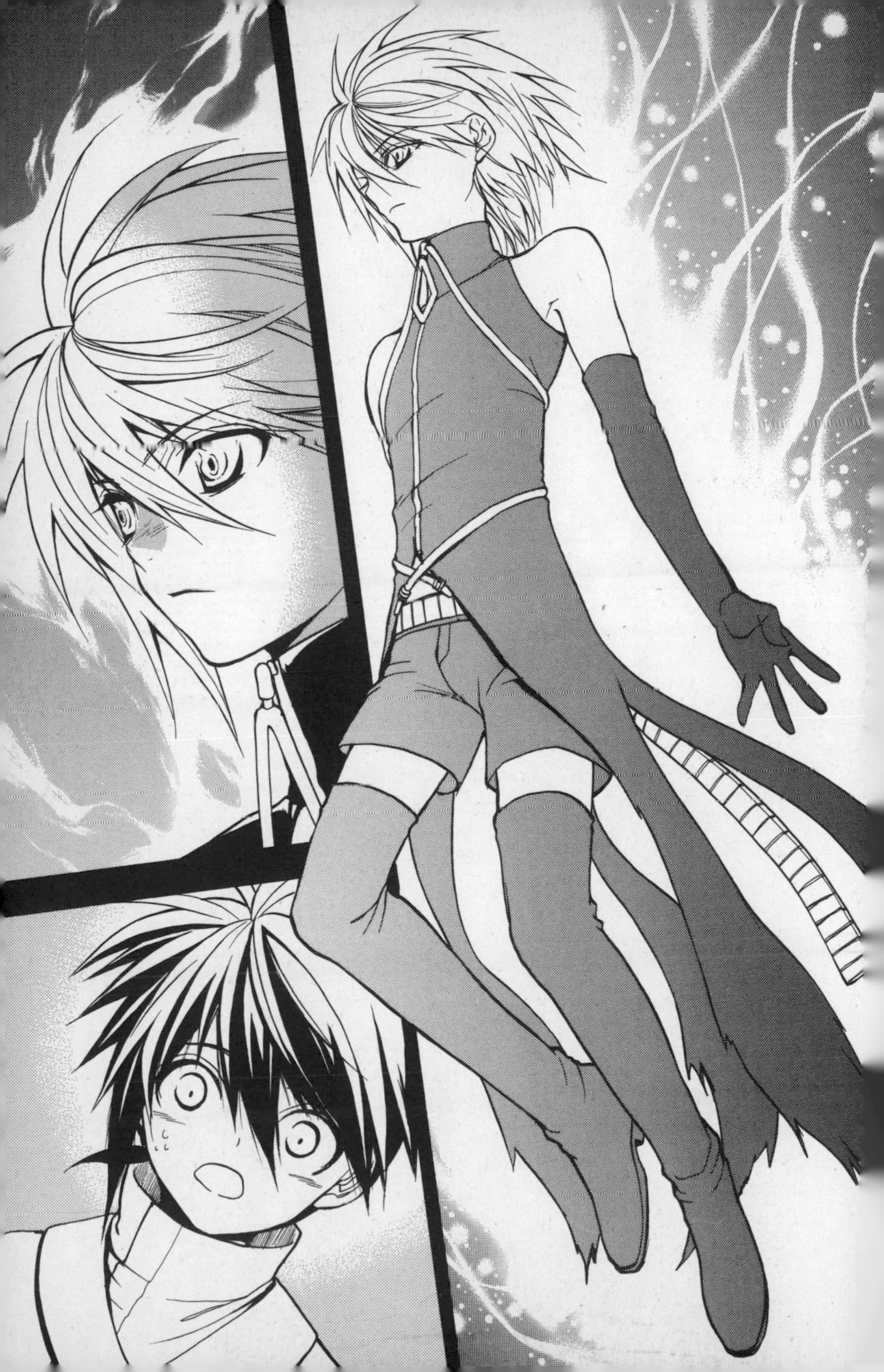

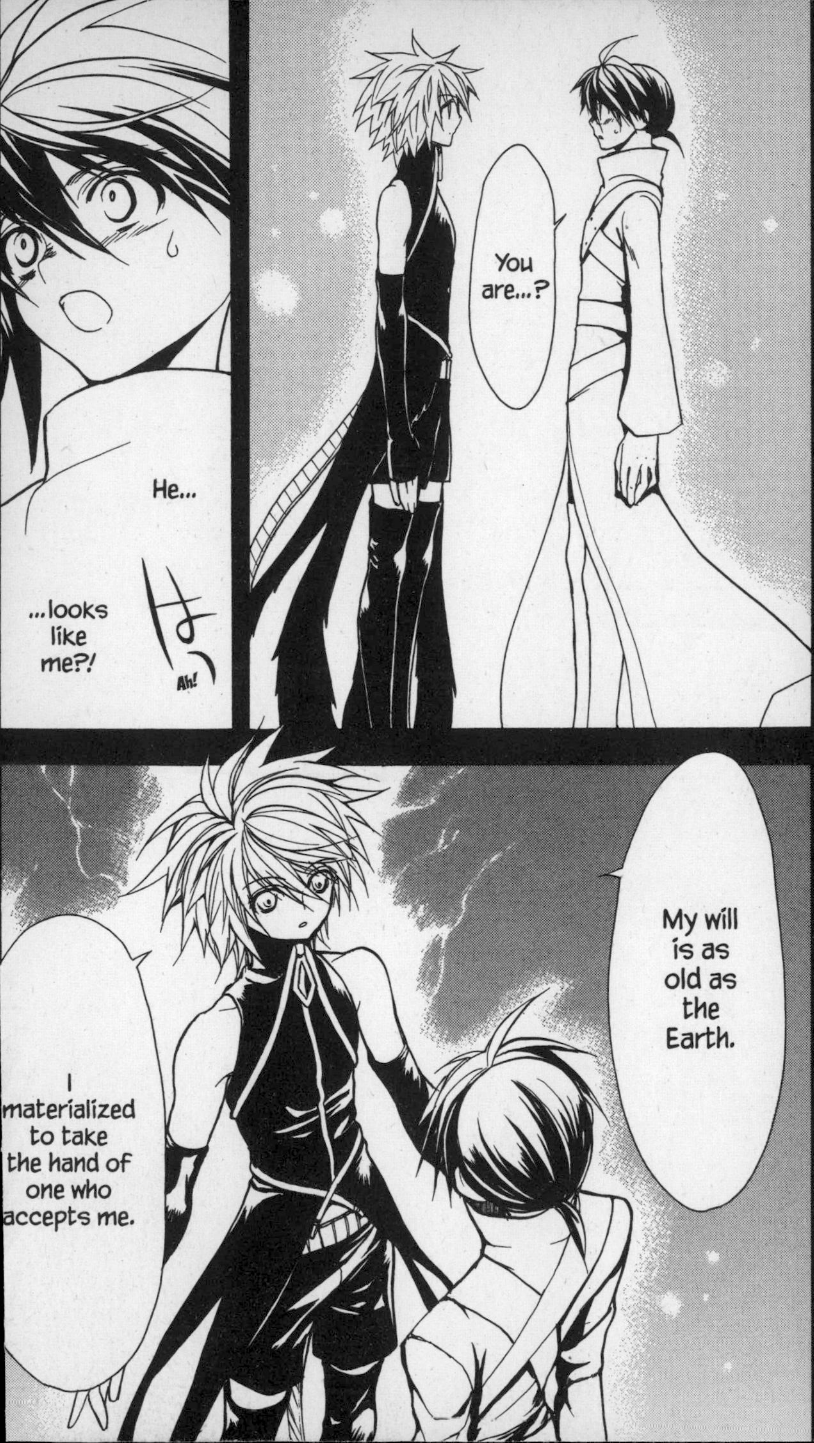
You are...?
He...
...looks like me?!
Ah!
My will is as old as the Earth.
I materialized to take the hand of one who accepts me.

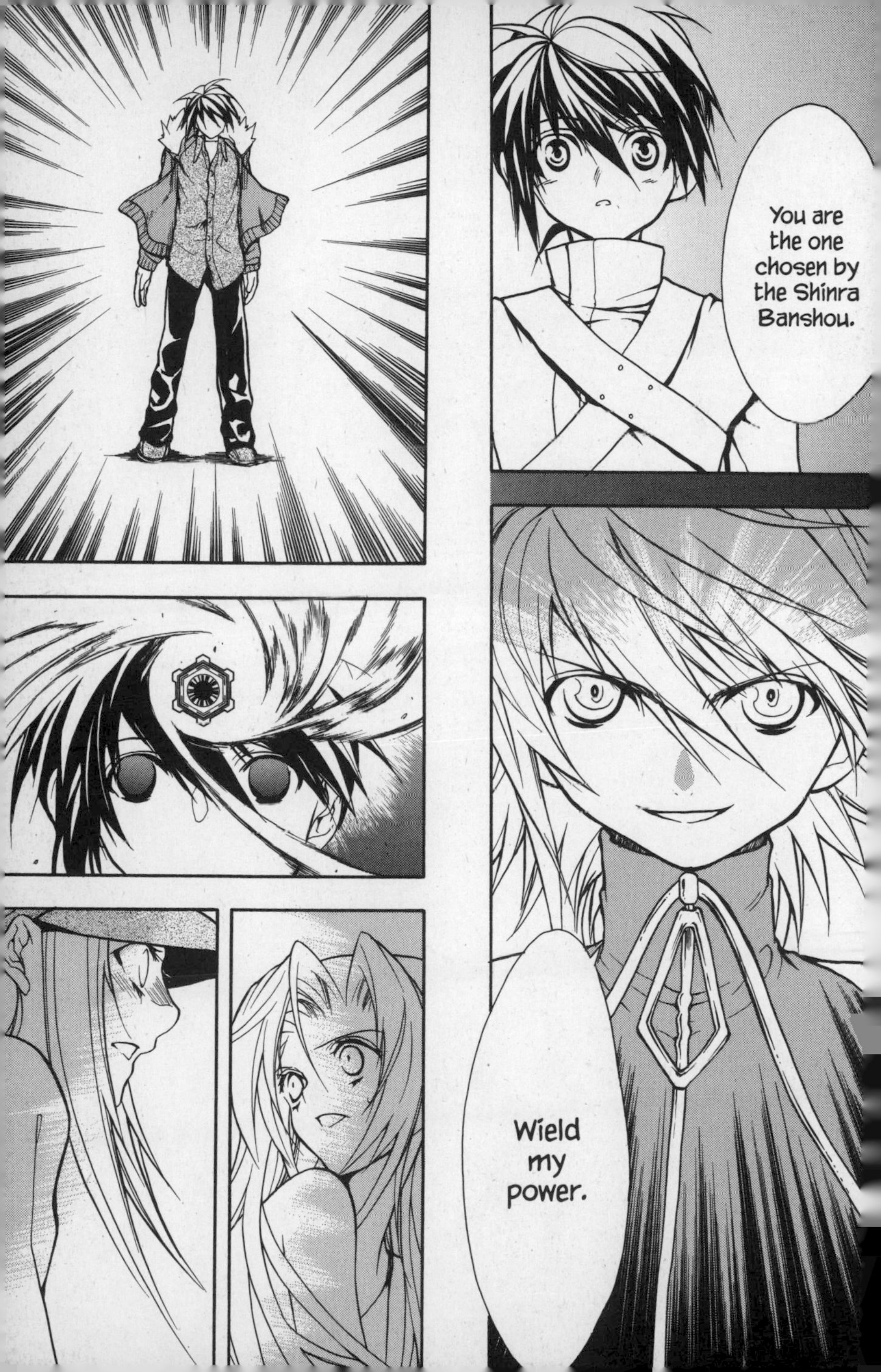
You are the one chosen by the Shinra Banshou.
Wield my power.

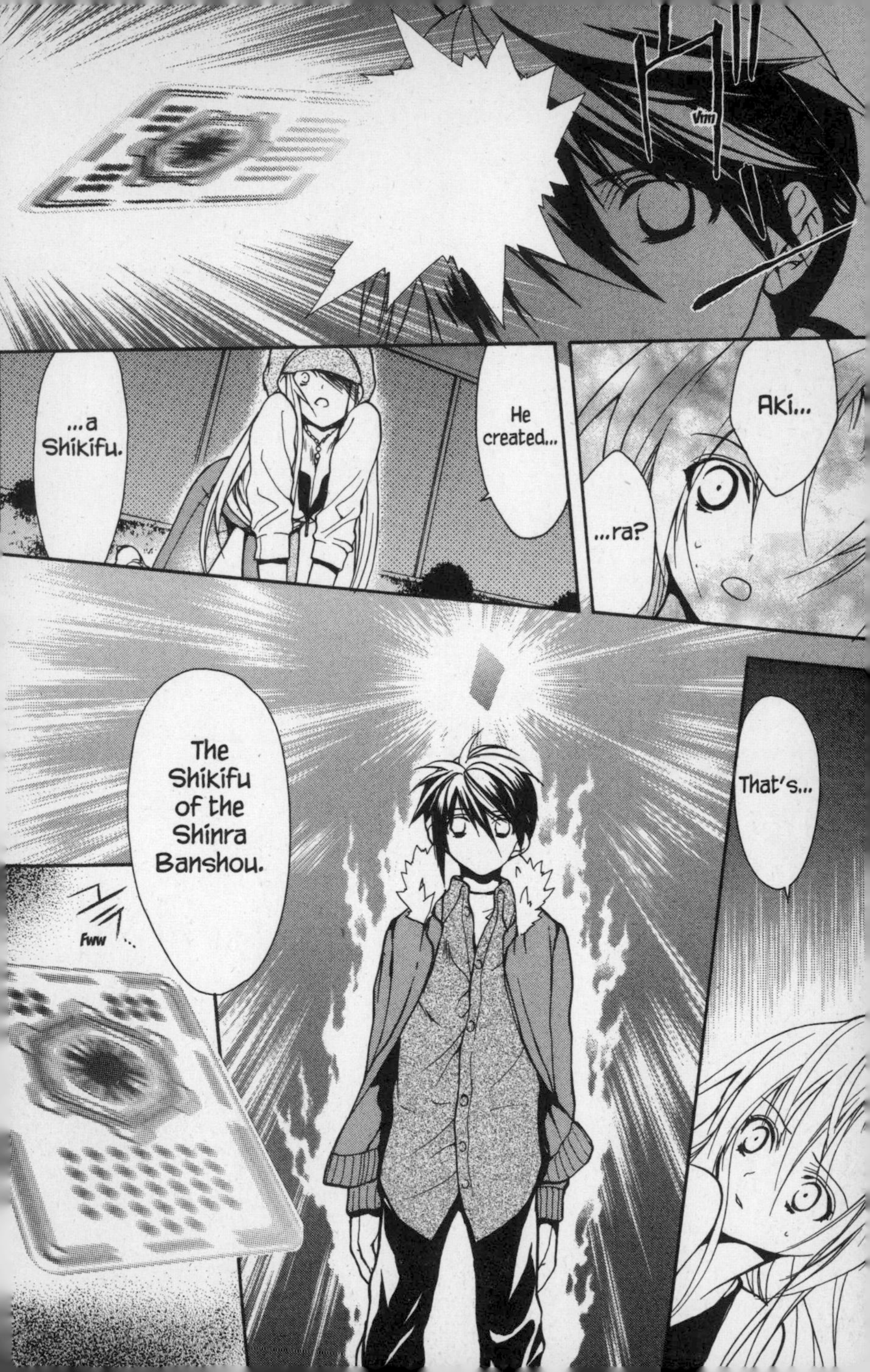
Vm
Aki...
...ra?
He created...
...a Shikifu.
That's...
The Shikifu of the Shinra Banshou.
Fww...

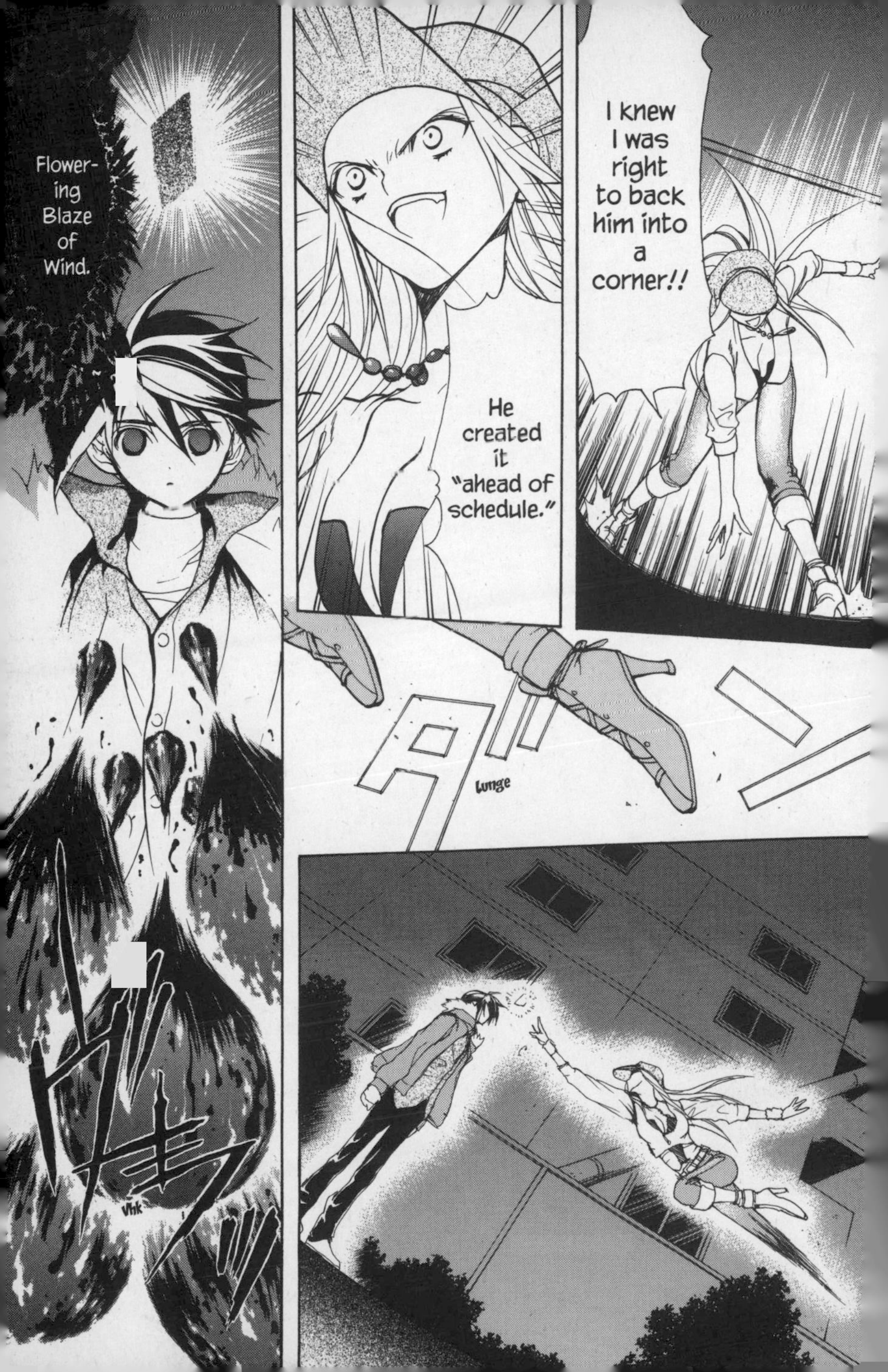
I knew I was right to back him into a corner!!
He created it "ahead of schedule."
Lunge
Flowering Blaze of Wind.
Vnk

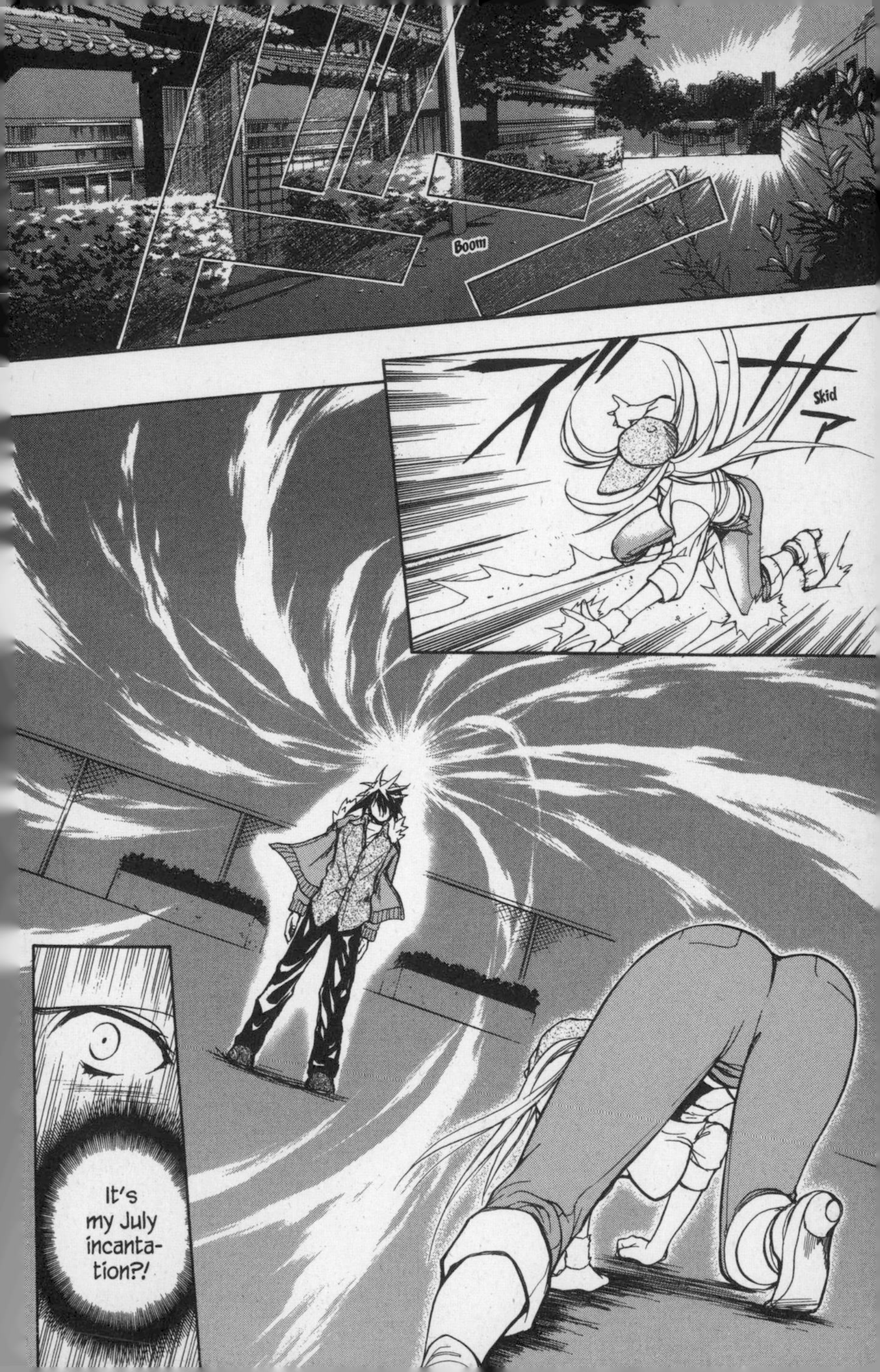
Boom
Skid
It's my July incantation?!

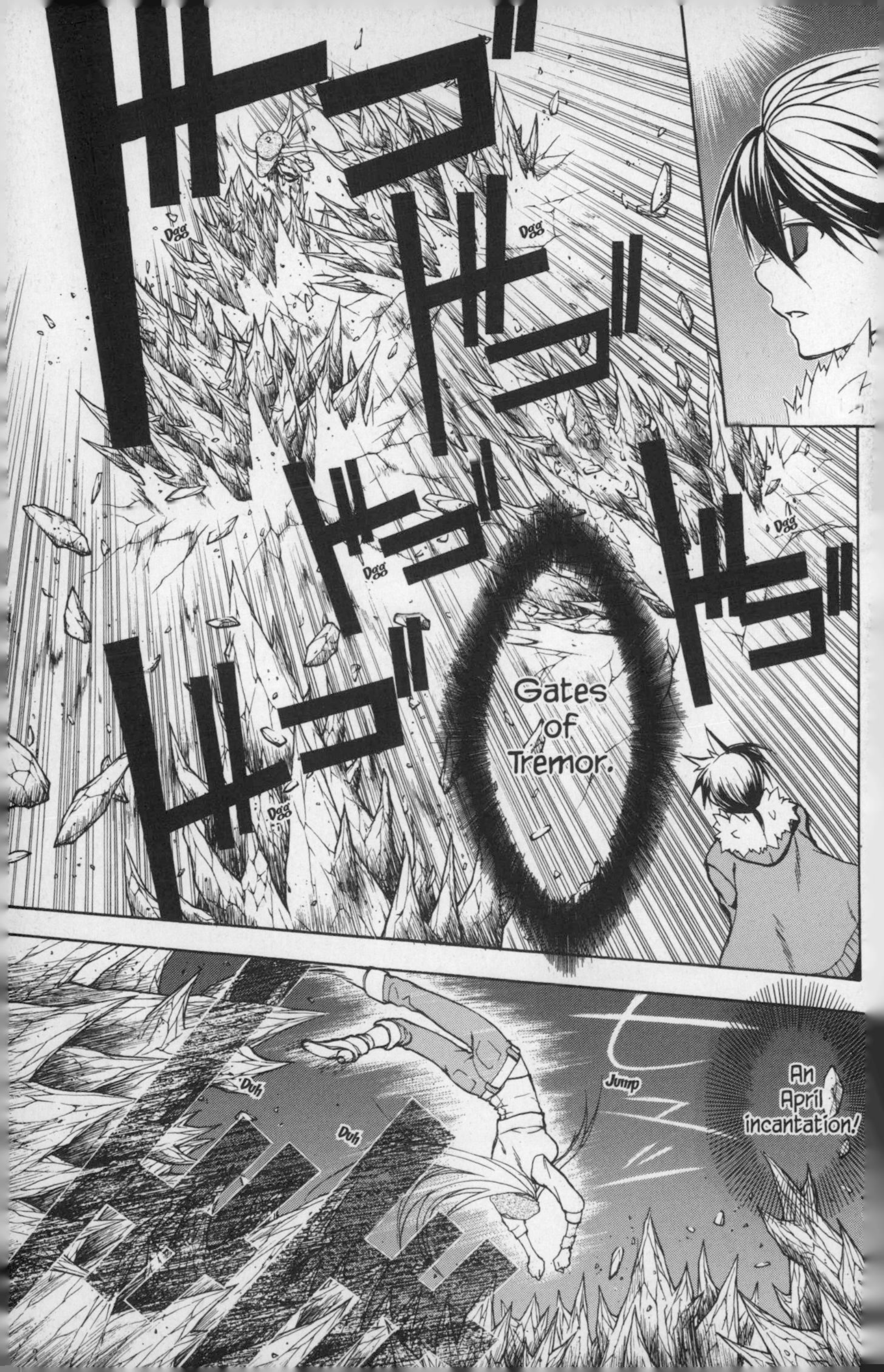
Dgg
Dgg
Dgg
Dgg
Gates of Tremor.
Dgg
An April incantation!
Jump
Duh
Duh

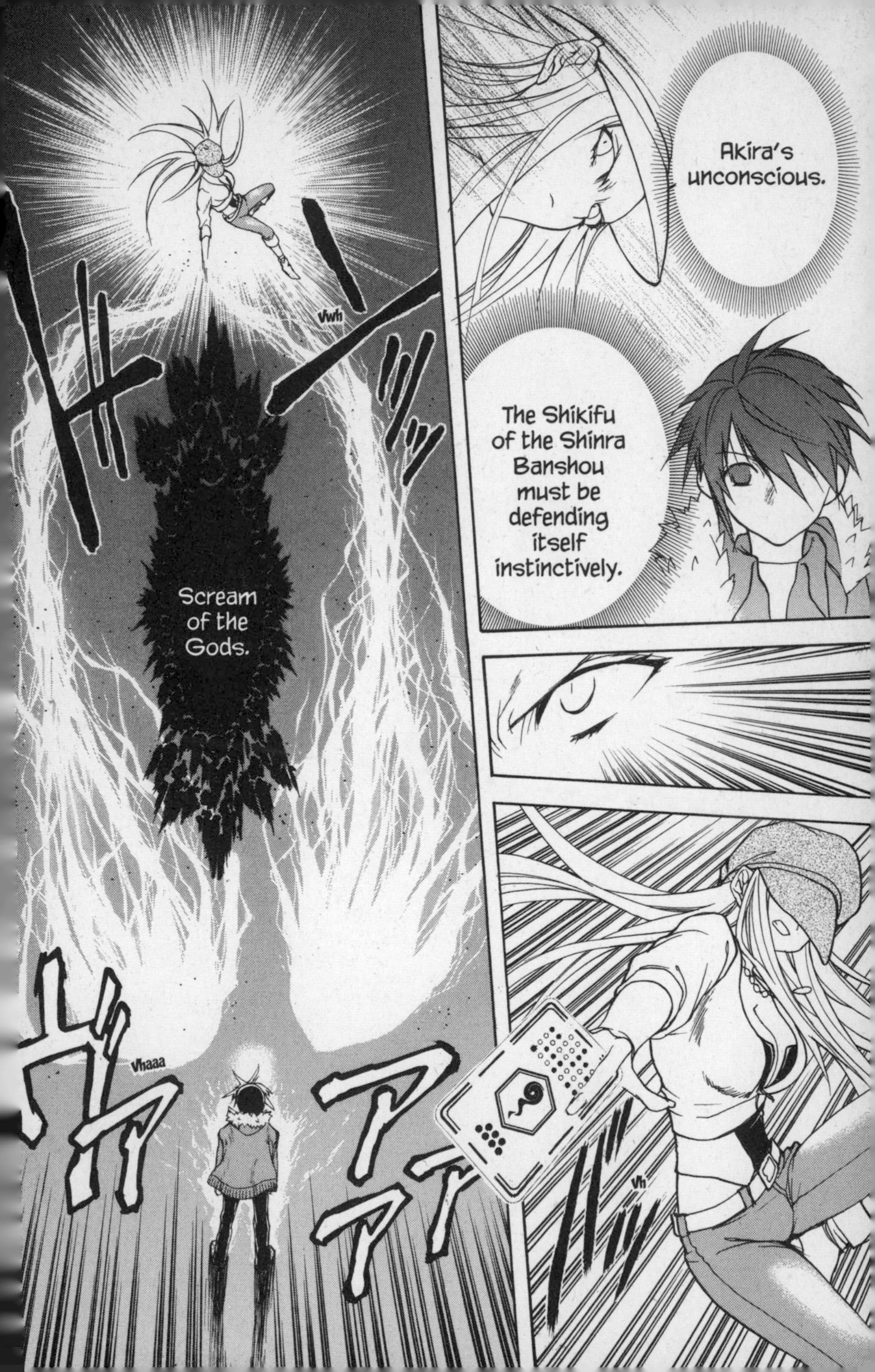
Akira's unconscious.
The Shikifu of the Shinra Banshou must be defending itself instinctively.
Vh
Vwh
Scream of the Gods.
Vhaaa

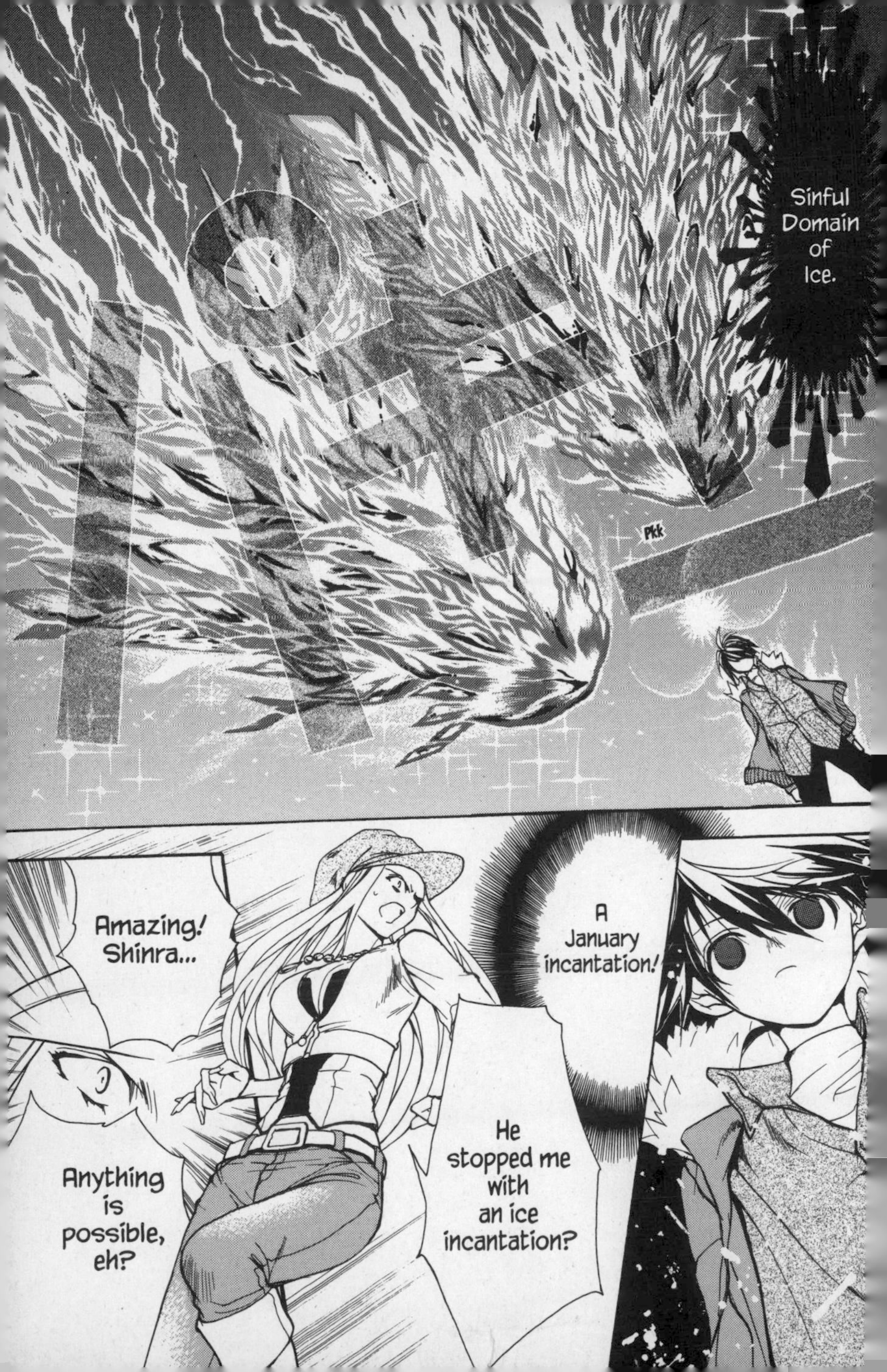
Sinful Domain of Ice.
Pkk
A January incantation!
He stopped me with an ice incantation?
Amazing! Shinra...
Anything is possible, eh?

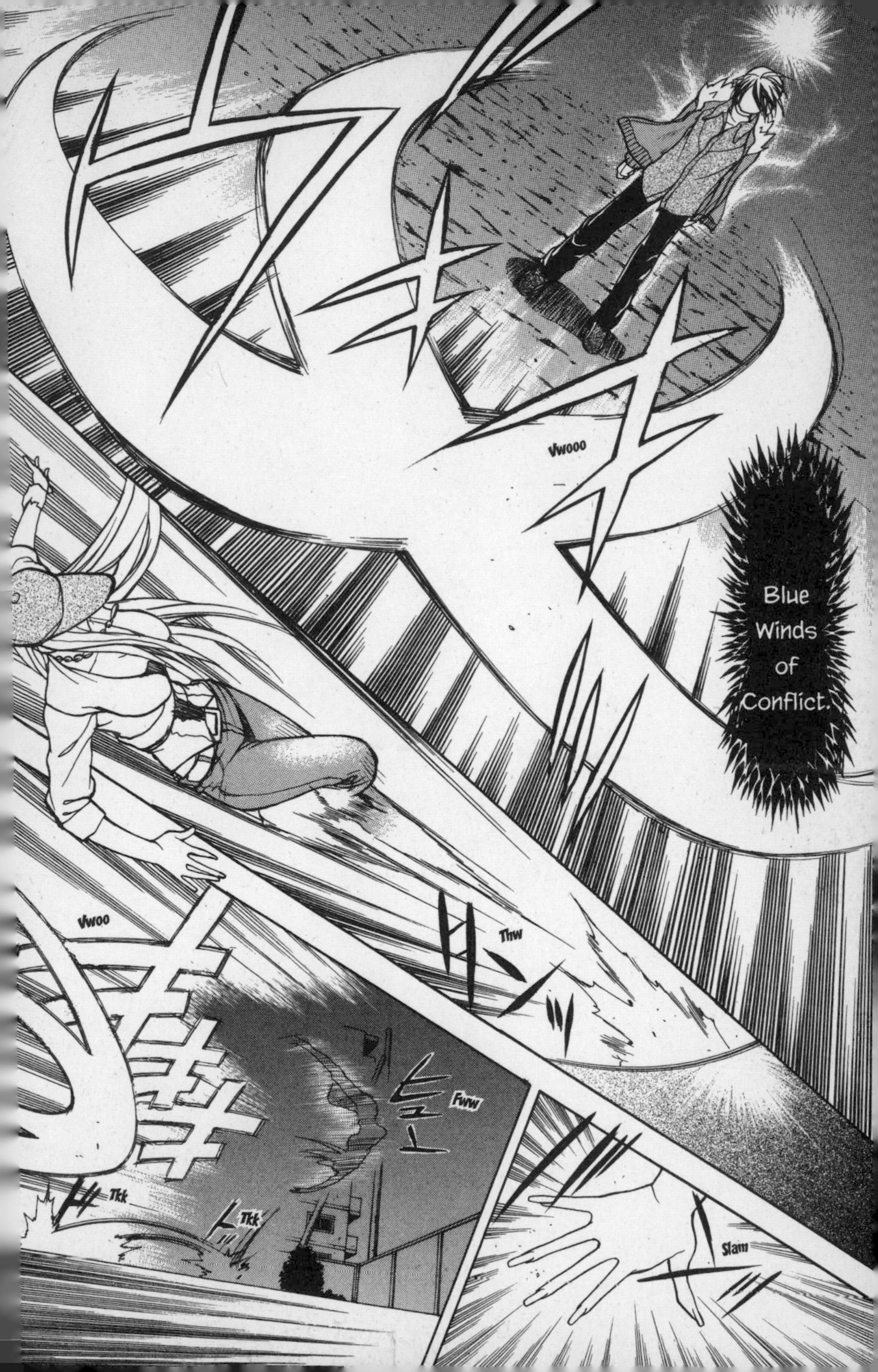
Blue Winds of Conflict.
Vwooo
Vwoo
Thw
Slam
Fww
Tkk
Tkk

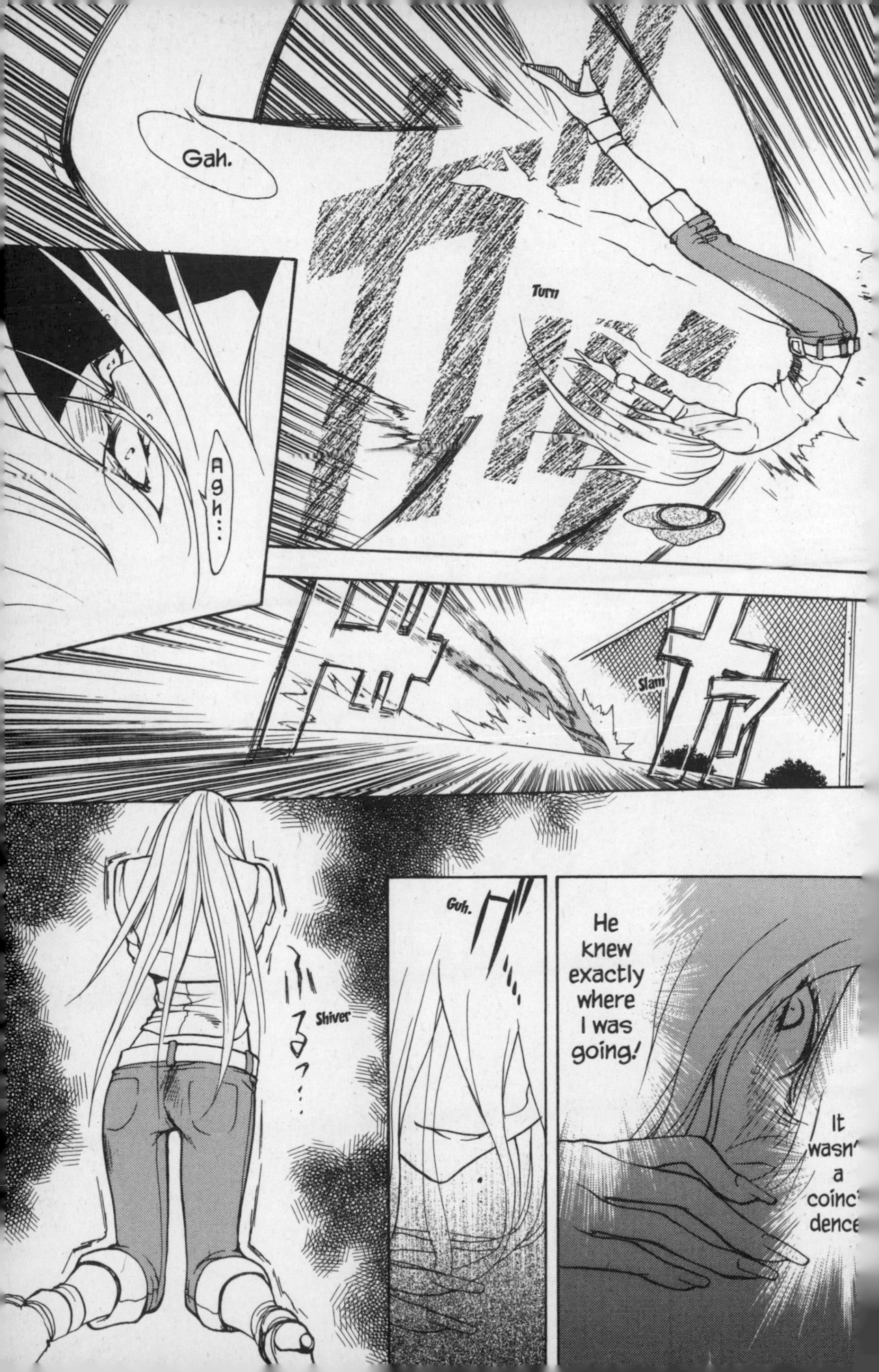
Gah.
Turn
Agh...
Slam
He knew exactly where I was going!
It wasn't a coinci dence
Guh.
Shiver

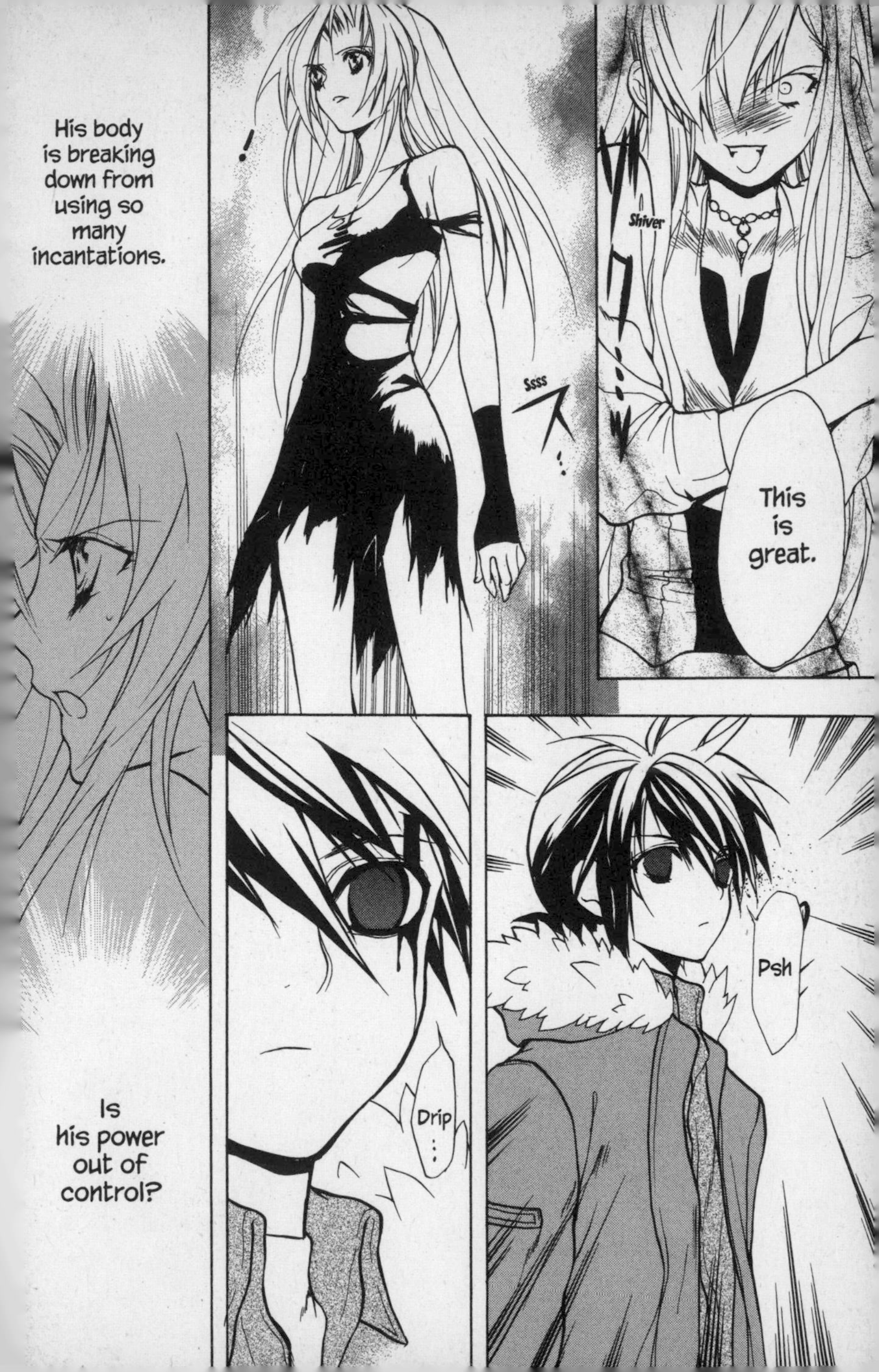
Shiver
This is great.
!
Ssss
Psh
Drip...
His body is breaking down from using so many incantations.
Is his power out of control?

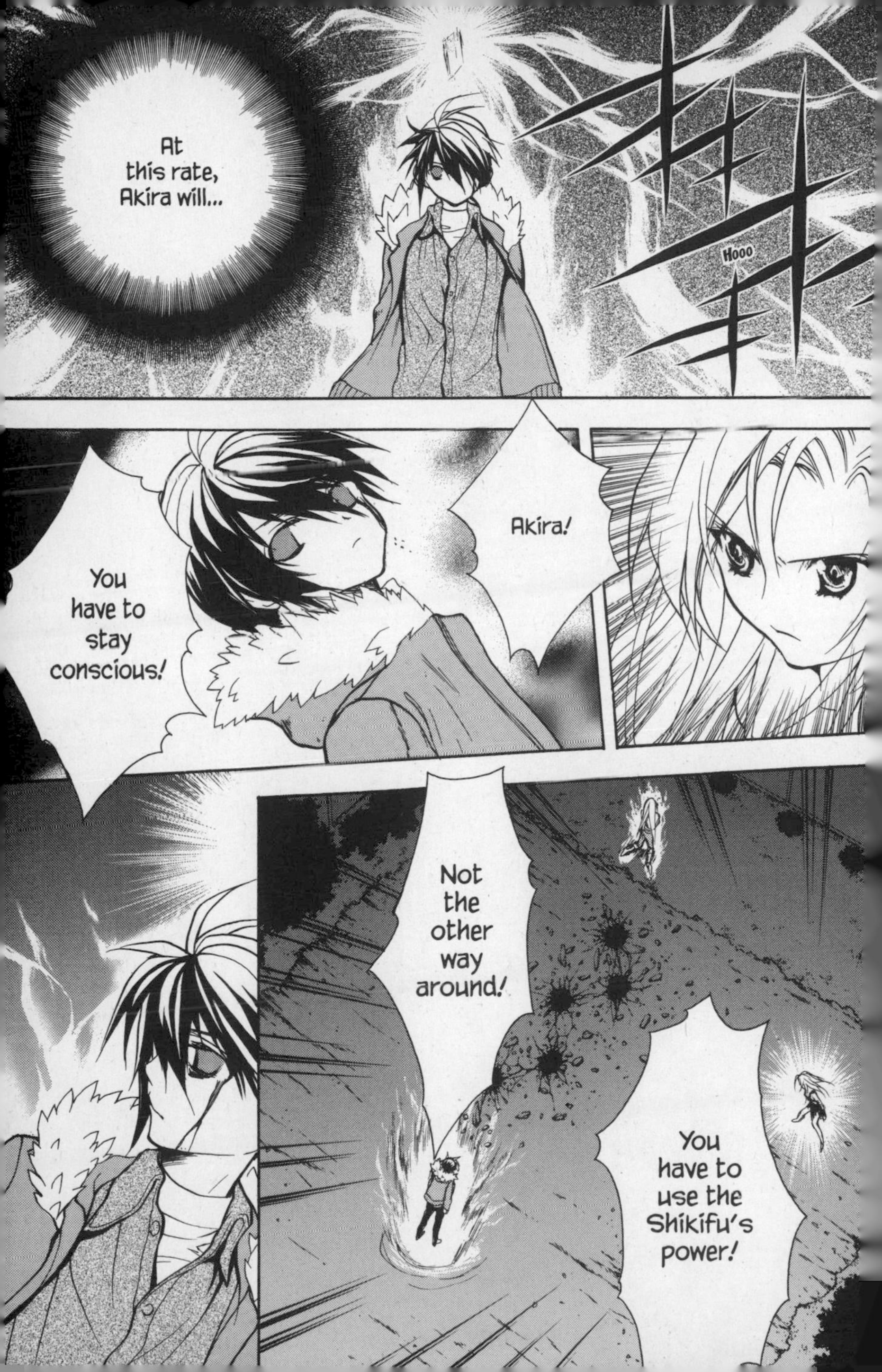
At this rate, Akira will...
Hooo
Akira!
You have to stay conscious!
Not the other way around!
You have to use the Shikifu's power!

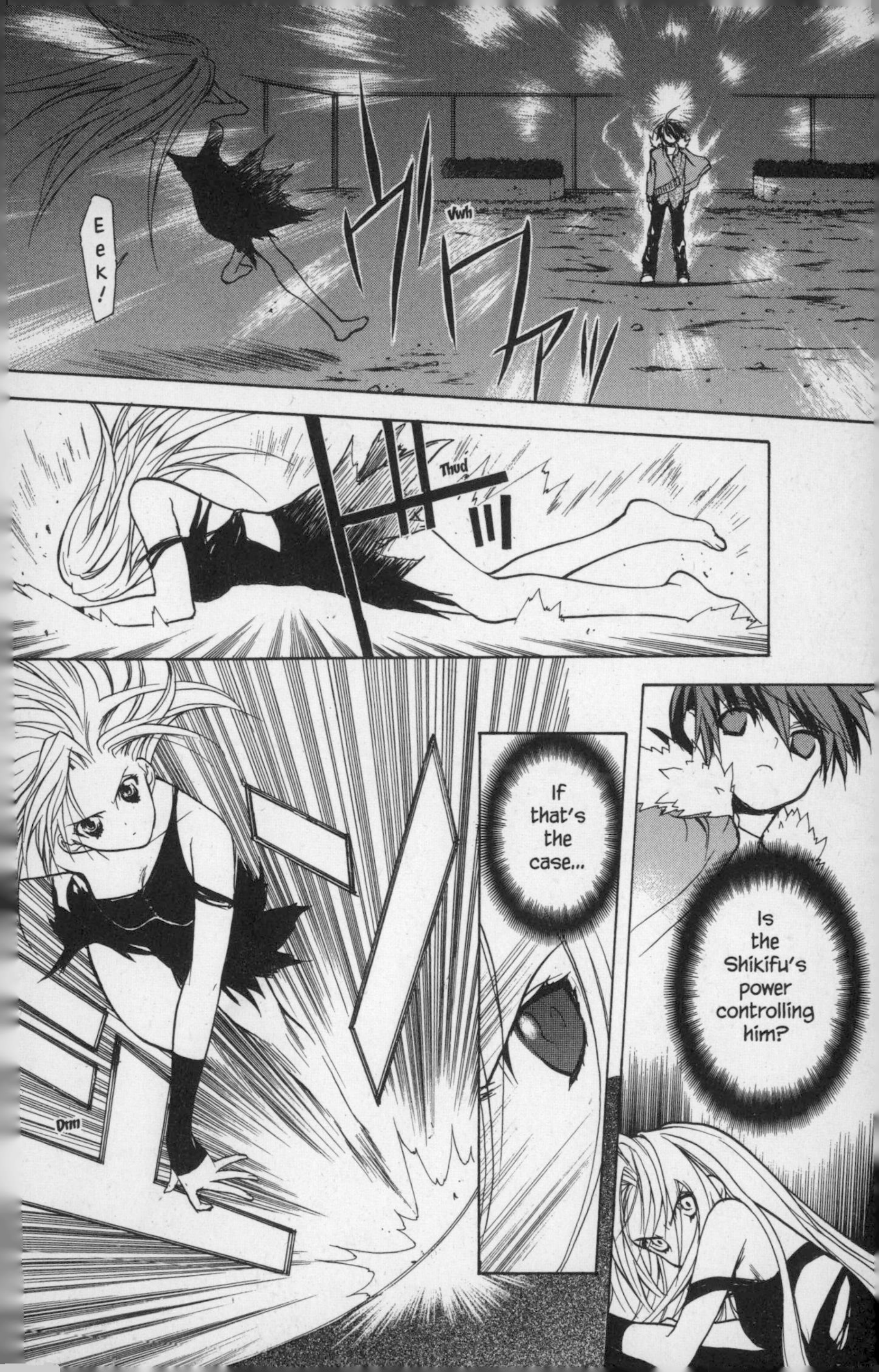
Eek!
Vwh
Thud
Is the Shikifu's power controlling him?
If that's the case...
Dm

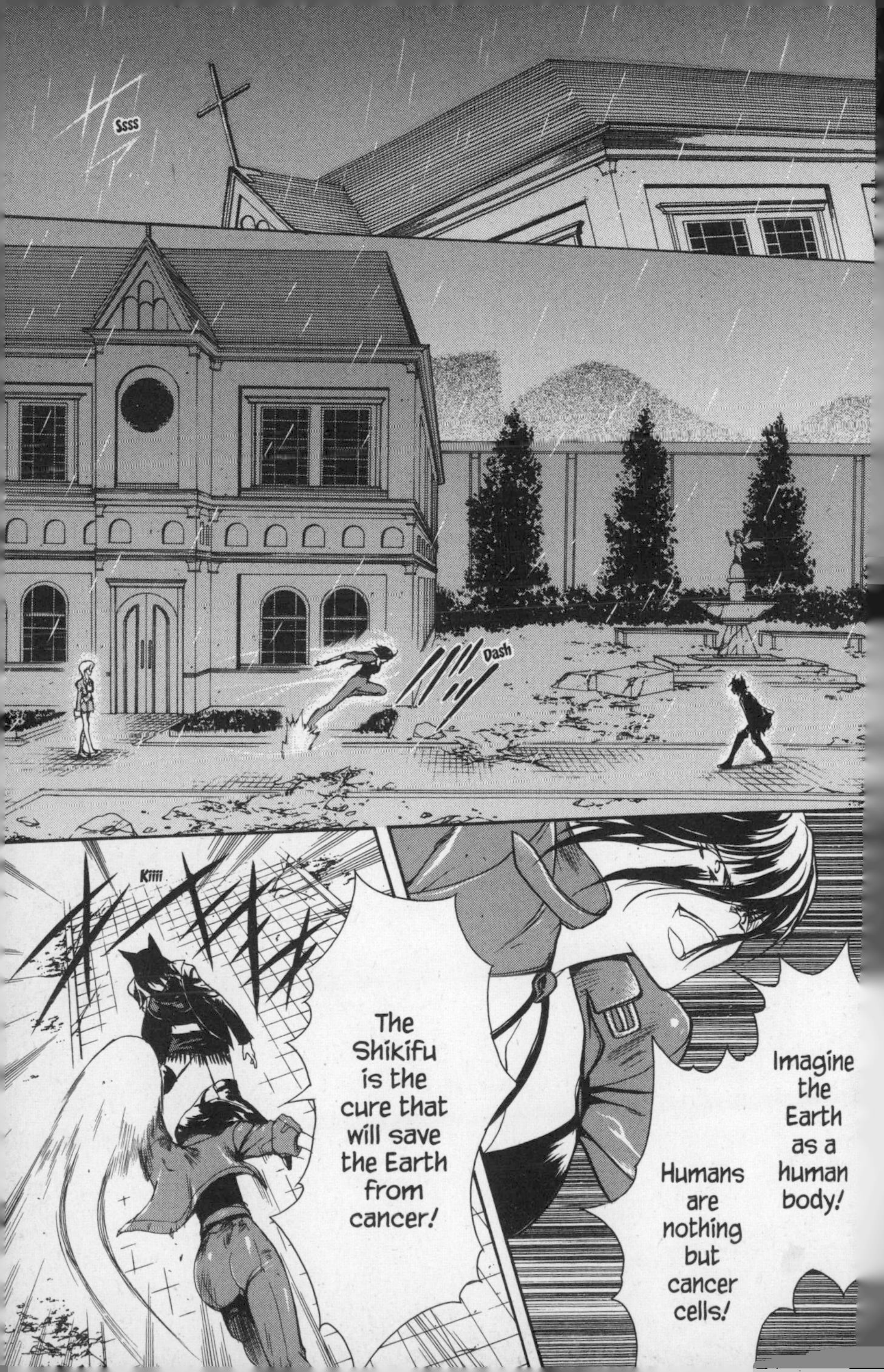
Ssss
Dash
Imagine the Earth as a human body!
Humans are nothing but cancer cells!
The Shikifu is the cure that will save the Earth from cancer!
Kiiii

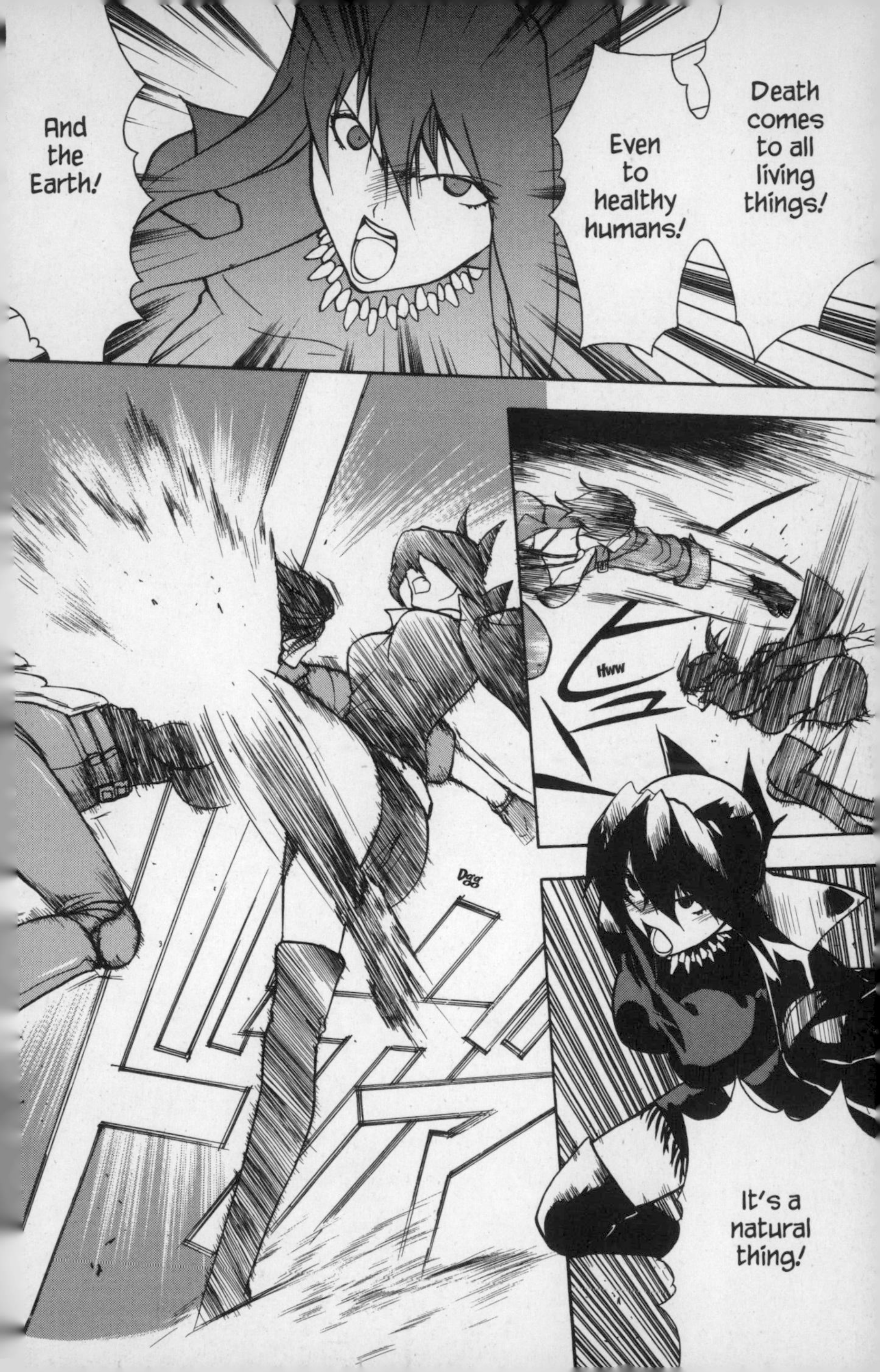
Death comes to all living things!
Even to healthy humans!
And the Earth!
Hww
It's a natural thing!
Dag

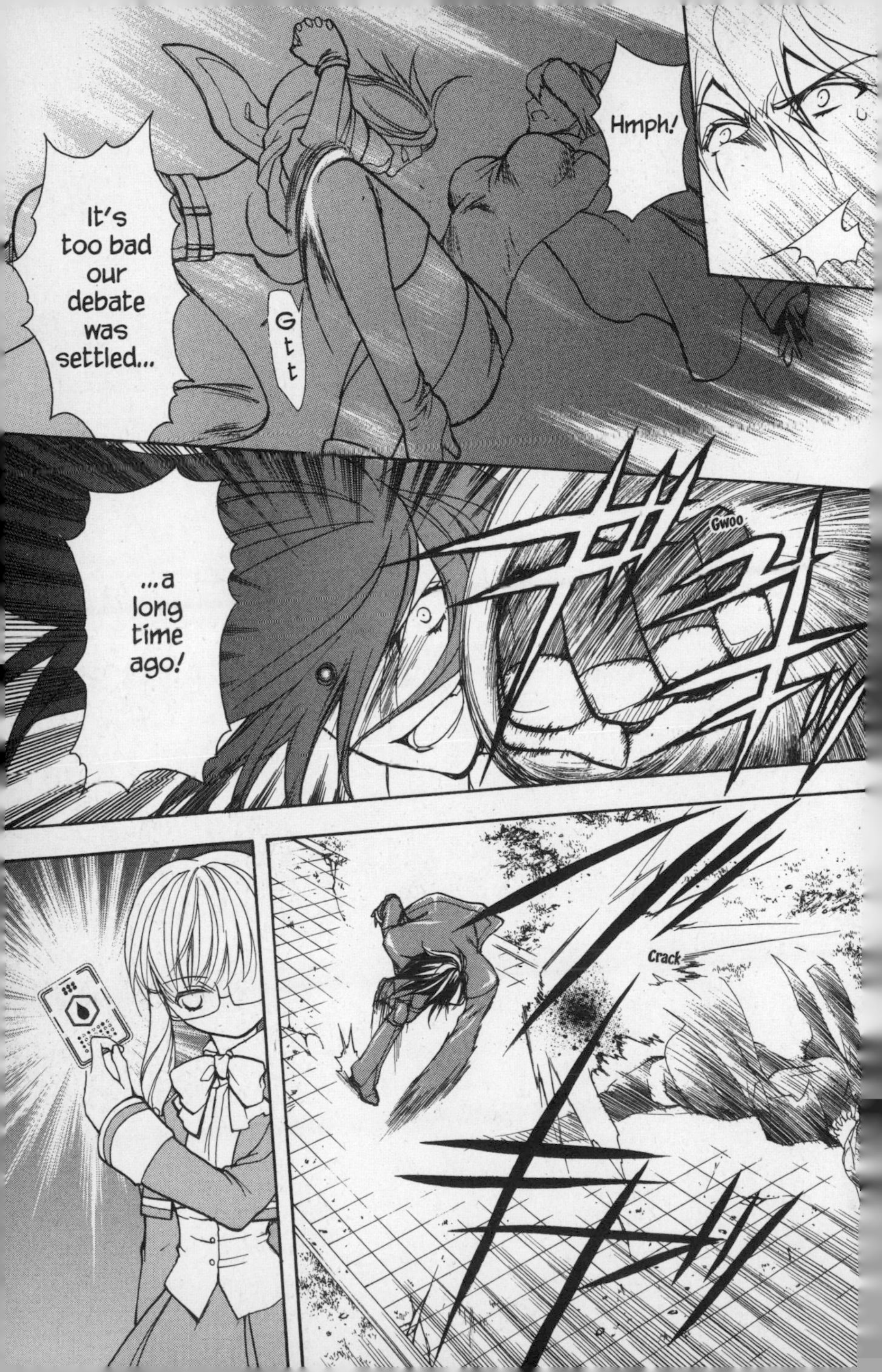
Hmph!
It's too bad our debate was settled...
Gtt
Gwoo
...a long time ago!
Crack

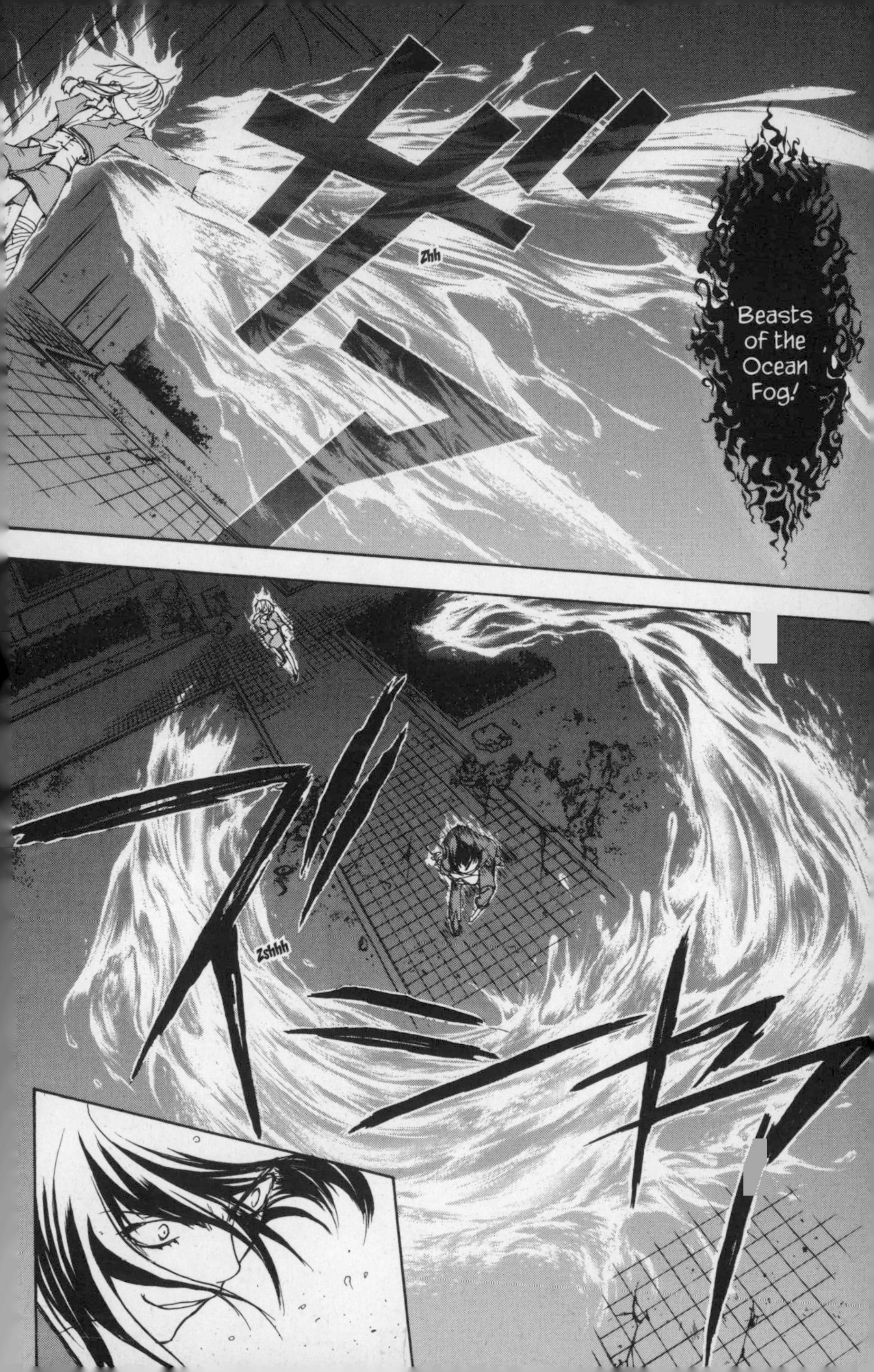
Beasts of the Ocean Fog!
Zhh
Zshhh

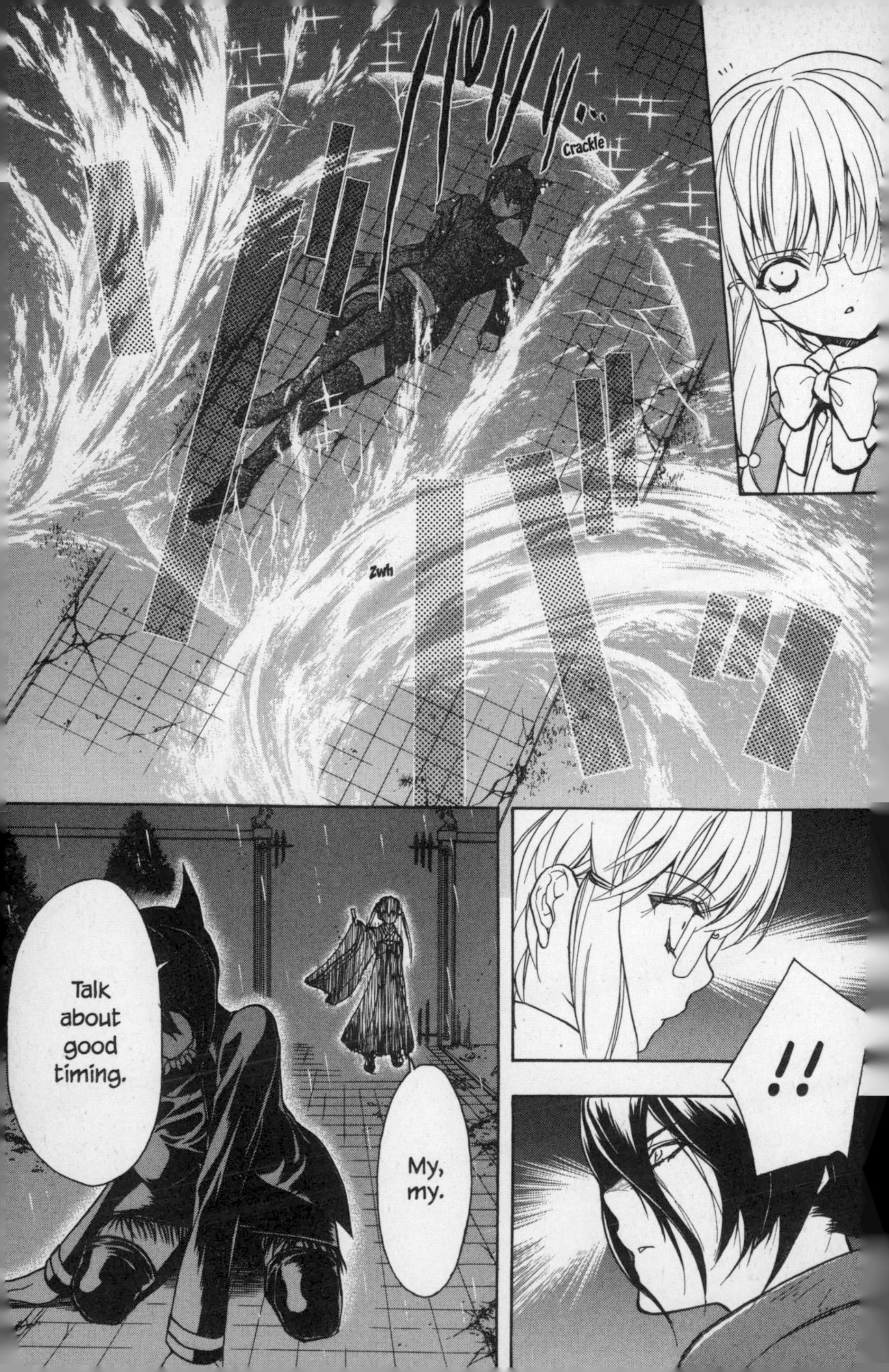

Crackle
Zwh
!!
My, my.
Talk about good timing.

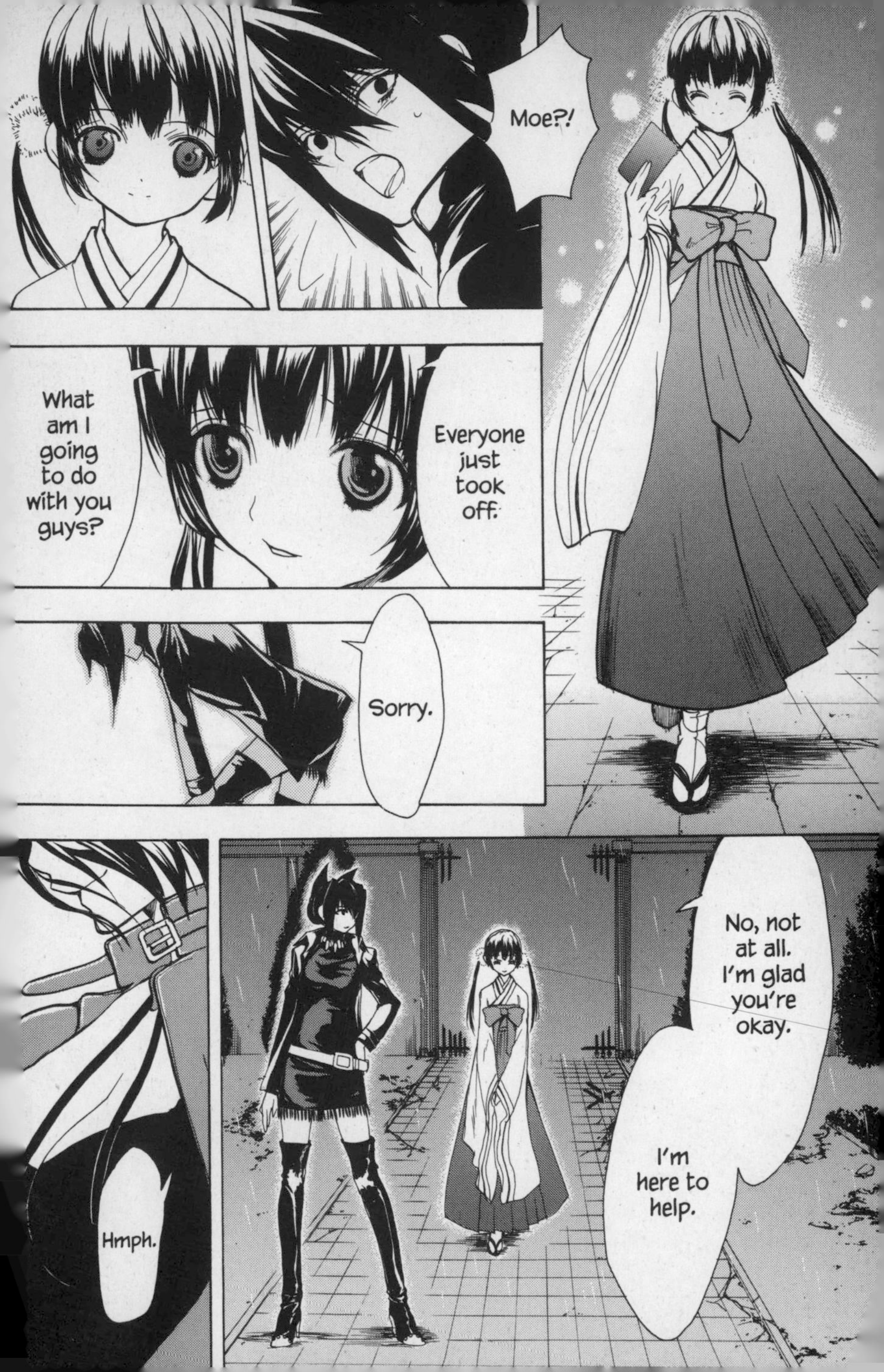
Moe?!
Everyone just took off.
What am I going to do with you guys?
Sorry.
No, not at all. I'm glad you're okay.
I'm here to help.
Hmph.

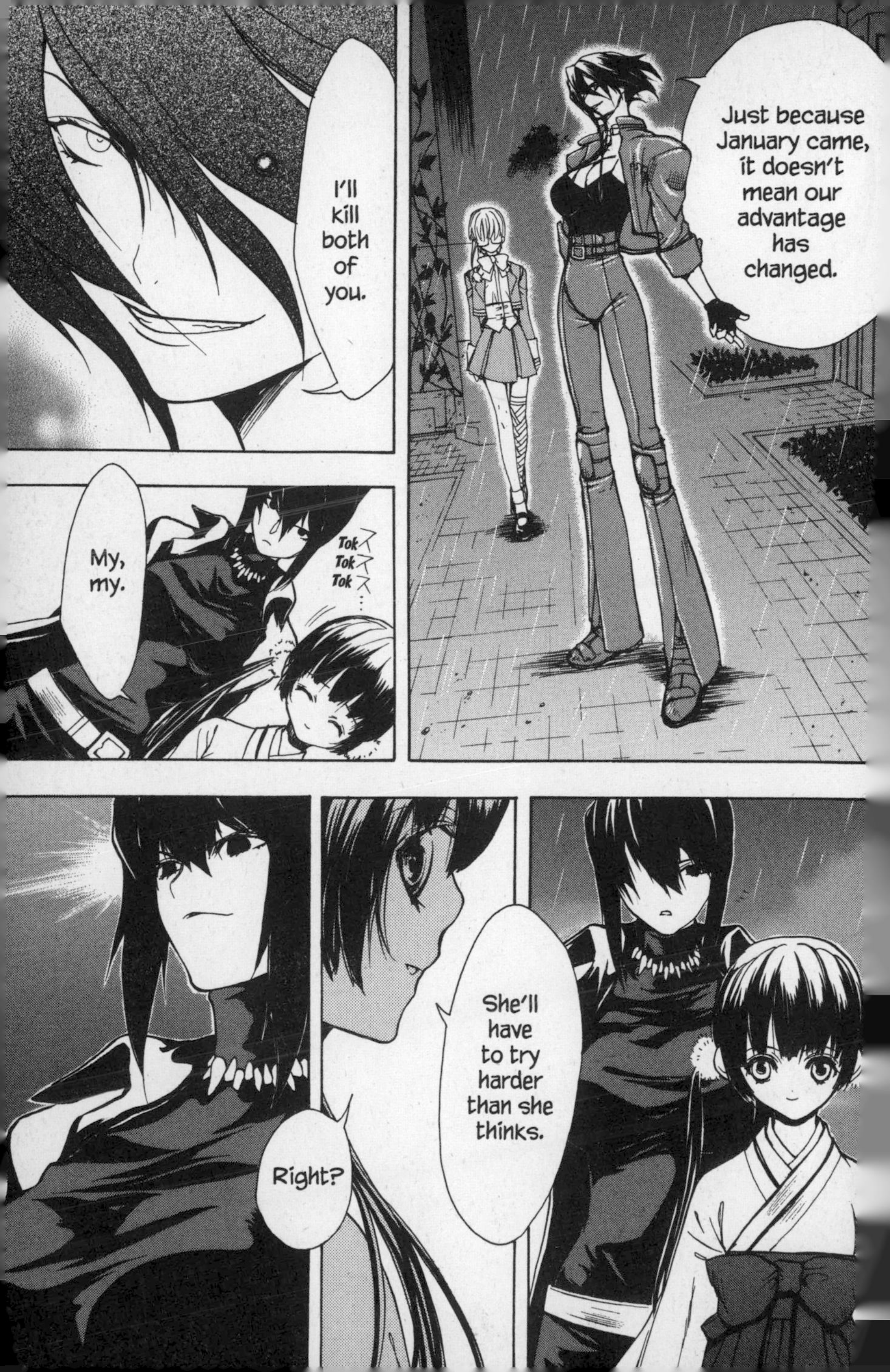
Just because January came, it doesn't mean our advantage has changed.
I'll kill both of you.
My, my.
Tok
Tok
Tok
She'll have to try harder than she thinks.
Right?

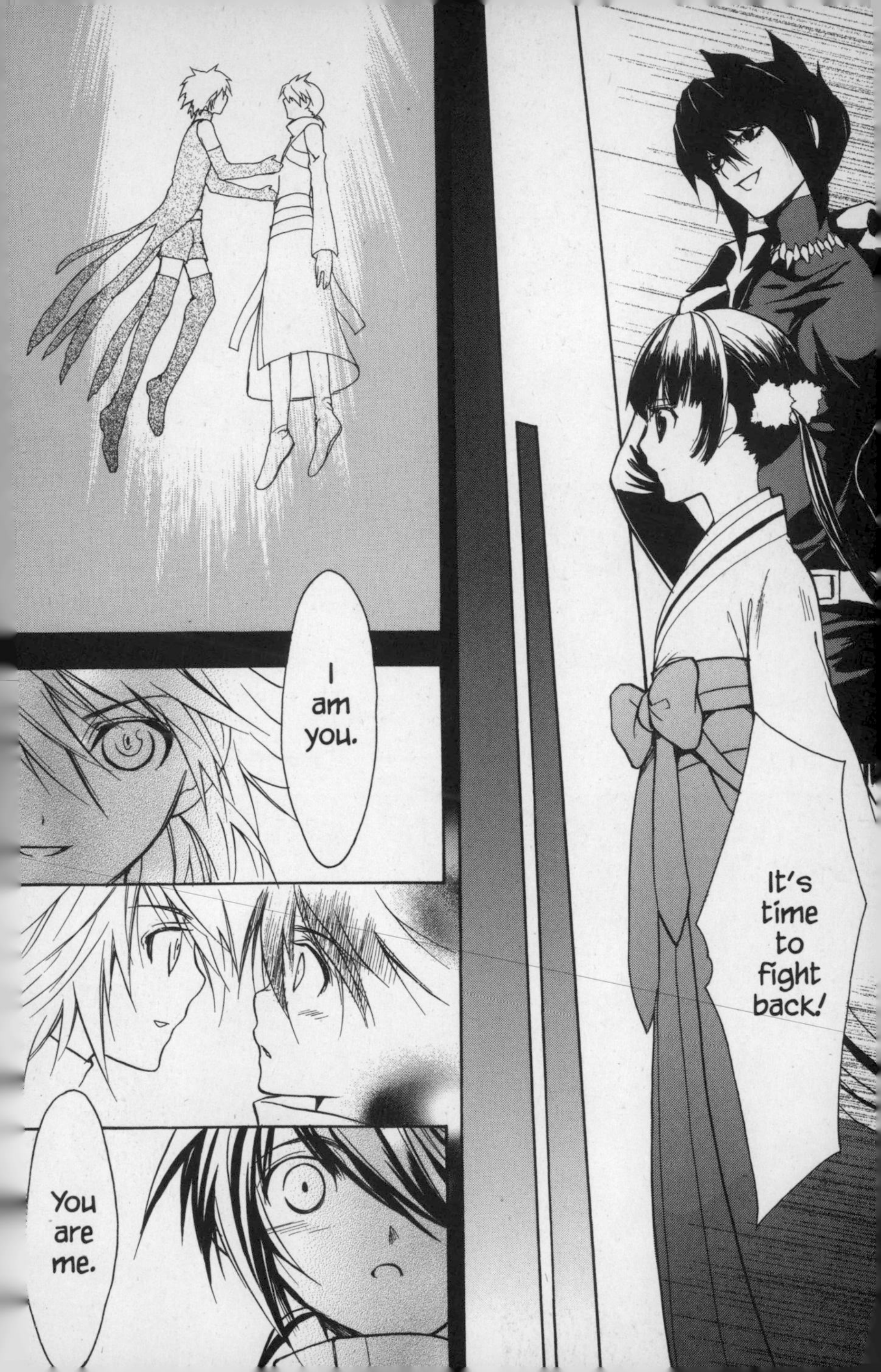

It's time to fight back!
I am you.
You are me.

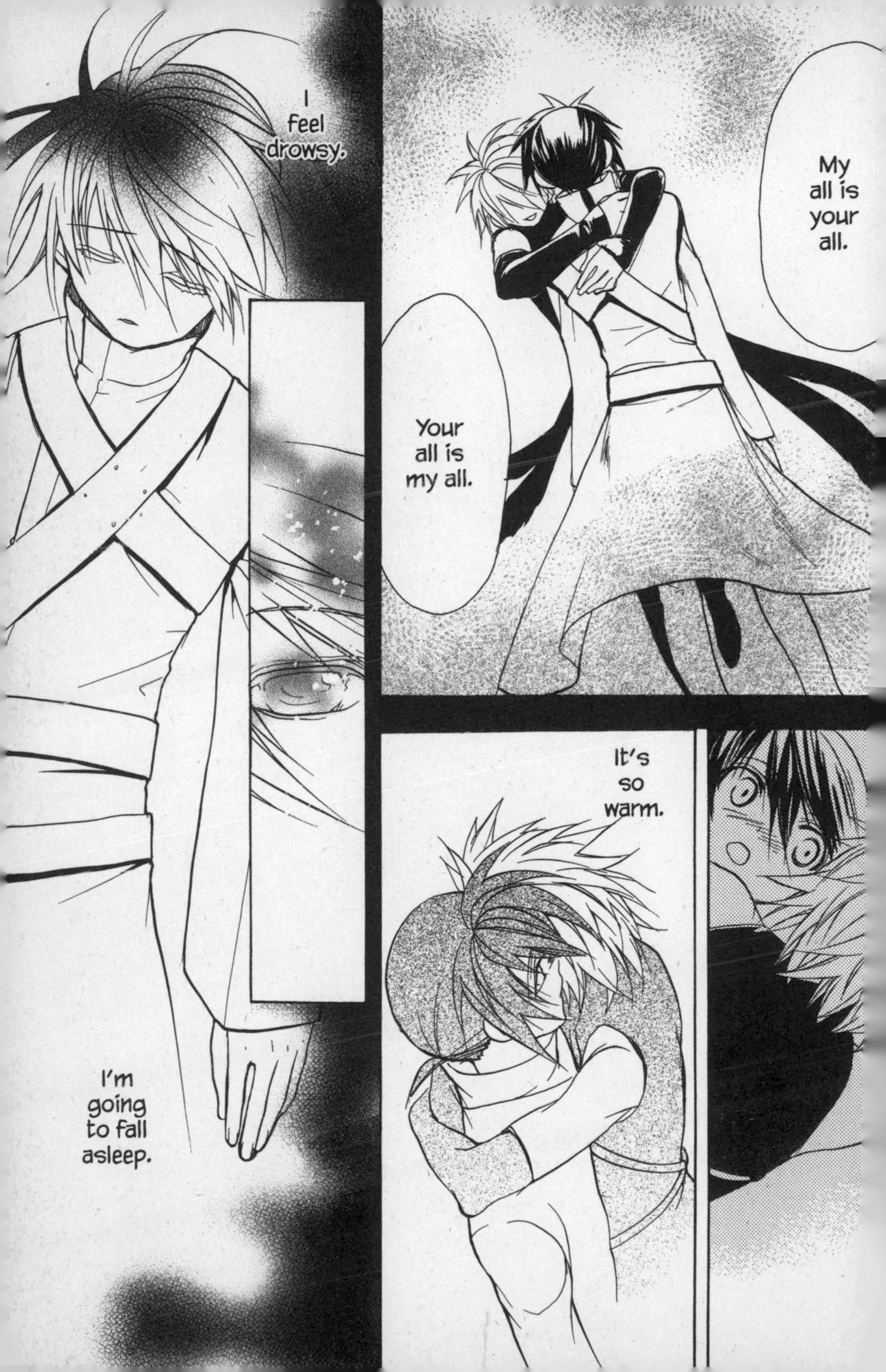
My all is your all.
Your all is my all.
It's so warm.
I feel drowsy.
I'm going to fall asleep.

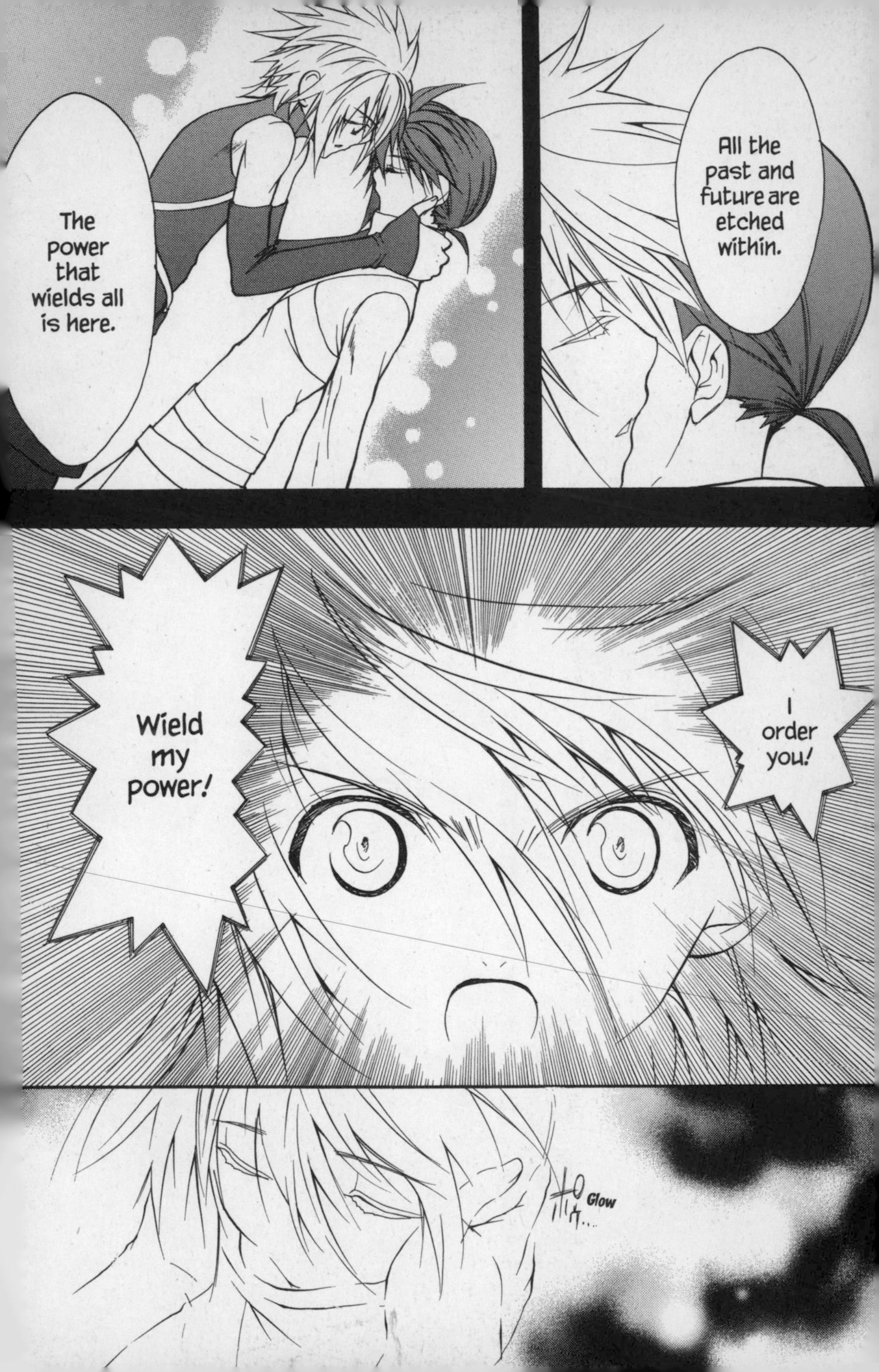
All the past and future are etched within.
The power that wields all is here.
I order you!
Wield my power!
Glow...

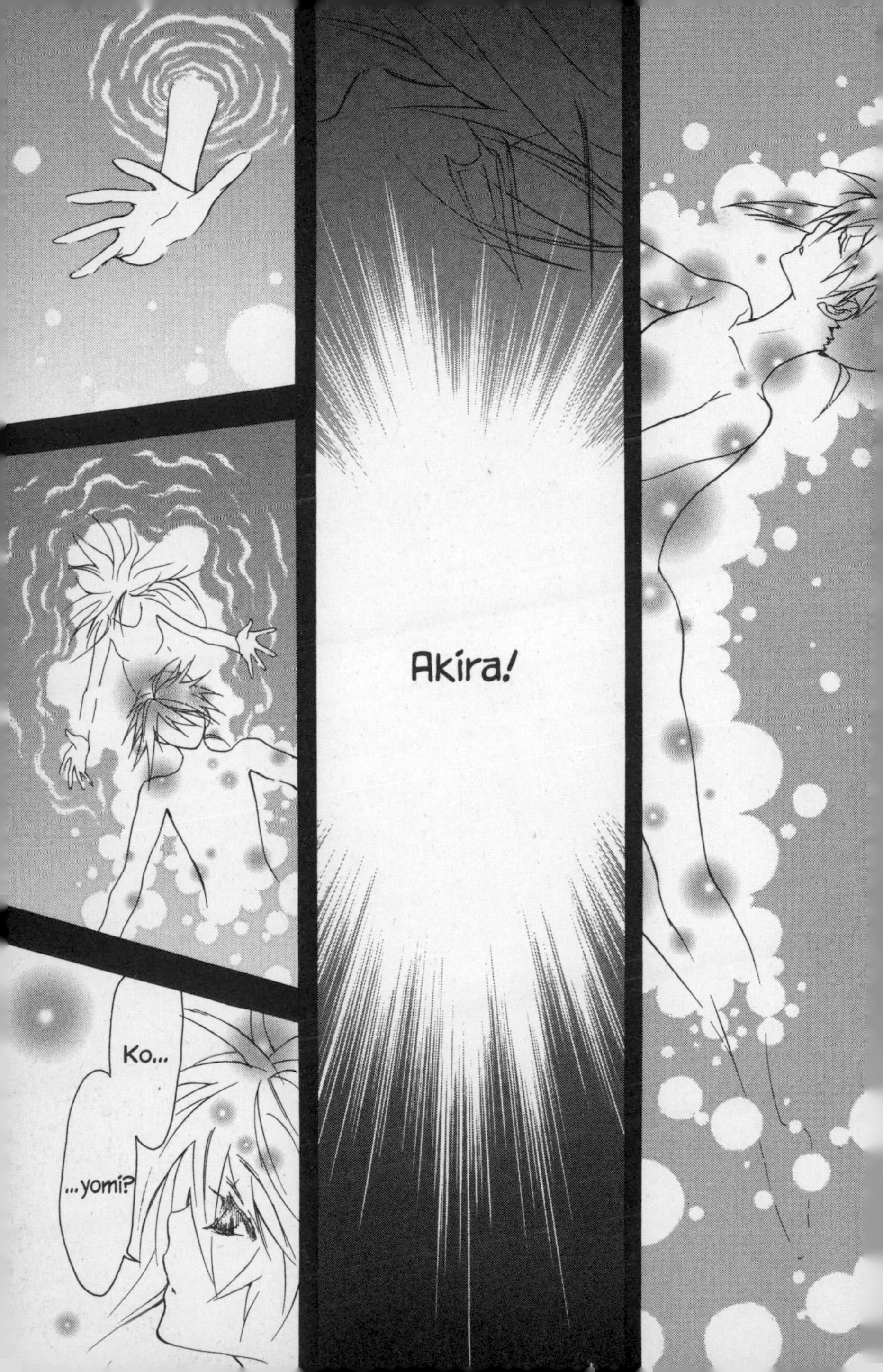
Akira!
Ko...
...yomi?

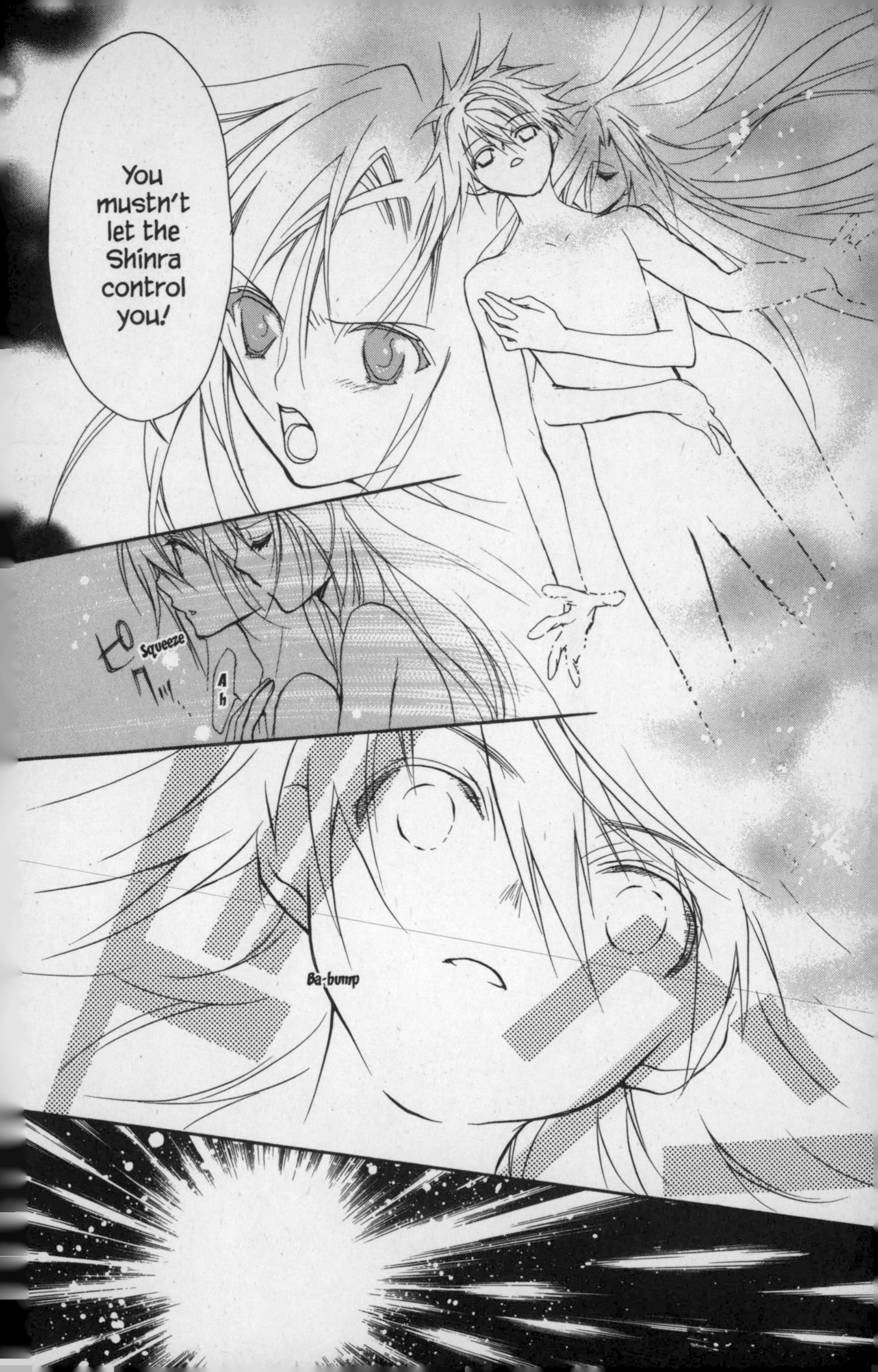
You mustn't let the Shinra control you!
Squeeze
Ah
Ba-bump

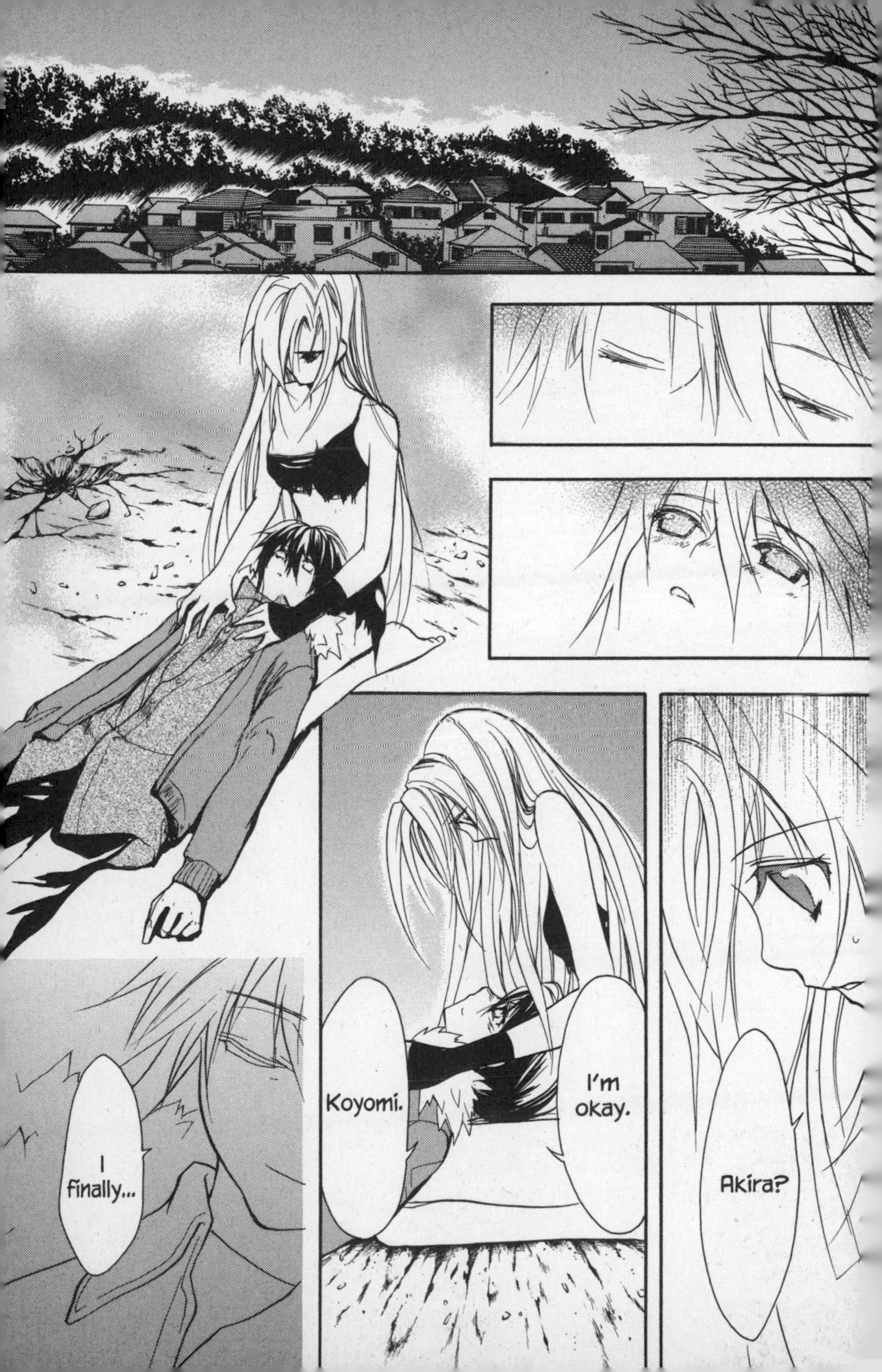
Akira?
I'm okay.
Koyomi.
I finally...

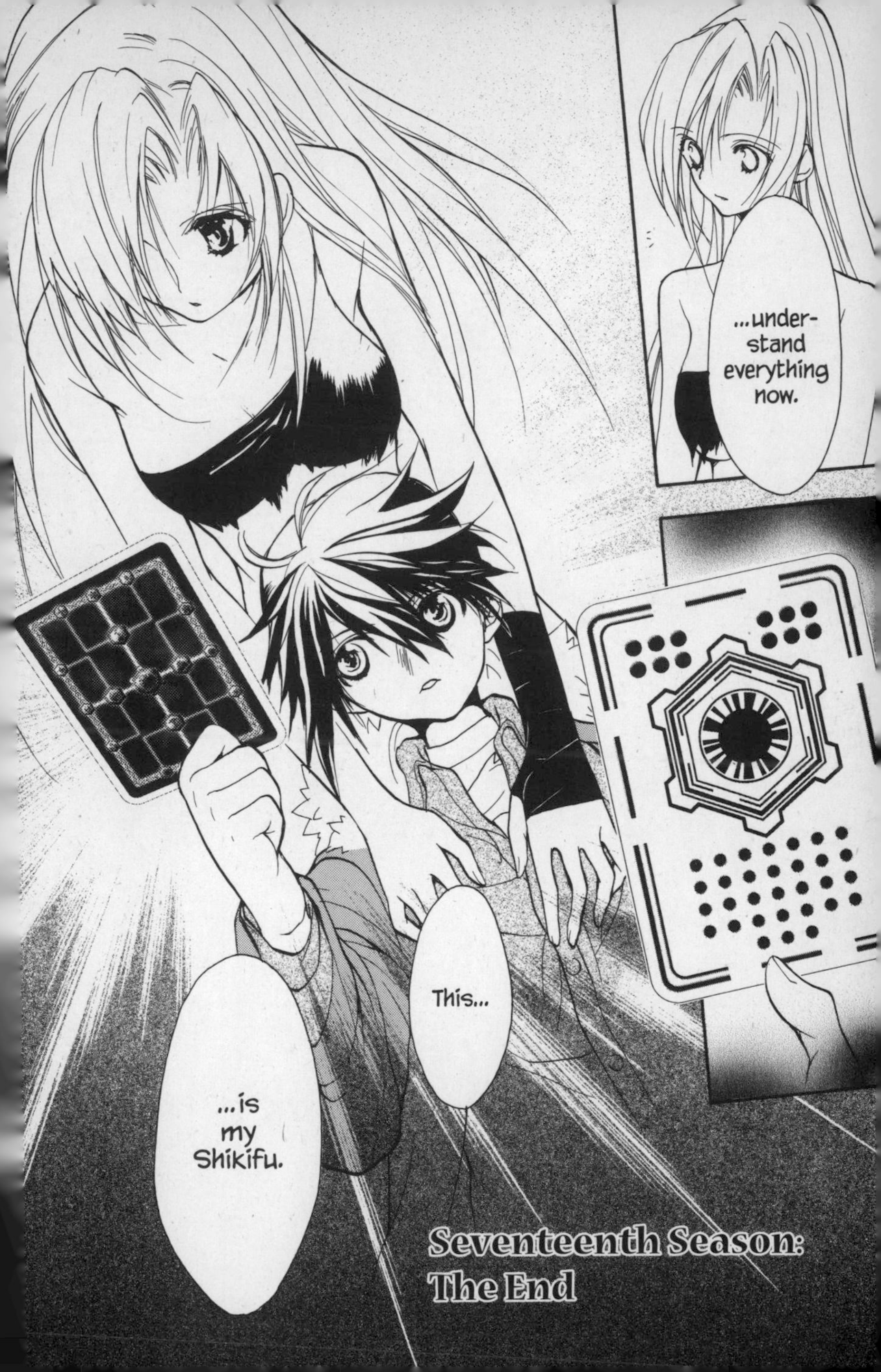
...under-stand everything now.
This...
...is my Shikifu.
Seventeenth Season: The End

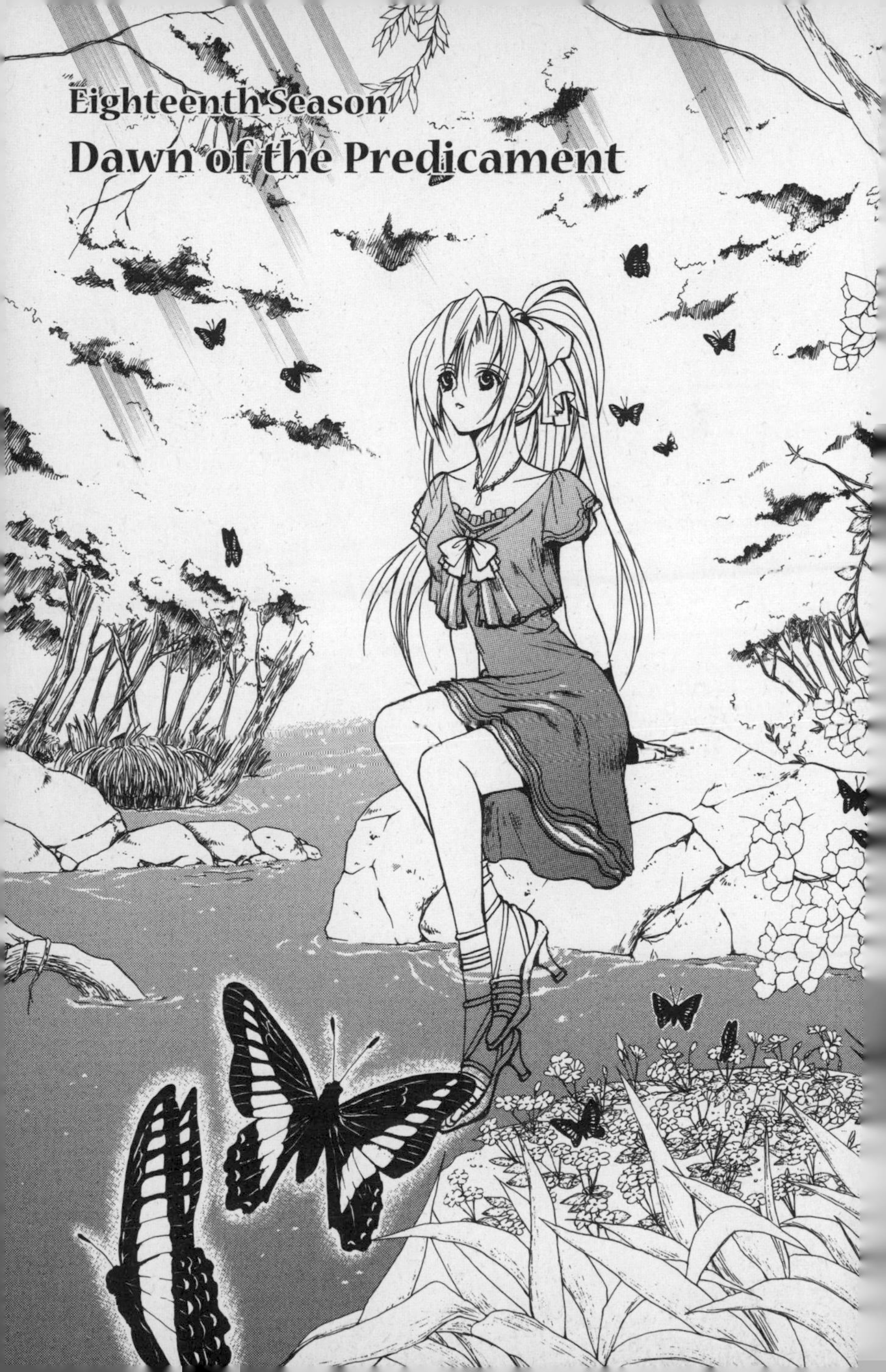
Eighteenth Season
Dawn of the Predicament

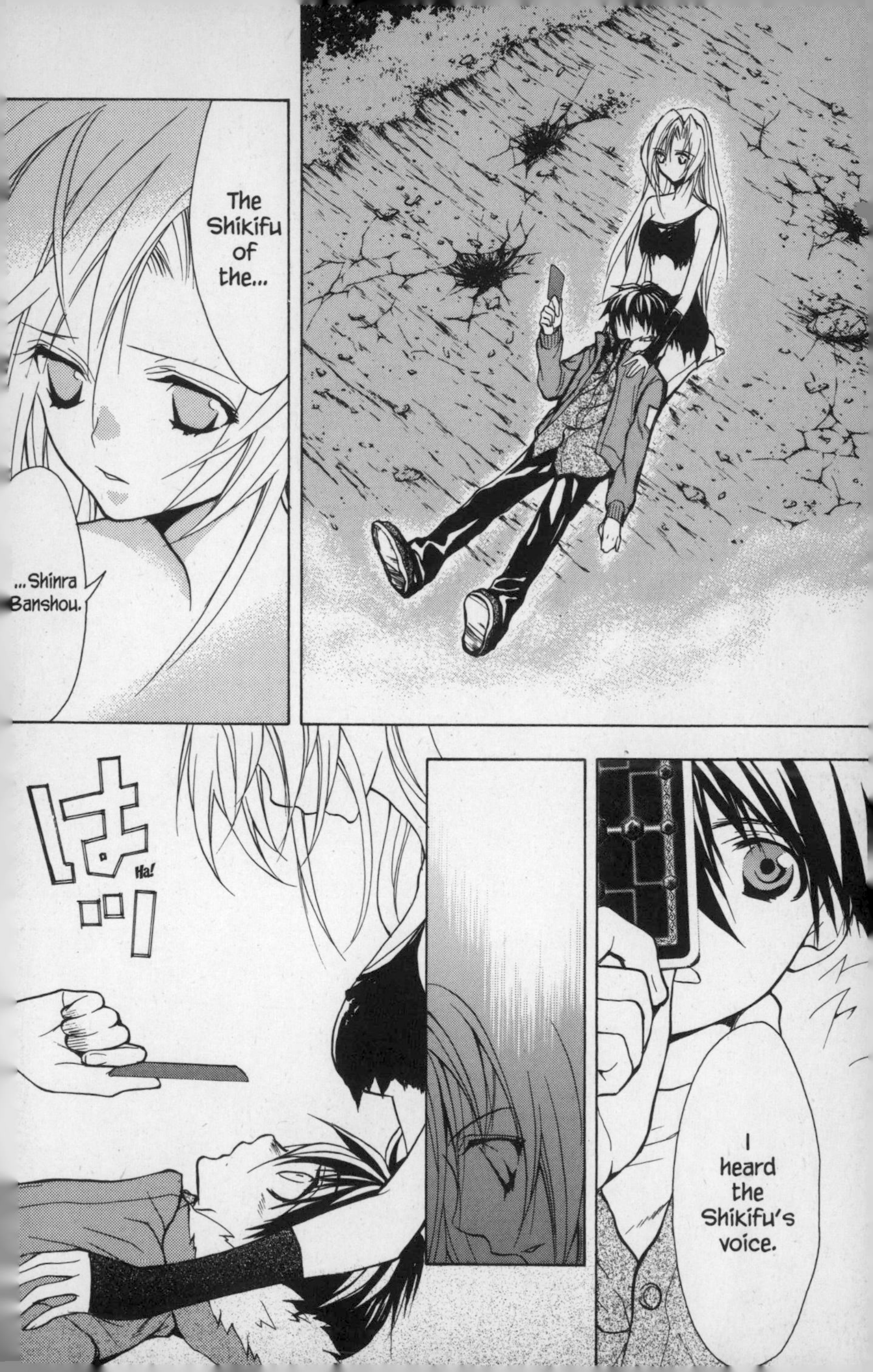
The Shikifu of the...
...Shinra Banshou.
I heard the Shikifu's voice.
はっ
Ha!

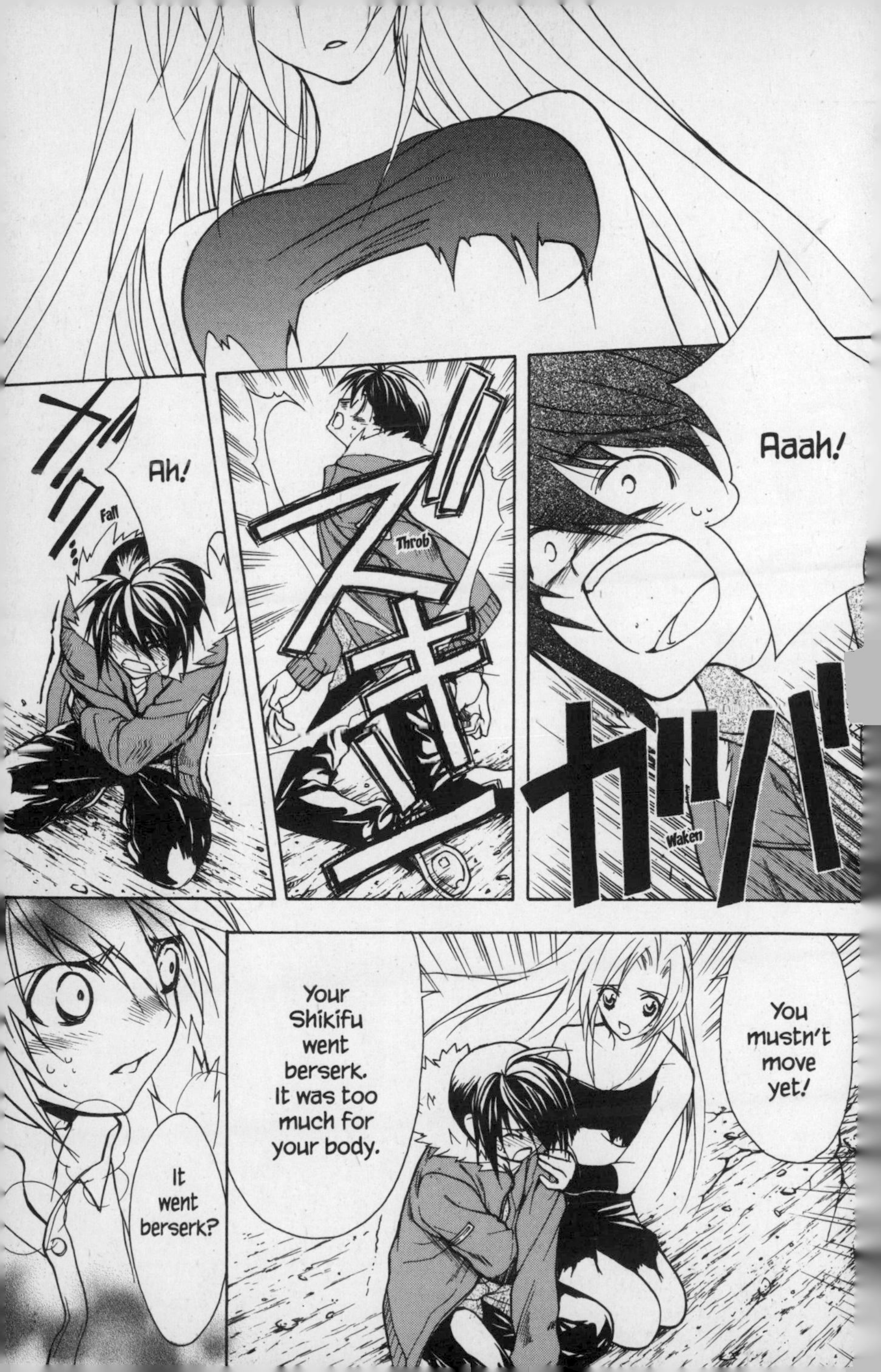
Aaah!
Waken
Throb
Ah!
Fall
You mustn't move yet!
Your Shikifu went berserk. It was too much for your body.
It went berserk?

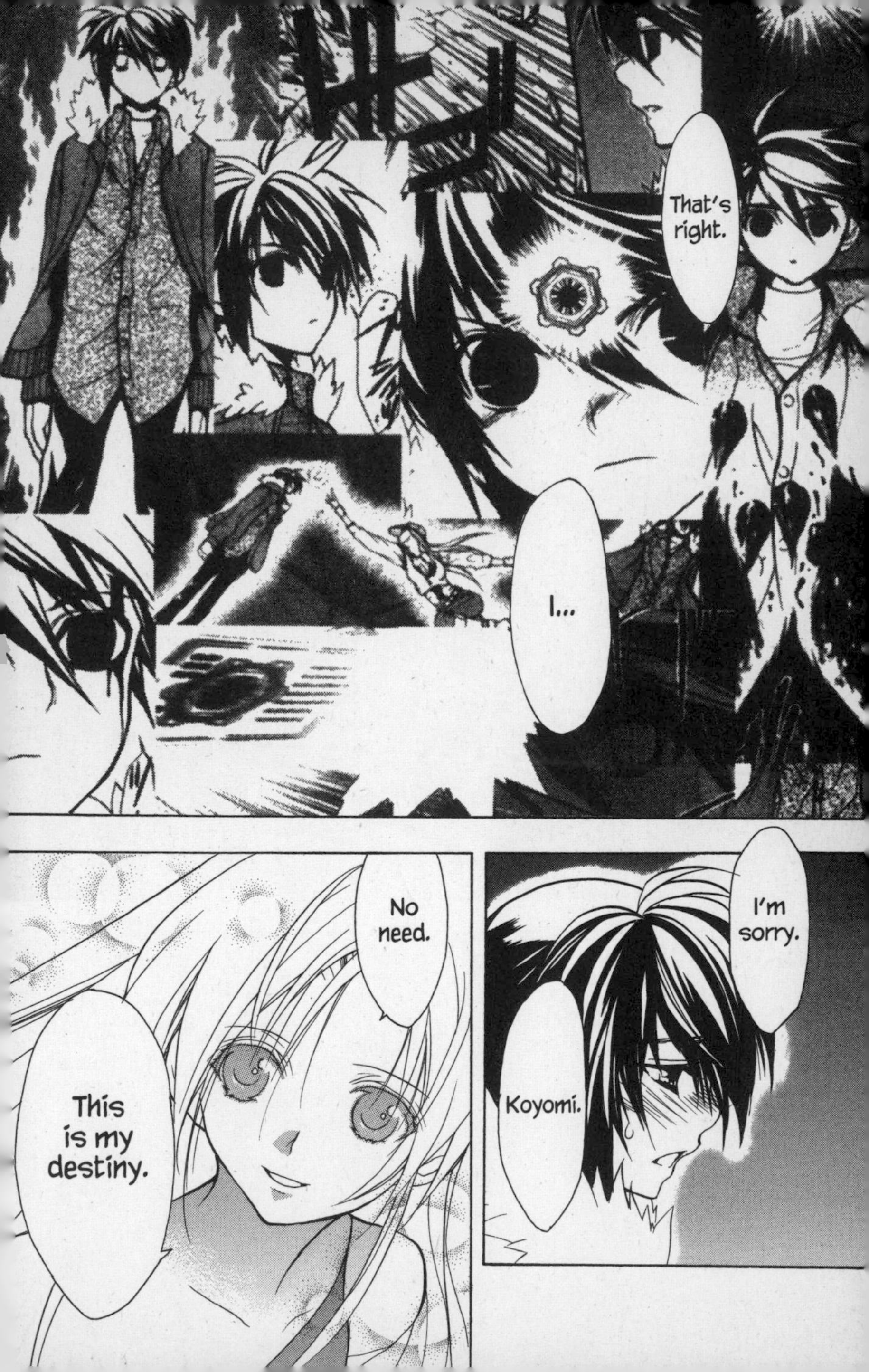
That's right.
I...
I'm sorry.
Koyomi.
No need.
This is my destiny.

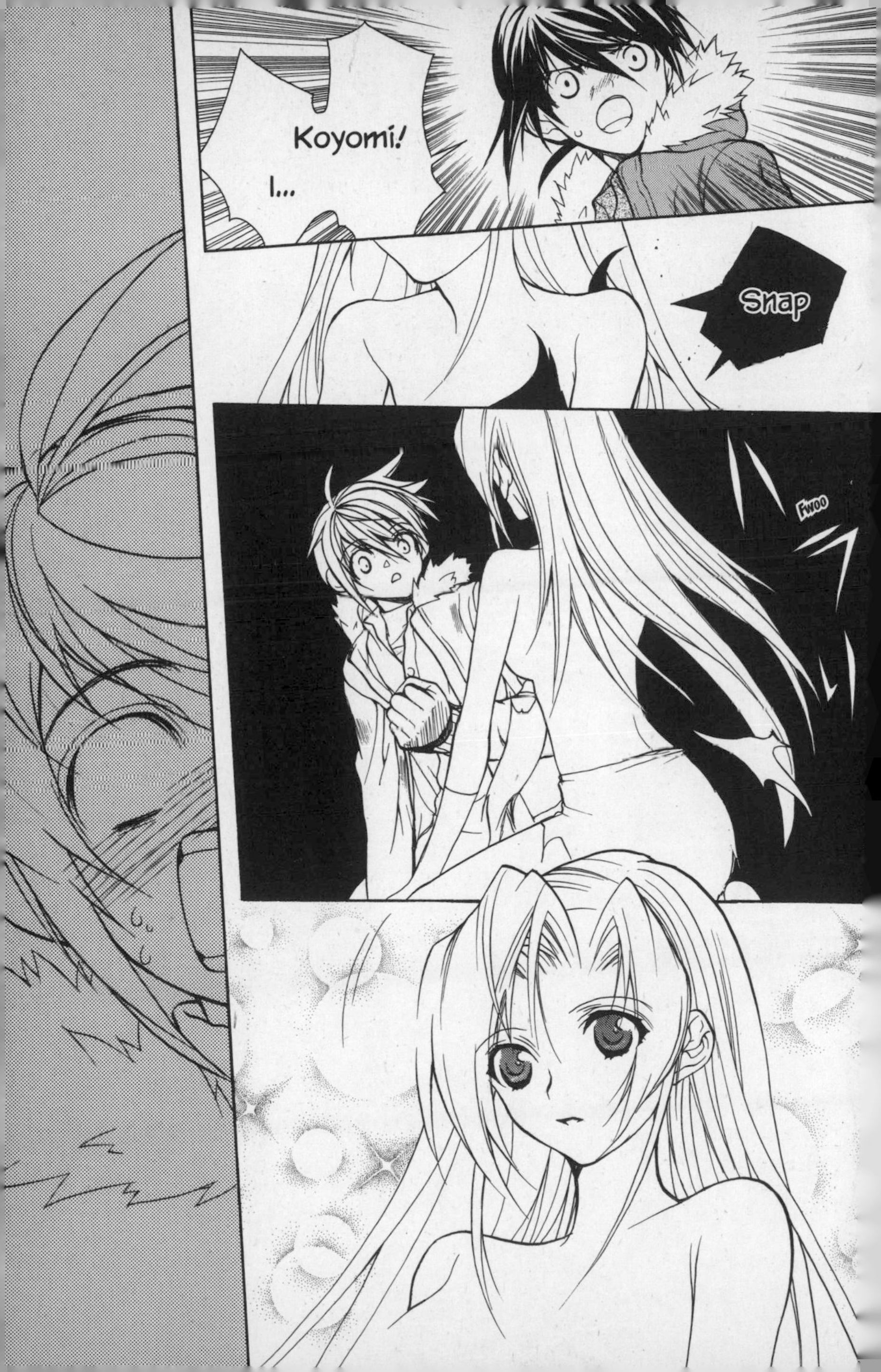
Koyomi!
I...
Snap
Fwoo

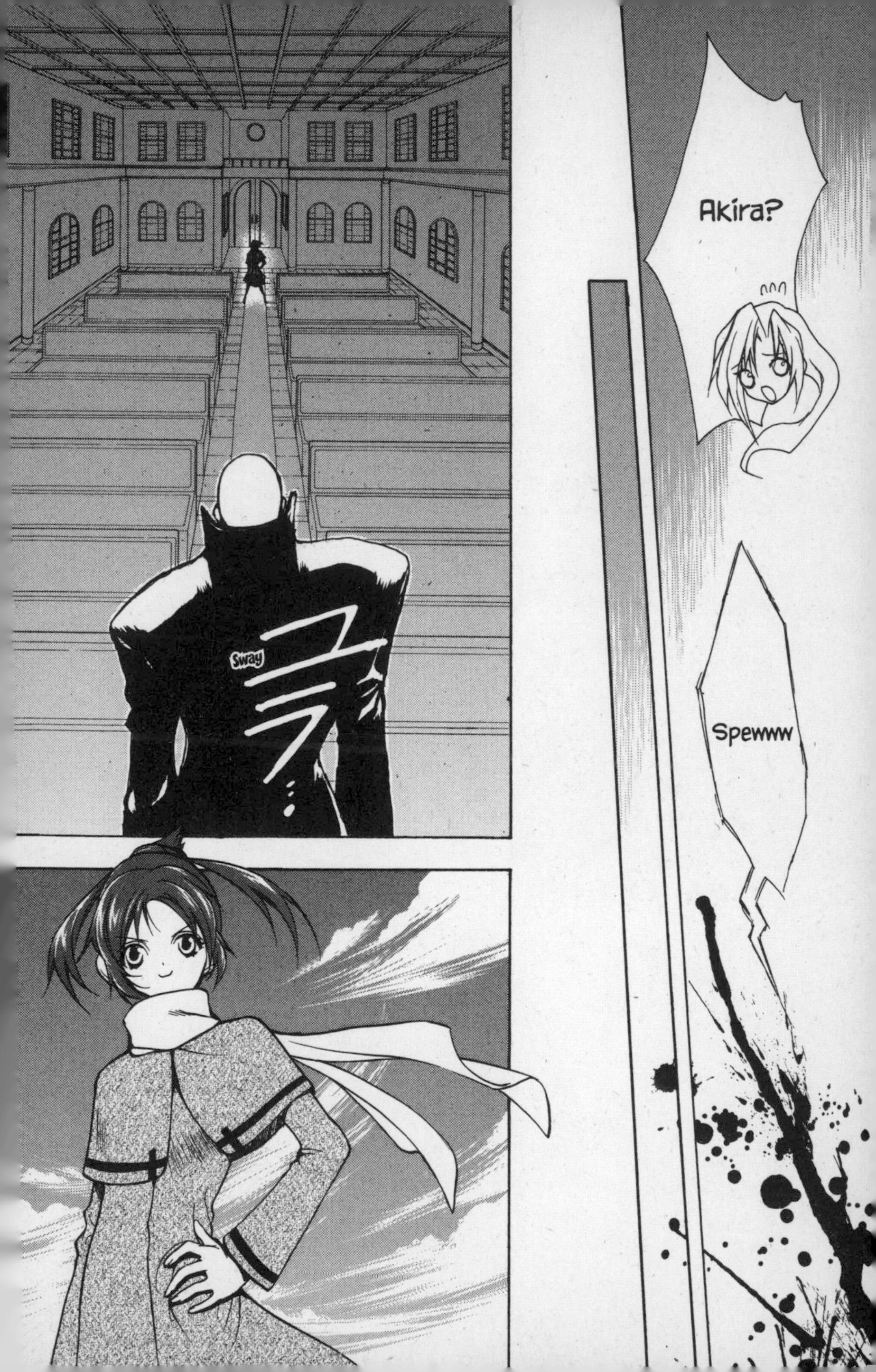
Akira?
Spewww
ユラ
Sway

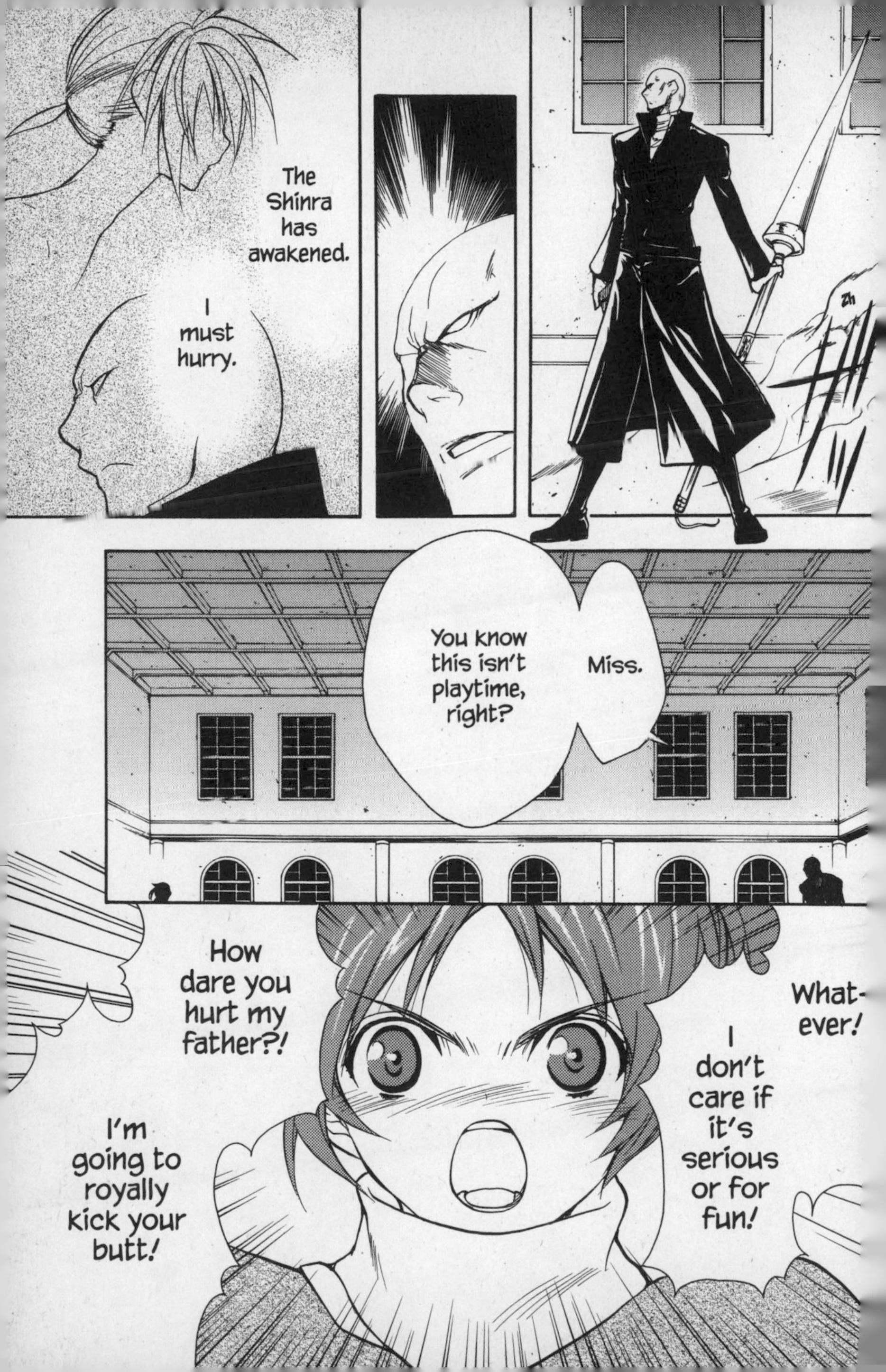
Zh
The Shinra has awakened.
I must hurry.
Miss.
You know this isn't playtime, right?
What-ever!
I don't care if it's serious or for fun!
How dare you hurt my father?!
I'm going to royally kick your butt!

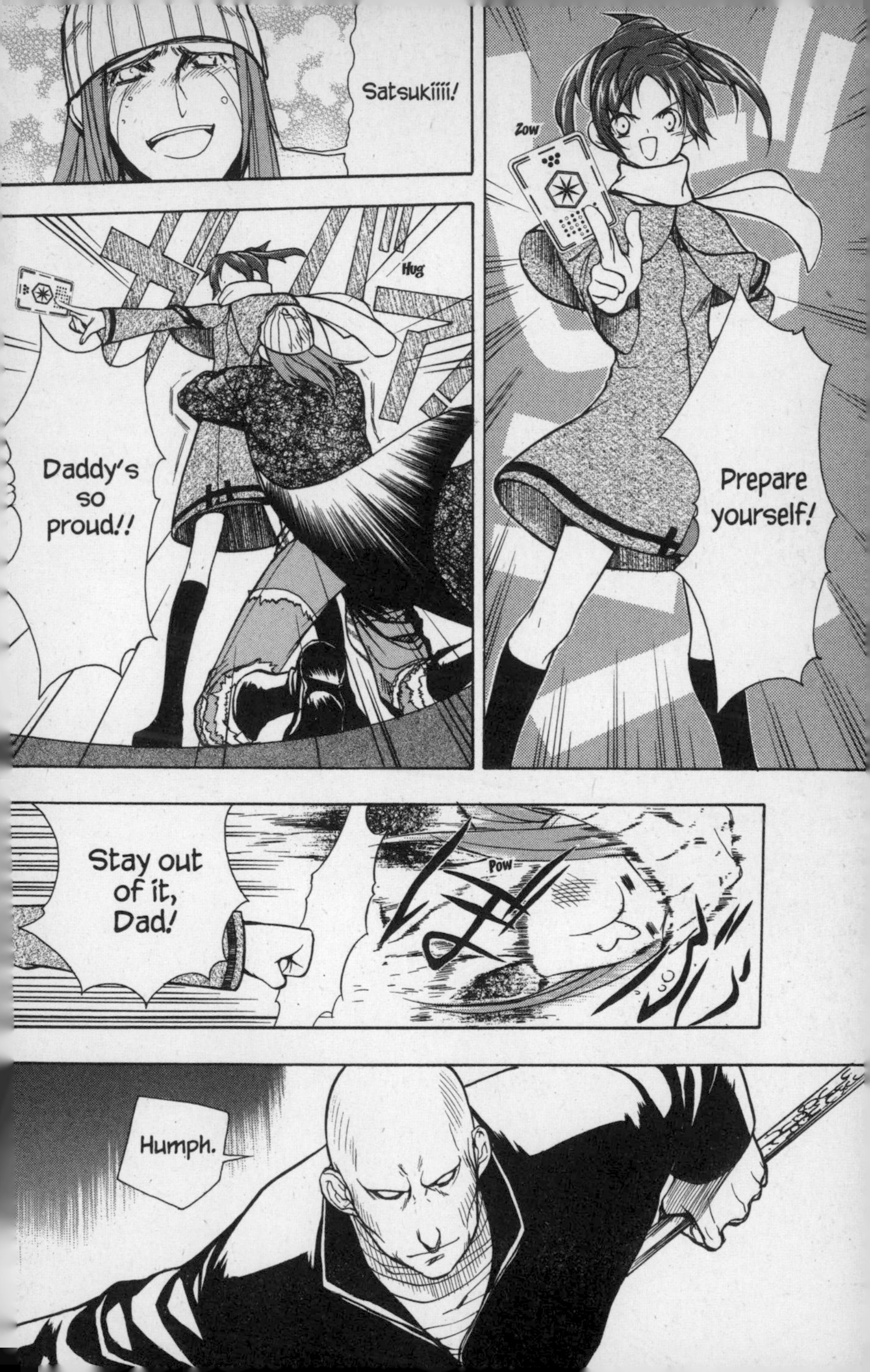
Zow
Prepare yourself!
Satsukiiii!
Hug
Daddy's so proud!!
Pow
Stay out of it, Dad!
Humph.

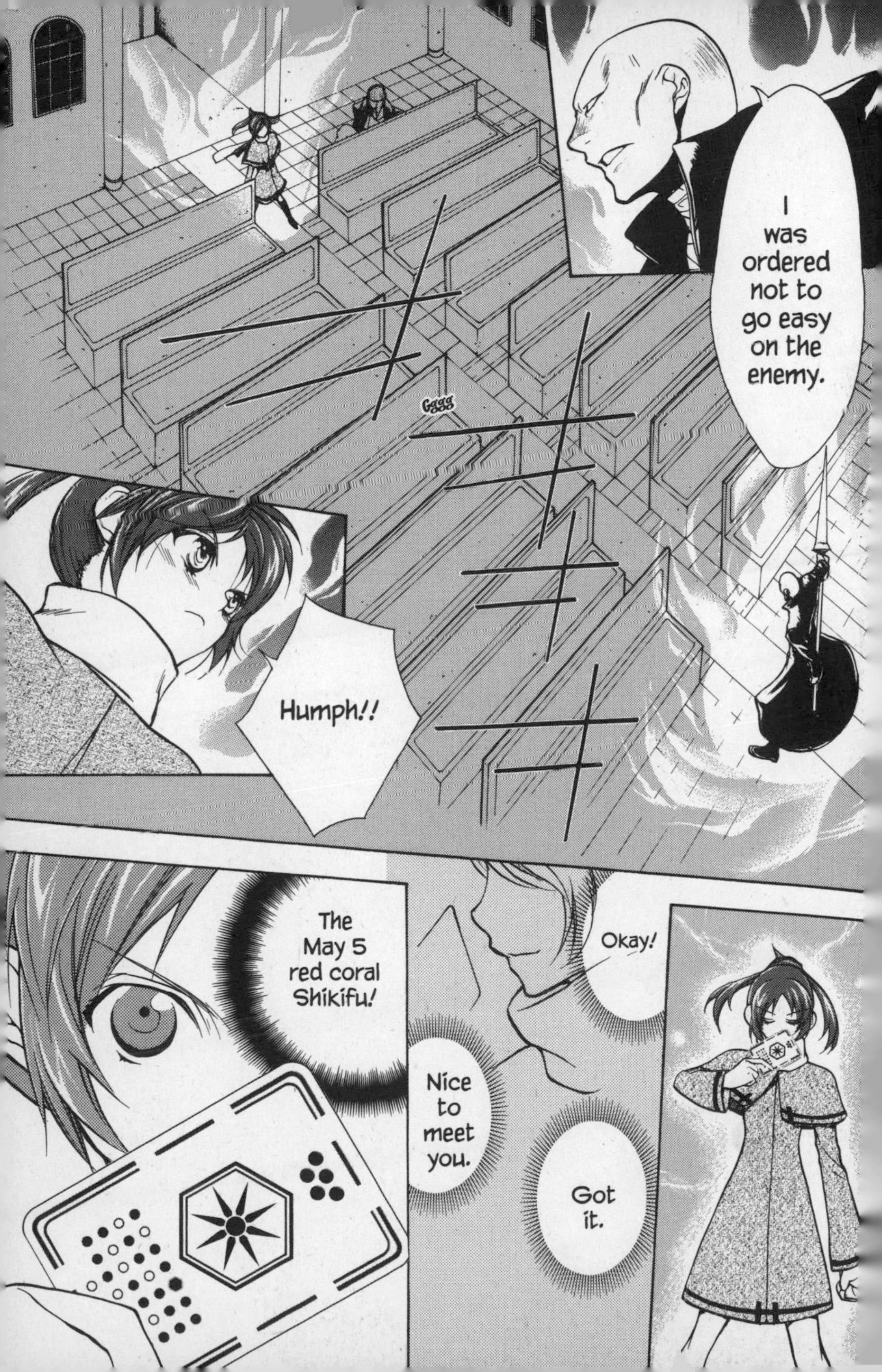
I was ordered not to go easy on the enemy.
Gggg
Humph!!
Okay!
Nice to meet you.
Got it.
The May 5 red coral Shikifu!

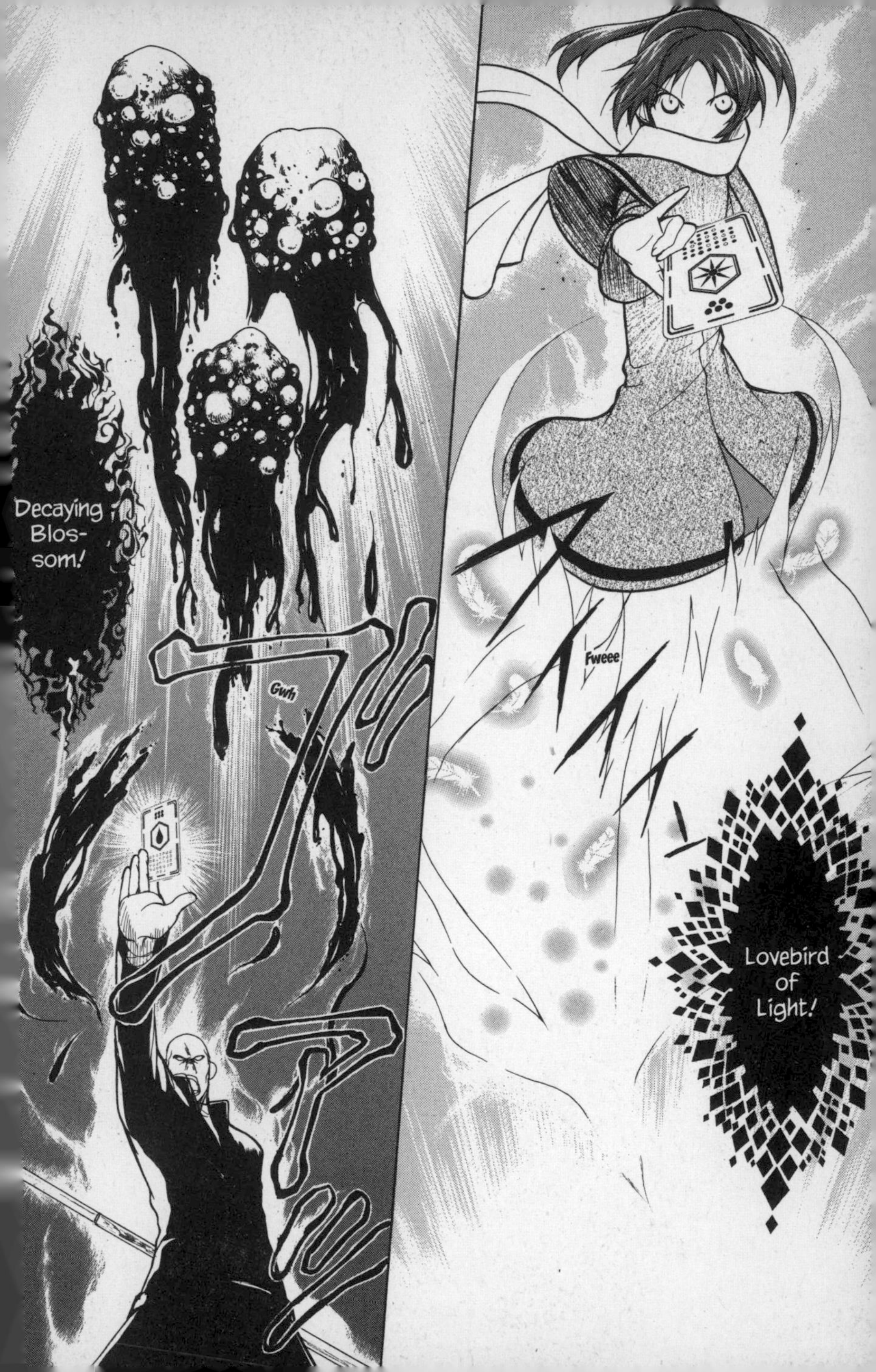
Fweee
Lovebird of Light!
Decaying Blos-som!
Gwh

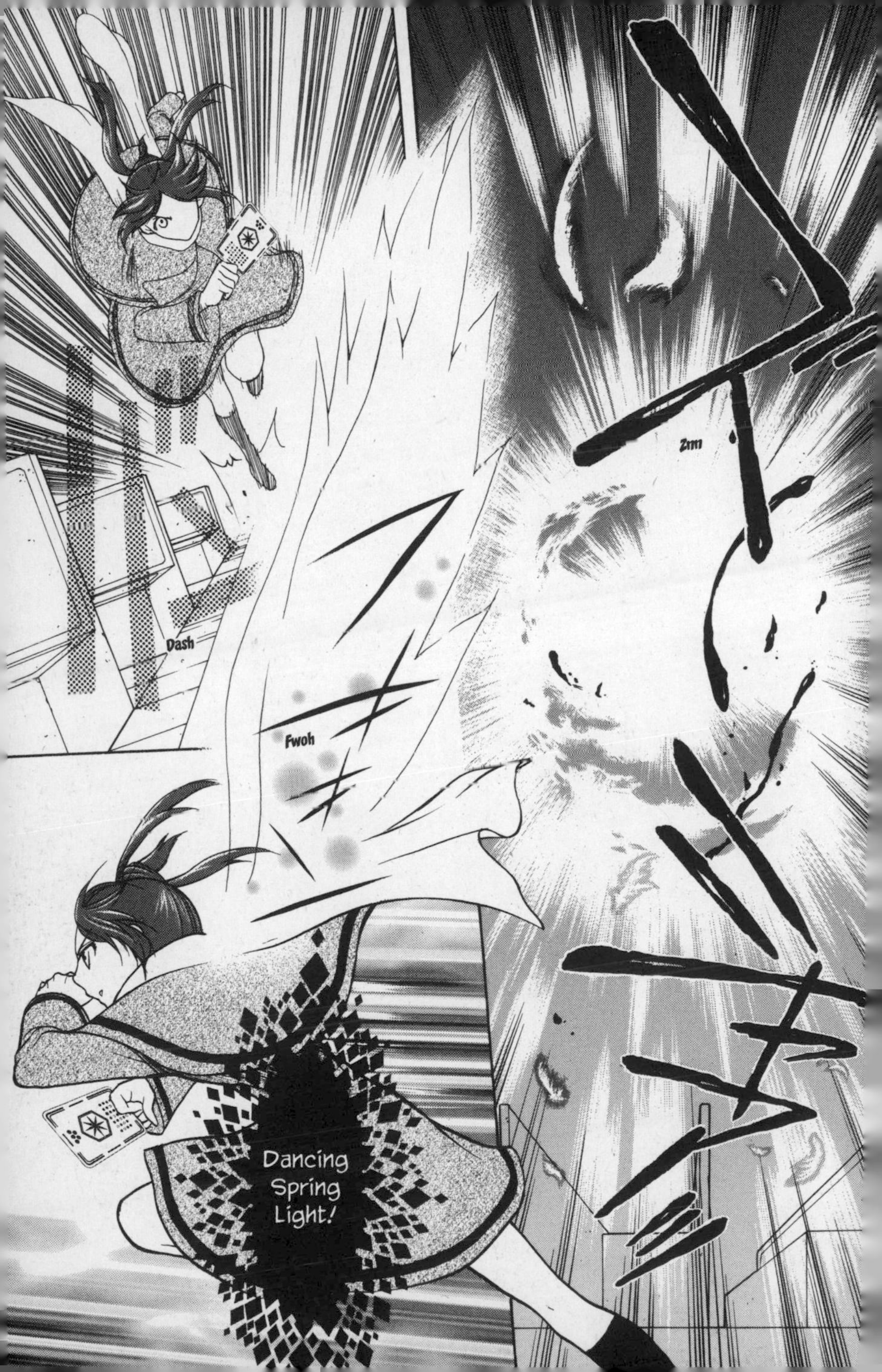
Zmm
Dash
Fwoh
Dancing Spring Light!

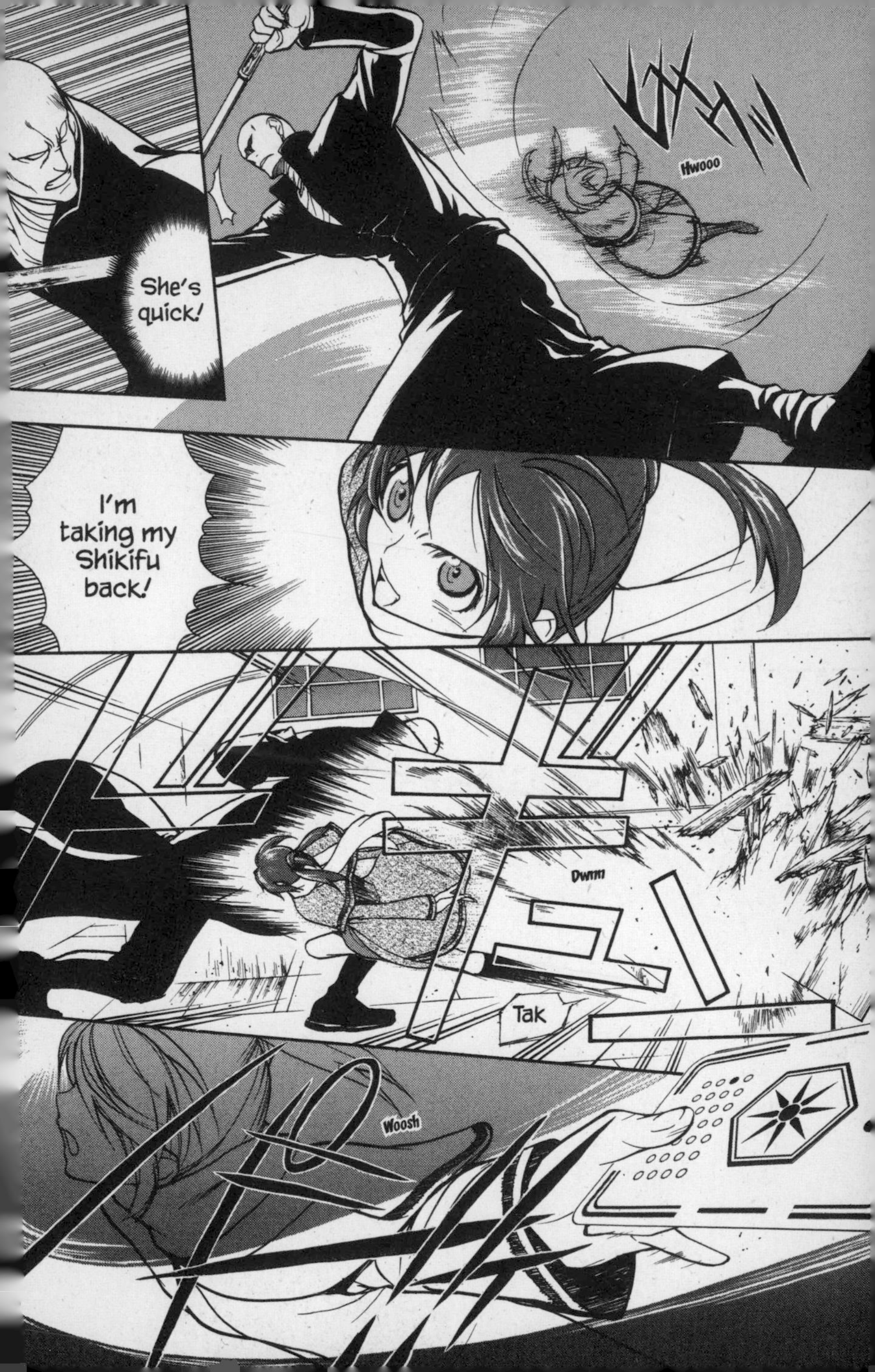
Hwooo
She's quick!
I'm taking my Shikifu back!
Dwmm
Tak
Woosh

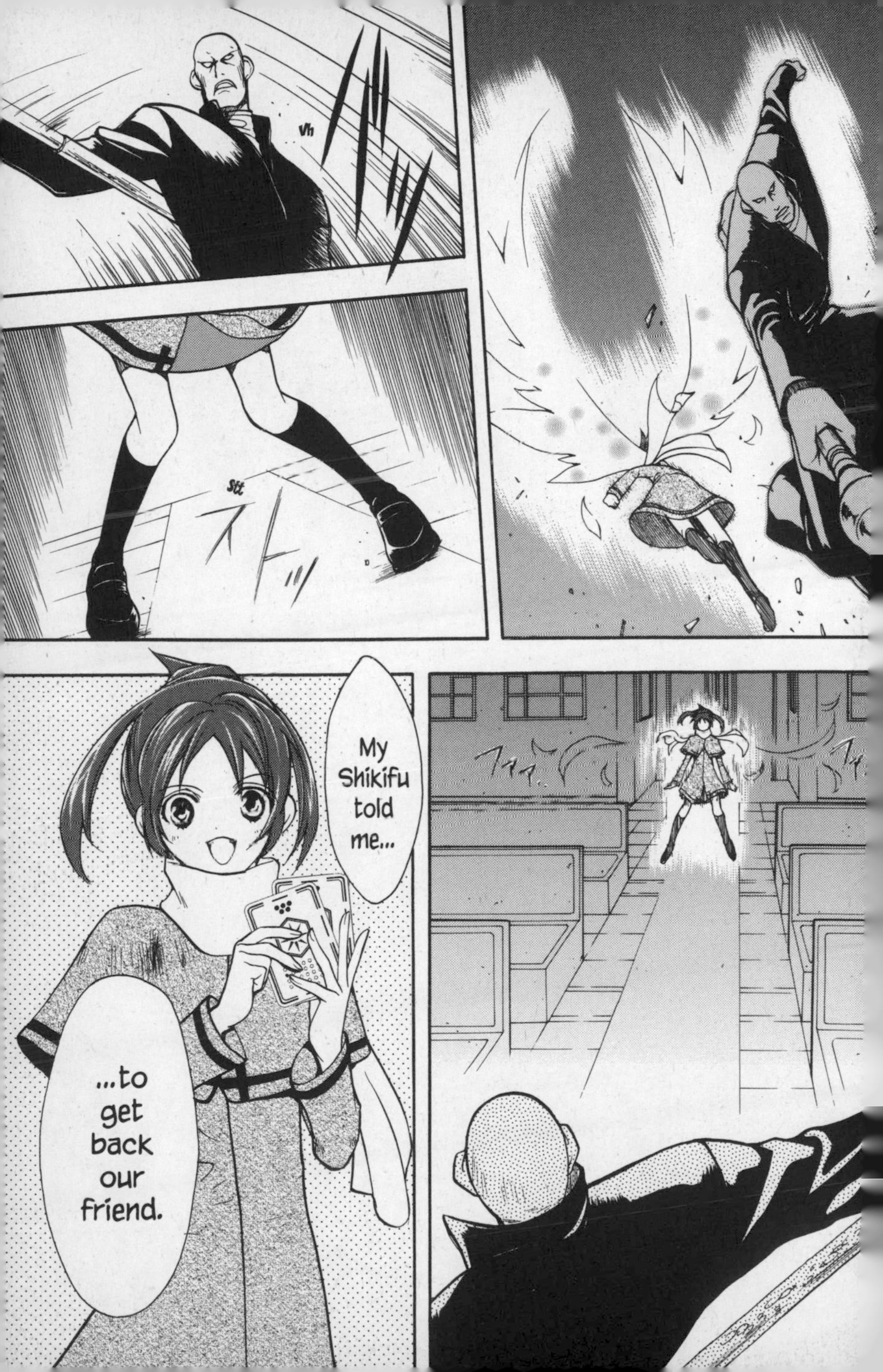
Vh
Stt
My Shikifu told me...
...to get back our friend.

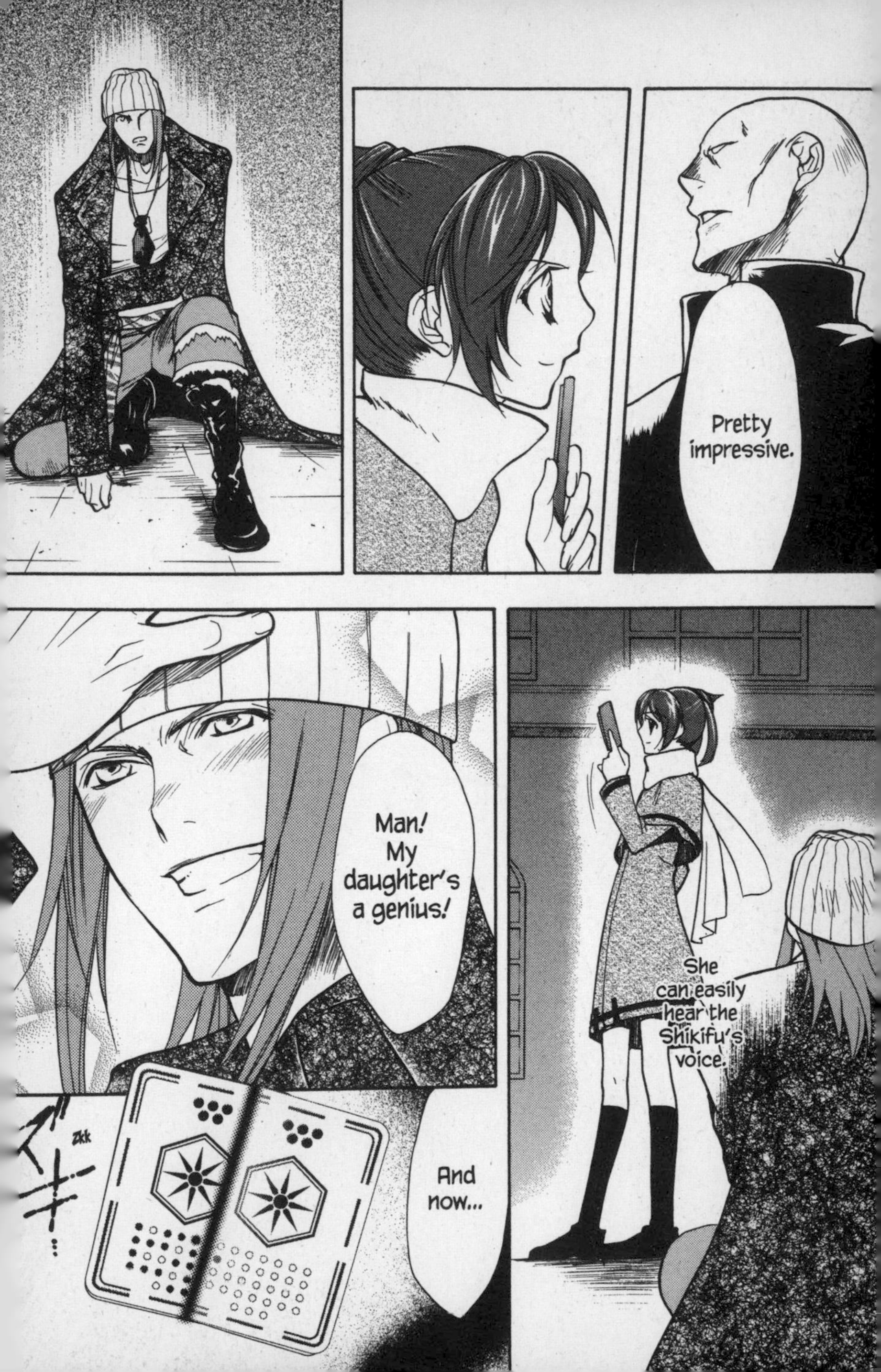
Pretty impressive.
She can easily hear the Shikifu's voice.
Man! My daughter's a genius!
Zkk
And now...

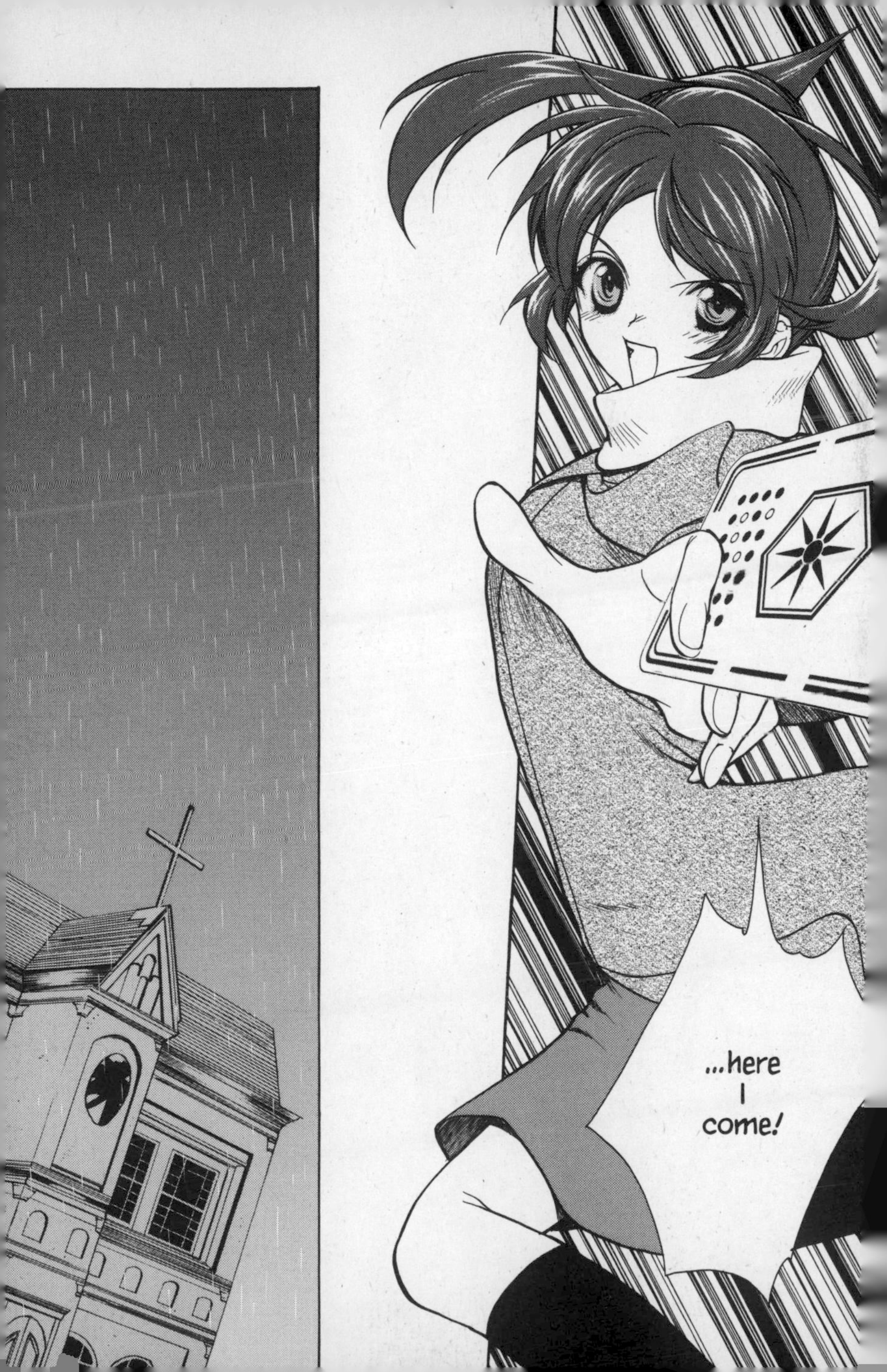
...here I come!

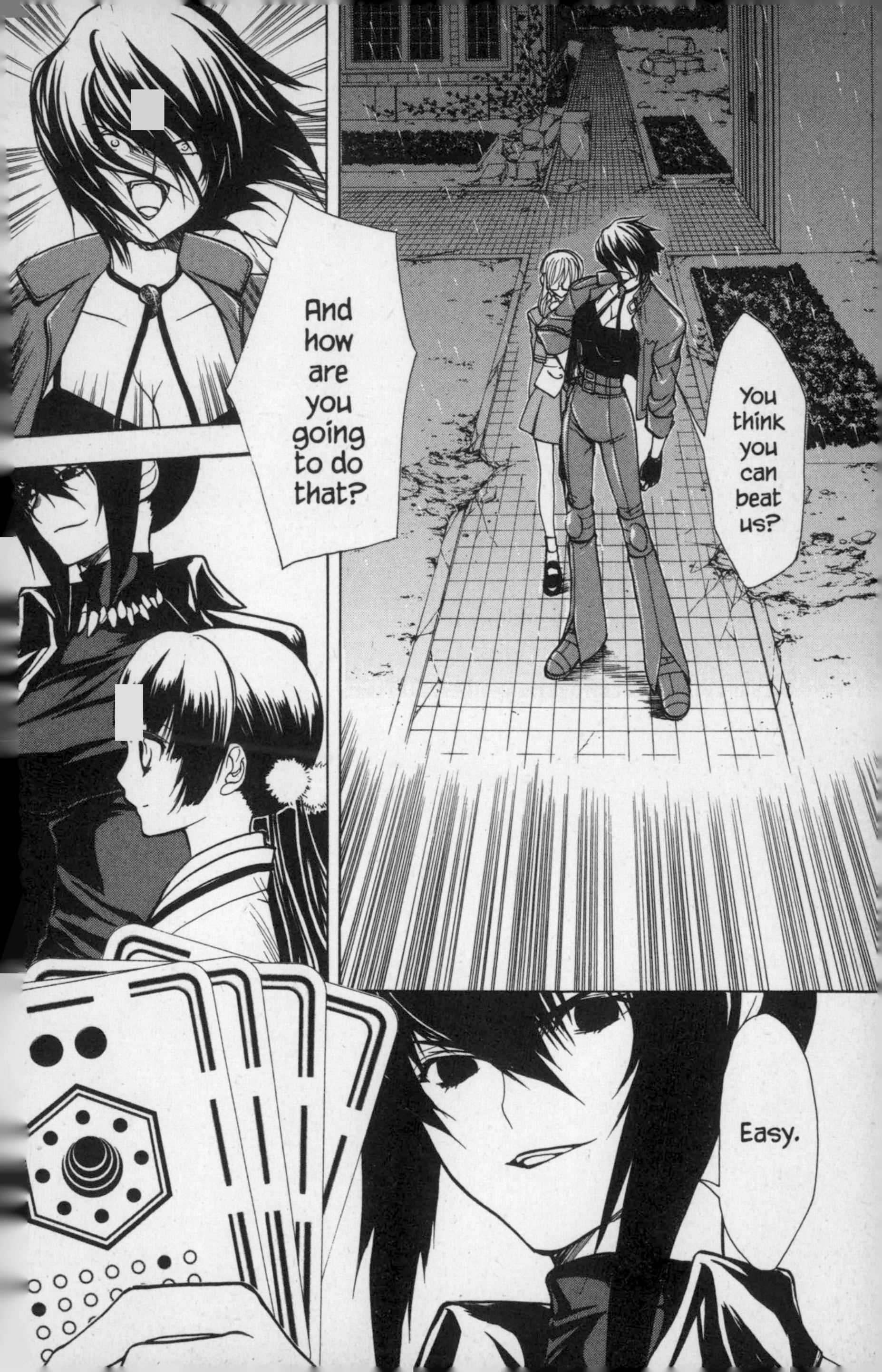
You think you can beat us?
And how are you going to do that?
Easy.

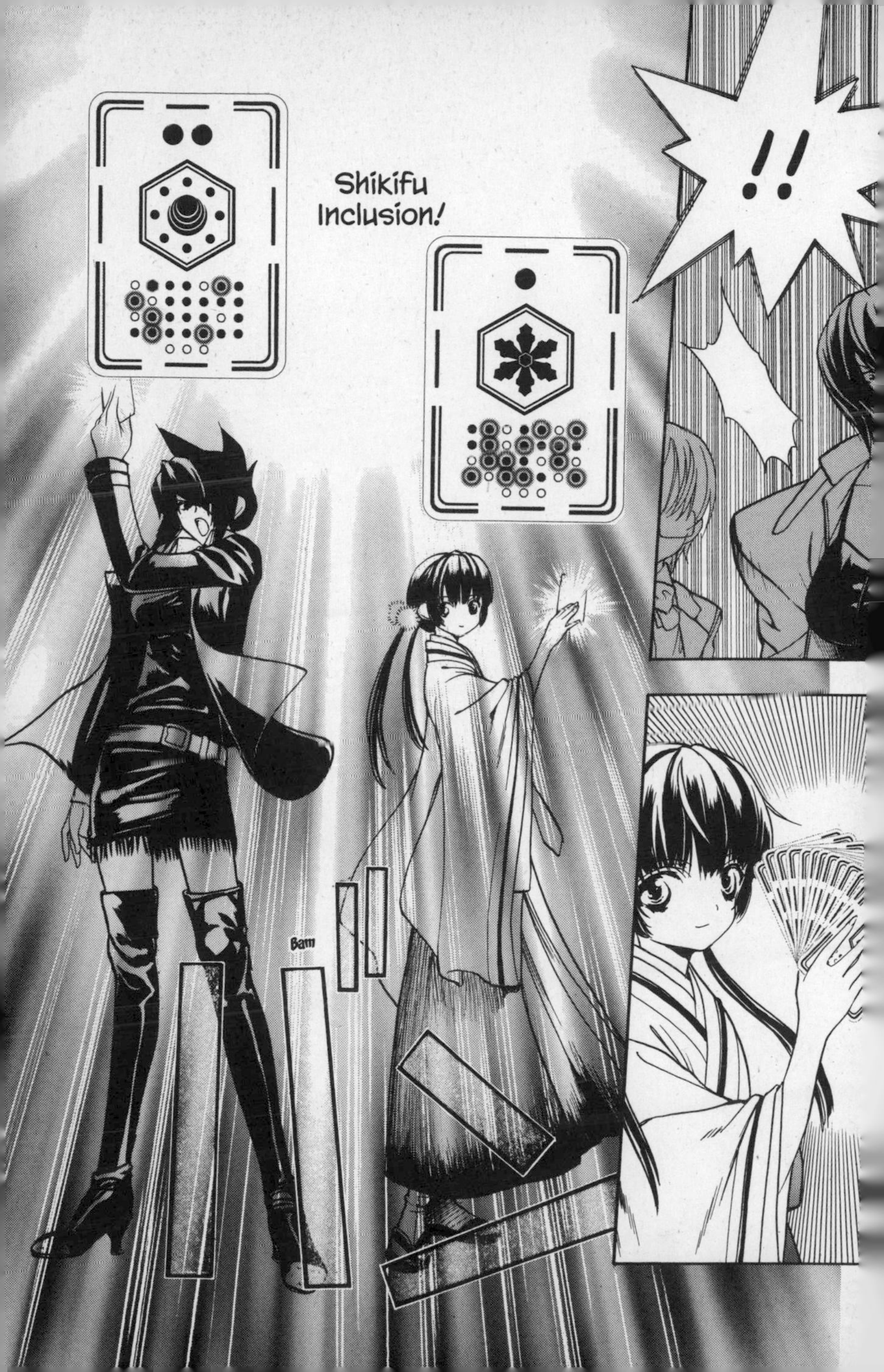
!!
Shikifu Inclusion!
Bam

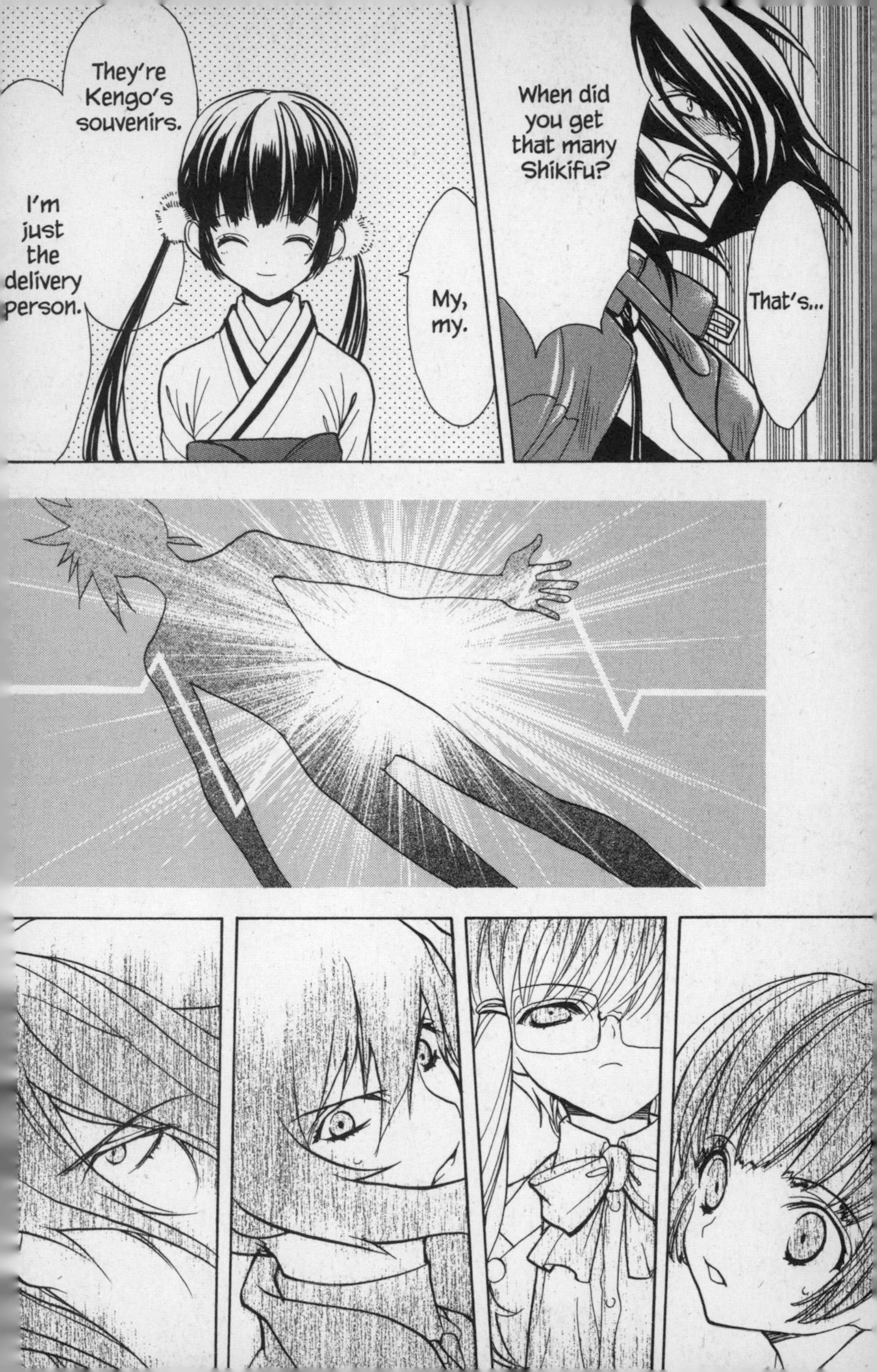
When did you get that many Shikifu?
That's...
My, my.
They're Kengo's souvenirs.
I'm just the delivery person.

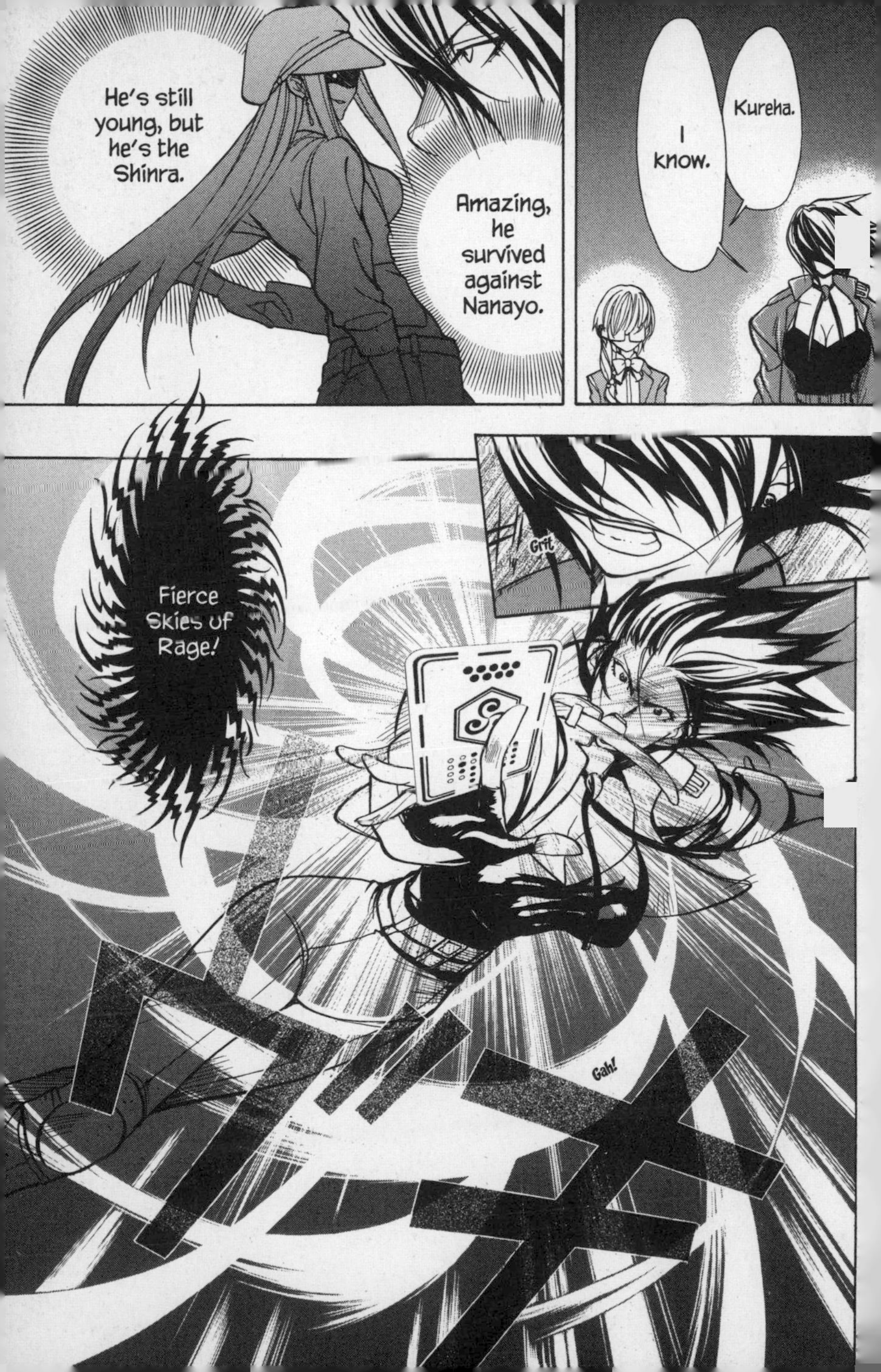
Kureha.
I know.
Amazing, he survived against Nanayo.
He's still young, but he's the Shinra.
Grit
Fierce Skies of Rage!
Gah!

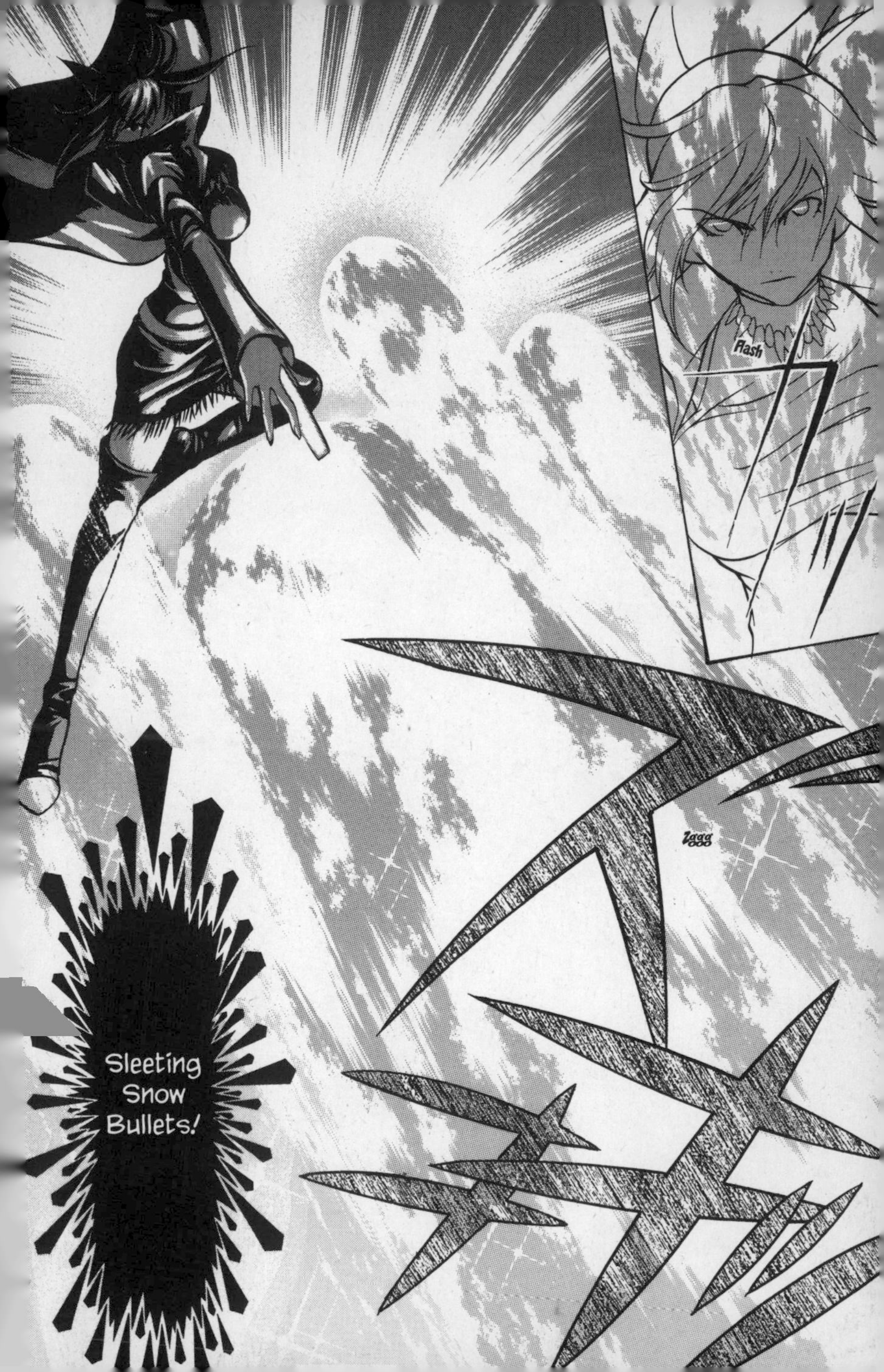
Flash
Zggg
Sleeting Snow Bullets!

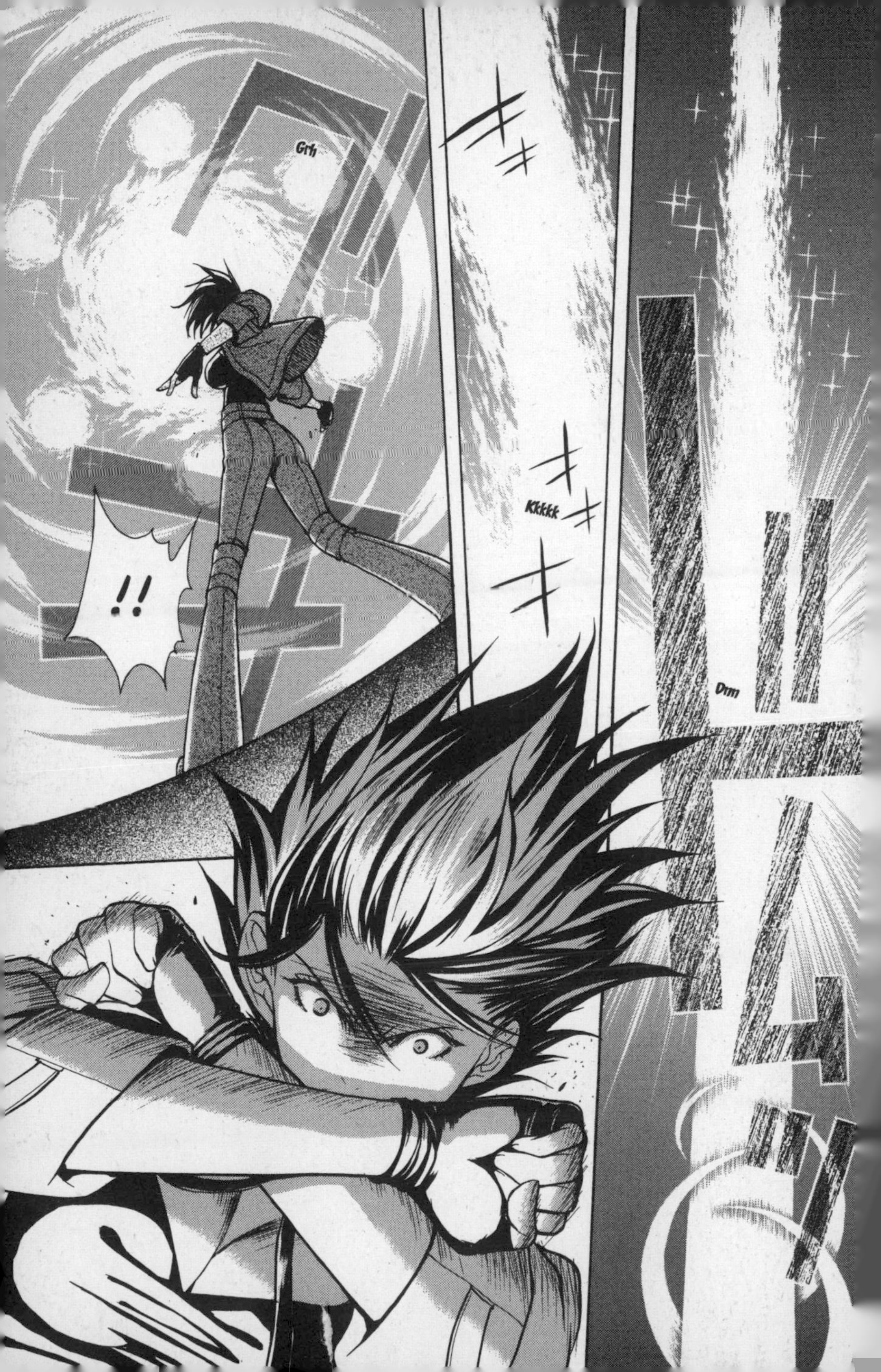
Dmn
Kkkkk
Grh
!!

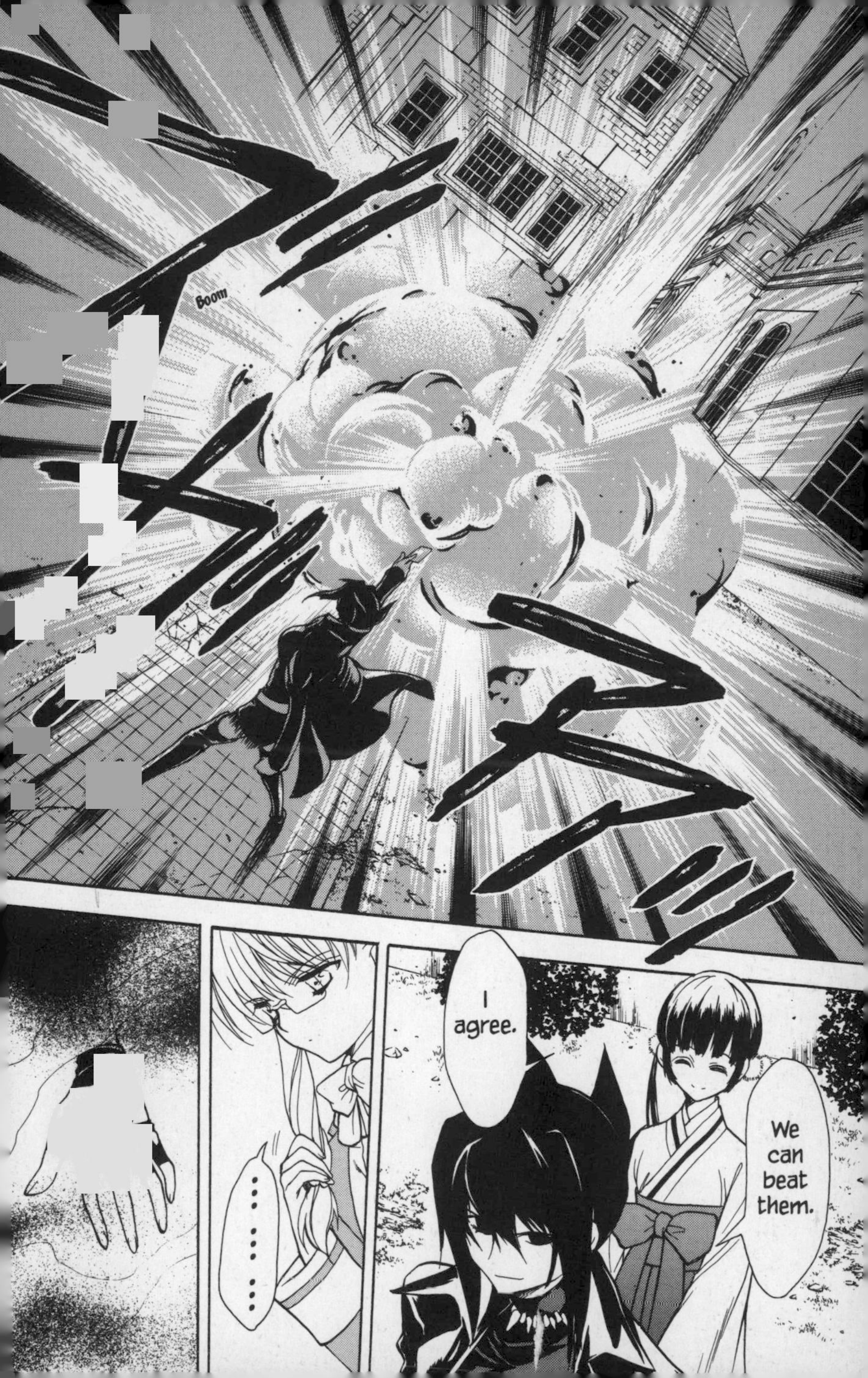
Boom
We can beat them.
I agree.
......

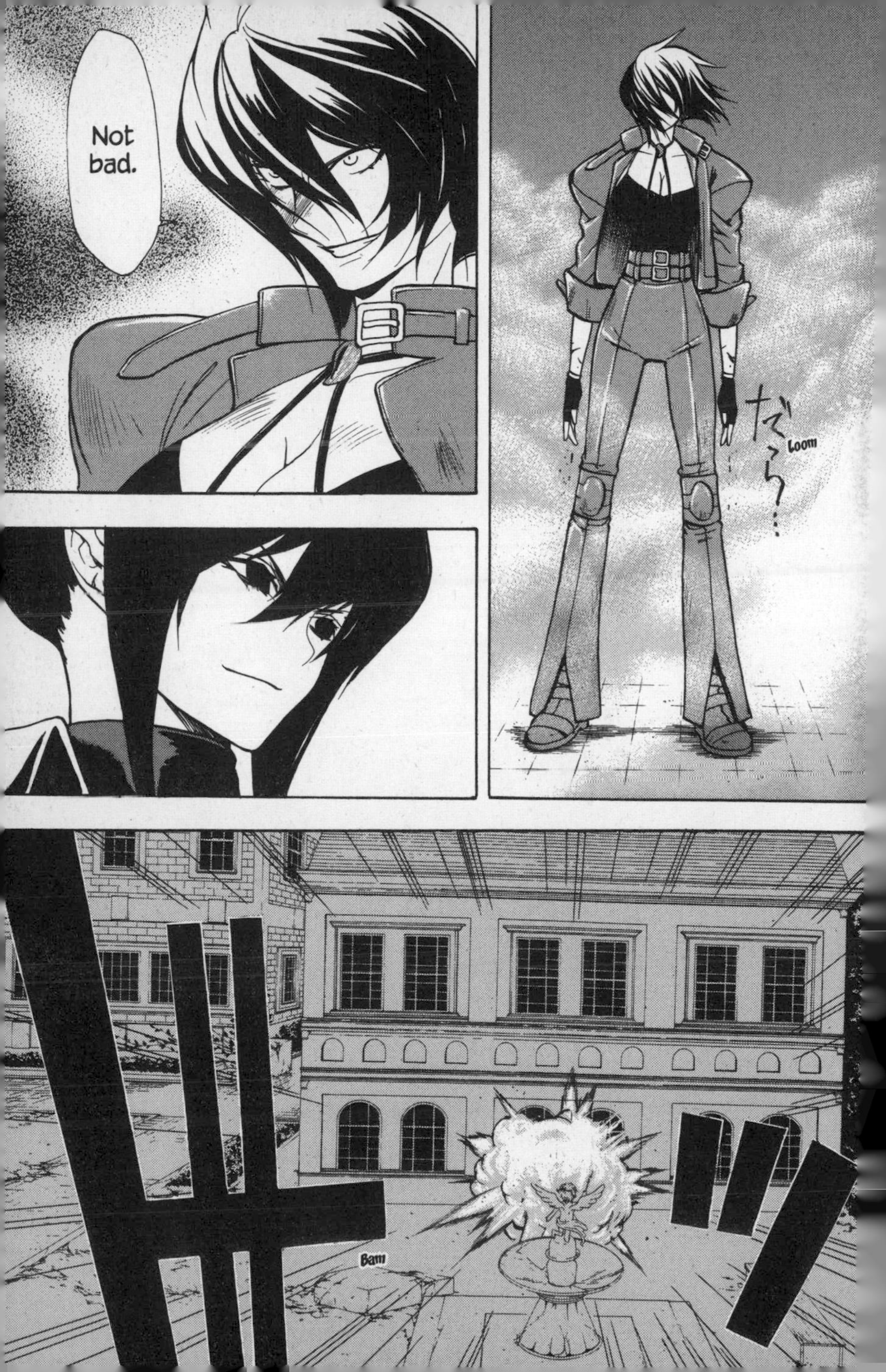
Loom
Not bad.
Bam

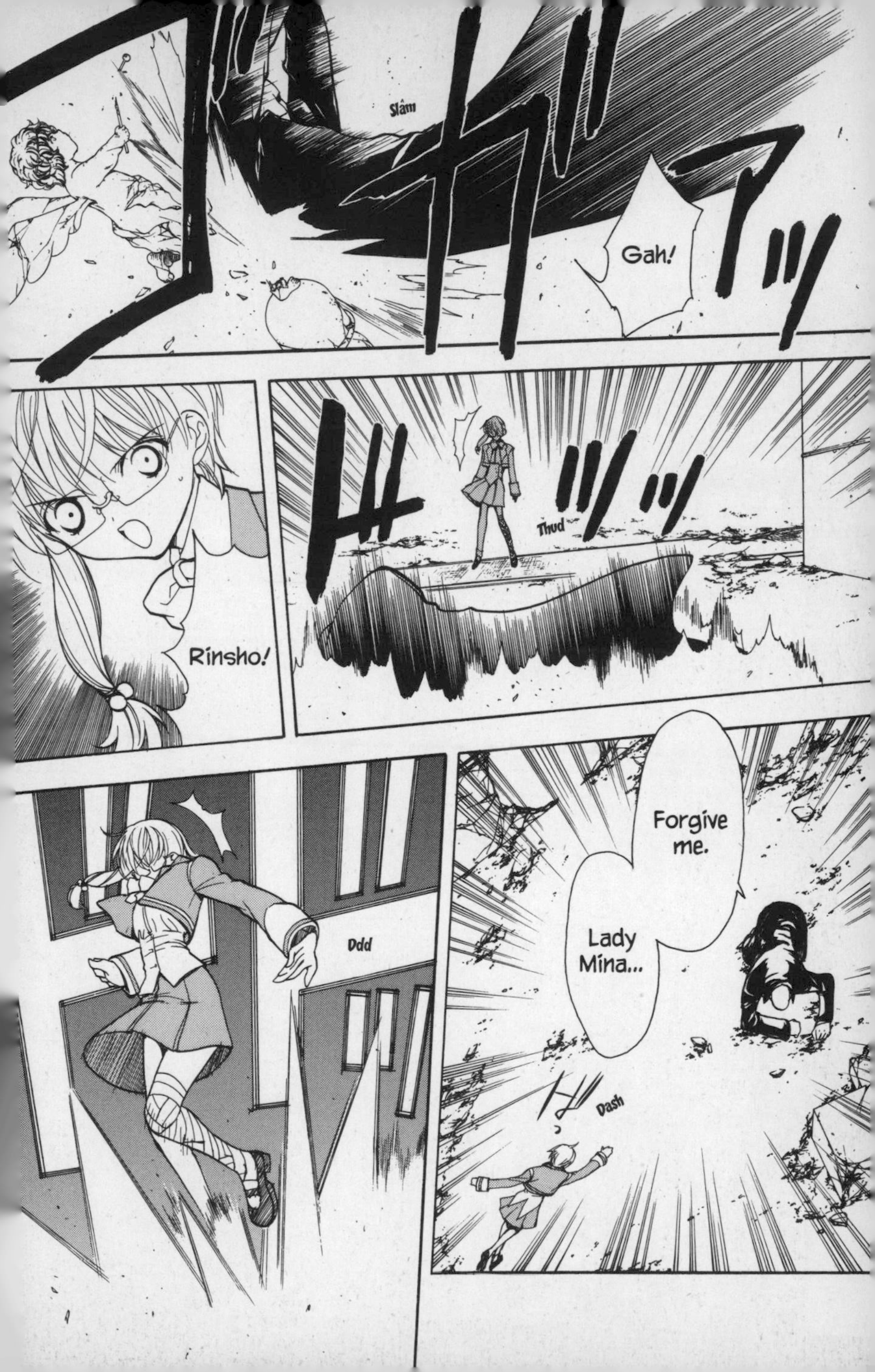
Slâm
Gah!
Thud
Rinsho!
Forgive me.
Lady Mina...
Dash
Ddd

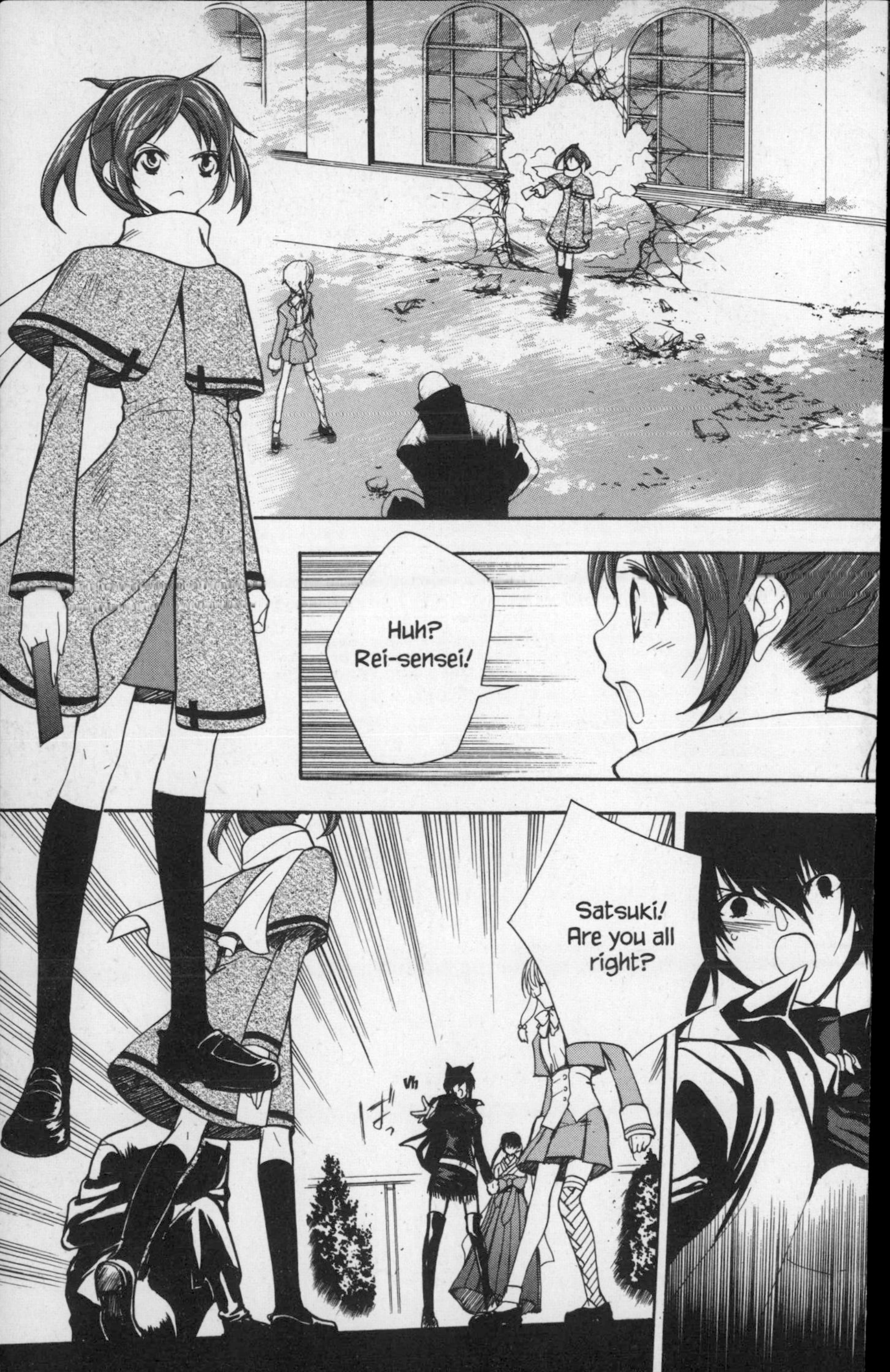
Huh?
Rei-sensei!
Satsuki!
Are you all right?
ばっ

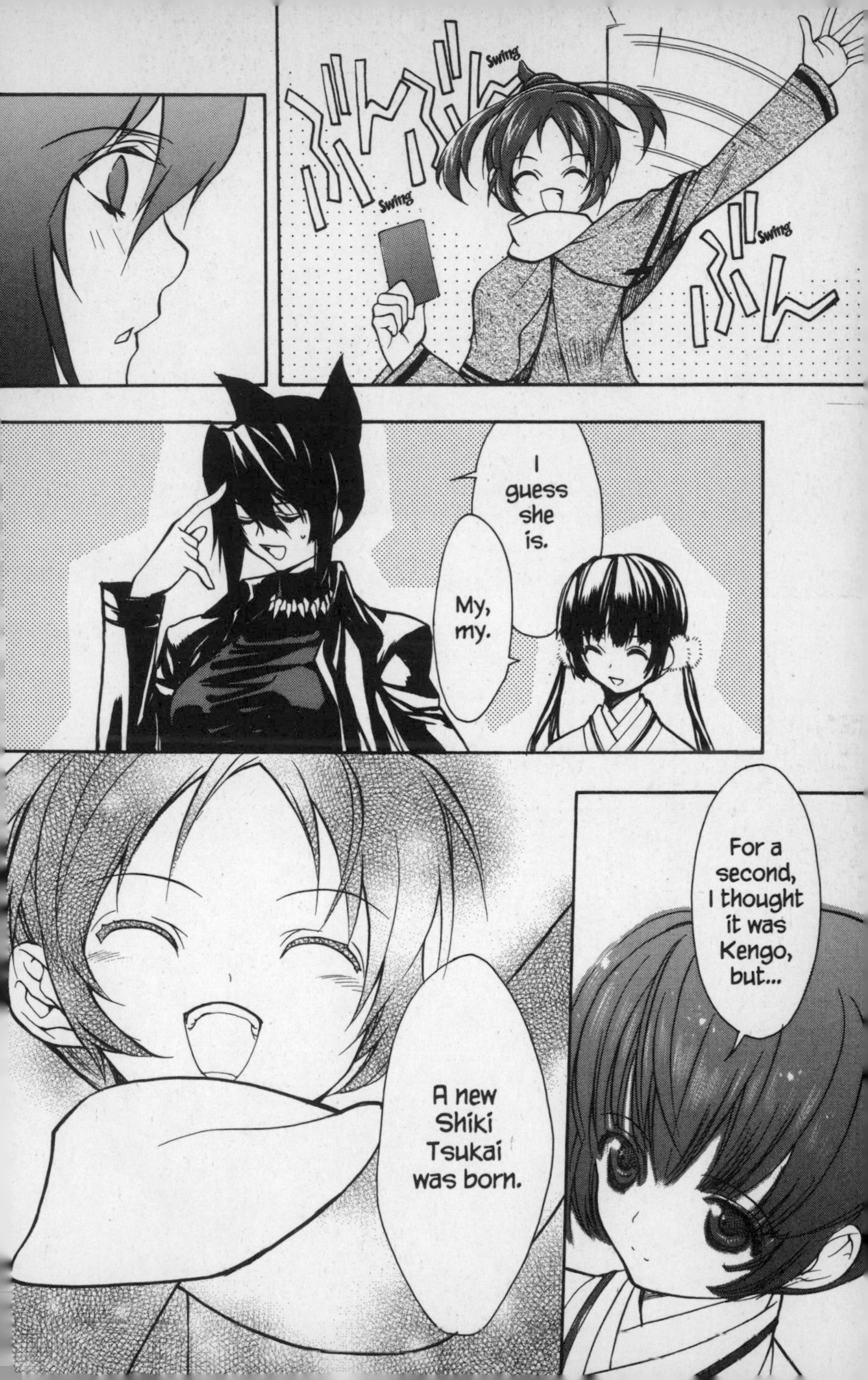
Swing
Swing
Swing
I guess she is.
My, my.
For a second, I thought it was Kengo, but...
A new Shiki Tsukai was born.

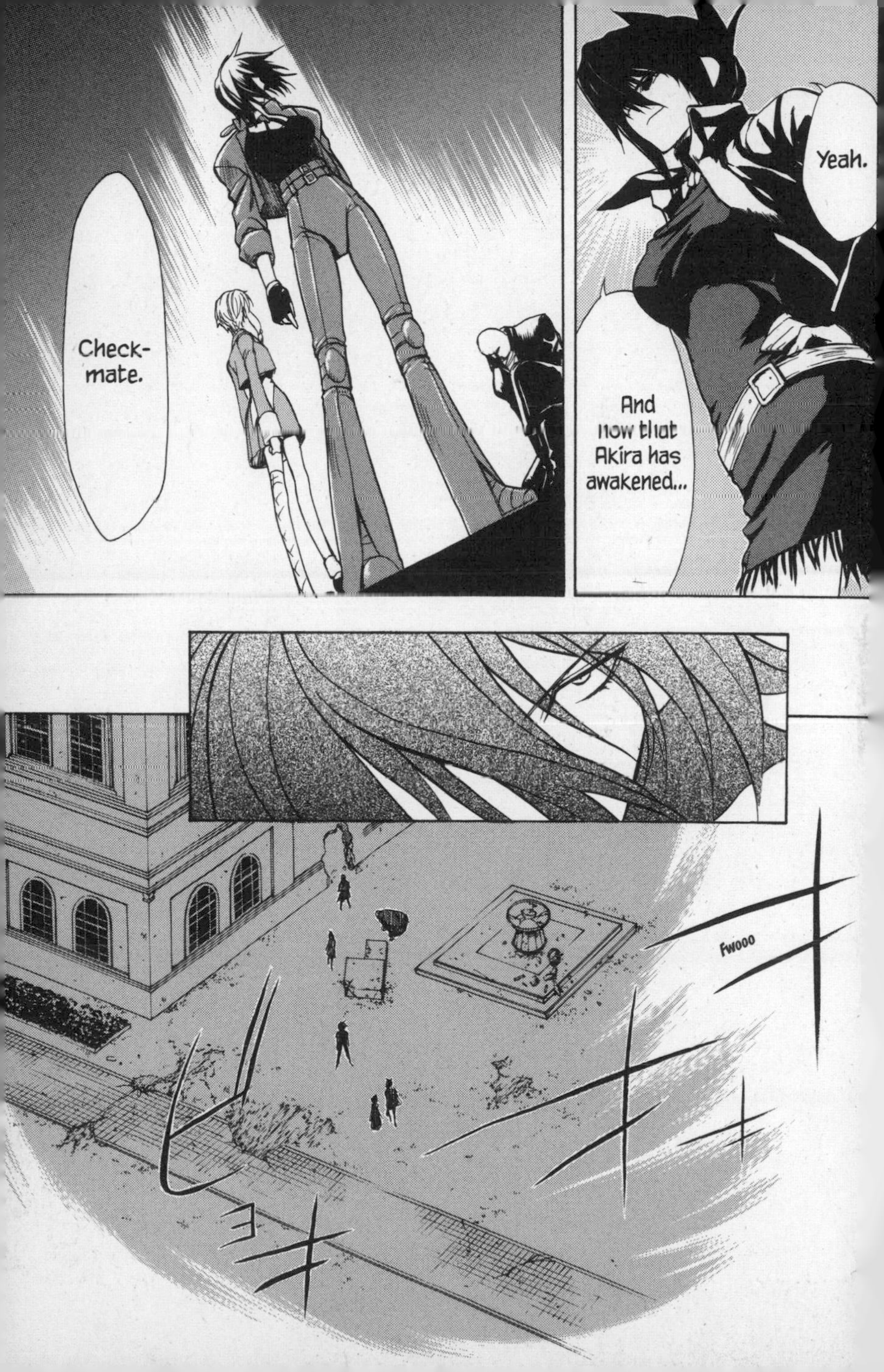
Yeah.
And now that Akira has awakened...
Check-mate.
Fwooo

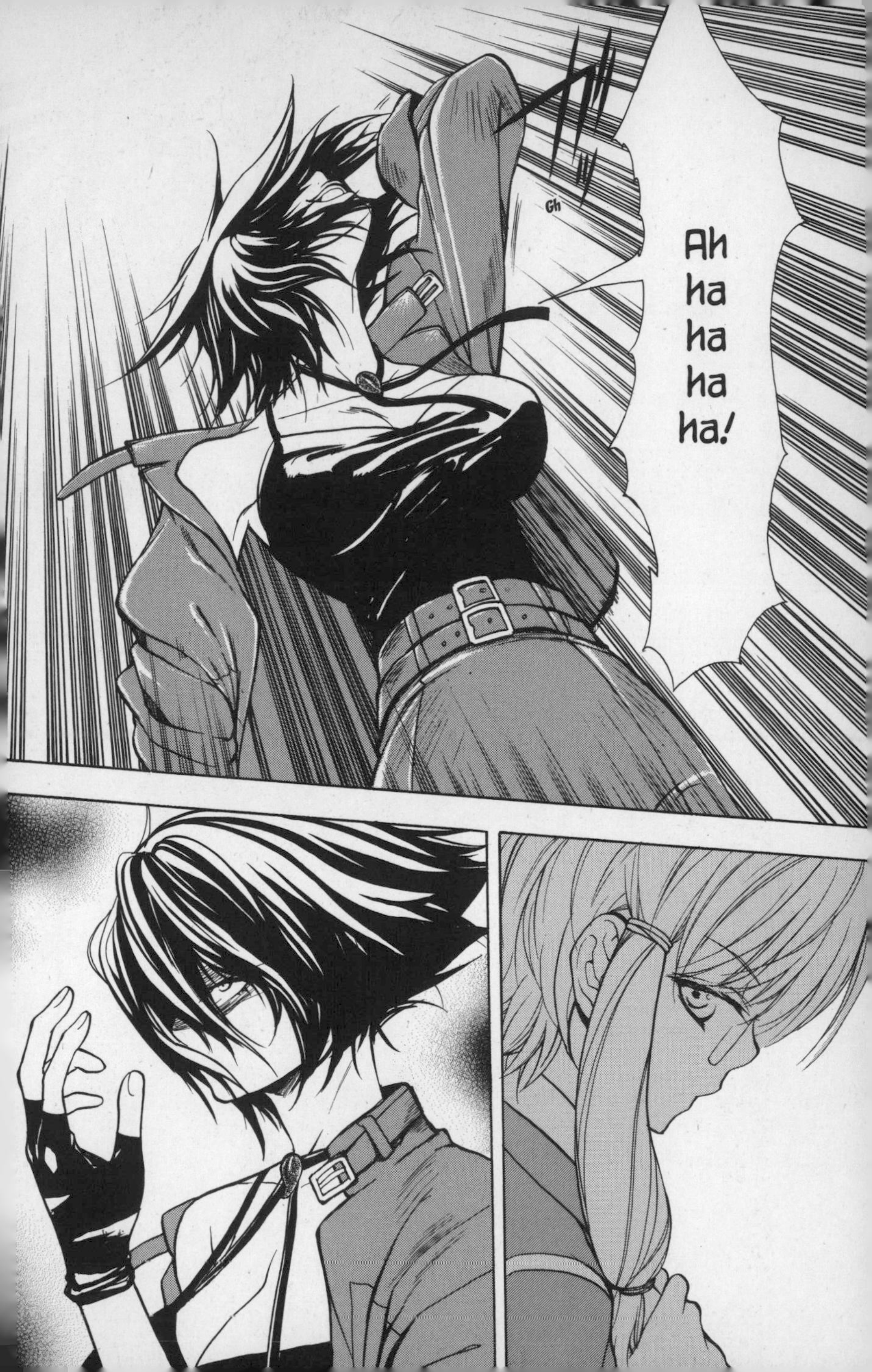
Ah ha ha ha ha!
Gh

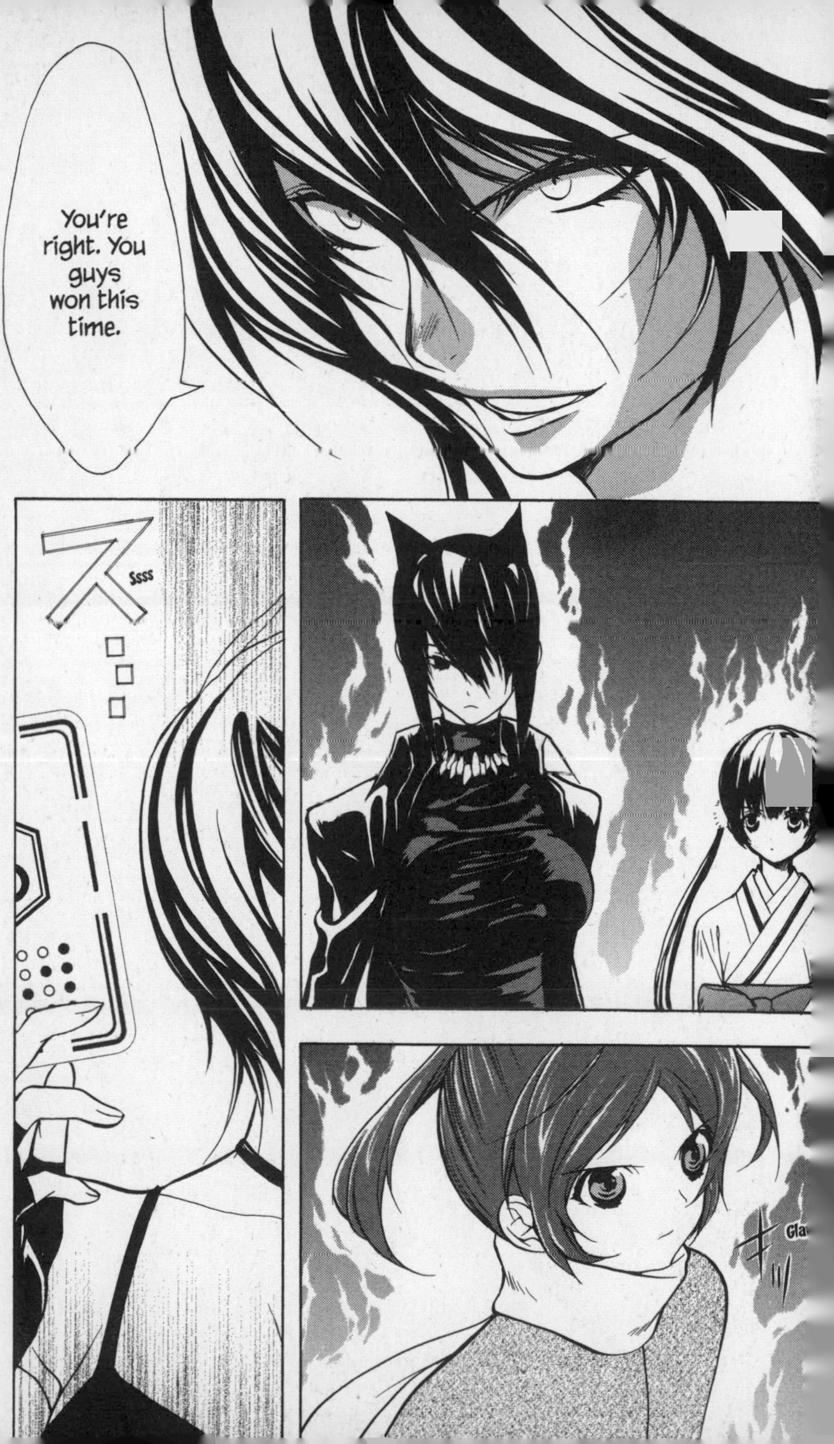
You're right. You guys won this time.
Gla
Ssss

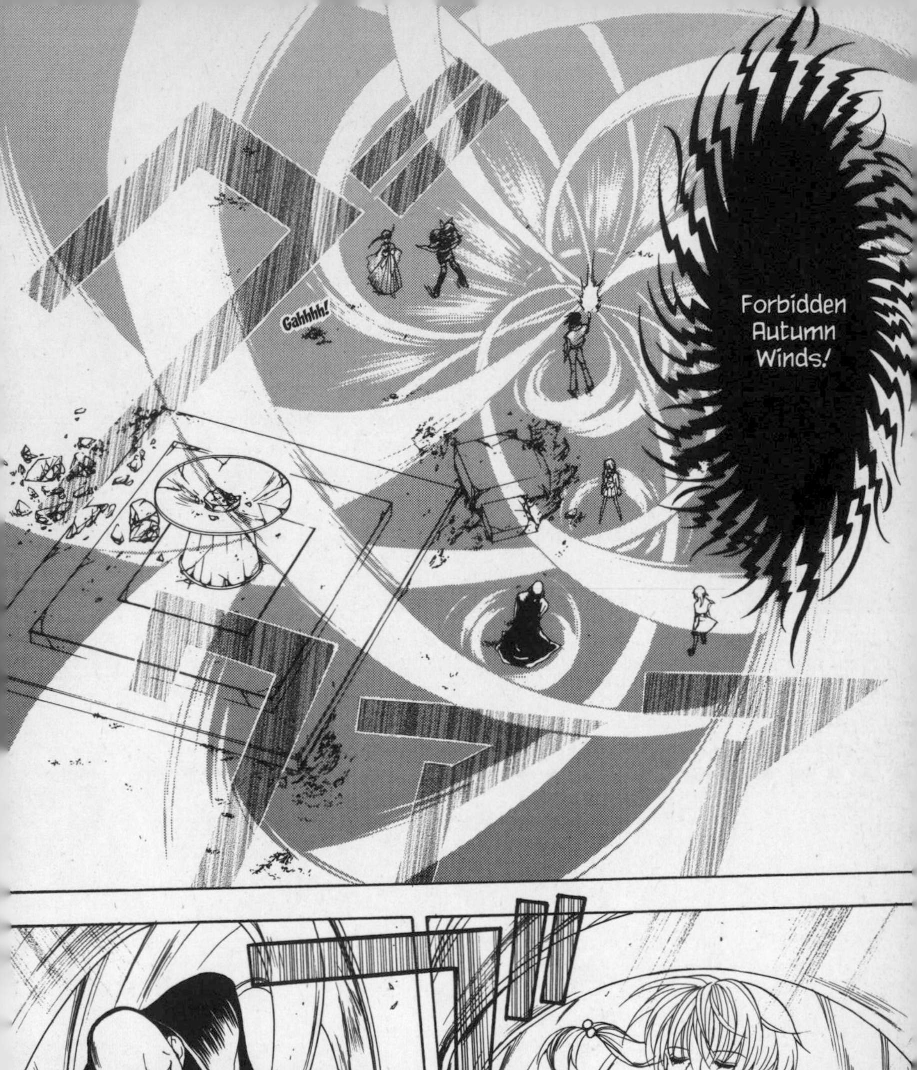
Forbidden Autumn Winds!
Gahhhh!
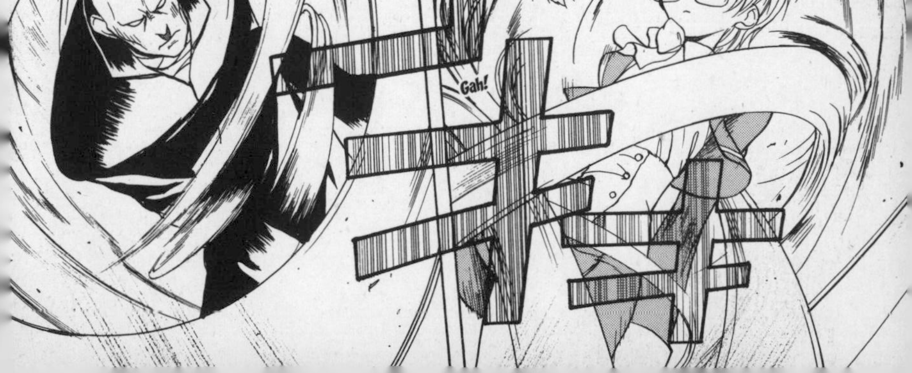
Gah!

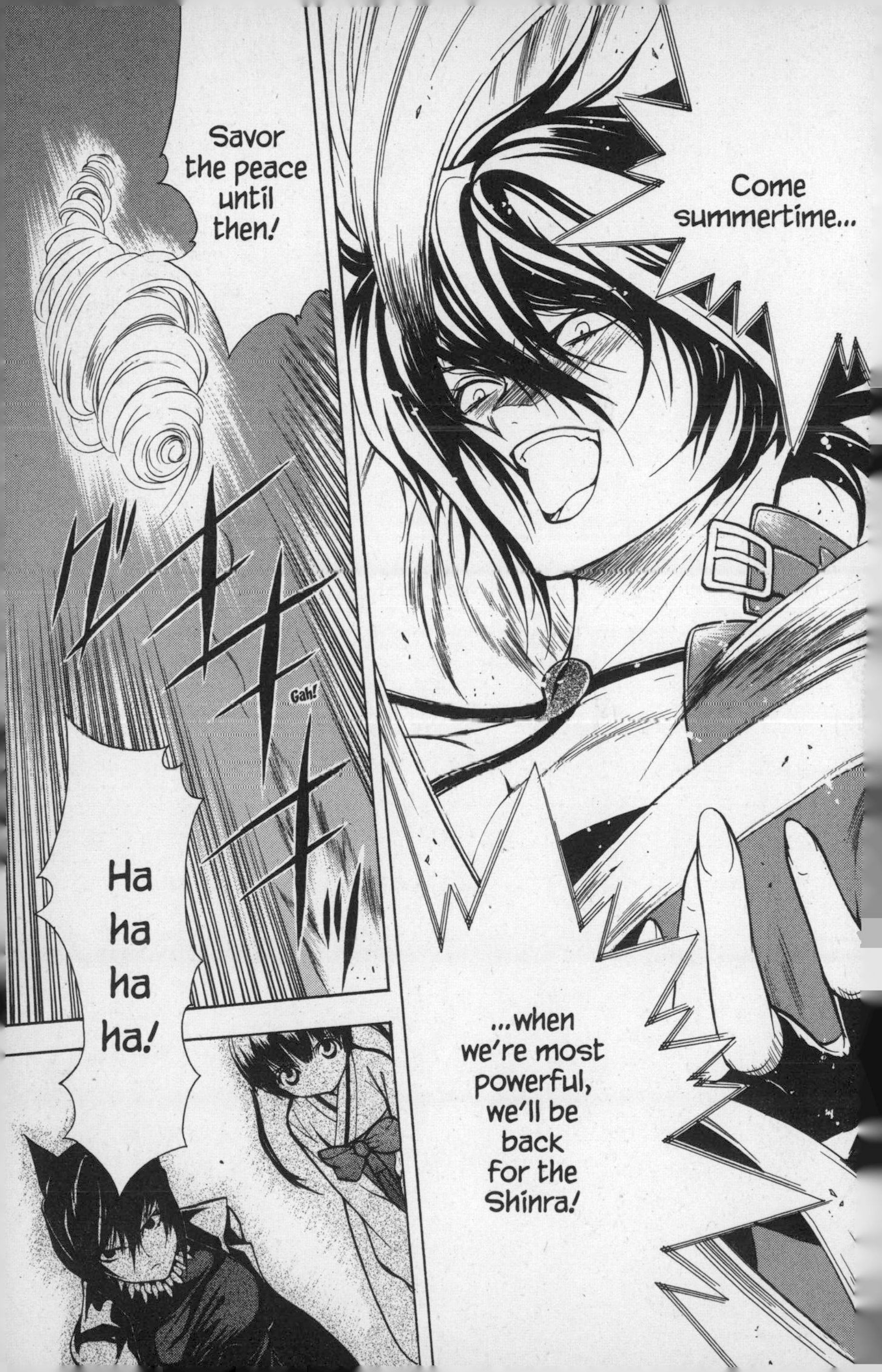
Come summertime...
...when we're most powerful, we'll be back for the Shinra!
Savor the peace until then!
Gah!
Ha ha ha ha!

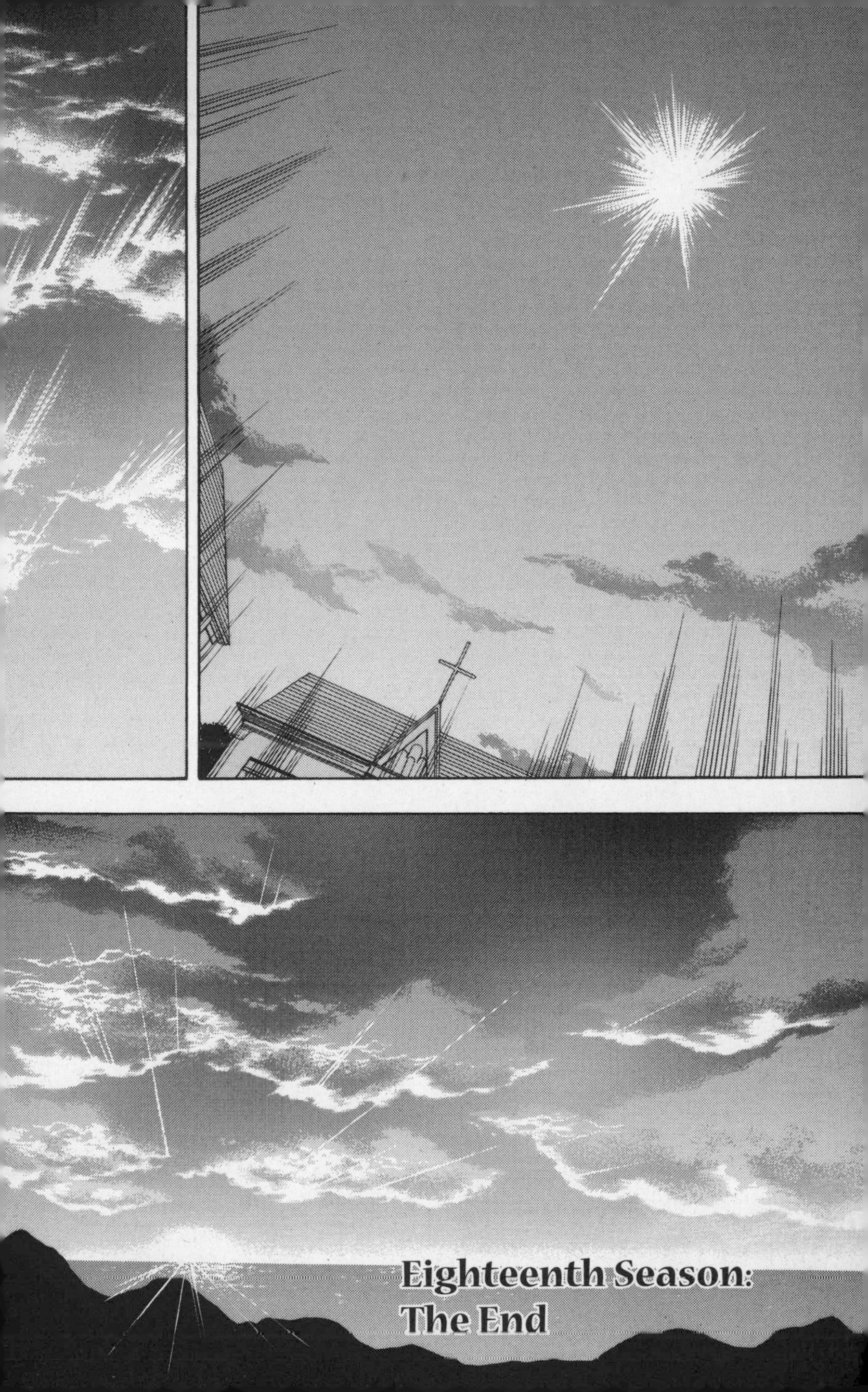
Eighteenth Season:
The End

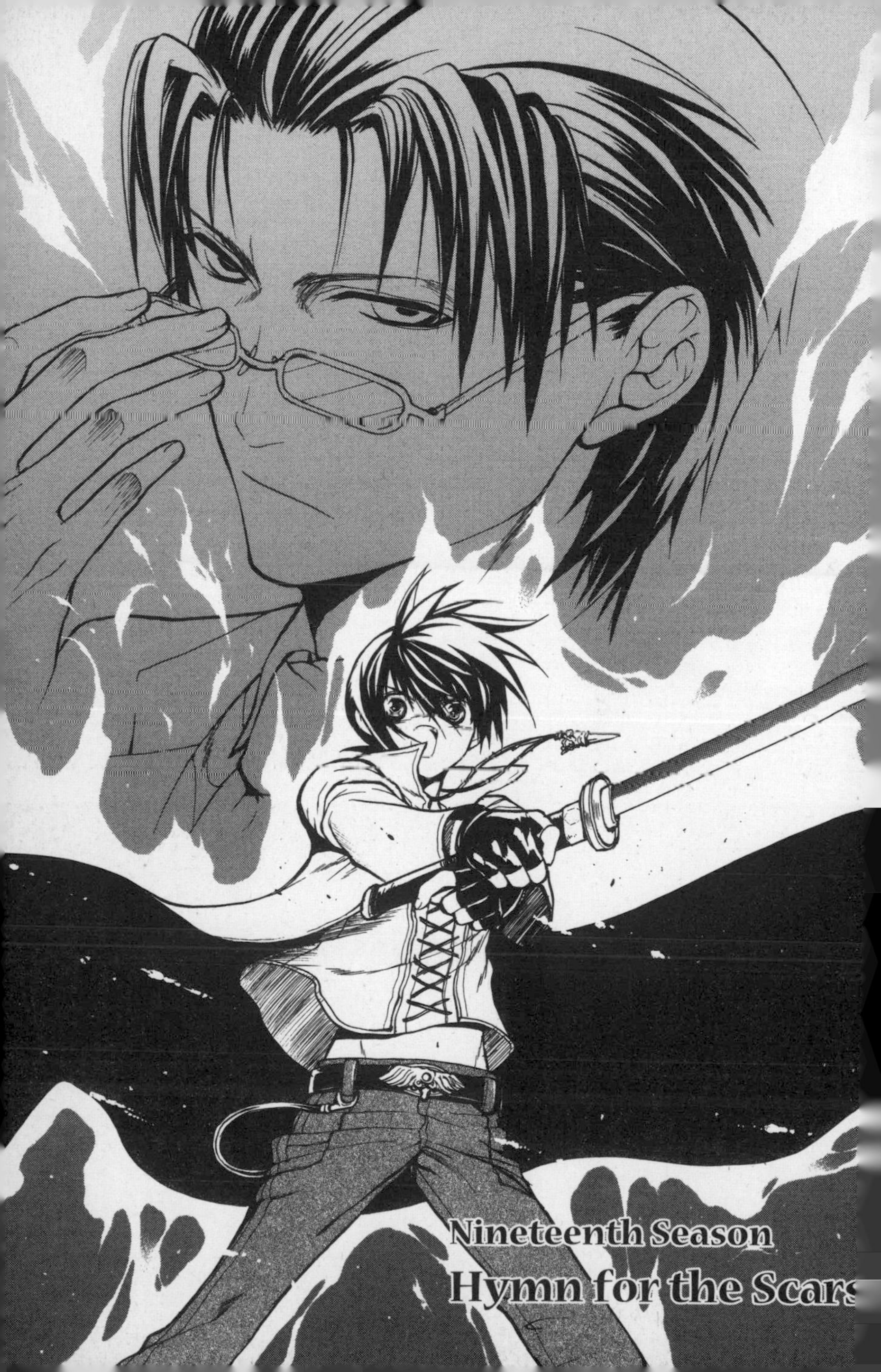
Nineteenth Season
Hymn for the Scars

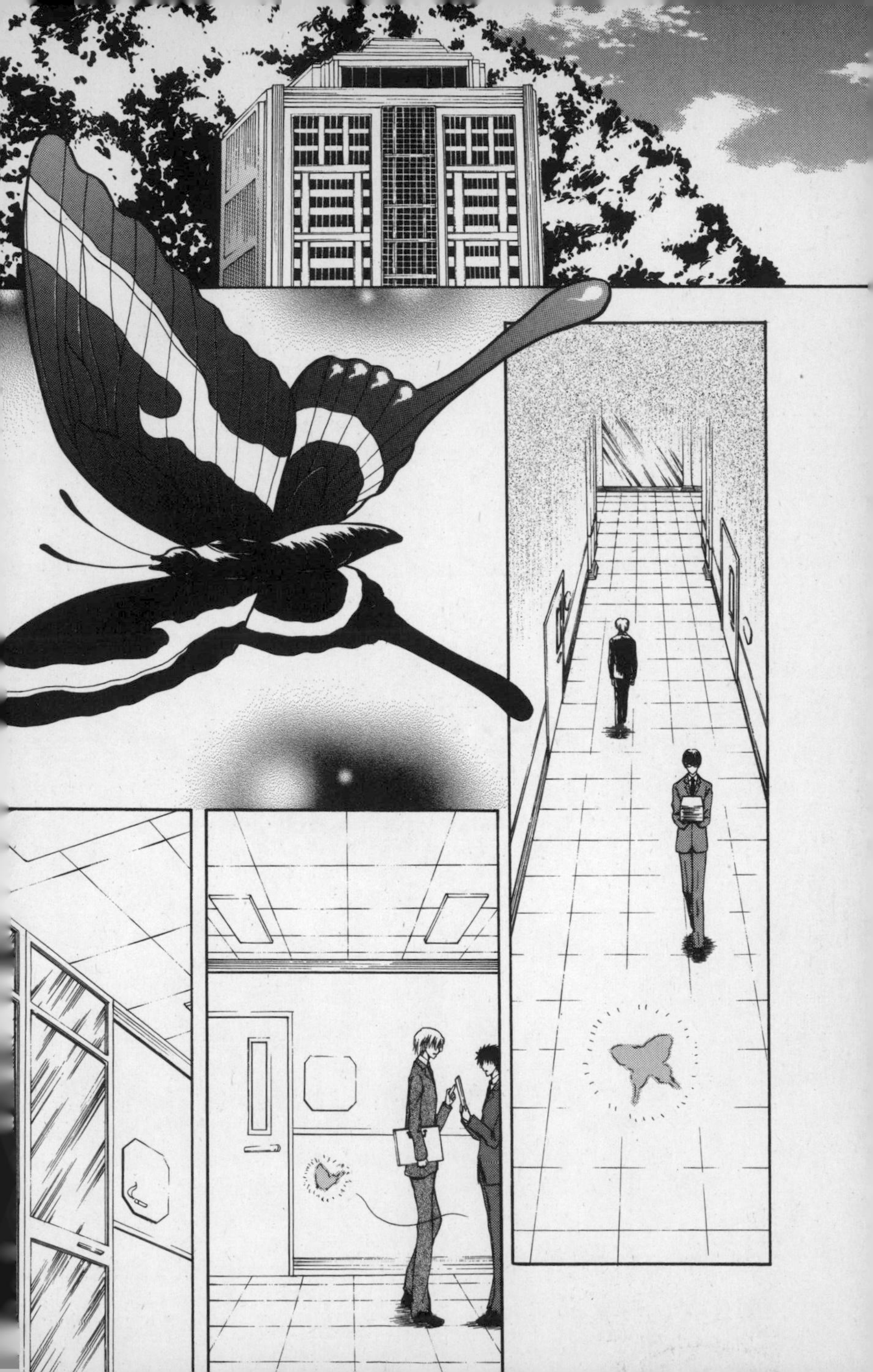

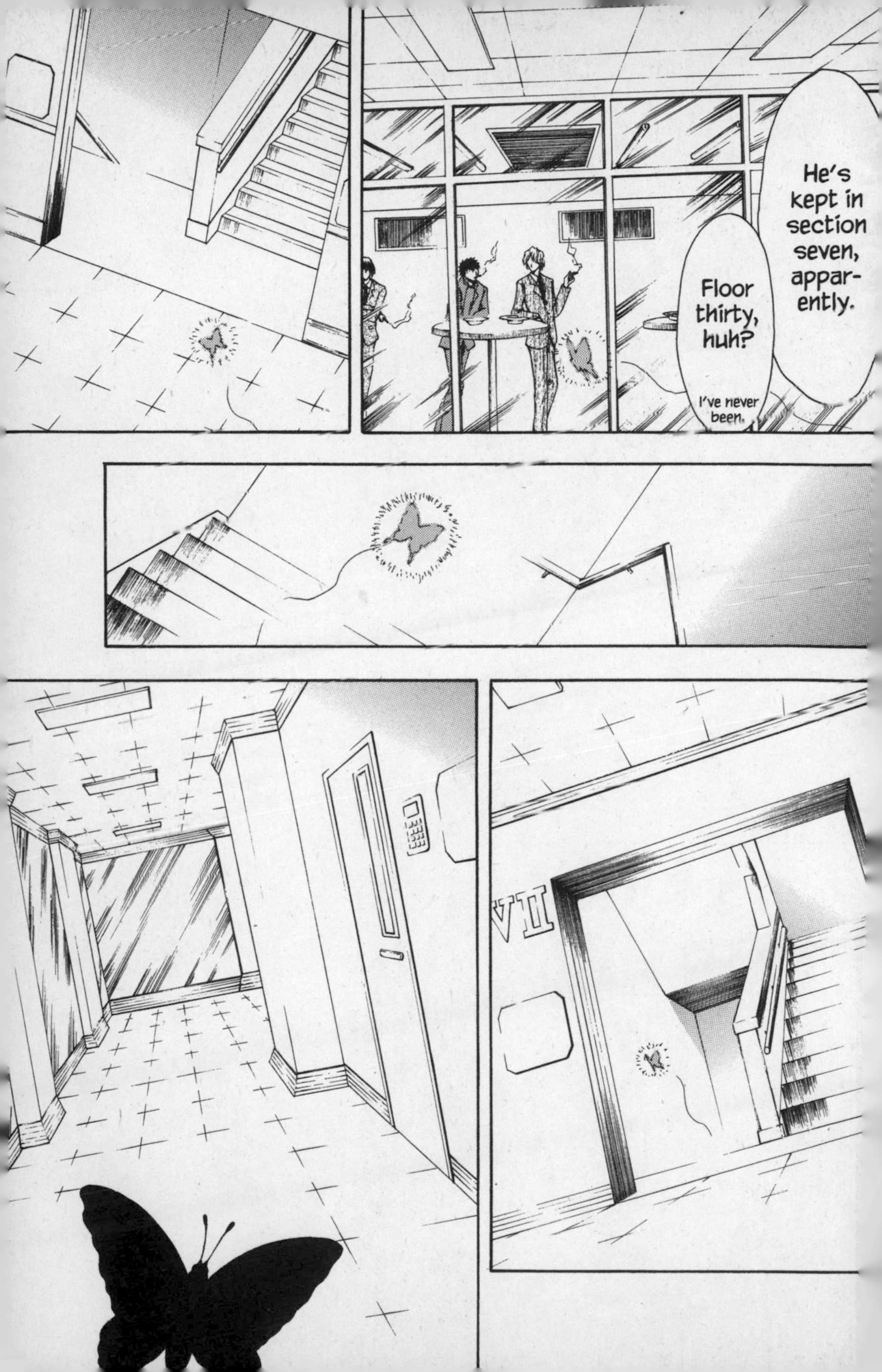
He's kept in section seven, apparently.
Floor thirty, huh?
I've never been.
VII

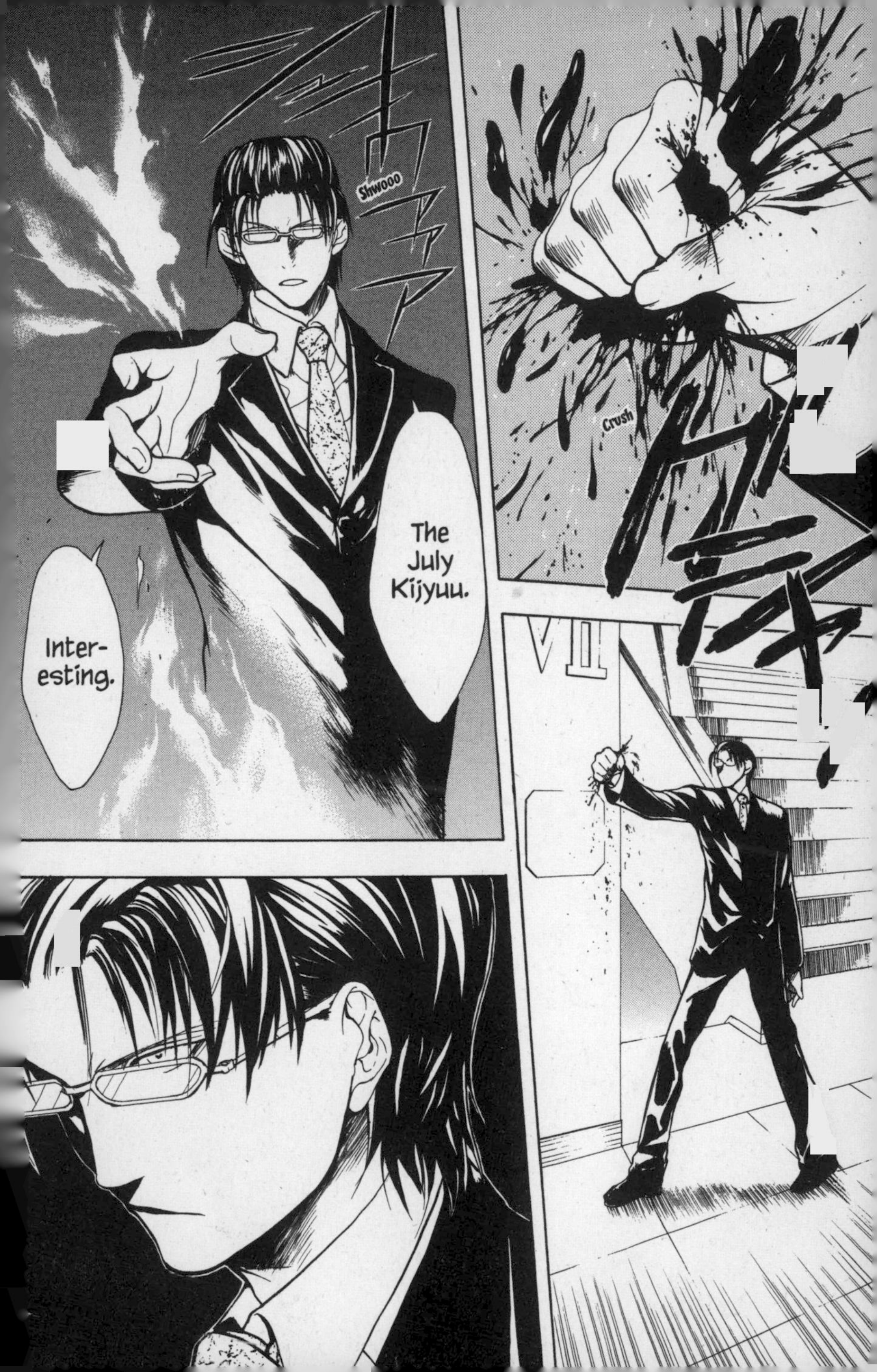
Crush
Shwooo
The July Kijyuu.
Inter-esting.

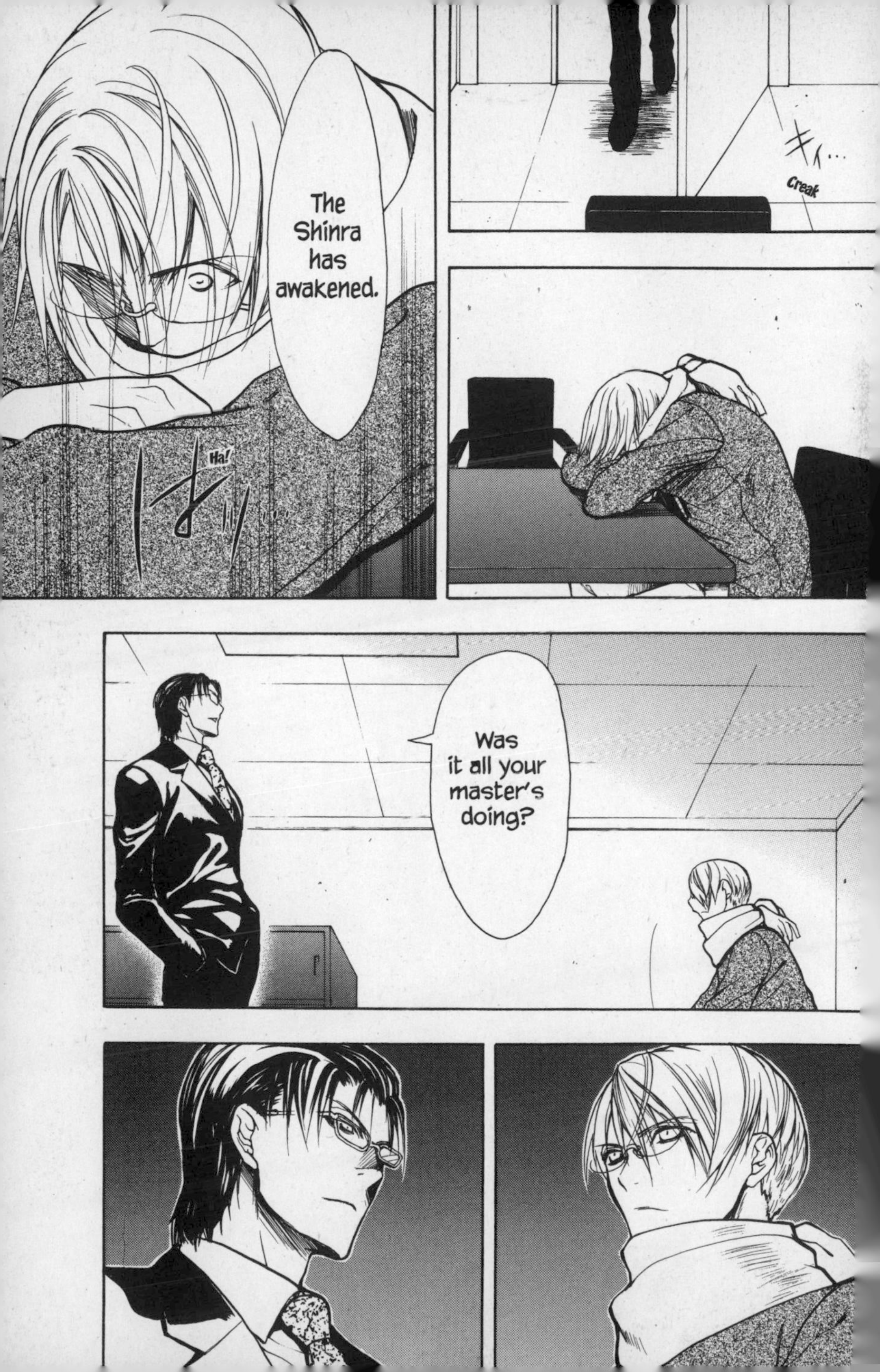
Creak
The Shinra has awakened.
Ha!
Was it all your master's doing?

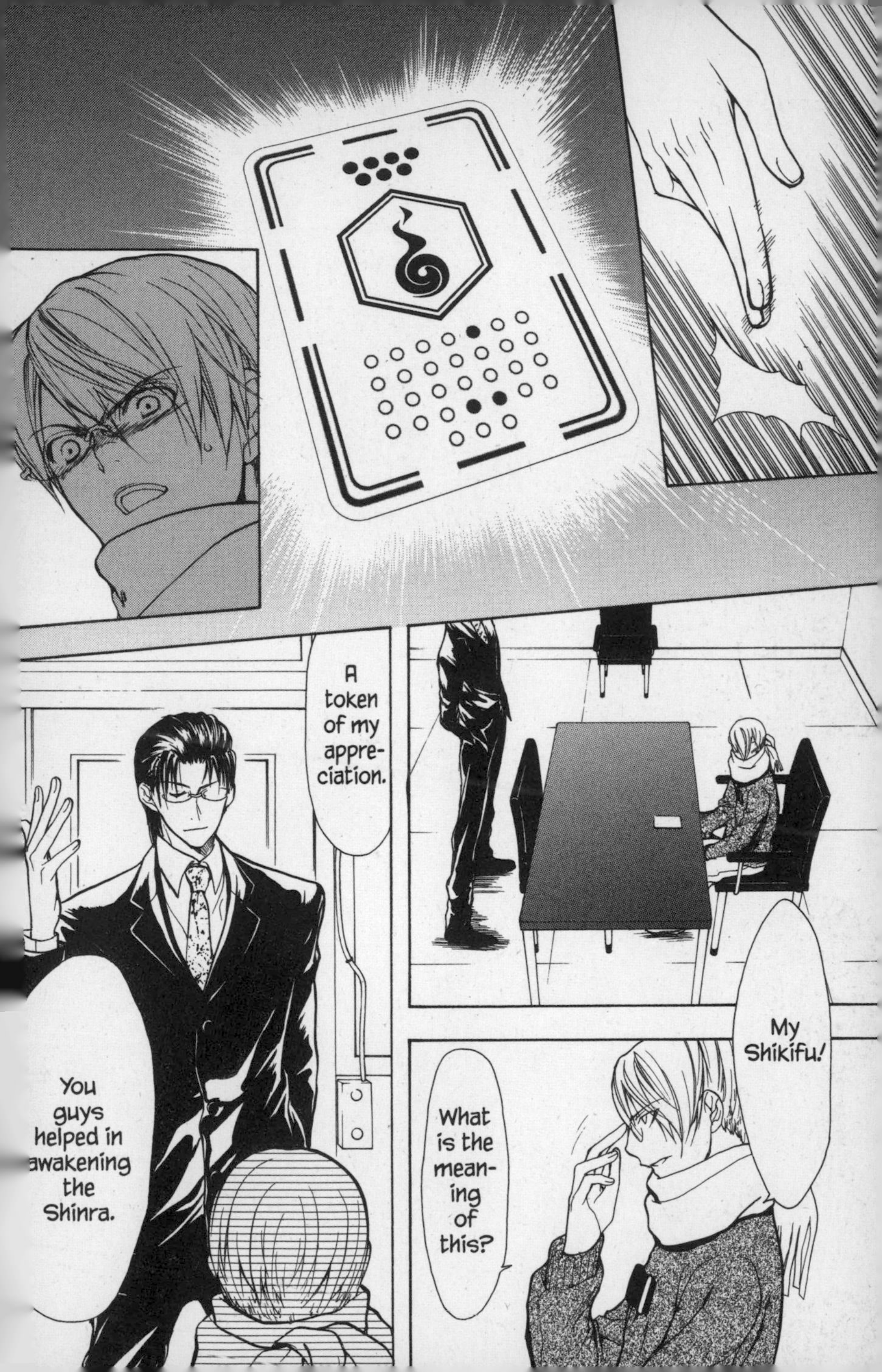
My Shikifu!
What is the meaning of this?
A token of my appreciation.
You guys helped in awakening the Shinra.

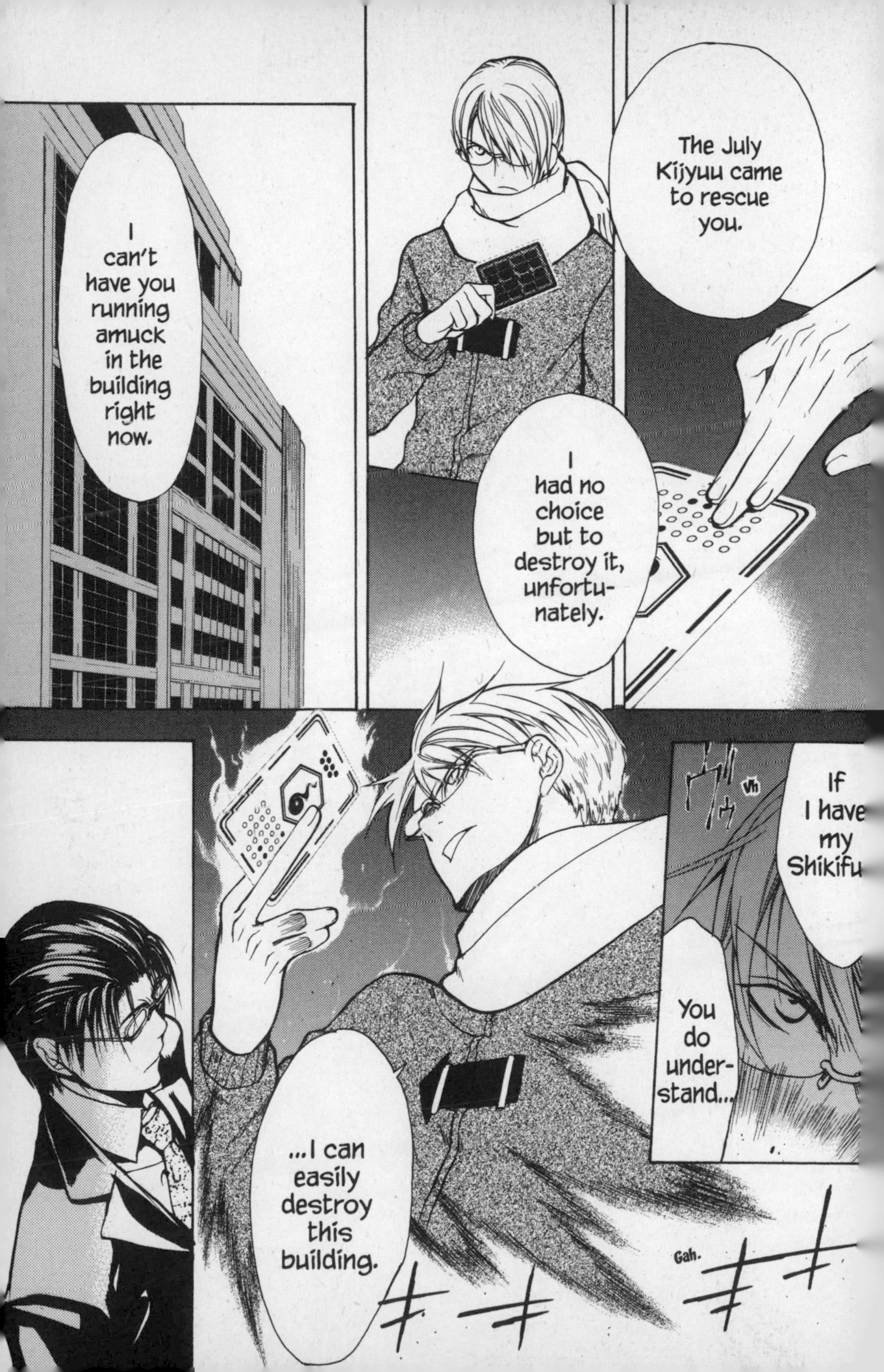
The July Kijyuu came to rescue you.
I had no choice but to destroy it, unfortunately.
I can't have you running amuck in the building right now.
Vh
If I have my Shikifu
You do understand...
...I can easily destroy this building.
Gah.

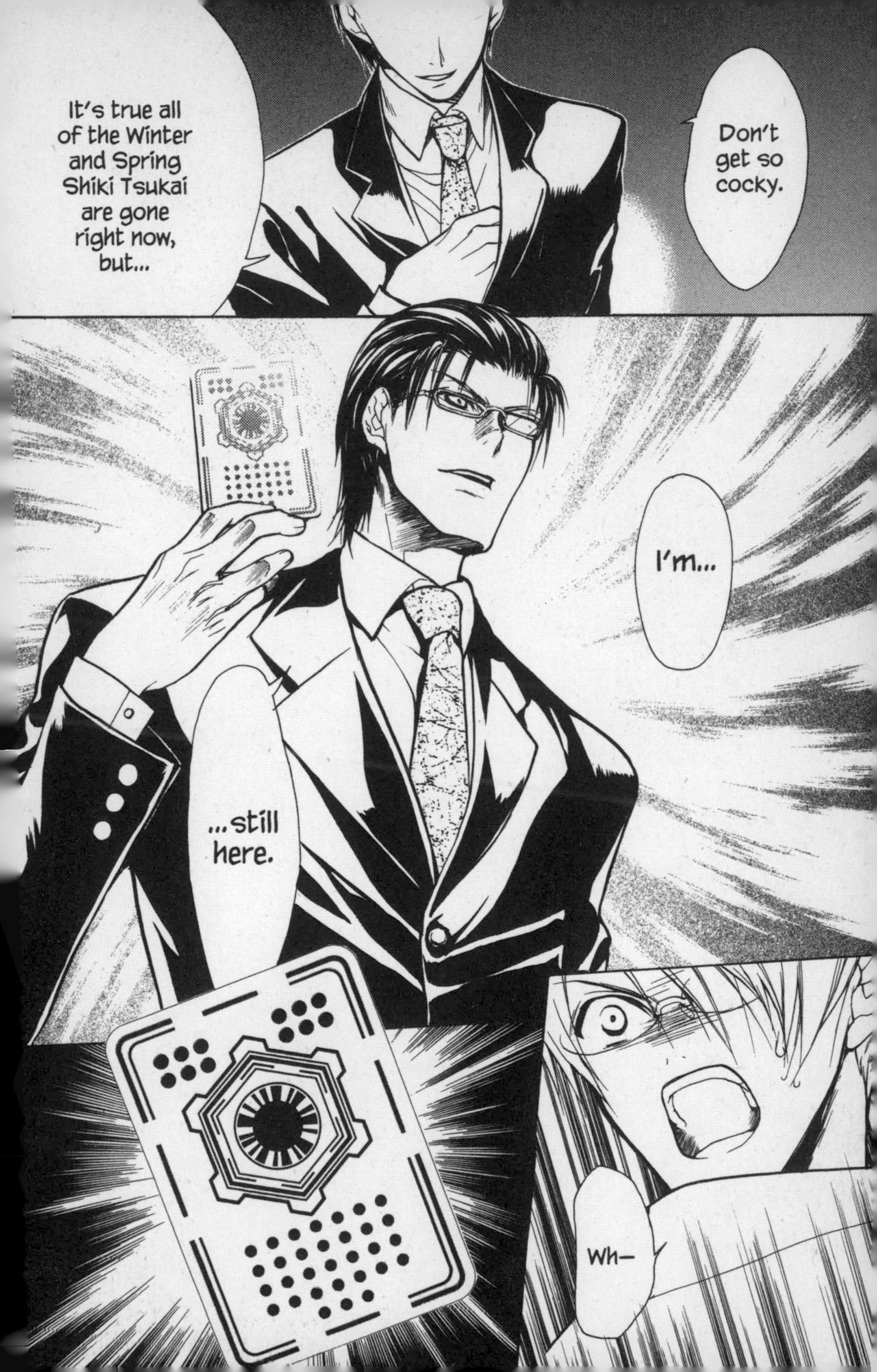
Don't get so cocky.
It's true all of the Winter and Spring Shiki Tsukai are gone right now, but...
I'm...
...still here.
Wh-

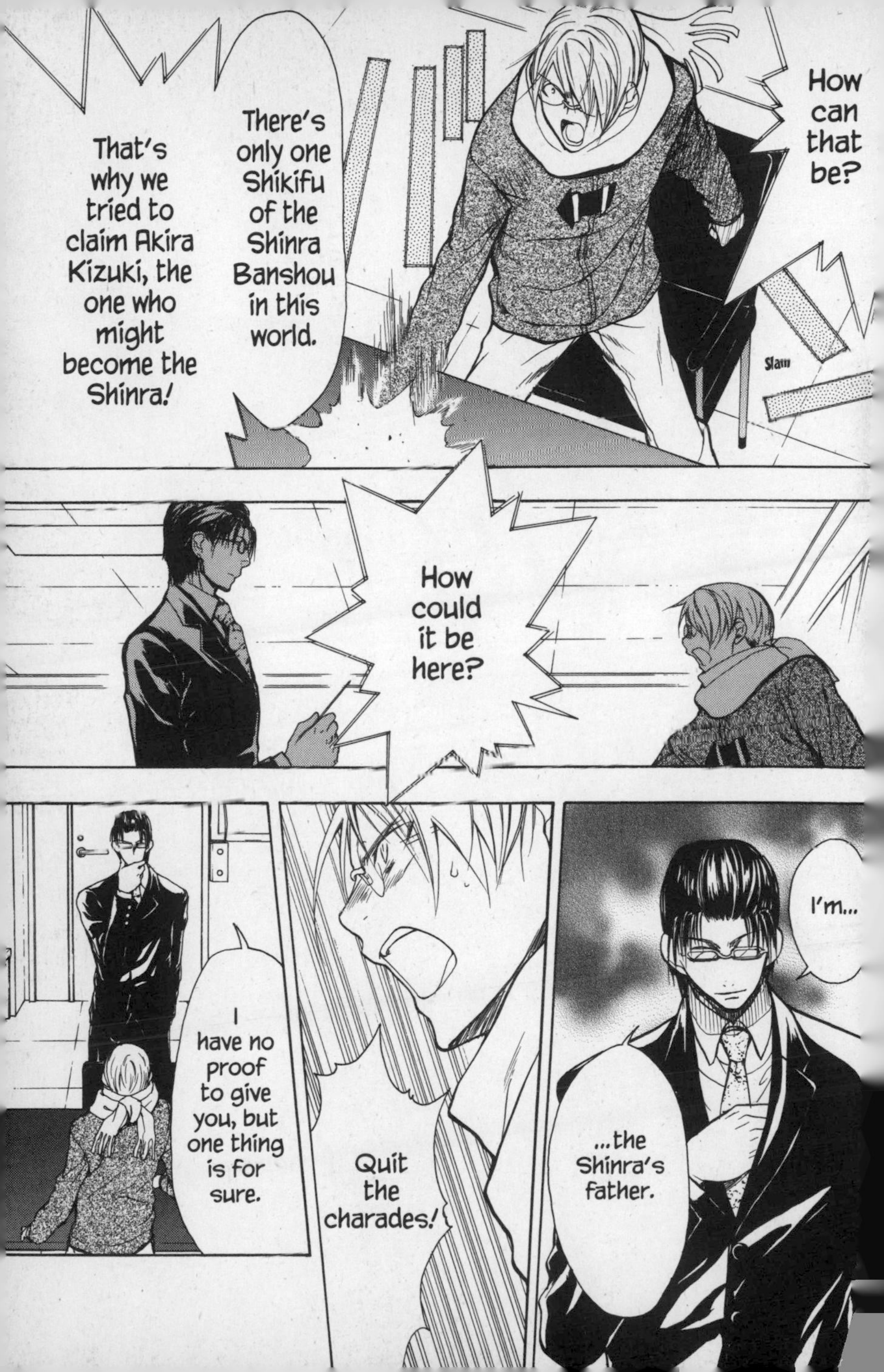
How can that be?
Slam
There's only one Shikifu of the Shinra Banshou in this world.
That's why we tried to claim Akira Kizuki, the one who might become the Shinra!
How could it be here?
I'm...
...the Shinra's father.
Quit the charades!
I have no proof to give you, but one thing is for sure.

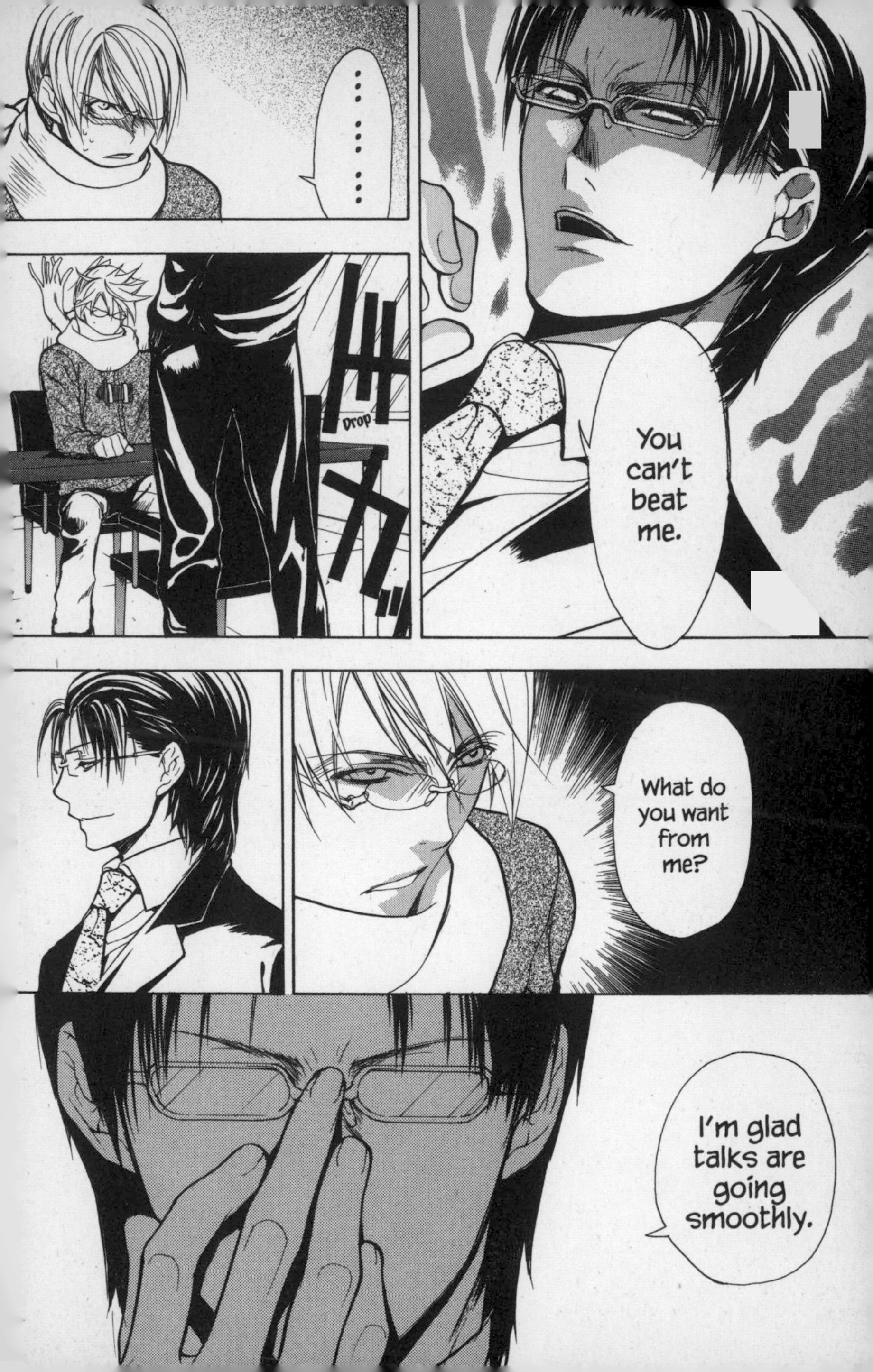
You can't beat me.
......
Drop
What do you want from me?
I'm glad talks are going smoothly.

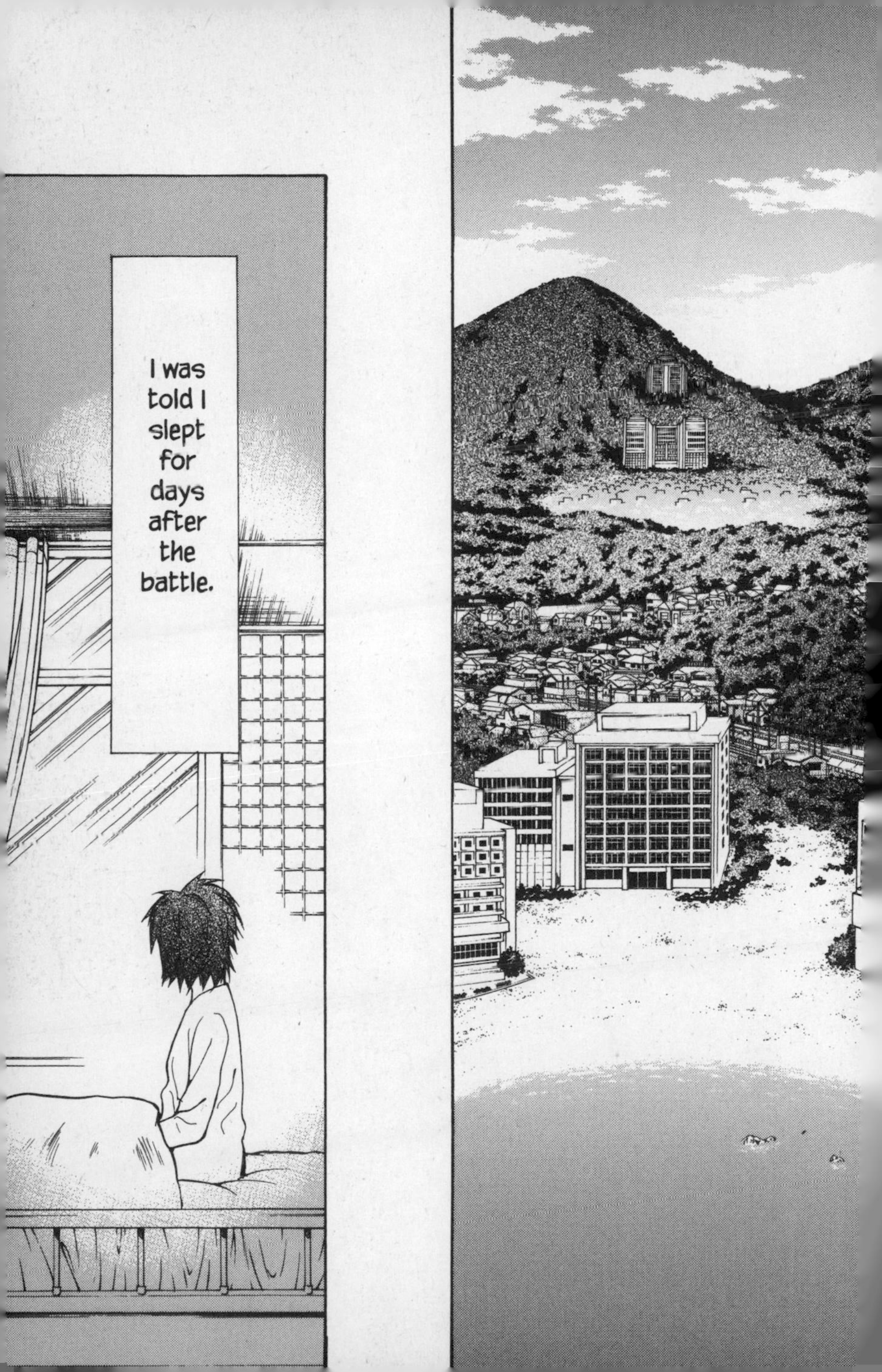
I was told I slept for days after the battle.

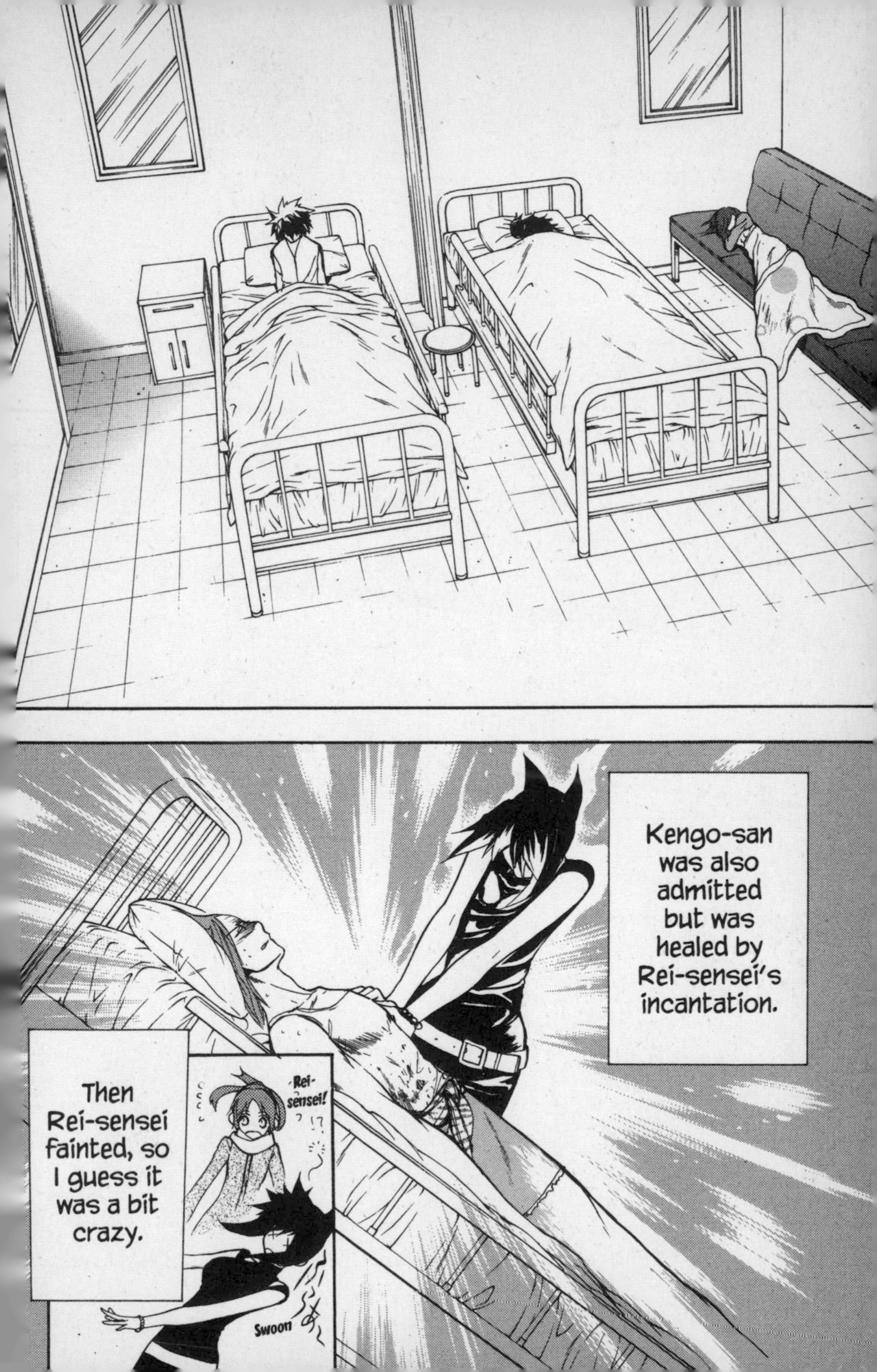
Kengo-san was also admitted but was healed by Rei-sensei's incantation.
Then Rei-sensei fainted, so I guess it was a bit crazy.
Rei-sensei!
!?
Swoon

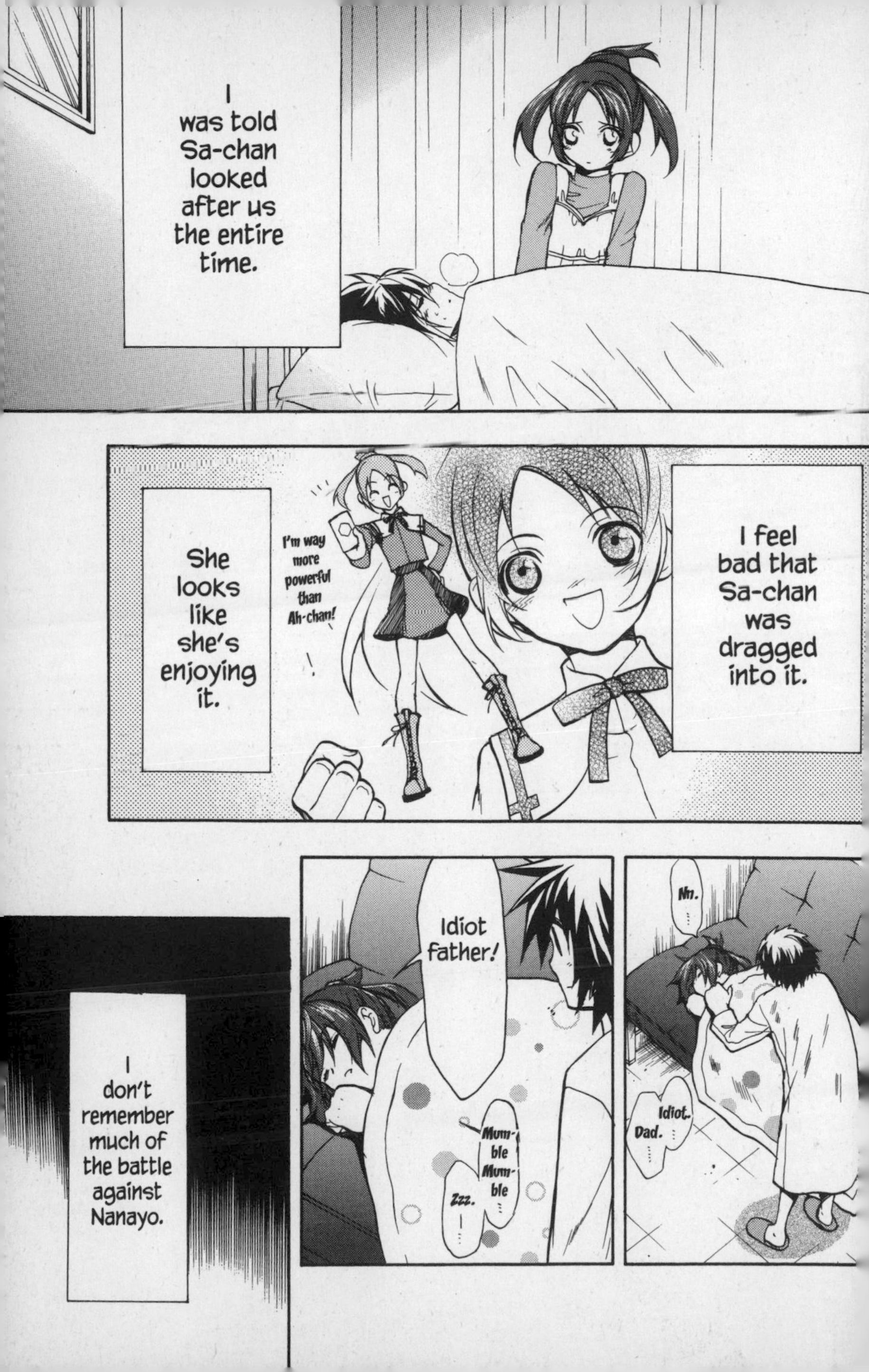
I was told Sa-chan looked after us the entire time.
I feel bad that Sa-chan was dragged into it.
I'm way more powerful than Ah-chan!
She looks like she's enjoying it.
Nn. ...
Idiot. Dad. ...
Idiot father!
Mumble Mumble ...
Zzz. ...
I don't remember much of the battle against Nanayo.

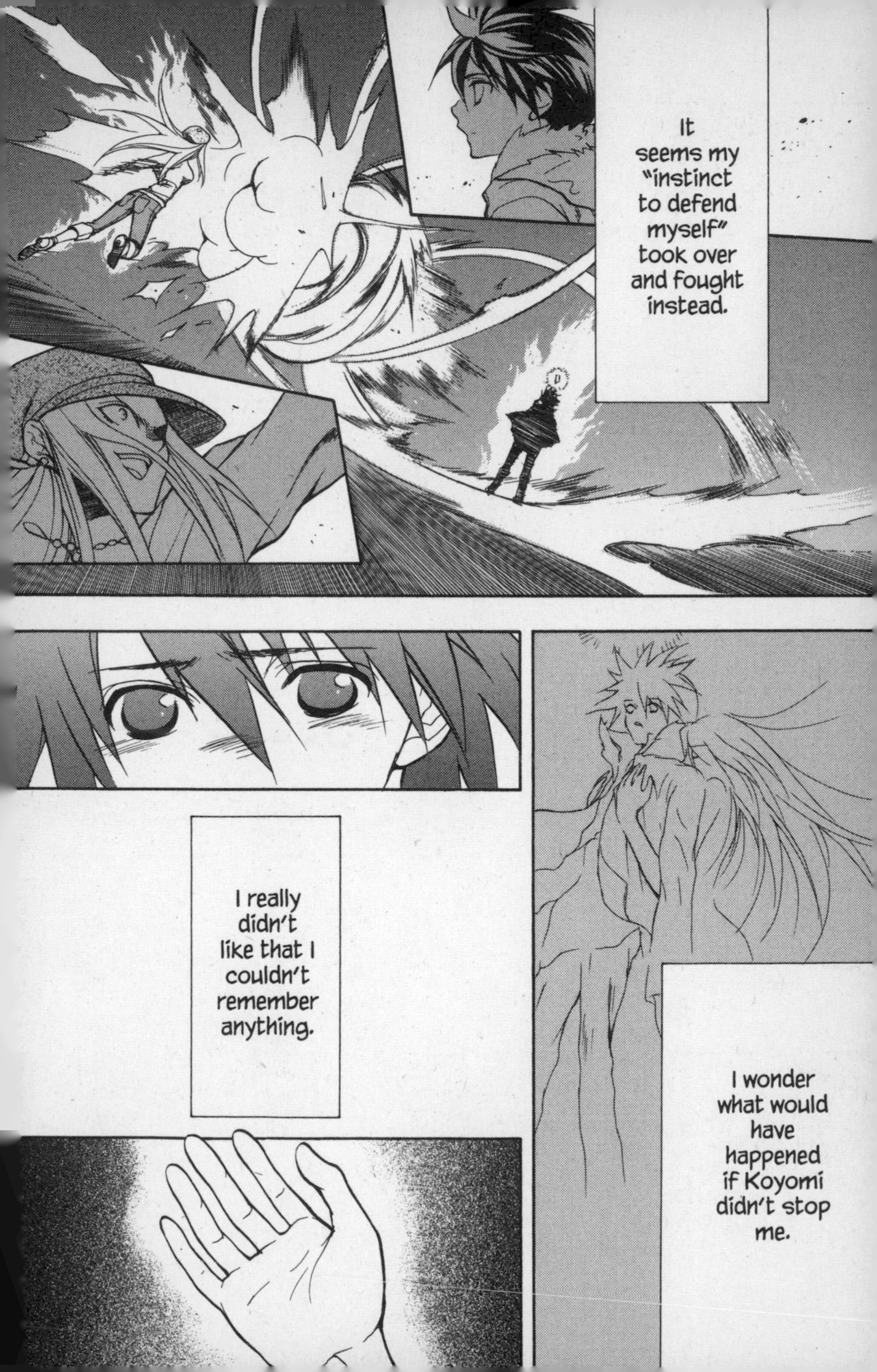
It seems my "instinct to defend myself" took over and fought instead.
I wonder what would have happened if Koyomi didn't stop me.
I really didn't like that I couldn't remember anything.

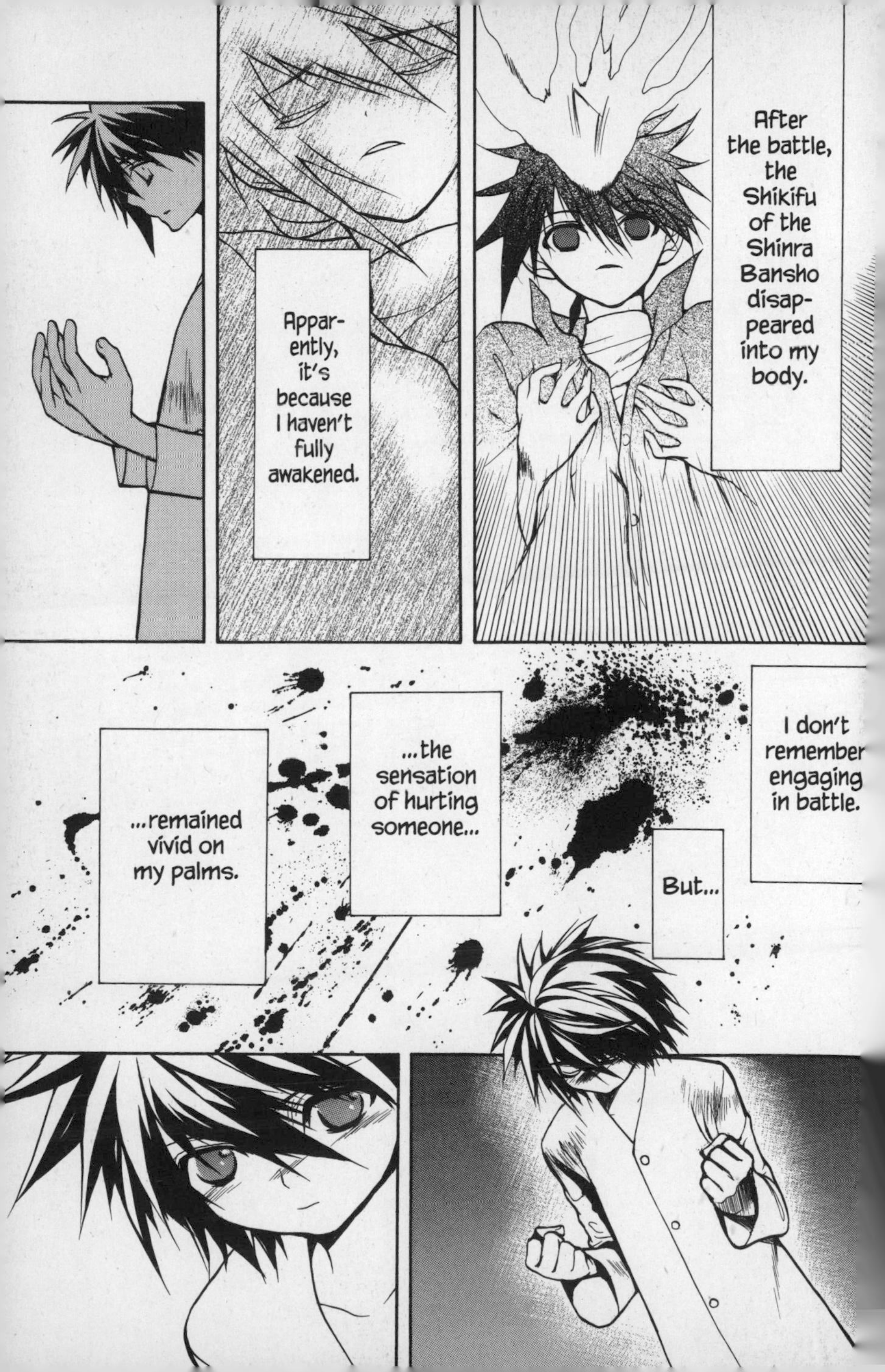
After the battle, the Shikifu of the Shinra Bansho disappeared into my body.
Apparently, it's because I haven't fully awakened.
I don't remember engaging in battle.
But...
...the sensation of hurting someone...
...remained vivid on my palms.

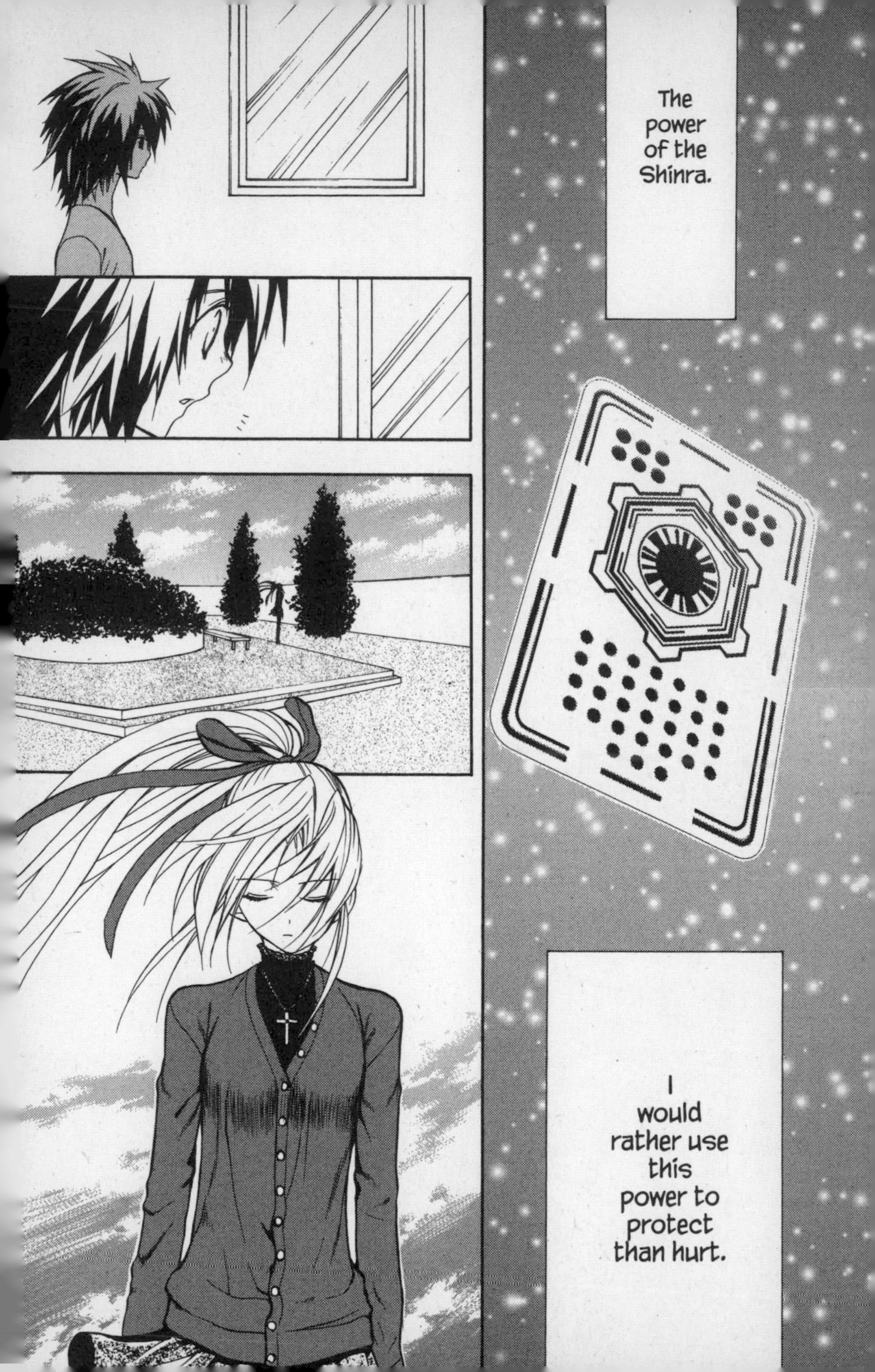
The power of the Shinra.
I would rather use this power to protect than hurt.

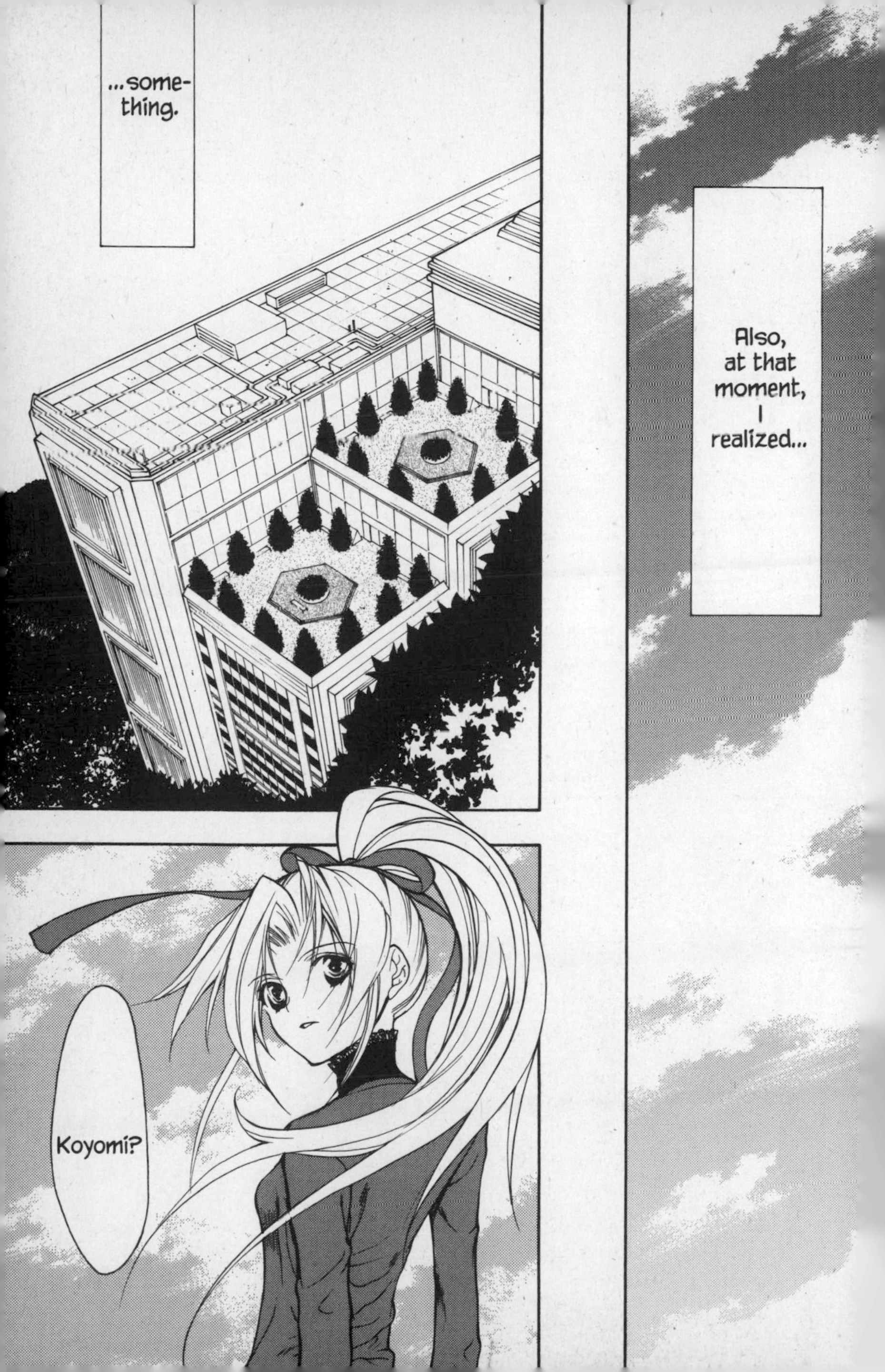
Also, at that moment, I realized...
...some-thing.
Koyomi?

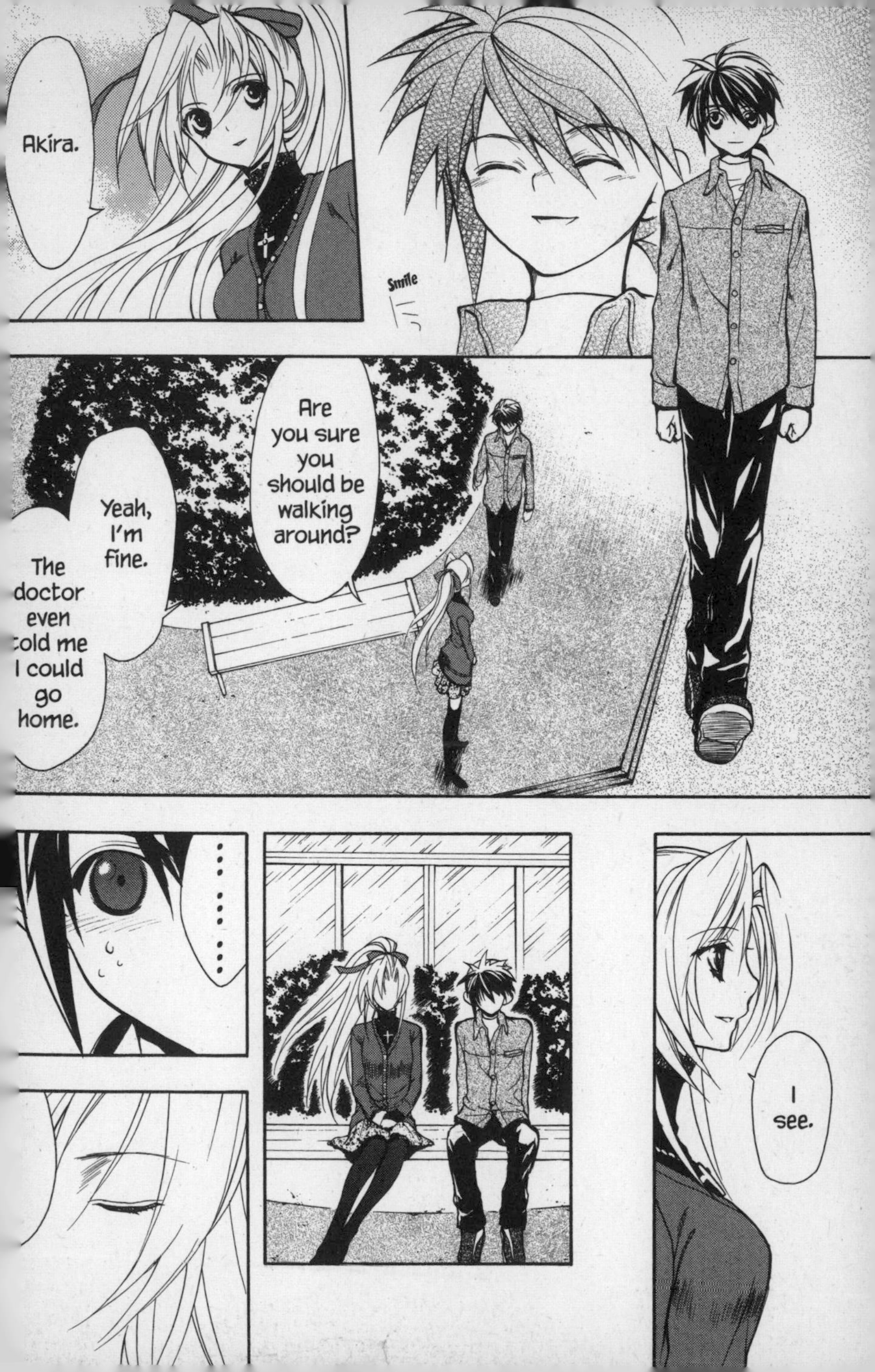
Smile
Akira.
Are you sure you should be walking around?
Yeah, I'm fine.
The doctor even told me I could go home.
I see.
......

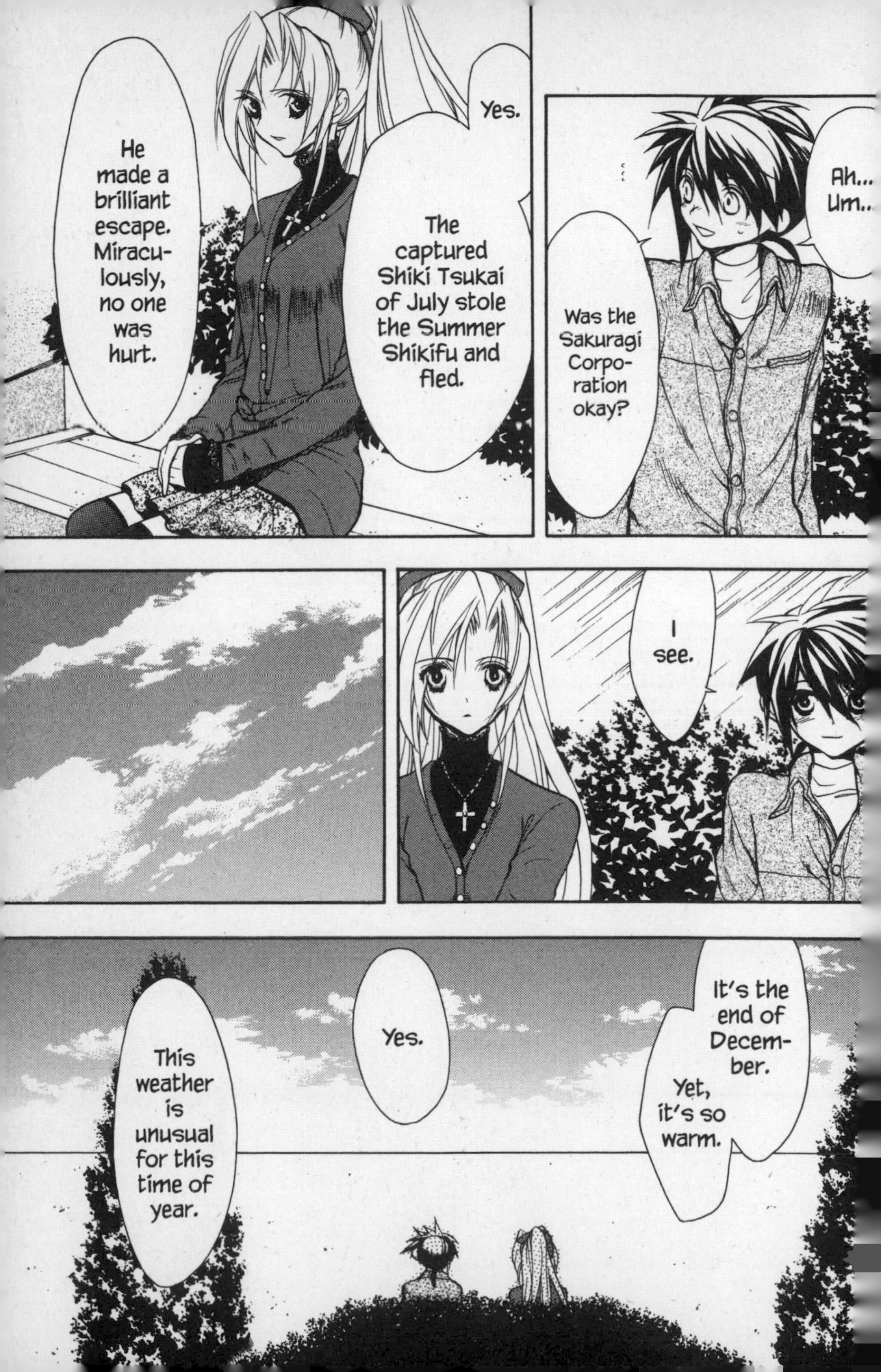
Ah... Um...
...
Was the Sakuragi Corporation okay?
Yes.
The captured Shiki Tsukai of July stole the Summer Shikifu and fled.
He made a brilliant escape. Miraculously, no one was hurt.
I see.
It's the end of December.
Yet, it's so warm.
Yes.
This weather is unusual for this time of year.

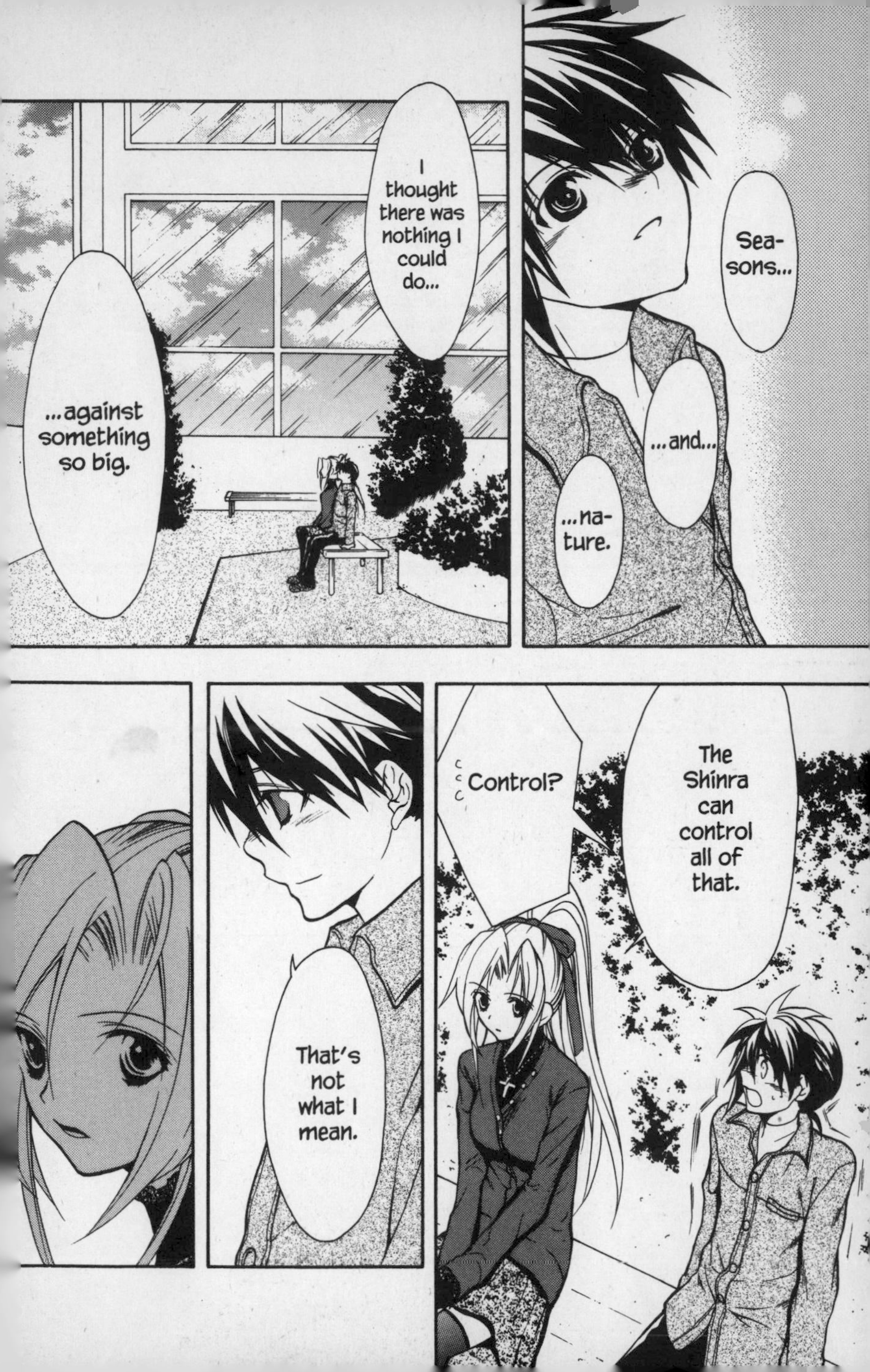
Sea-sons...
...and...
...na-ture.
I thought there was nothing I could do...
...against something so big.
The Shinra can control all of that.
Control?
That's not what I mean.

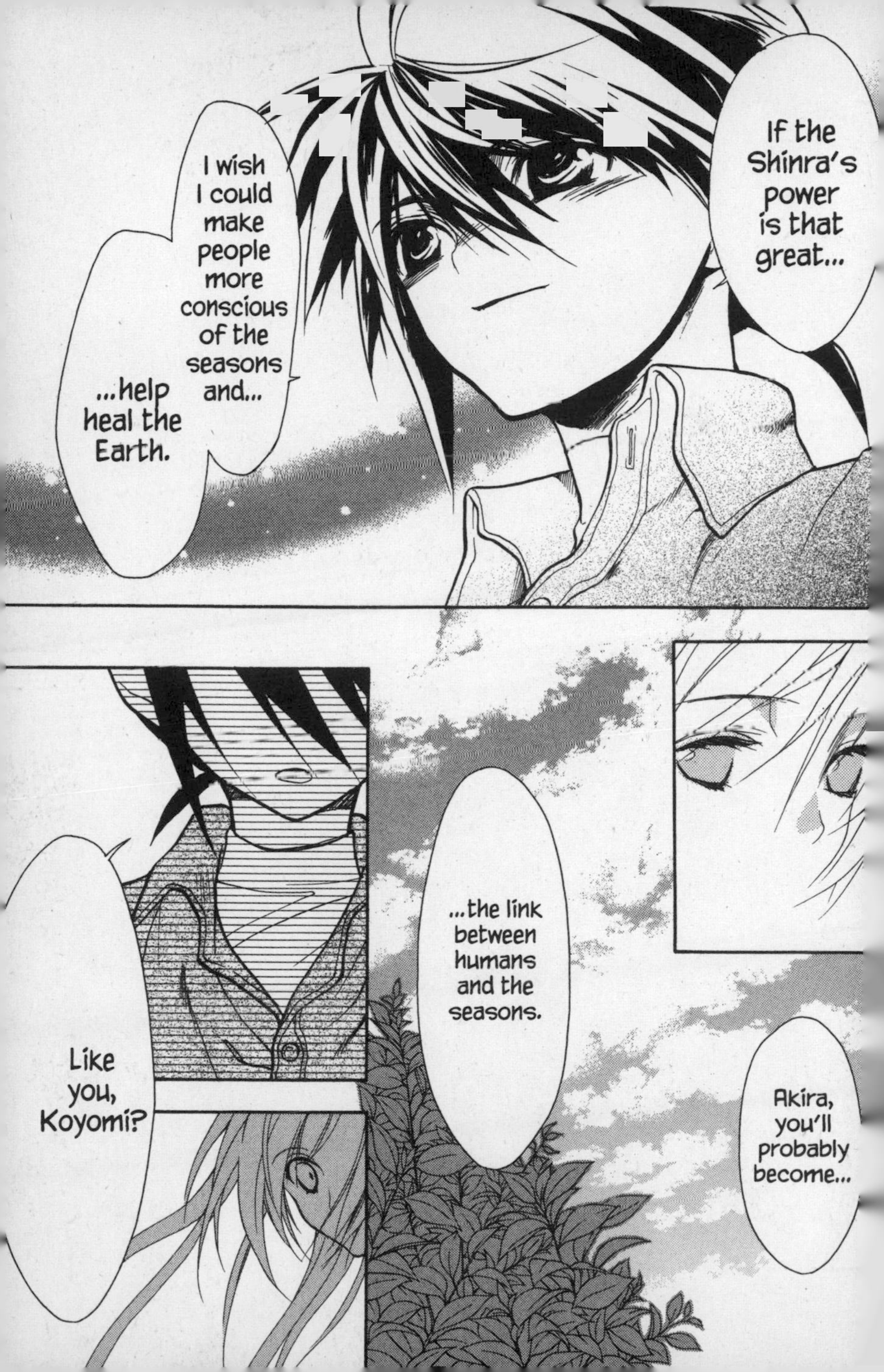
If the Shinra's power is that great...
I wish I could make people more conscious of the seasons and...
...help heal the Earth.
Akira, you'll probably become...
...the link between humans and the seasons.
Like you, Koyomi?

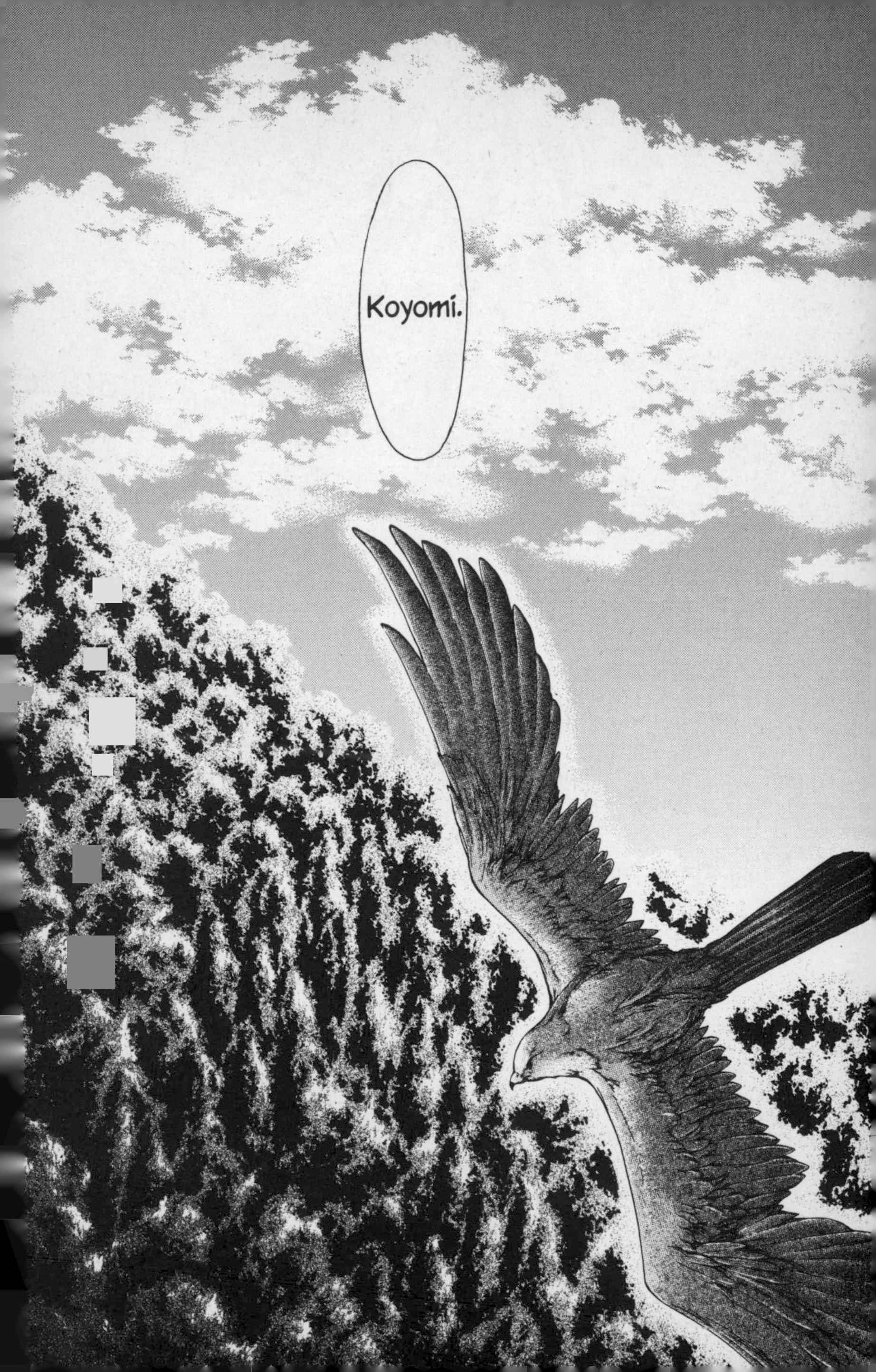
Koyomi.

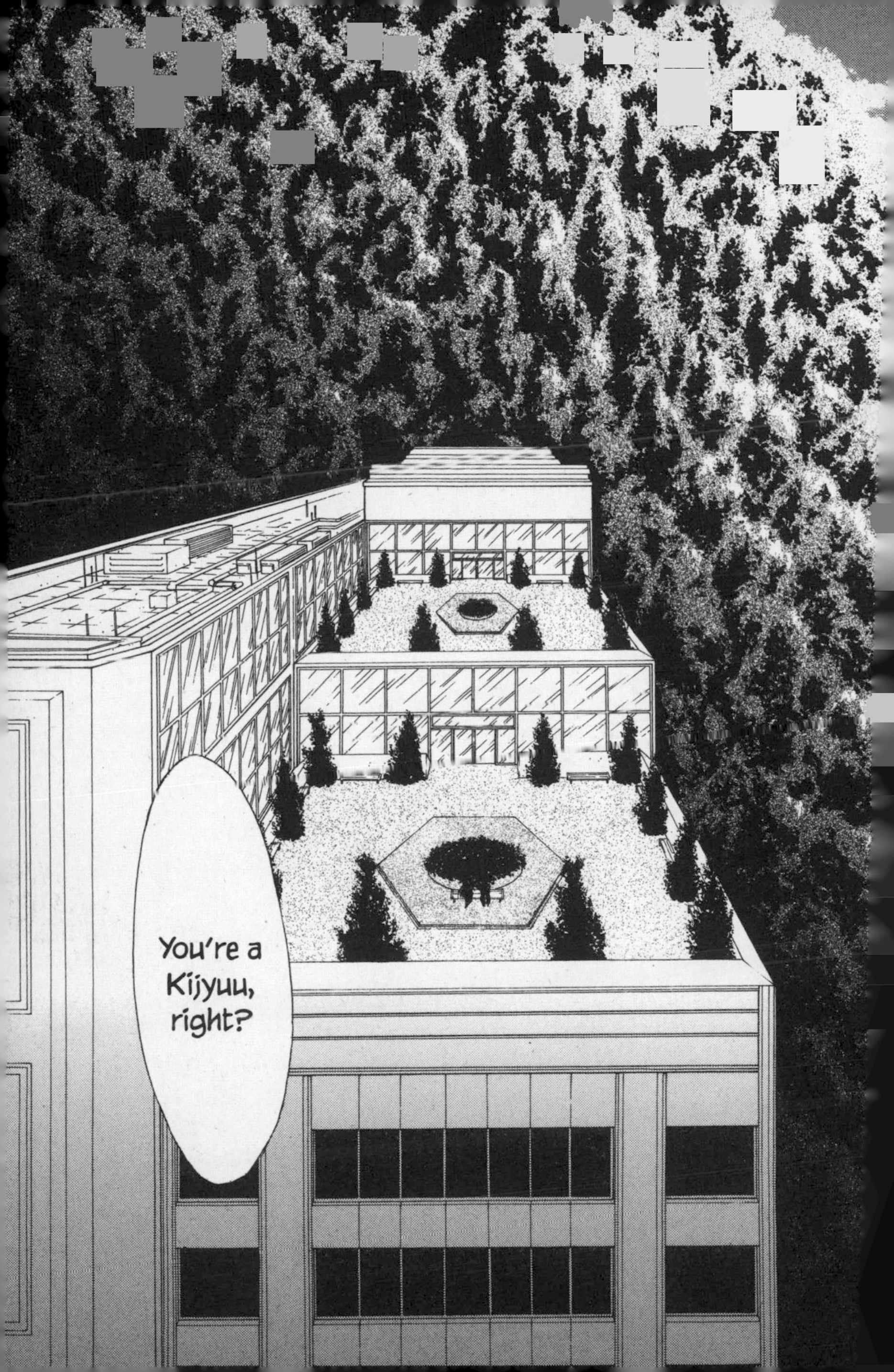
You're a Kijyuu, right?

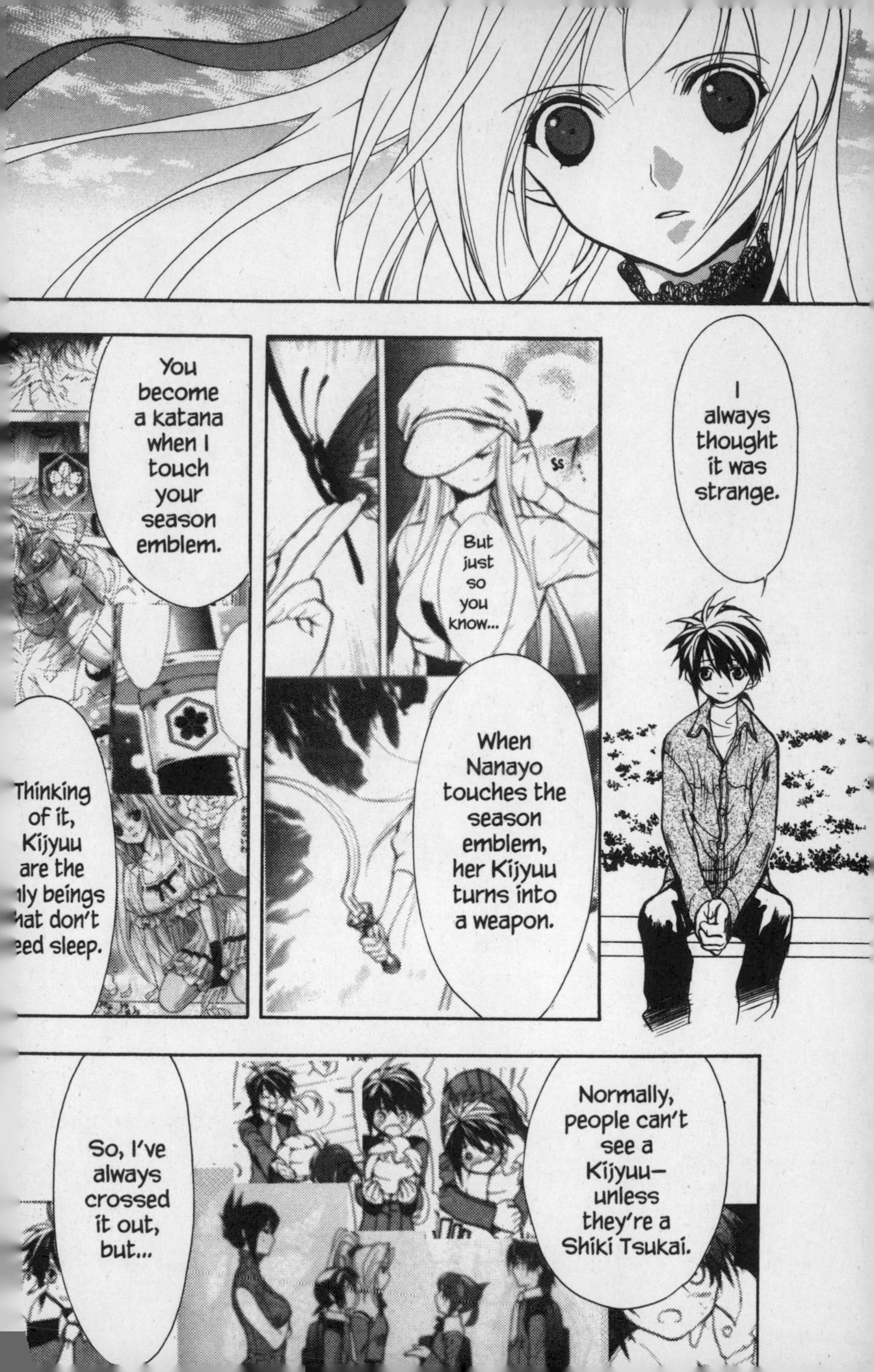
I always thought it was strange.
SS
But just so you know...
When Nanayo touches the season emblem, her Kijyuu turns into a weapon.
You become a katana when I touch your season emblem.
Thinking of it, Kijyuu are the nly beings hat don't eed sleep.
Normally, people can't see a Kijyuu—unless they're a Shiki Tsukai.
So, I've always crossed it out, but...

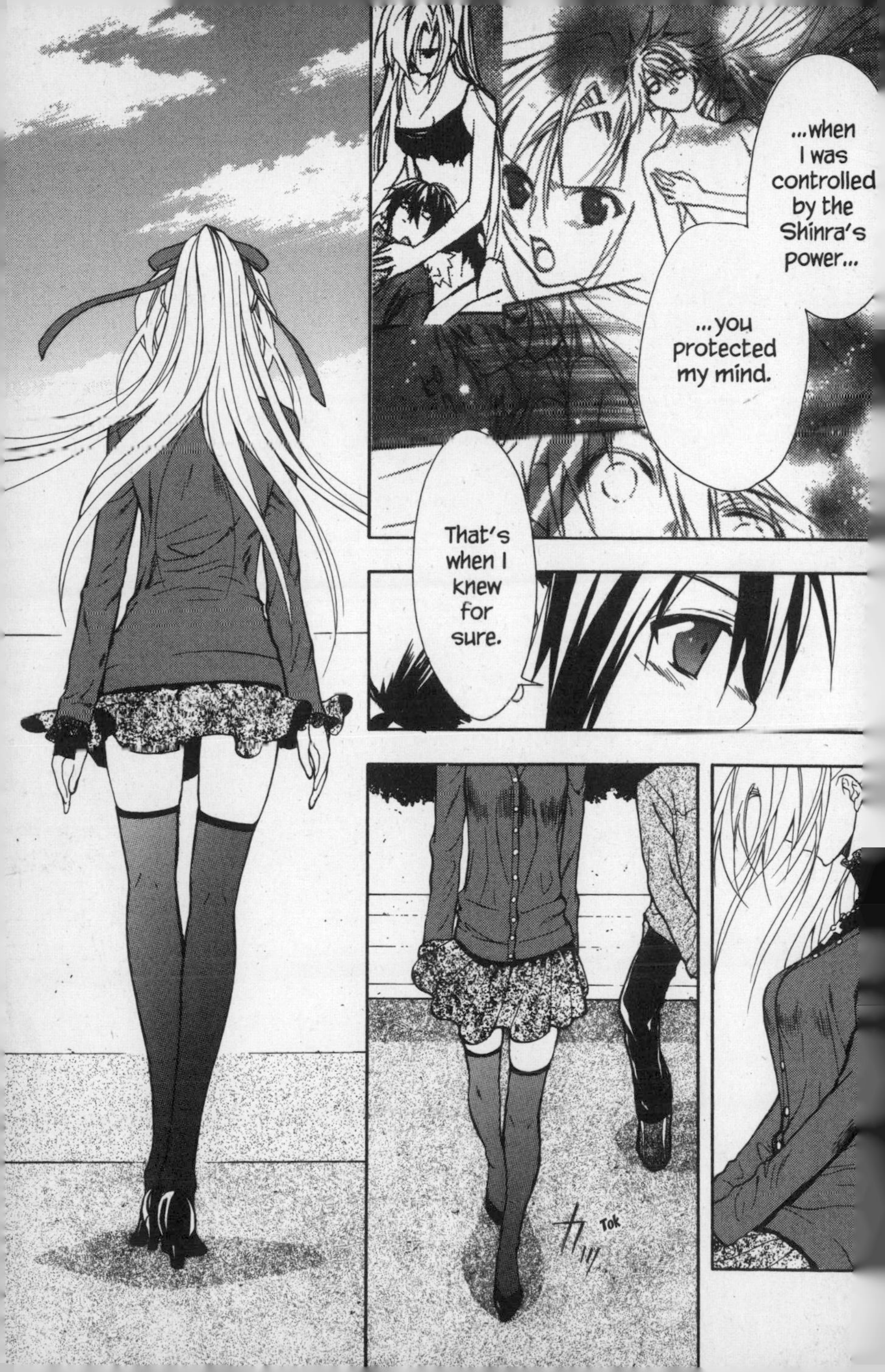
...when I was controlled by the Shinra's power...
...you protected my mind.
That's when I knew for sure.
Tok

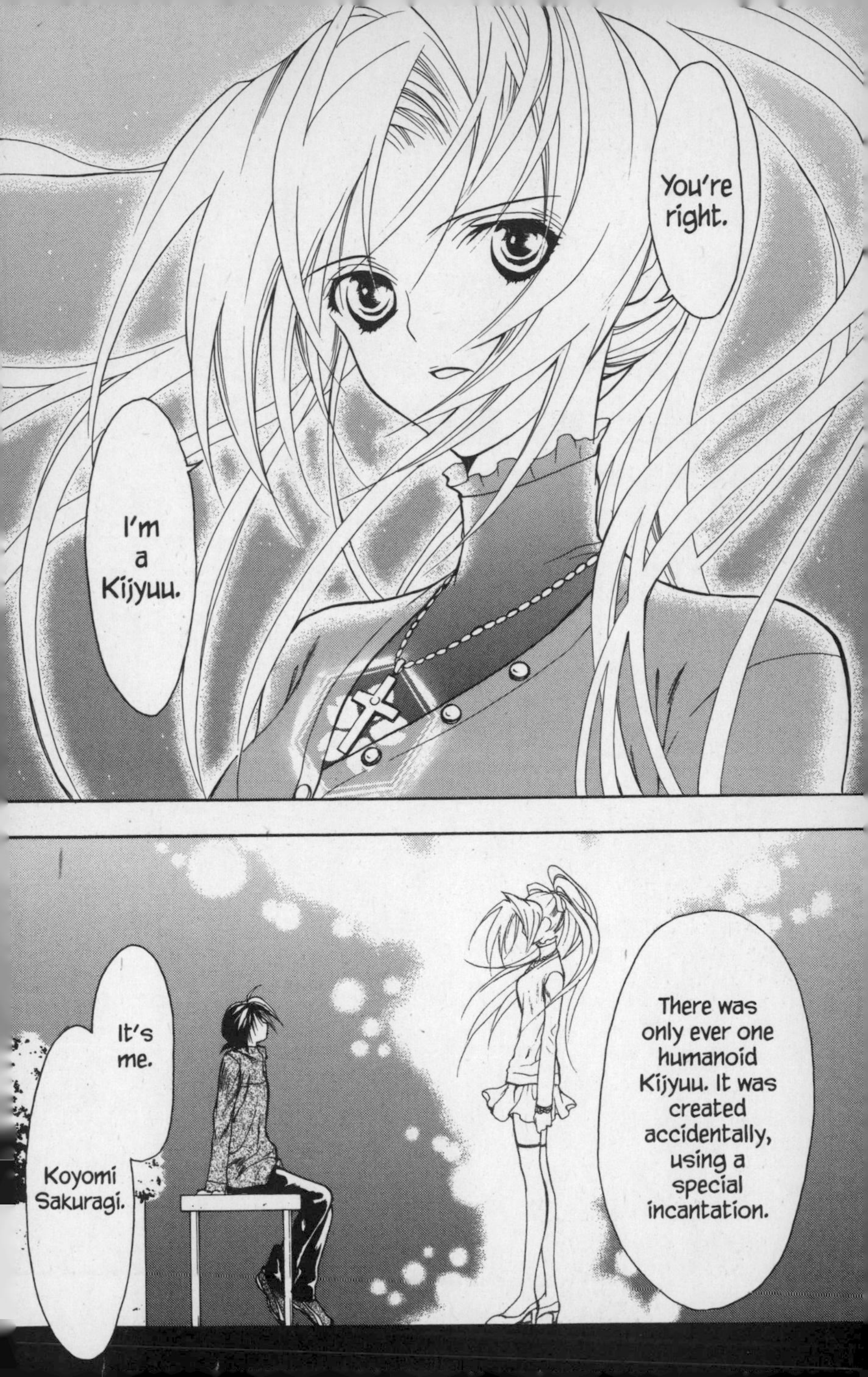
You're right.
I'm a Kijyuu.
There was only ever one humanoid Kijyuu. It was created accidentally, using a special incantation.
It's me.
Koyomi Sakuragi.

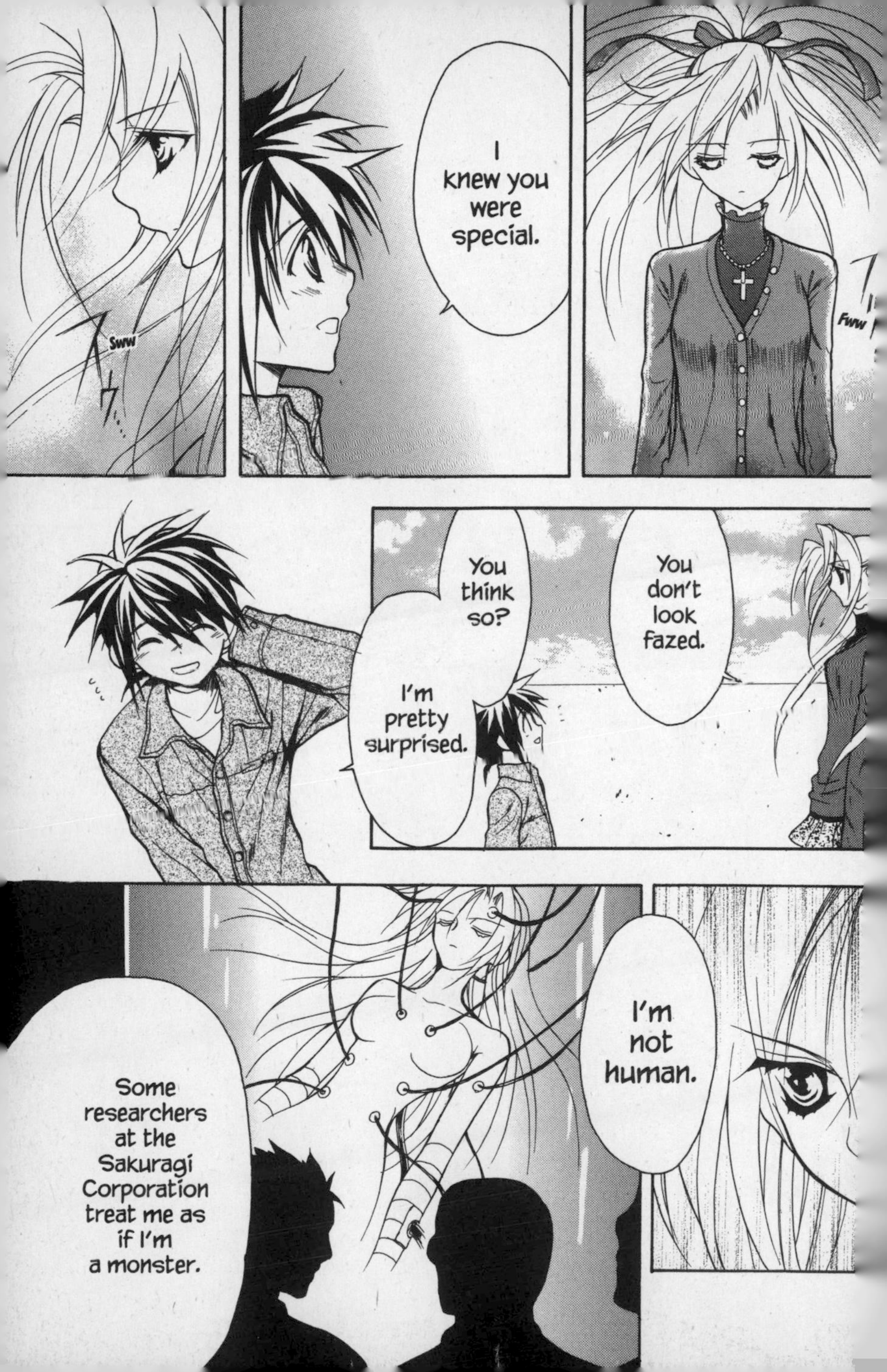
Fww
I knew you were special.
Sww
You don't look fazed.
You think so?
I'm pretty surprised.
I'm not human.
Some researchers at the Sakuragi Corporation treat me as if I'm a monster.

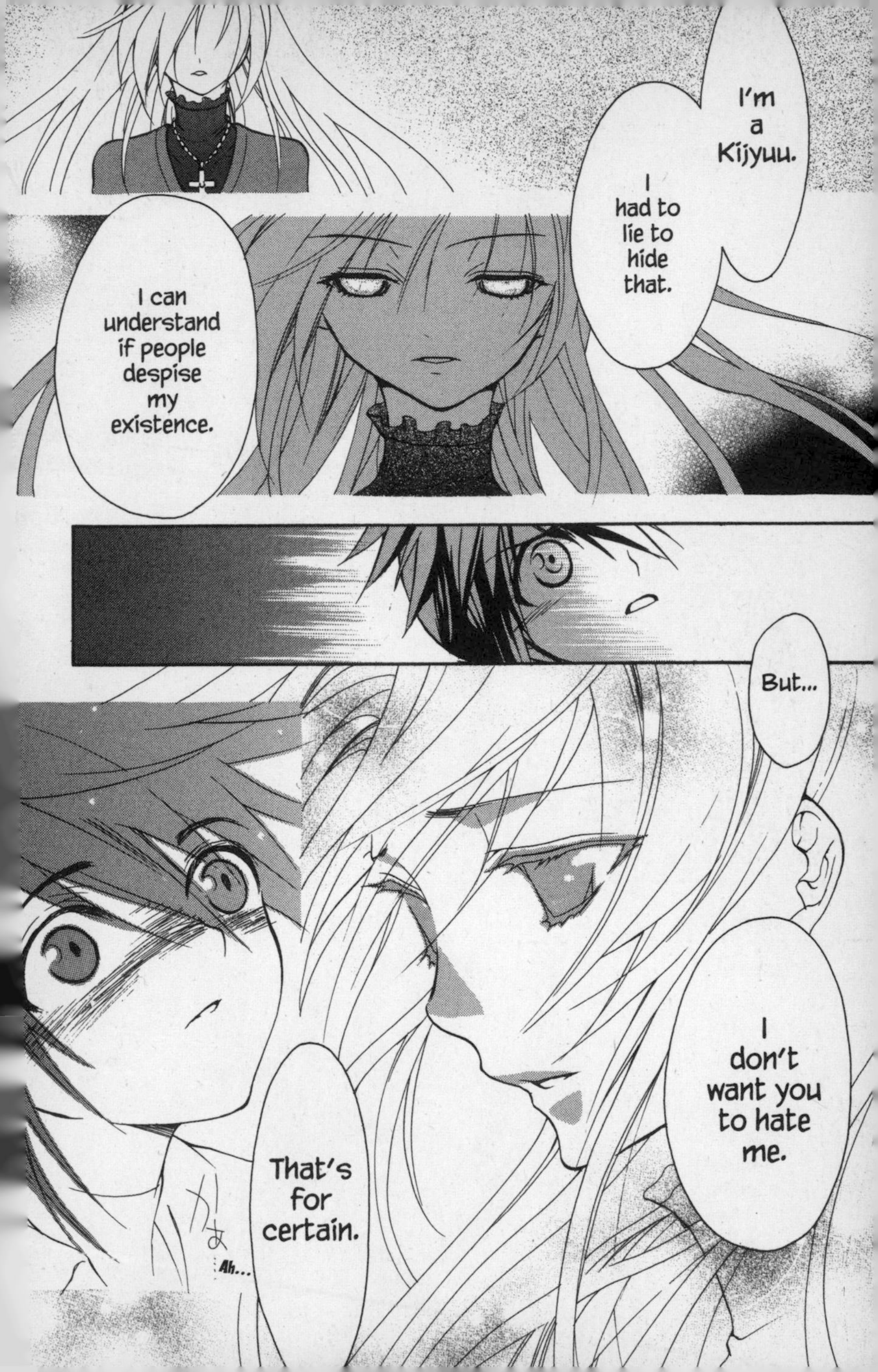
I'm a Kijyuu.
I had to lie to hide that.
I can understand if people despise my existence.
But...
I don't want you to hate me.
That's for certain.
Ah...

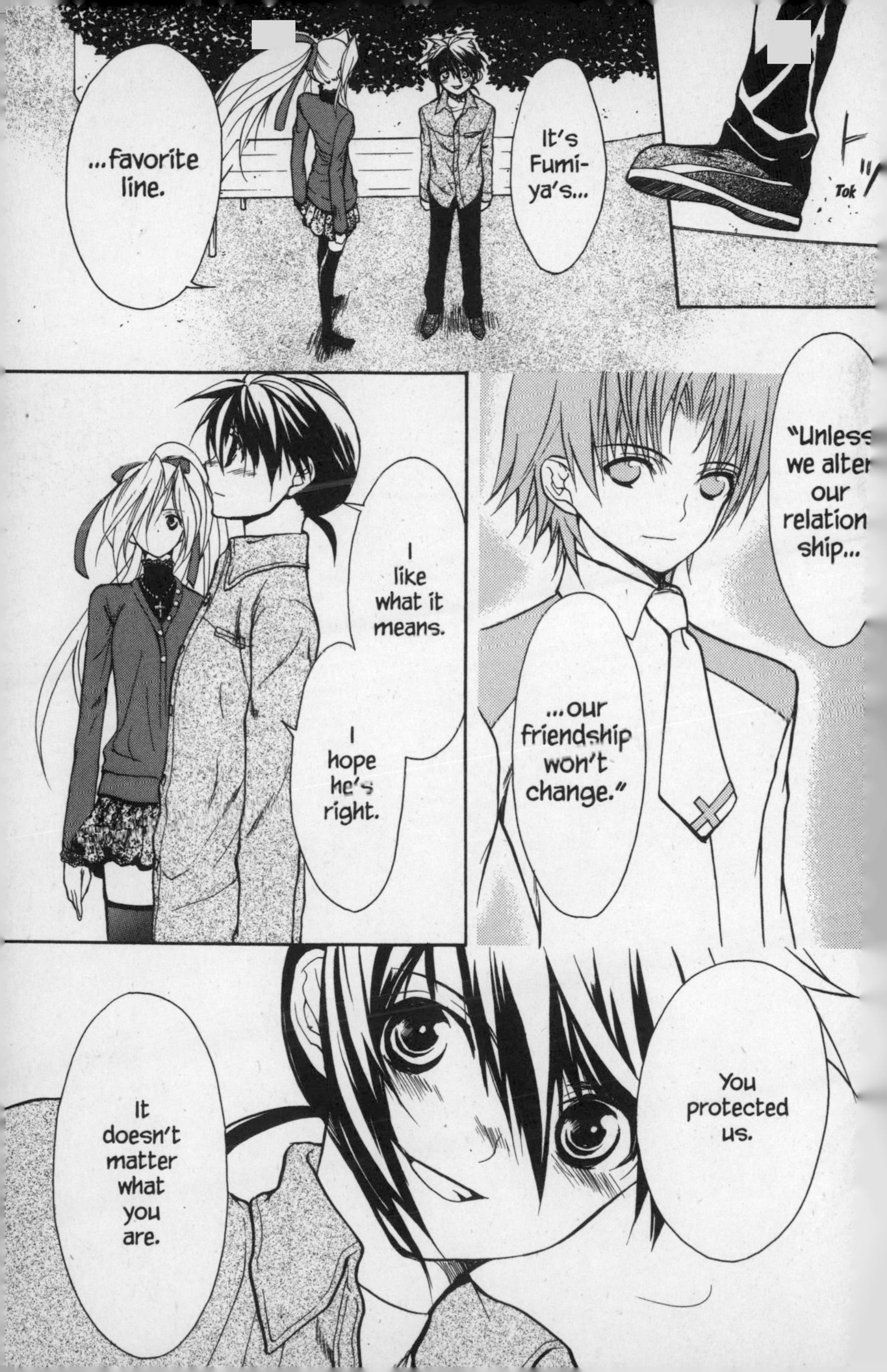

Tok
It's Fumi-ya's...
...favorite line.
"Unless we alter our relationship...
...our friendship won't change."
I like what it means.
I hope he's right.
You protected us.
It doesn't matter what you are.

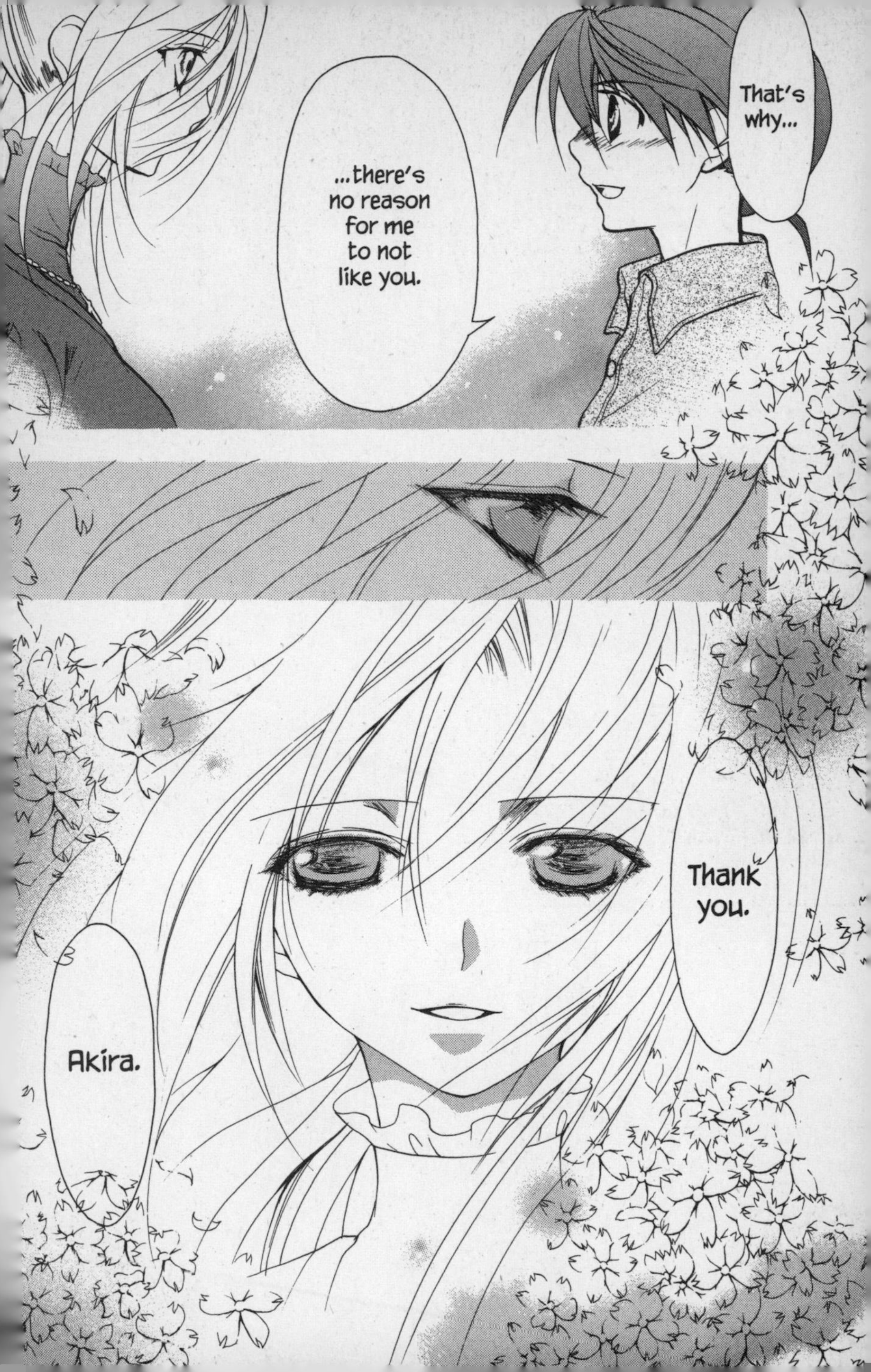
That's why...
...there's no reason for me to not like you.
Thank you.
Akira.

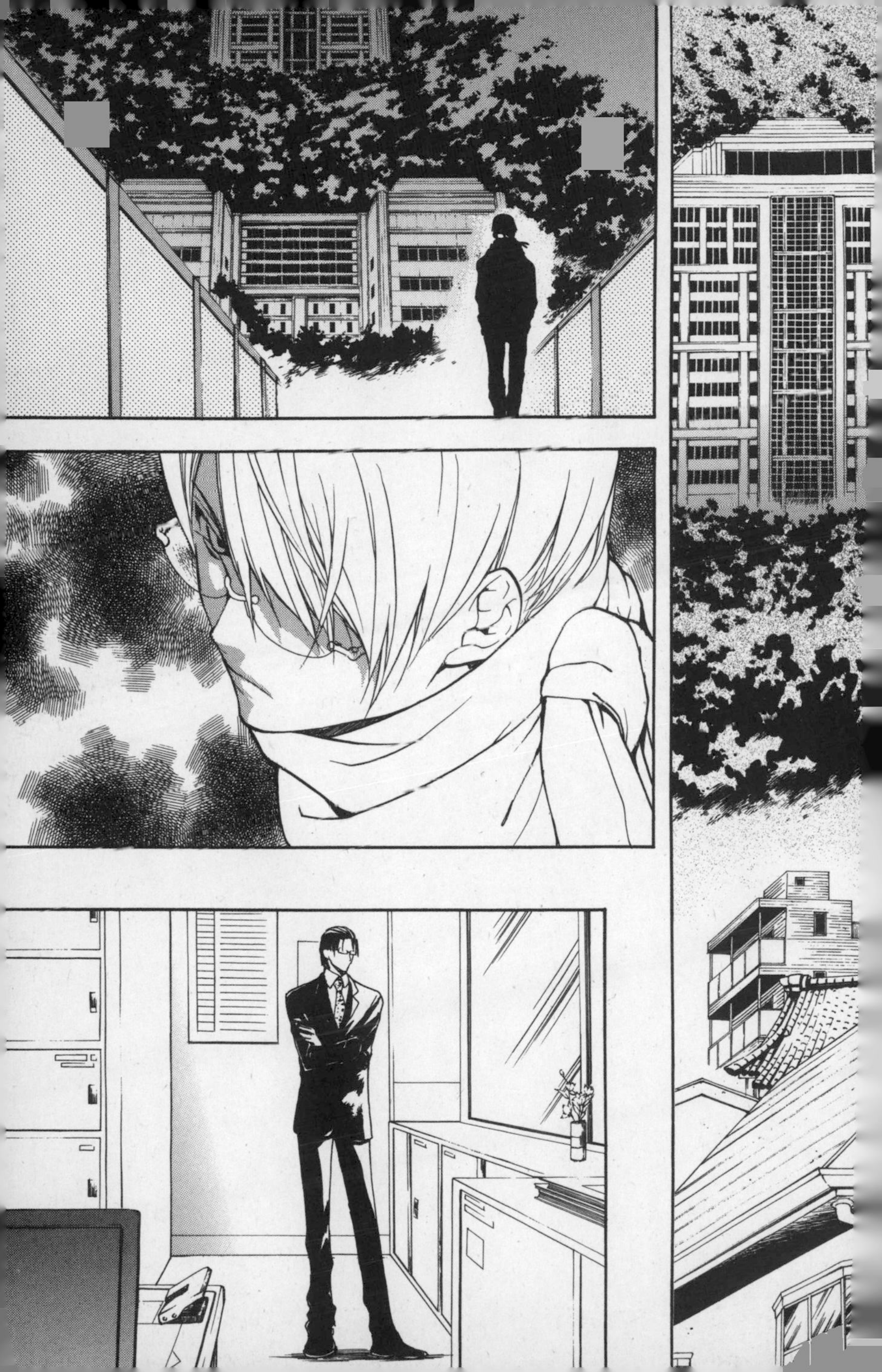

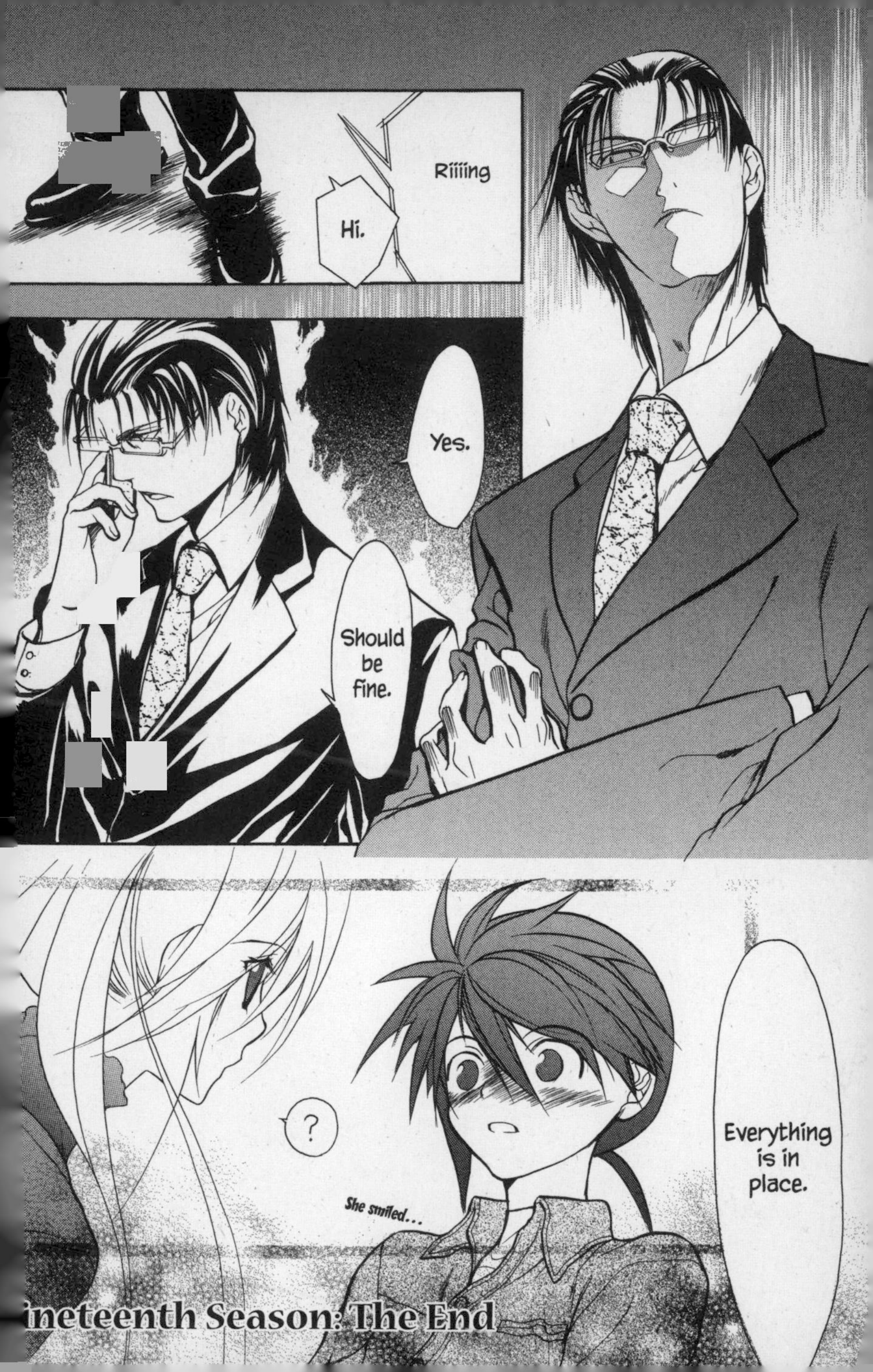
Riiiing
Hi.
Yes.
Should be fine.
Everything is in place.
?
She smiled...
ineteenth Season: The End

Twentieth Season

Chaos and Reflection

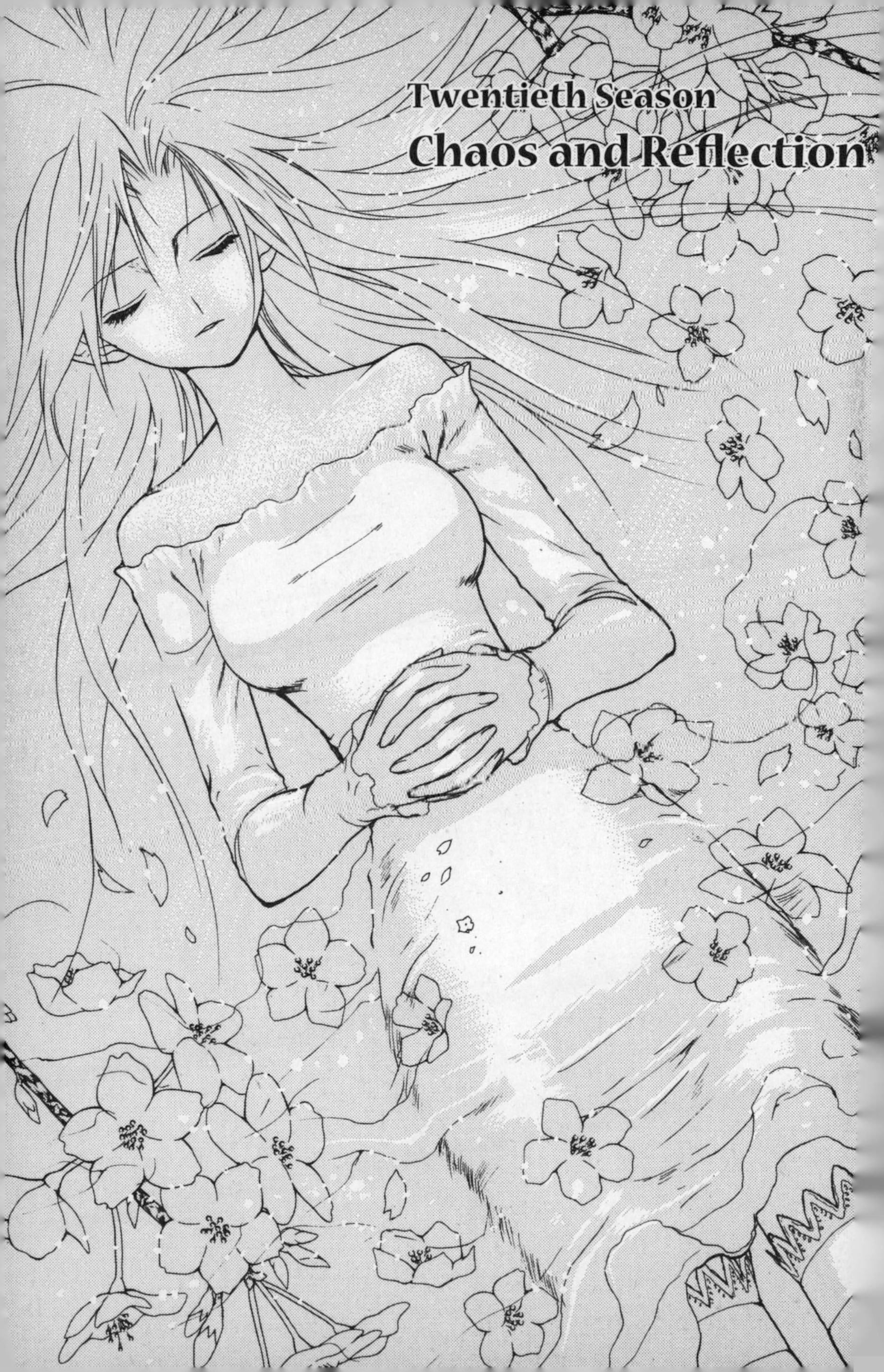

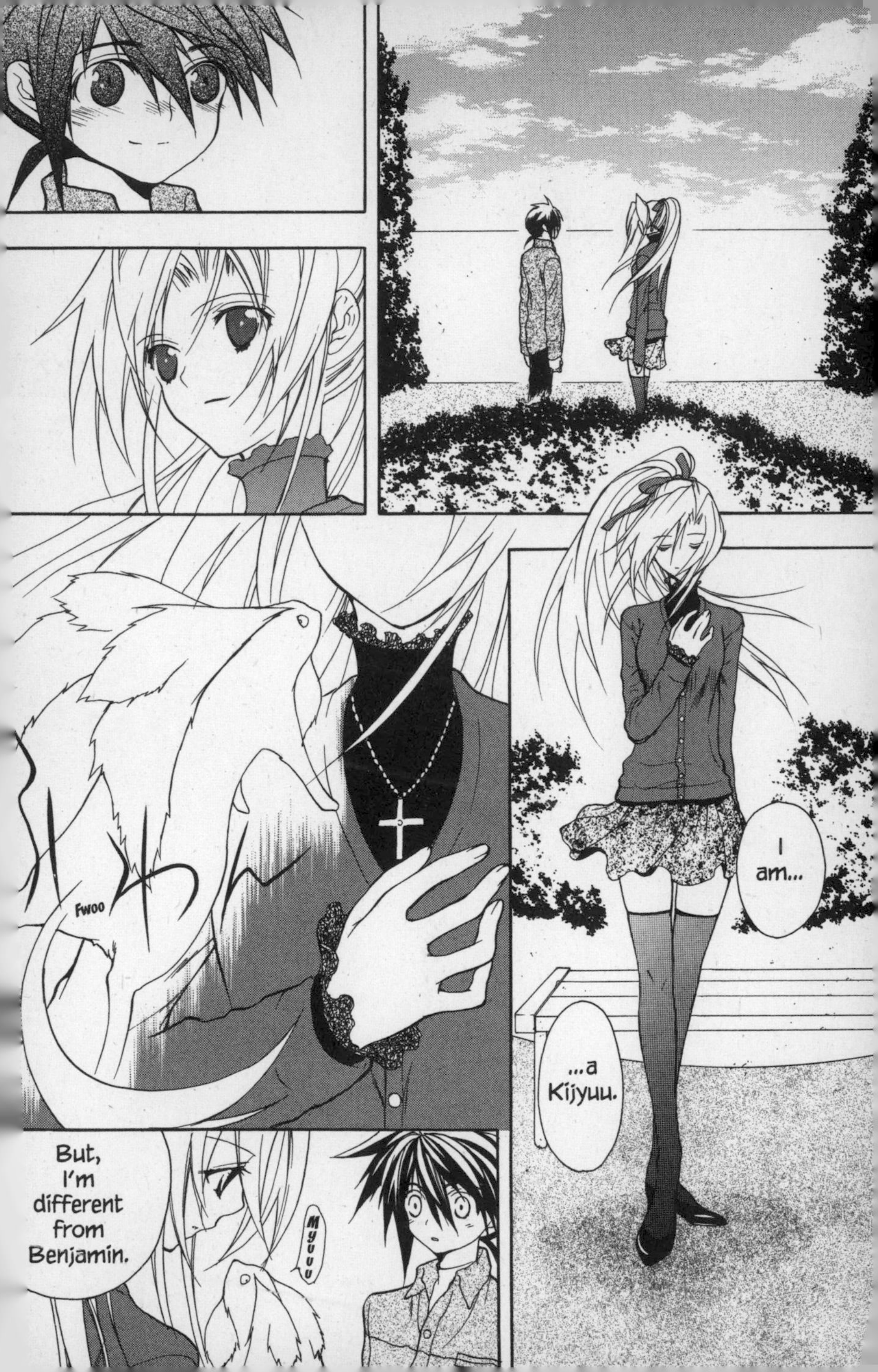
I am...
...a Kijyuu.
Fwoo
But, I'm different from Benjamin.
Myuuu

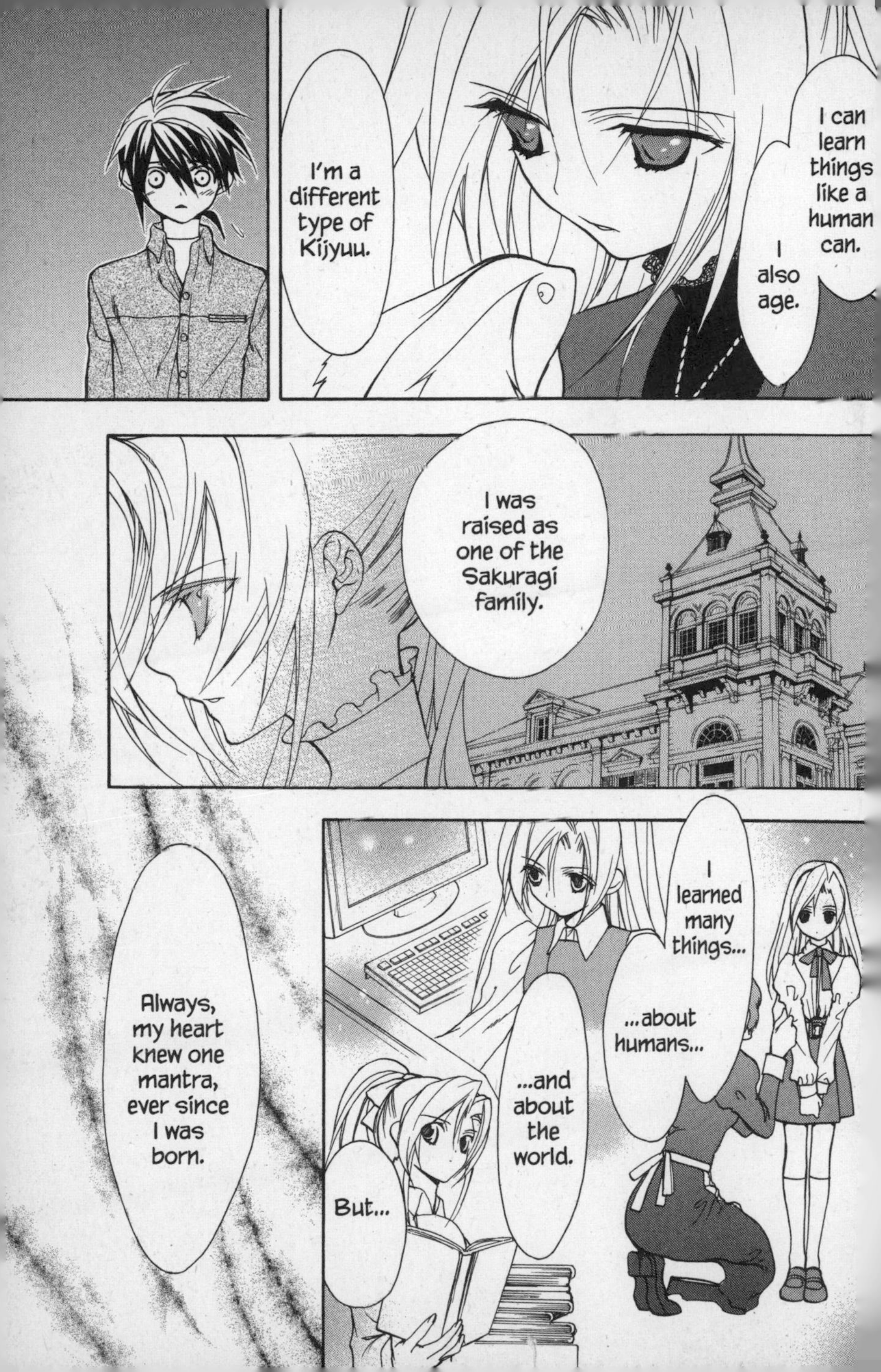
I can learn things like a human can.
I also age.
I'm a different type of Kijyuu.
I was raised as one of the Sakuragi family.
I learned many things...
...about humans...
...and about the world.
But...
Always, my heart knew one mantra, ever since I was born.

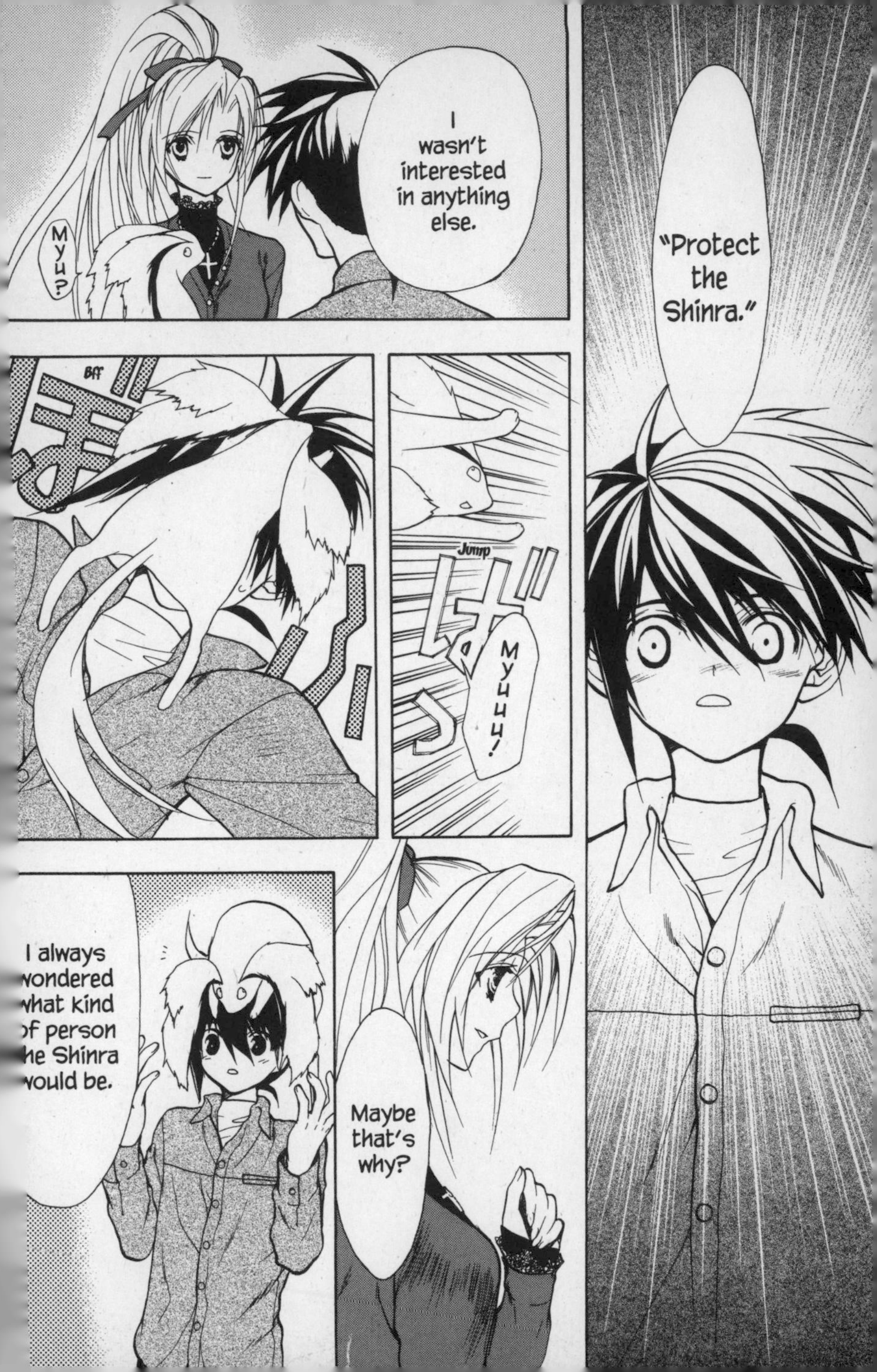
"Protect the Shinra."
I wasn't interested in anything else.
Myu?
Jump
Myuuu!
Bff
Maybe that's why?
I always wondered what kind of person the Shinra would be.

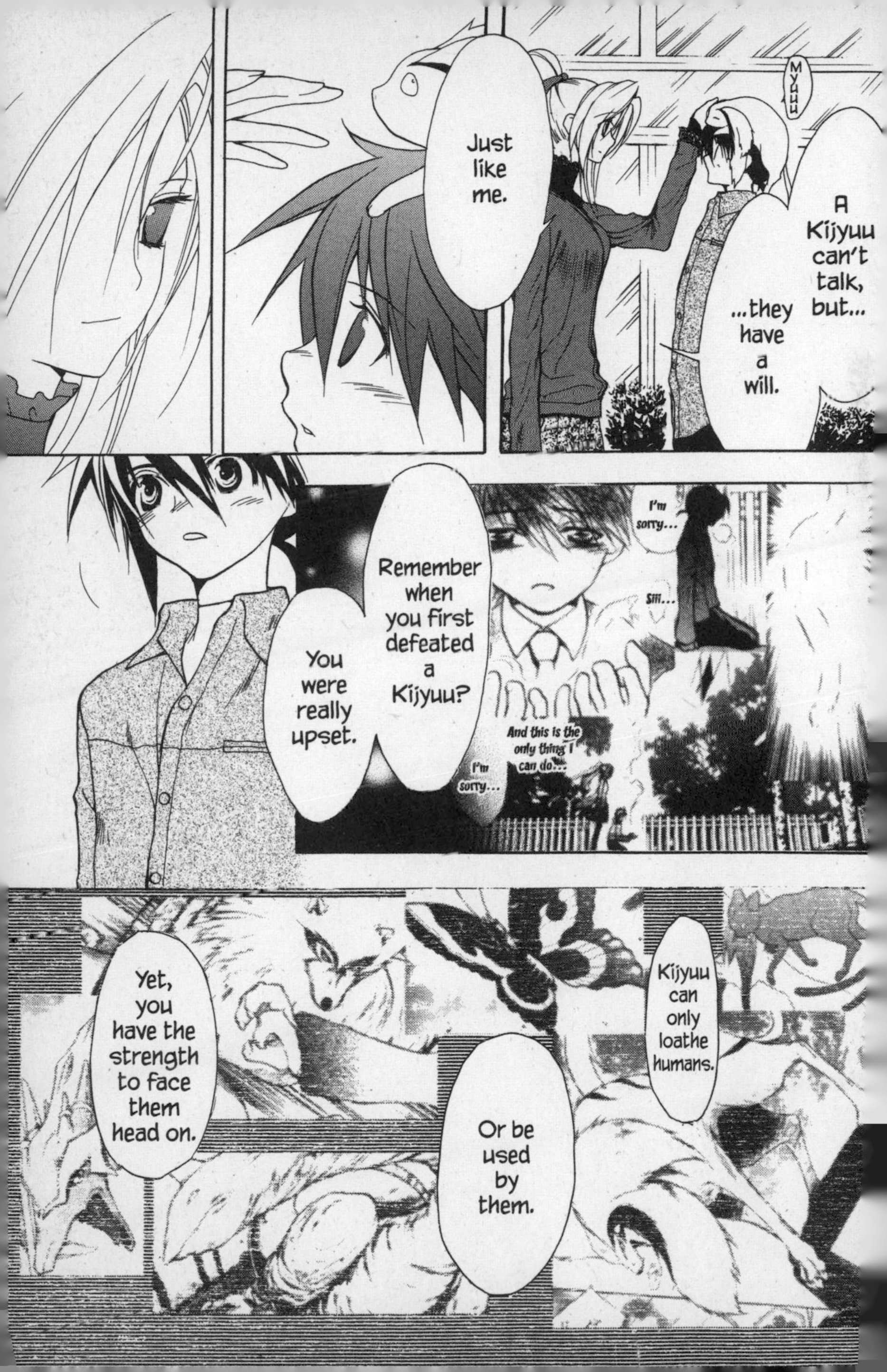
MYUUU
A Kijyuu can't talk, but...
...they have a will.
Just like me.
I'm sorry...
Siii...
And this is the only thing I can do...
I'm sorry...
Remember when you first defeated a Kijyuu?
You were really upset.
Kijyuu can only loathe humans.
Or be used by them.
Yet, you have the strength to face them head on.

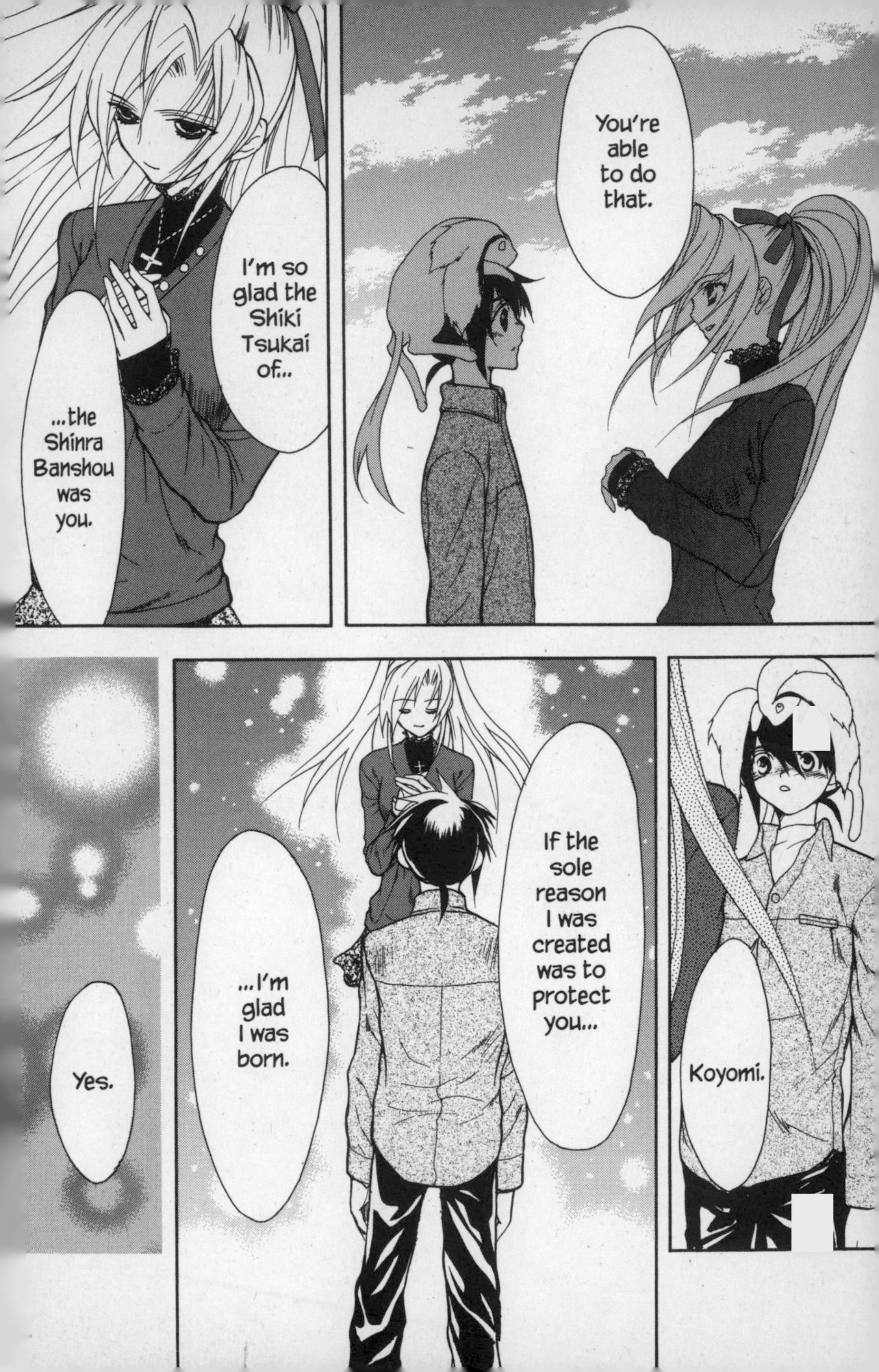
You're able to do that.
I'm so glad the Shiki Tsukai of...
...the Shinra Banshou was you.
Koyomi.
If the sole reason I was created was to protect you...
...I'm glad I was born.
Yes.

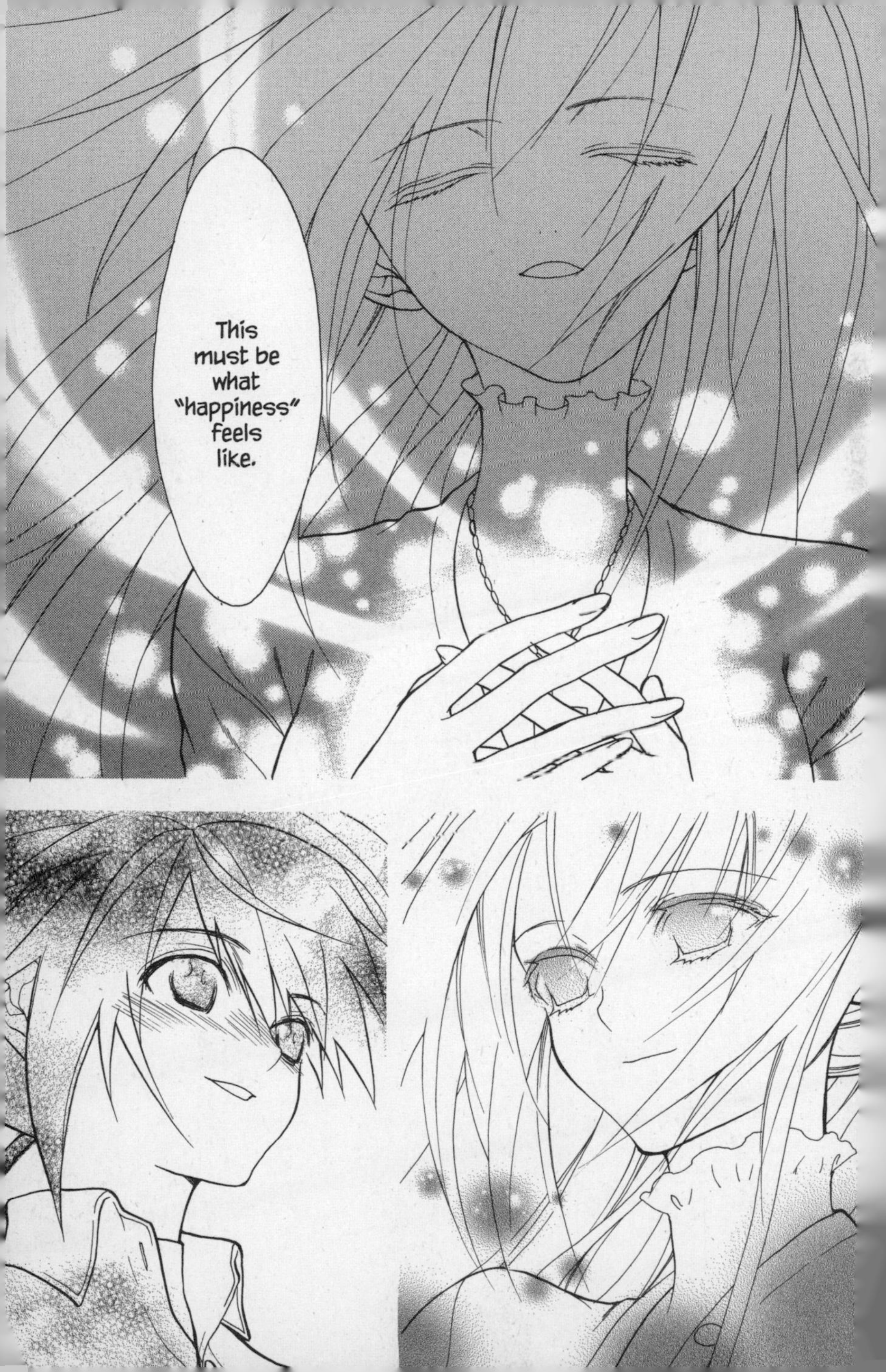
This must be what "happiness" feels like.

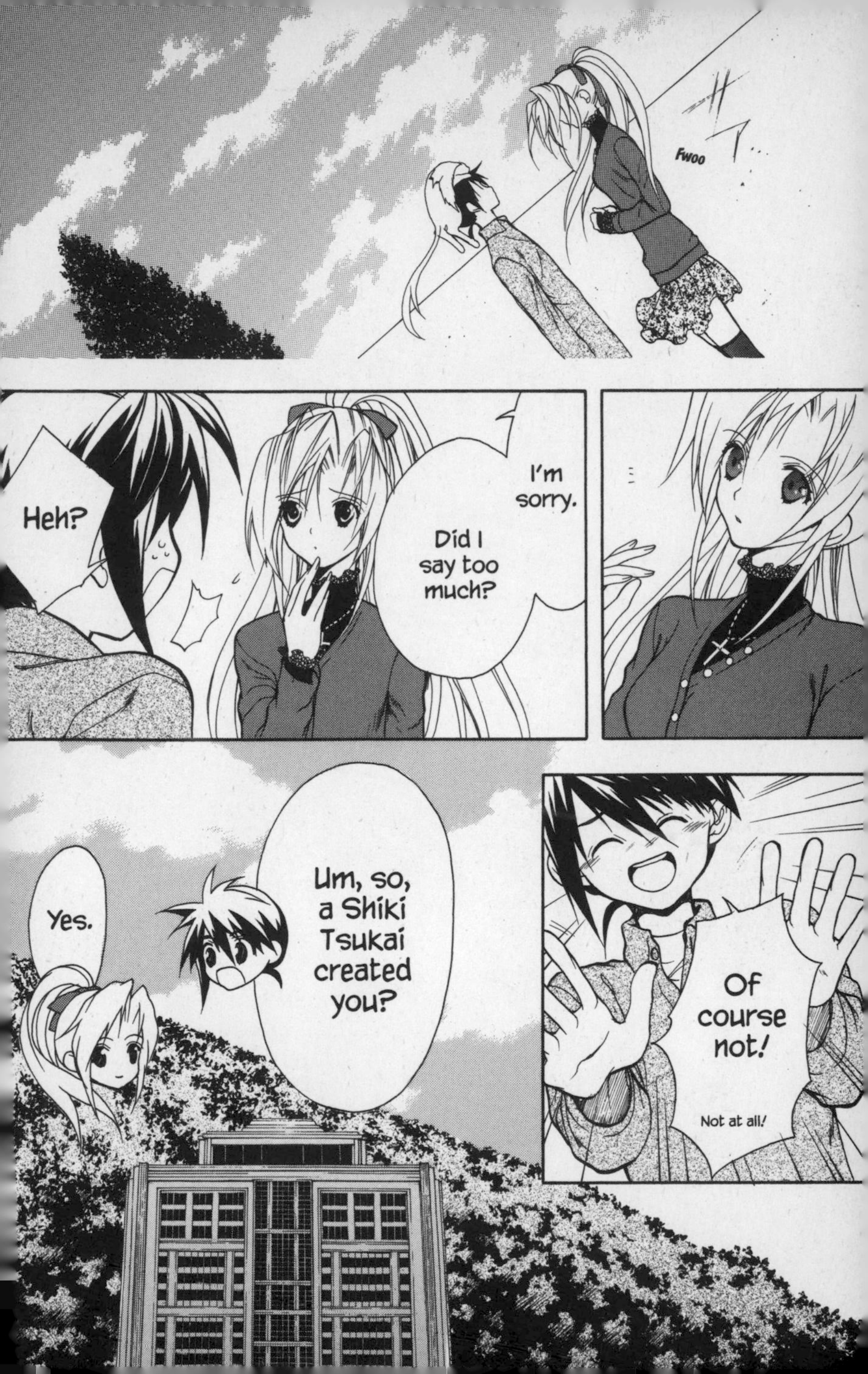
Fwoo
I'm sorry.
Did I say too much?
Heh?
Of course not!
Not at all!
Um, so, a Shiki Tsukai created you?
Yes.

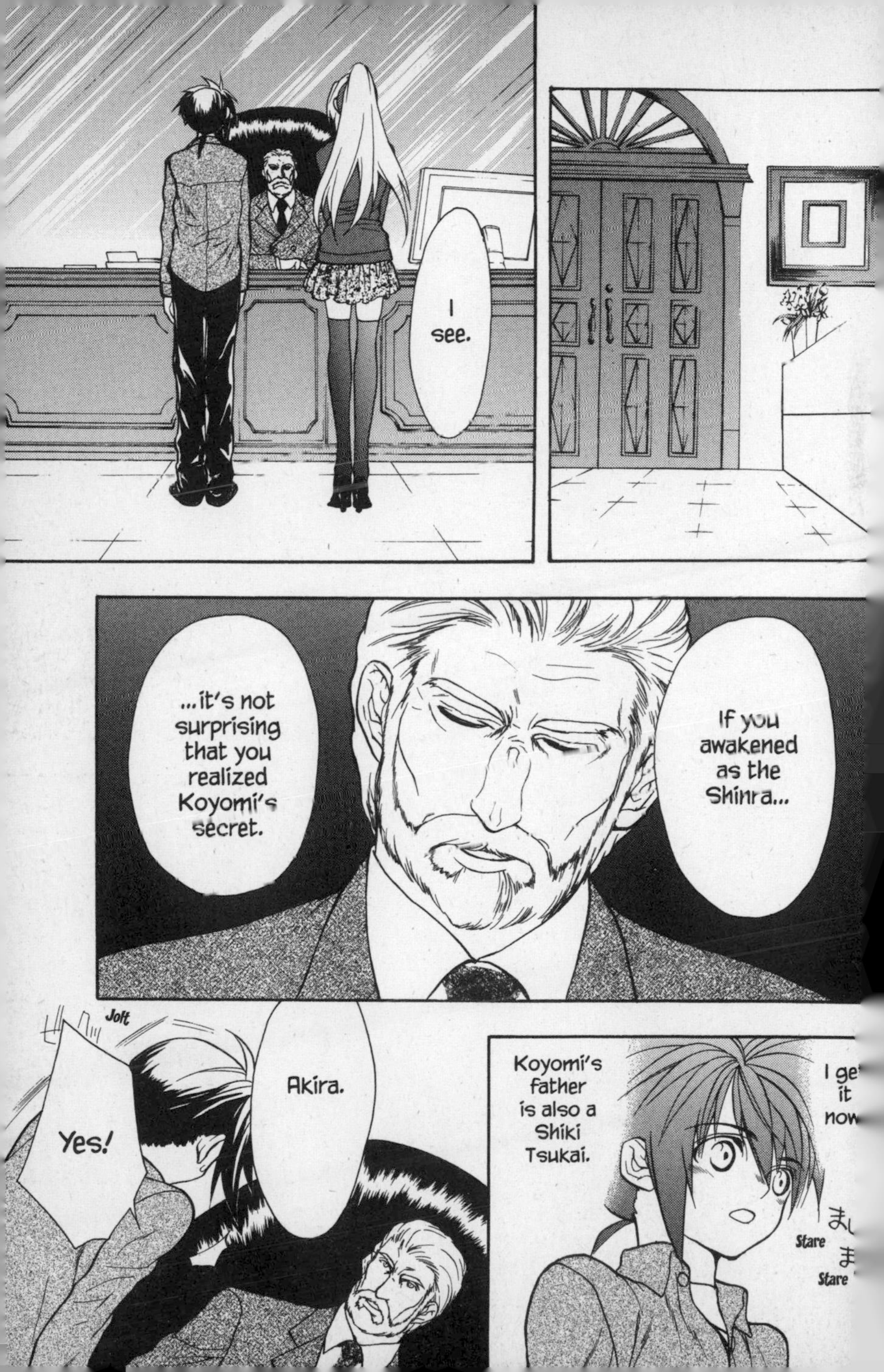
I see.
If you awakened as the Shinra...
...it's not surprising that you realized Koyomi's secret.
I ge it now
Koyomi's father is also a Shiki Tsukai.
Stare
Stare
Akira.
Jolt
Yes!

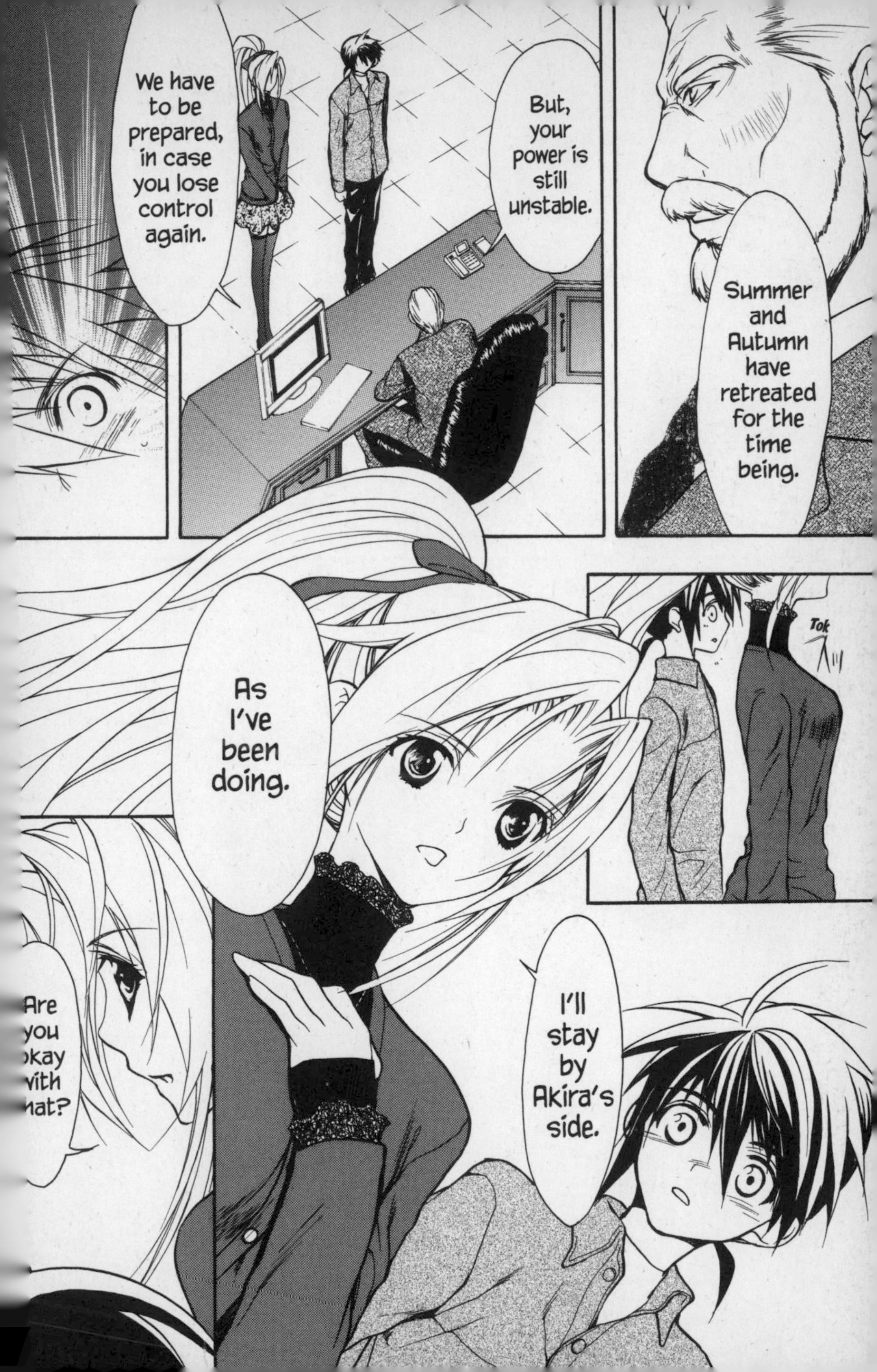
Summer and Autumn have retreated for the time being.
But, your power is still unstable.
We have to be prepared, in case you lose control again.
Tok
As I've been doing.
I'll stay by Akira's side.
Are you okay with that?

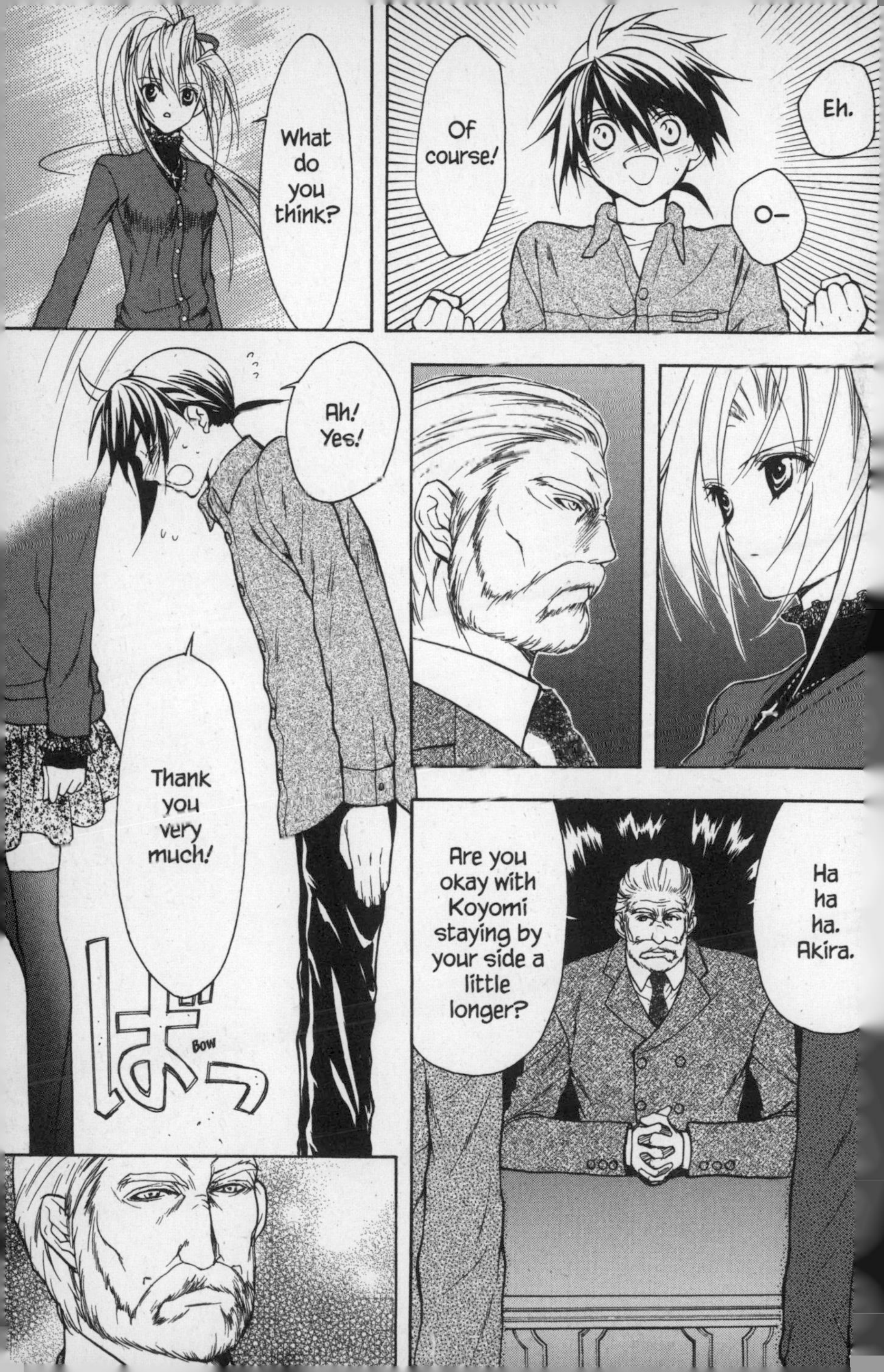
Eh.
O–
Of course!
What do you think?
Ah! Yes!
Thank you very much!
Bow
Ha ha ha. Akira.
Are you okay with Koyomi staying by your side a little longer?

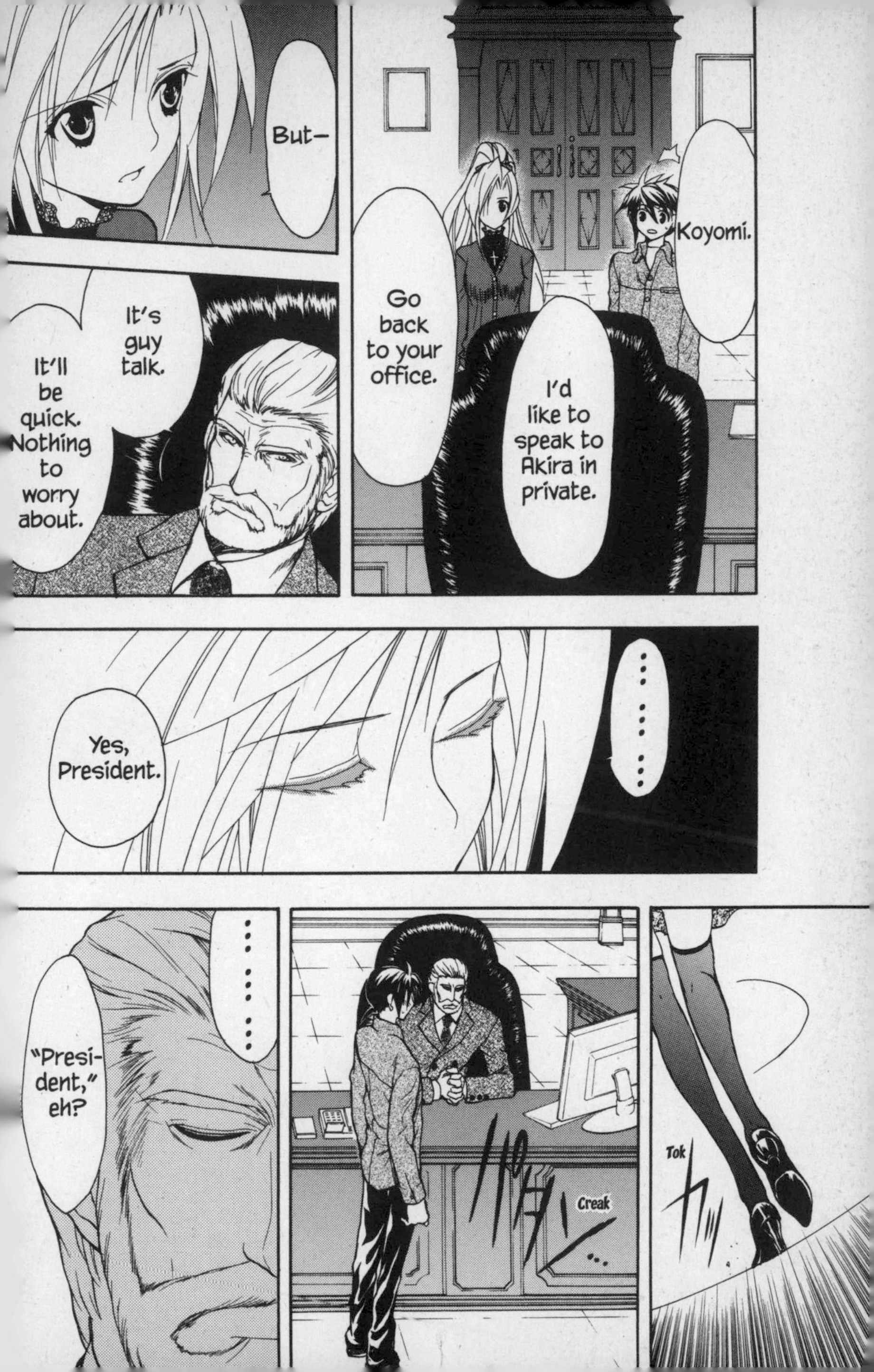
Koyomi.
I'd like to speak to Akira in private.
Go back to your office.
But—
It's guy talk.
It'll be quick. Nothing to worry about.
......
Yes, President.
Tok
Creak
......
"President," eh?

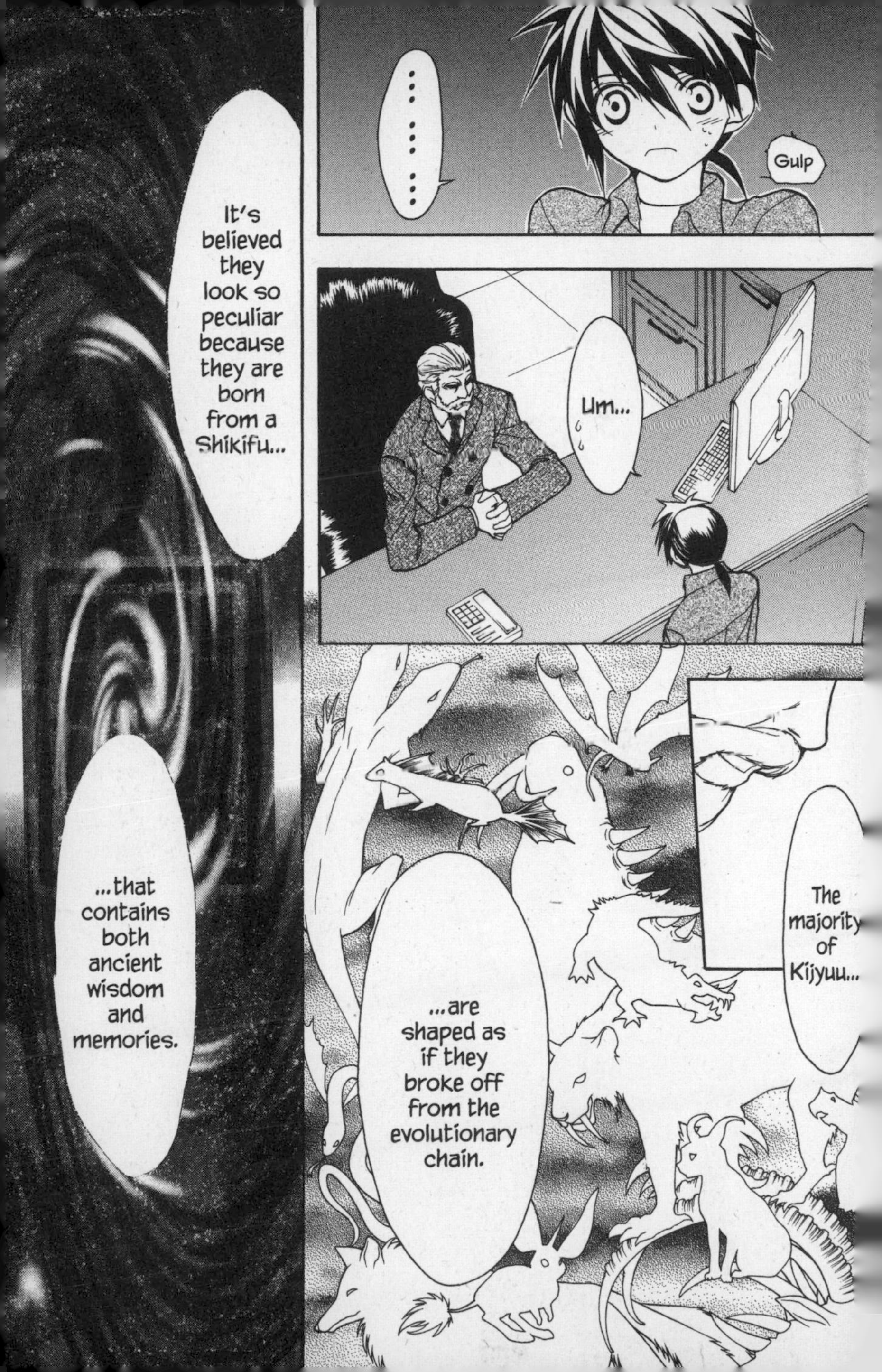
......
Gulp
Um...
The majority of Kijyuu...
...are shaped as if they broke off from the evolutionary chain.
It's believed they look so peculiar because they are born from a Shikifu...
...that contains both ancient wisdom and memories.

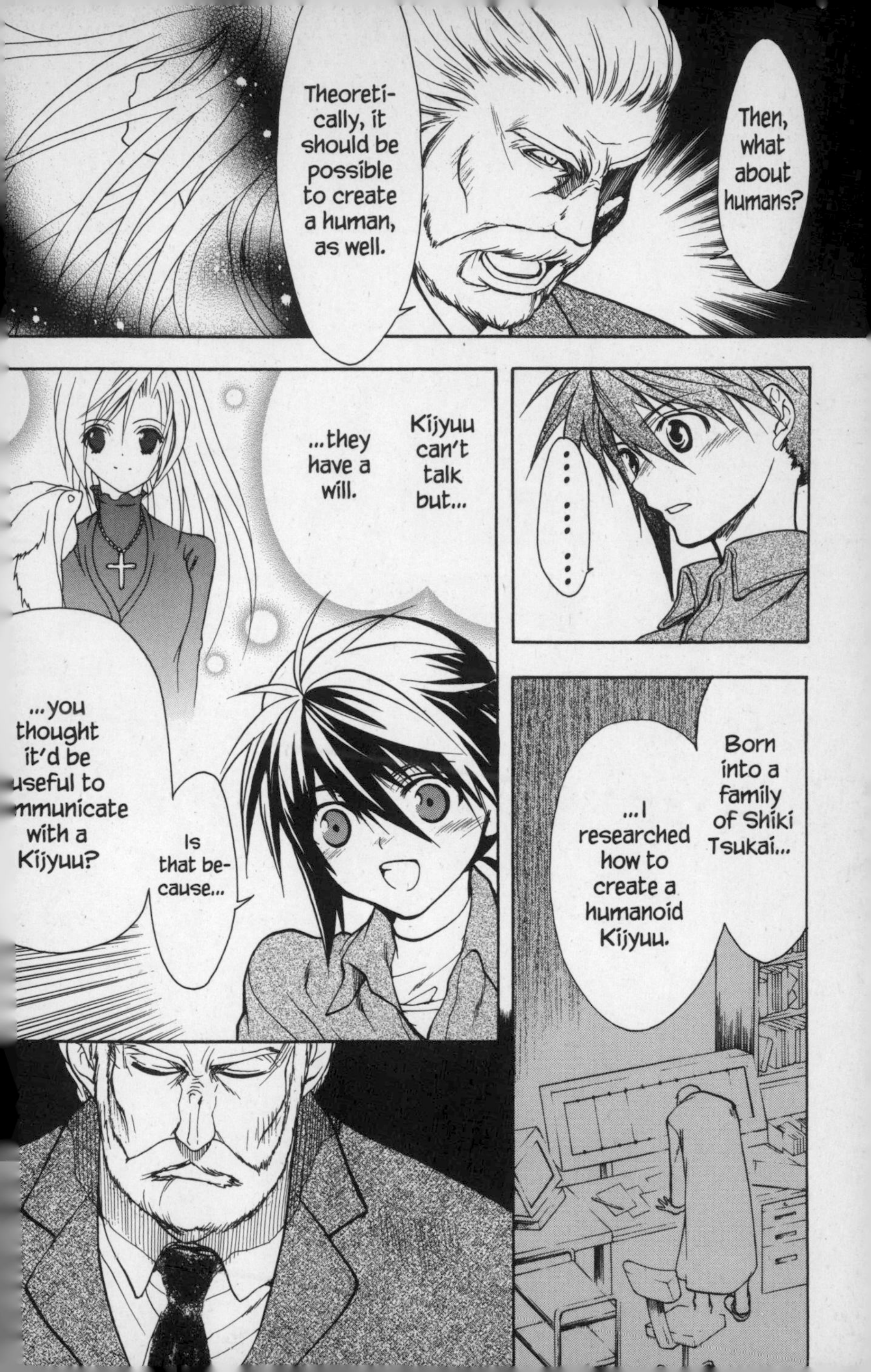
Then, what about humans?
Theoretically, it should be possible to create a human, as well.
......
Kijyuu can't talk but...
...they have a will.
Is that because...
...you thought it'd be seful to mmunicate with a Kijyuu?
Born into a family of Shiki Tsukai...
...I researched how to create a humanoid Kijyuu.

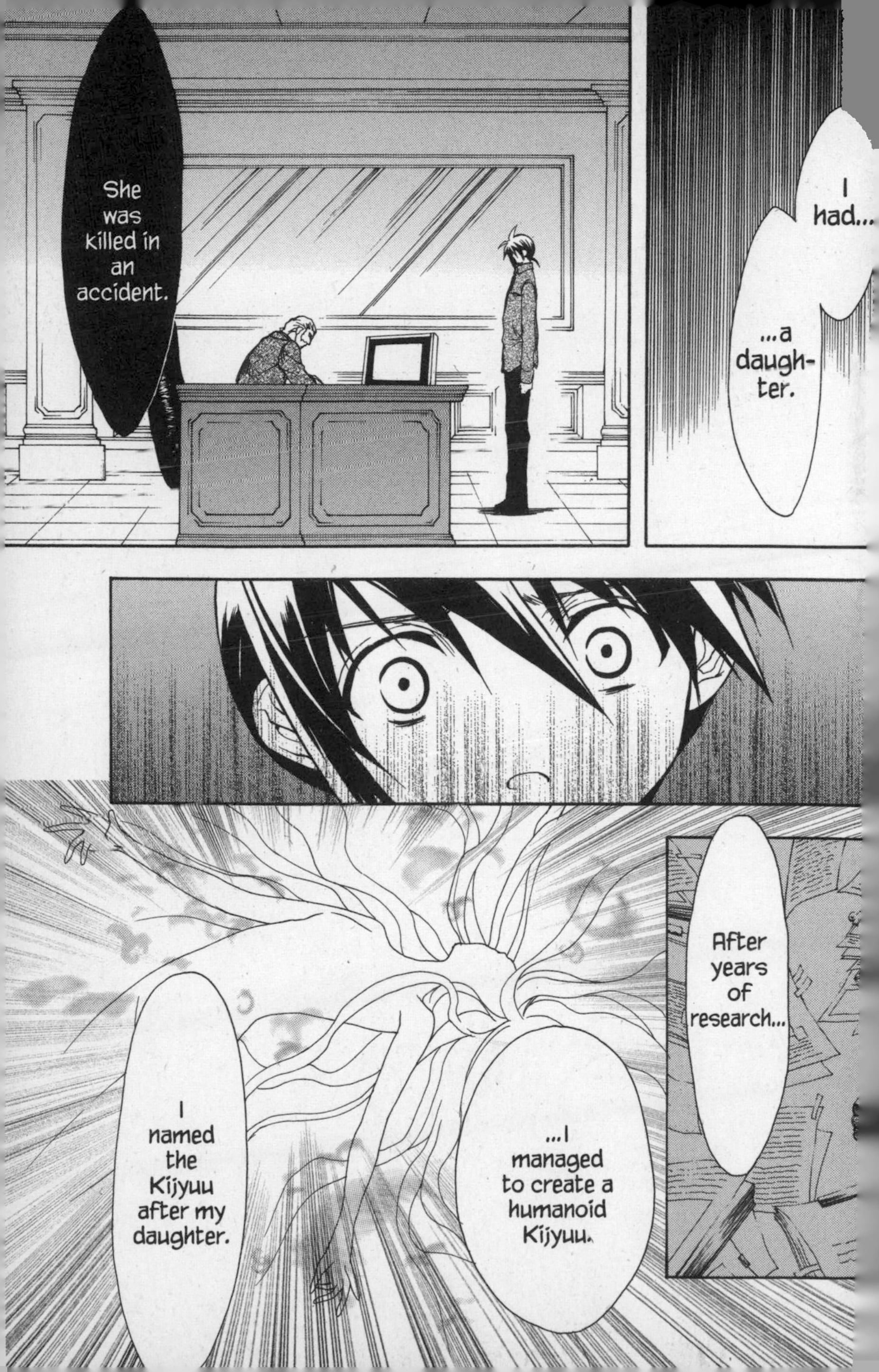
I had...
...a daughter.
She was killed in an accident.
After years of research...
...I managed to create a humanoid Kijyuu.
I named the Kijyuu after my daughter.

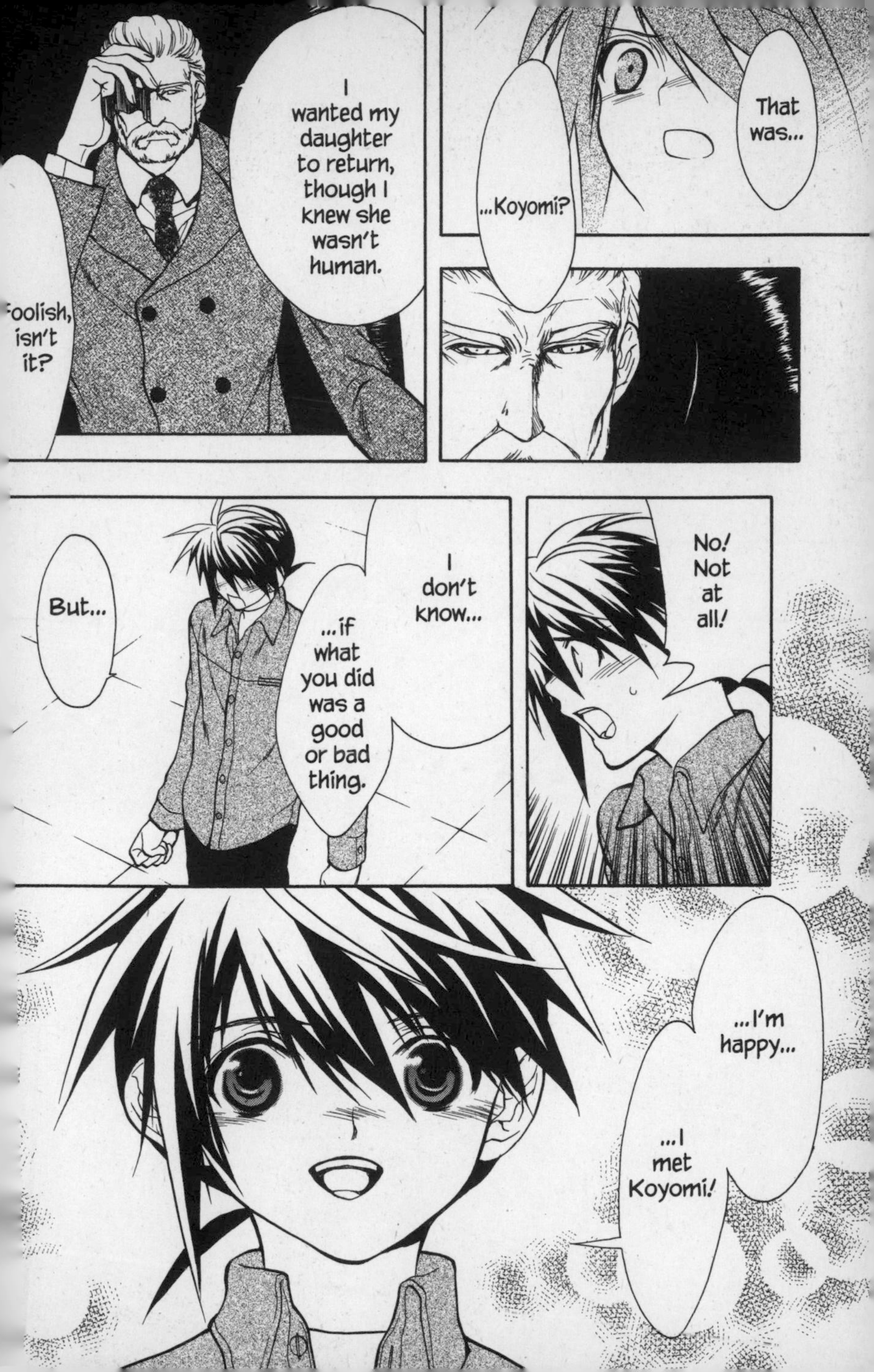
That was...
...Koyomi?
I wanted my daughter to return, though I knew she wasn't human.
Foolish, isn't it?
No! Not at all!
I don't know...
...if what you did was a good or bad thing.
But...
...I'm happy...
...I met Koyomi!

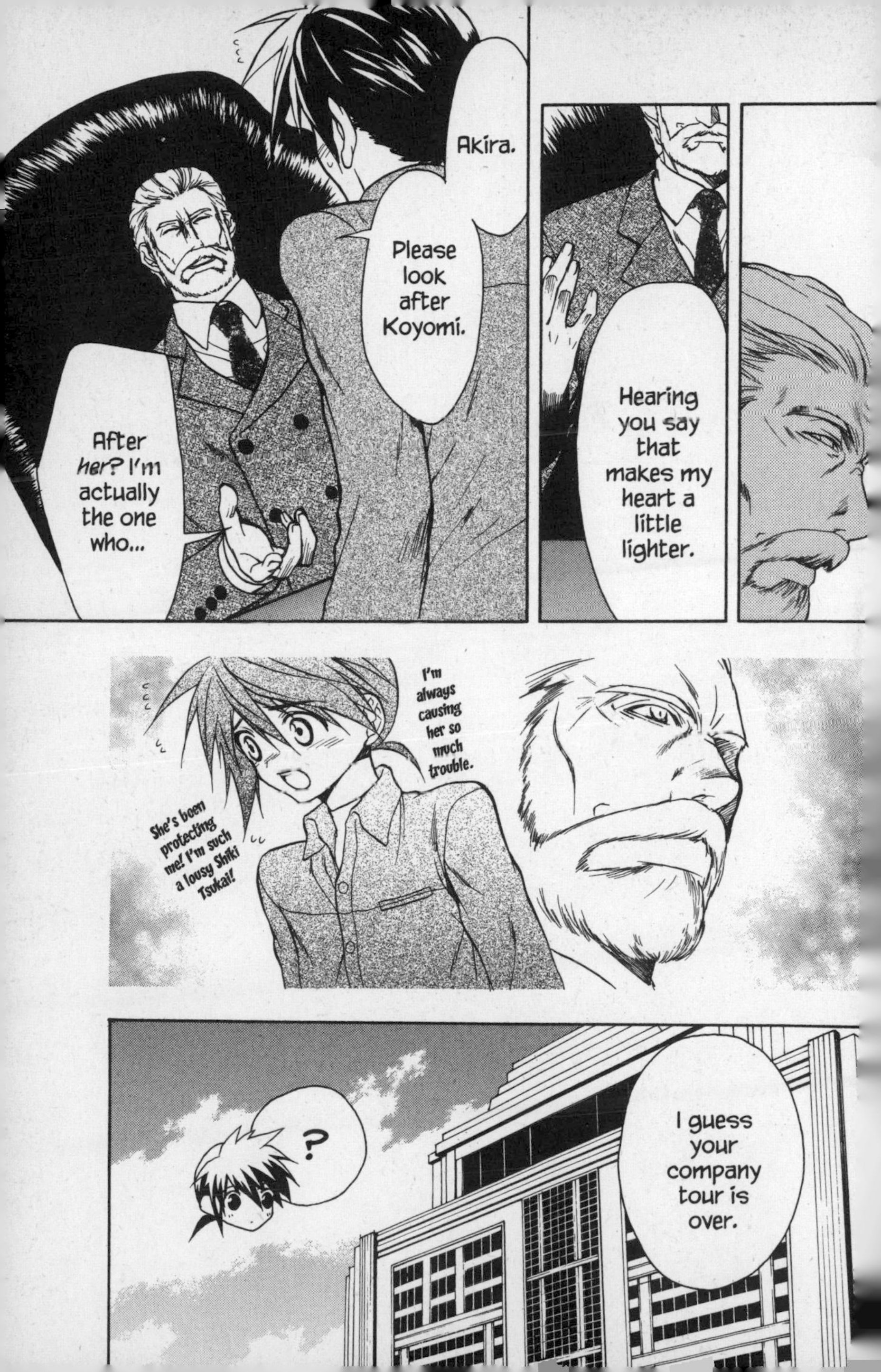
Hearing you say that makes my heart a little lighter.
Akira.
Please look after Koyomi.
After *her*? I'm actually the one who...
I'm always causing her so much trouble.
She's been protecting me! I'm such a lousy Shiki Tsukai!
I guess your company tour is over.
?

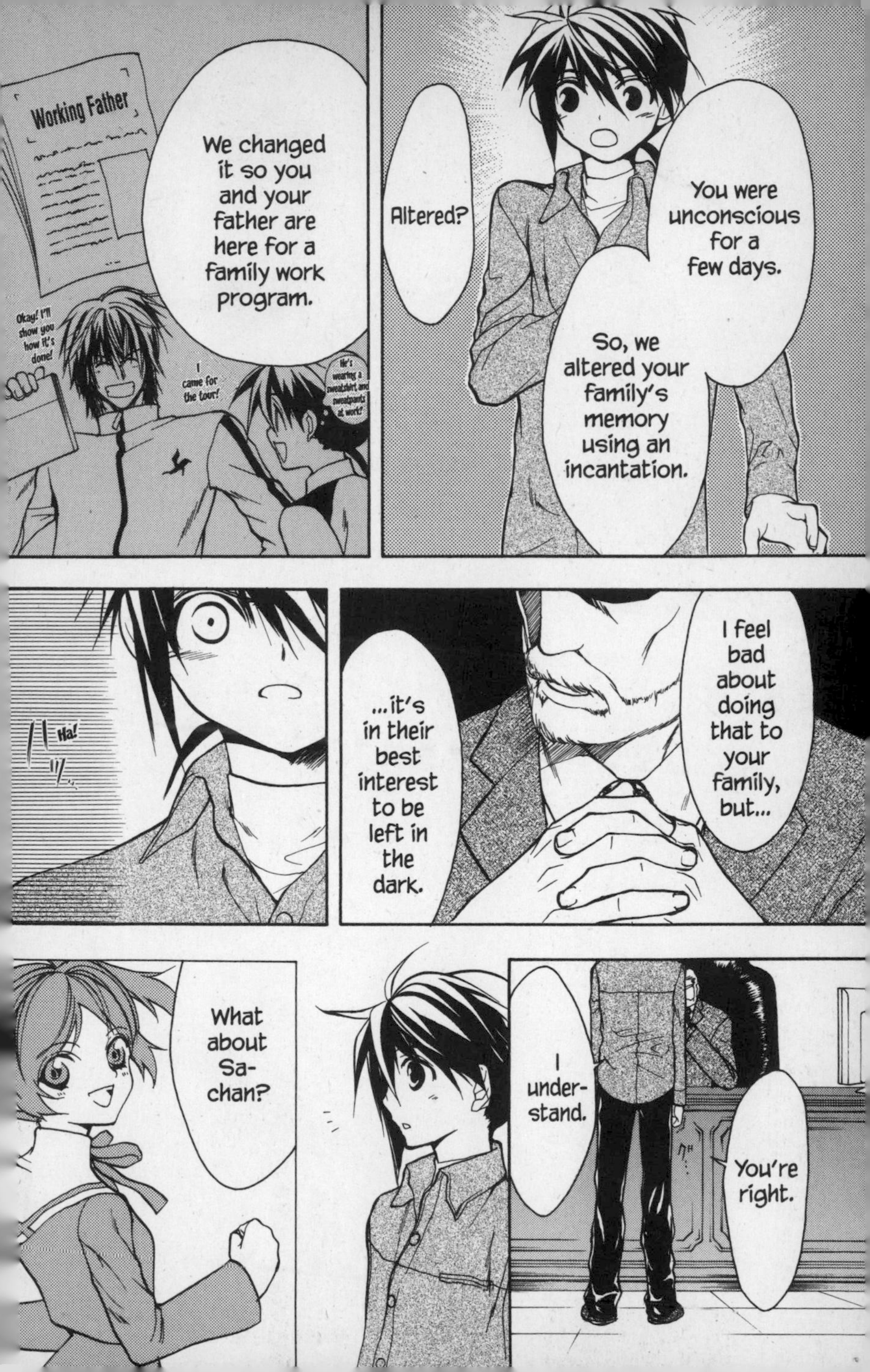
You were unconscious for a few days.
So, we altered your family's memory using an incantation.
Altered?
We changed it so you and your father are here for a family work program.
Working Father
He's wearing a sweatshirt and sweatpants at work?
I came for the tour!
Okay! I'll show you how it's done!
I feel bad about doing that to your family, but...
...it's in their best interest to be left in the dark.
Ha!
You're right.
I understand.
What about Sa-chan?

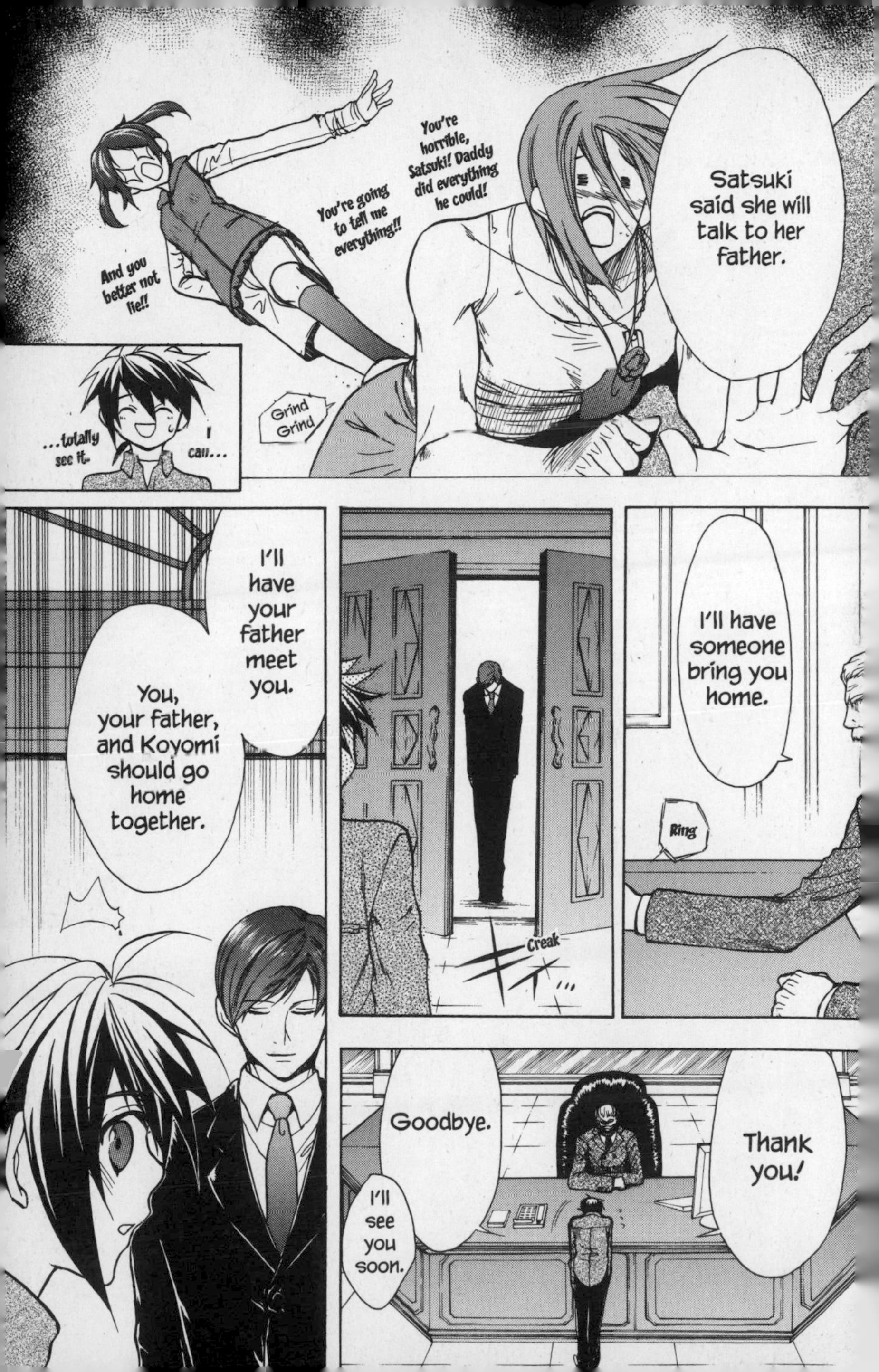
Satsuki said she will talk to her father.
You're horrible, Satsuki! Daddy did everything he could!
You're going to tell me everything!!
And you better not lie!!
Grind Grind
I call...
...totally see it.
I'll have someone bring you home.
Ring
Creak
Thank you!
Goodbye.
I'll see you soon.
I'll have your father meet you.
You, your father, and Koyomi should go home together.

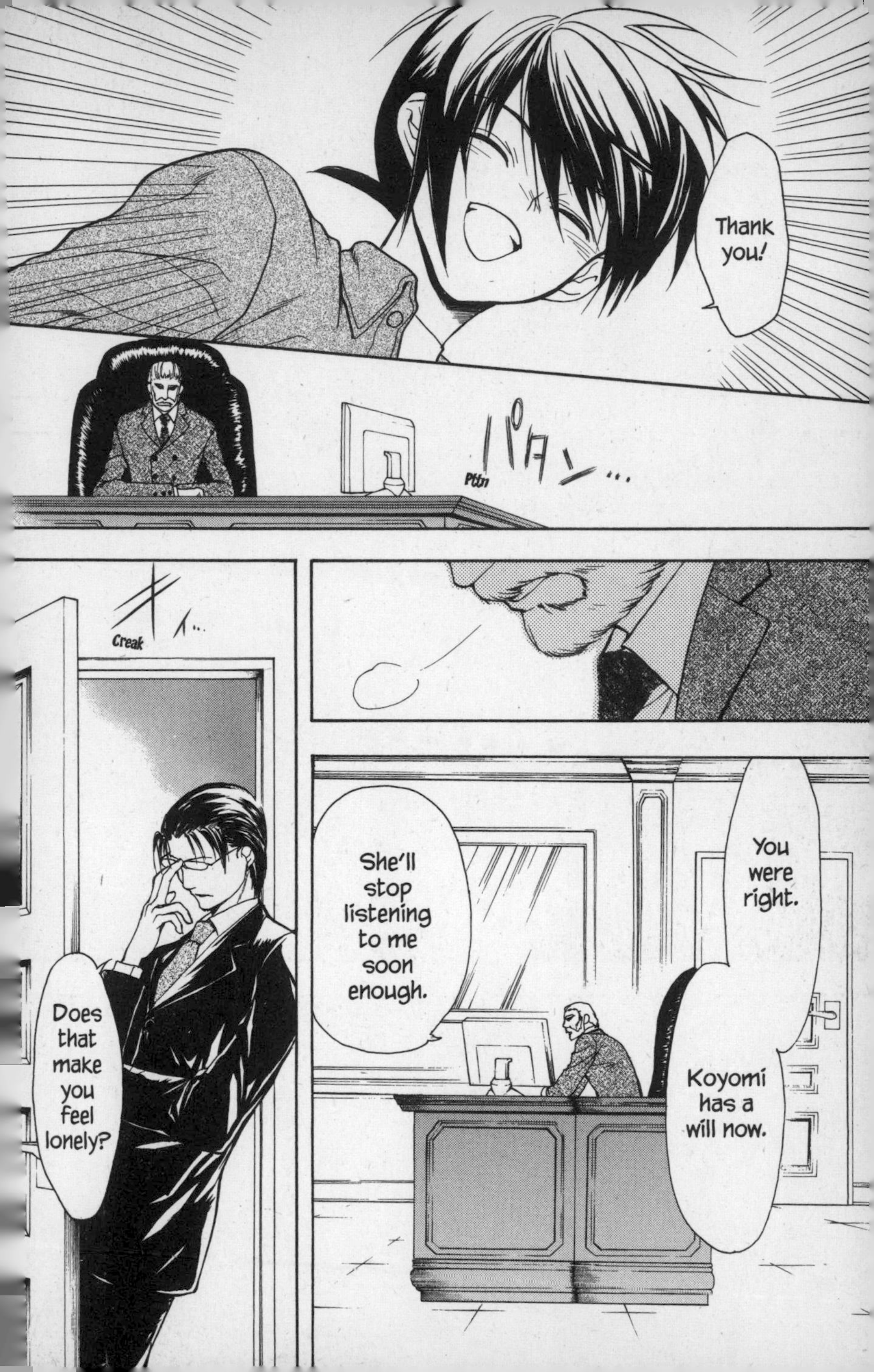
Thank you!
パタン…
Pttn
You were right.
Koyomi has a will now.
She'll stop listening to me soon enough.
ギイ…
Creak
Does that make you feel lonely?

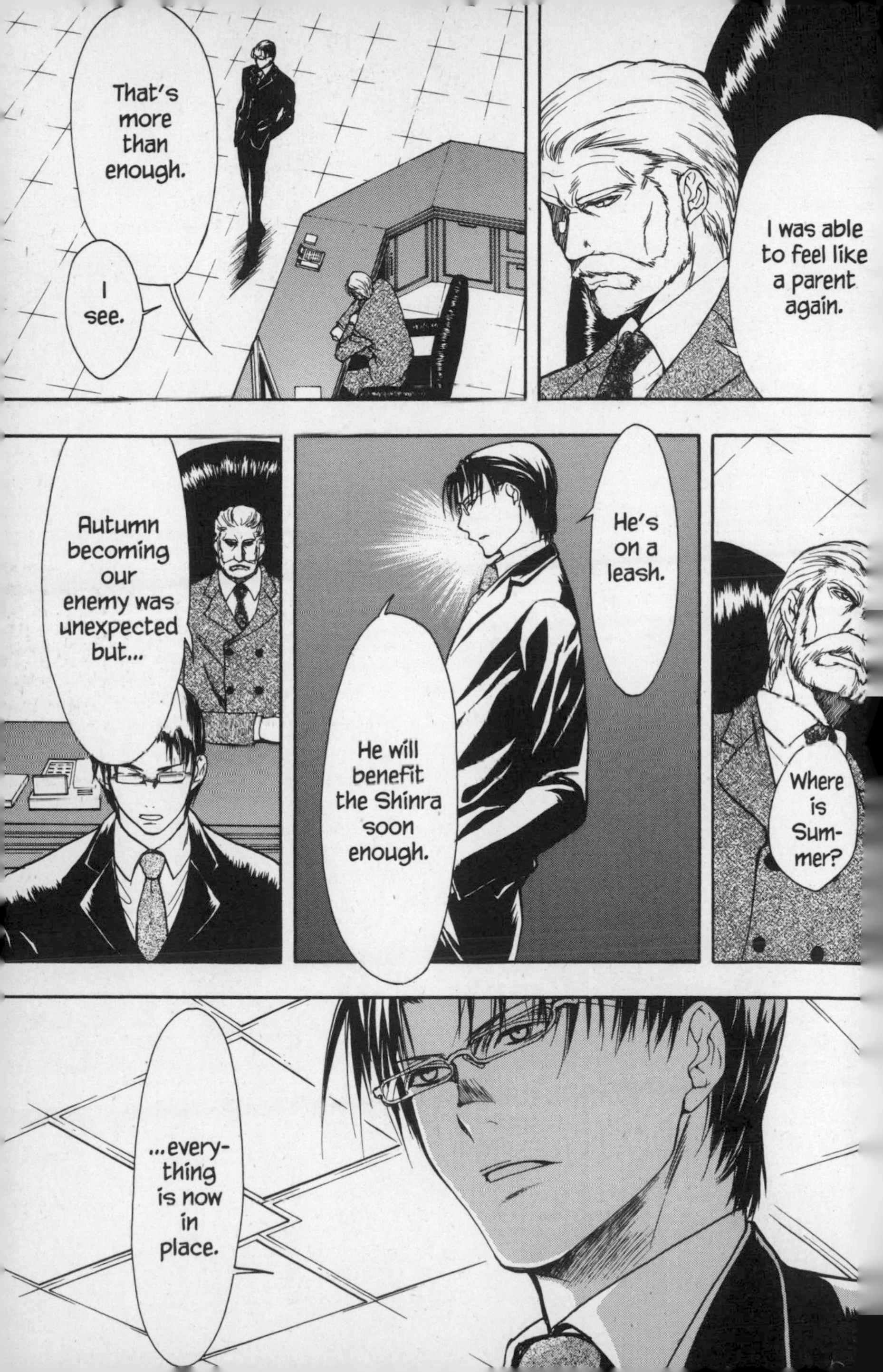
I was able to feel like a parent again.
That's more than enough.
I see.
Where is Sum-mer?
He's on a leash.
He will benefit the Shinra soon enough.
Autumn becoming our enemy was unexpected but...
...every-thing is now in place.

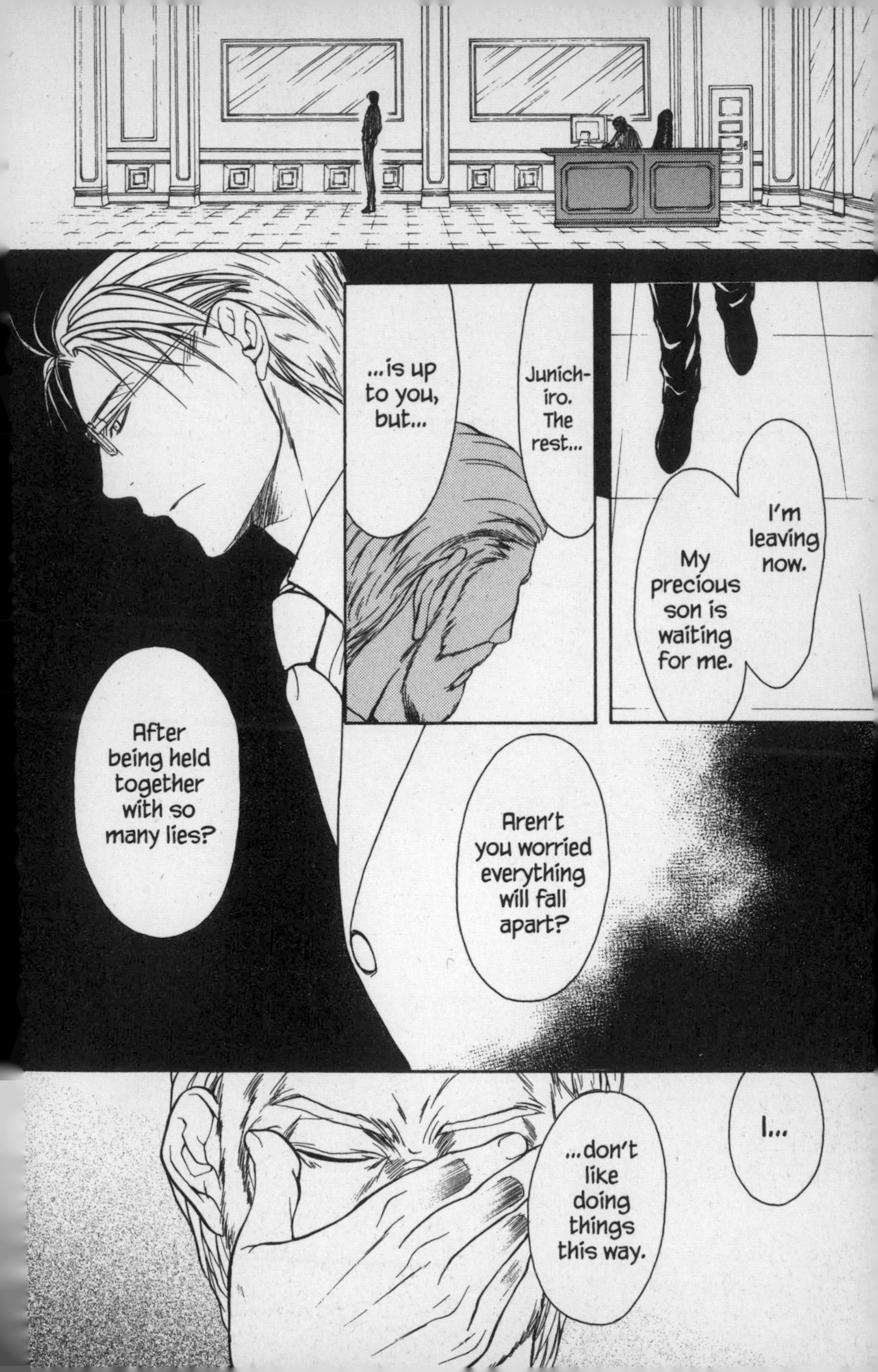
I'm leaving now.
My precious son is waiting for me.
Junichiro. The rest...
...is up to you, but...
Aren't you worried everything will fall apart?
After being held together with so many lies?
I...
...don't like doing things this way.

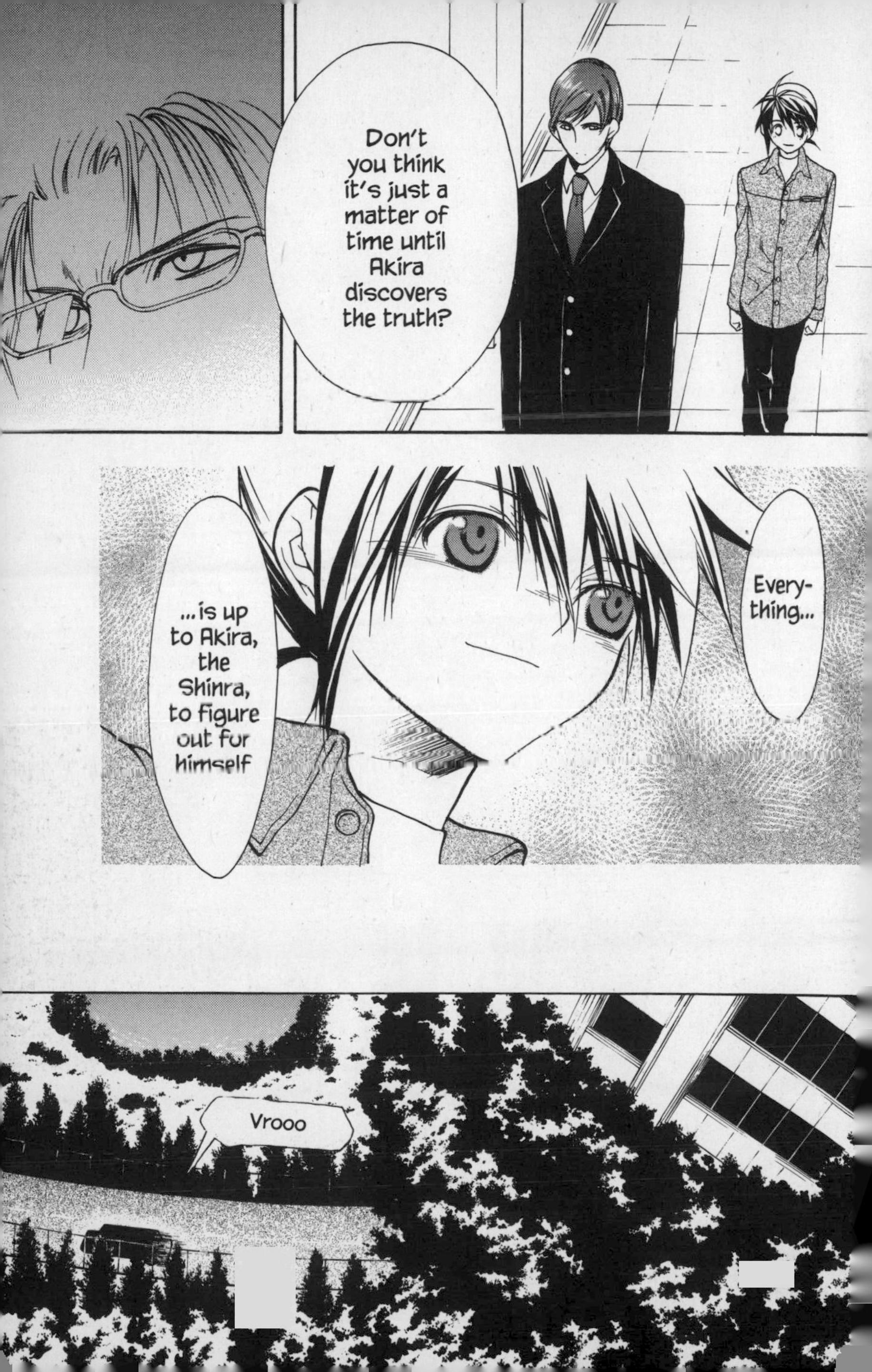
Don't you think it's just a matter of time until Akira discovers the truth?
Every-thing...
...is up to Akira, the Shinra, to figure out for himself
Vrooo

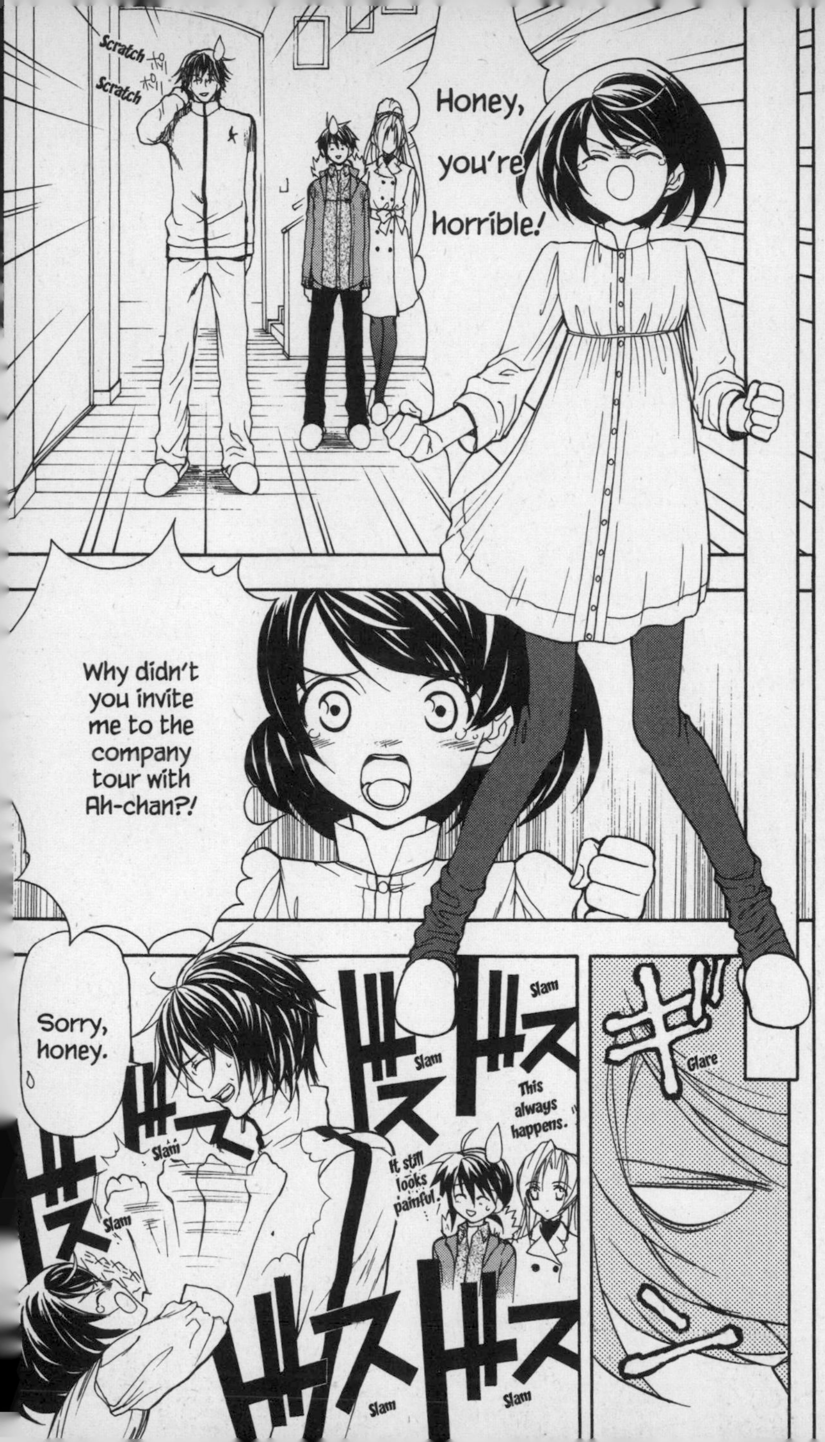
Honey, you're horrible!
Scratch
Scratch
Why didn't you invite me to the company tour with Ah-chan?!
Glare
Slam
Slam
This always happens.
It still looks painful...
Sorry, honey.
Slam
Slam
Slam
Slam

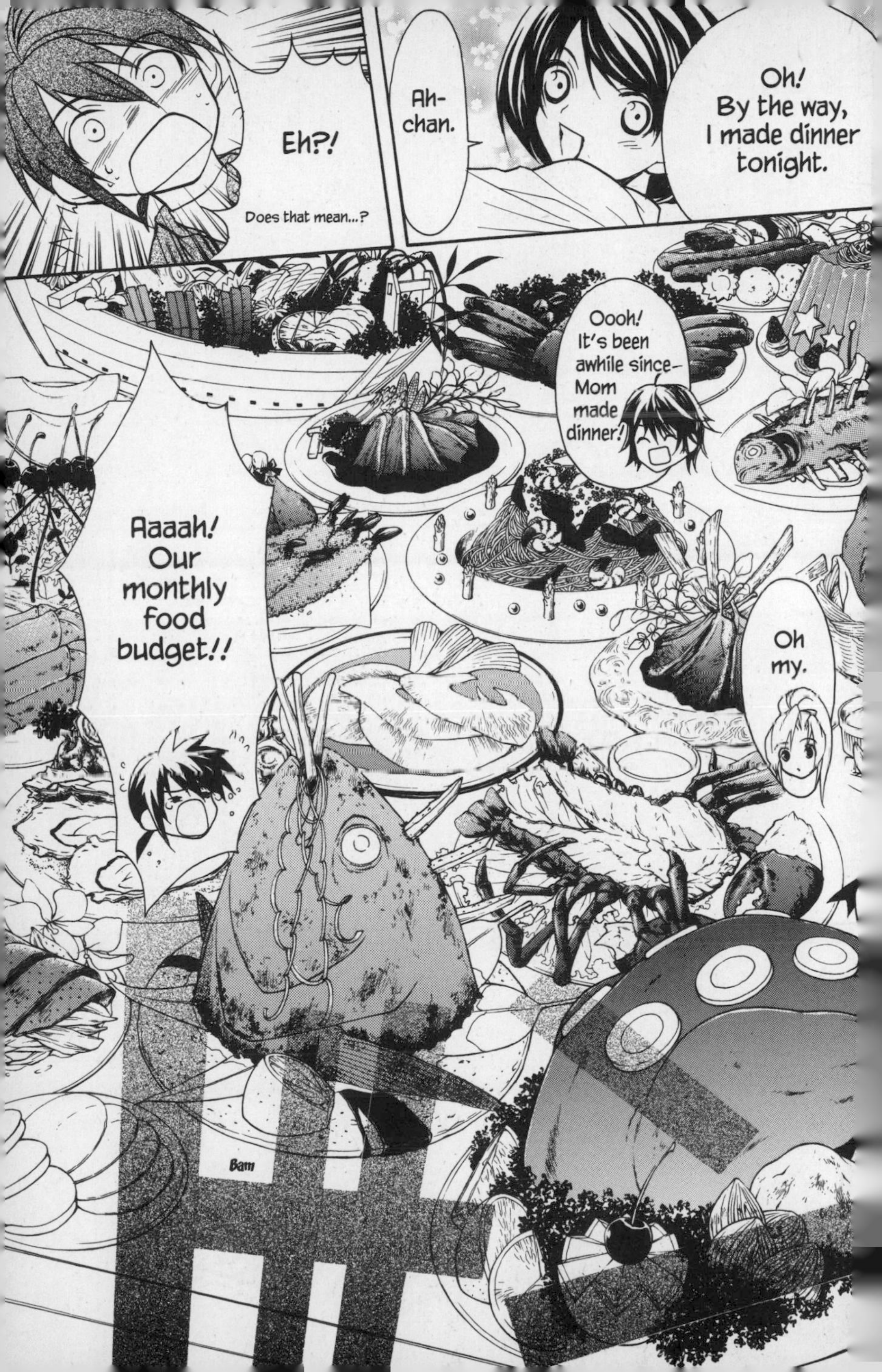
Oh! By the way, I made dinner tonight.
Ah-chan.
Eh?!
Does that mean...?
Oooh! It's been awhile since- Mom made dinner!
Oh my.
Aaaah! Our monthly food budget!!
Bam

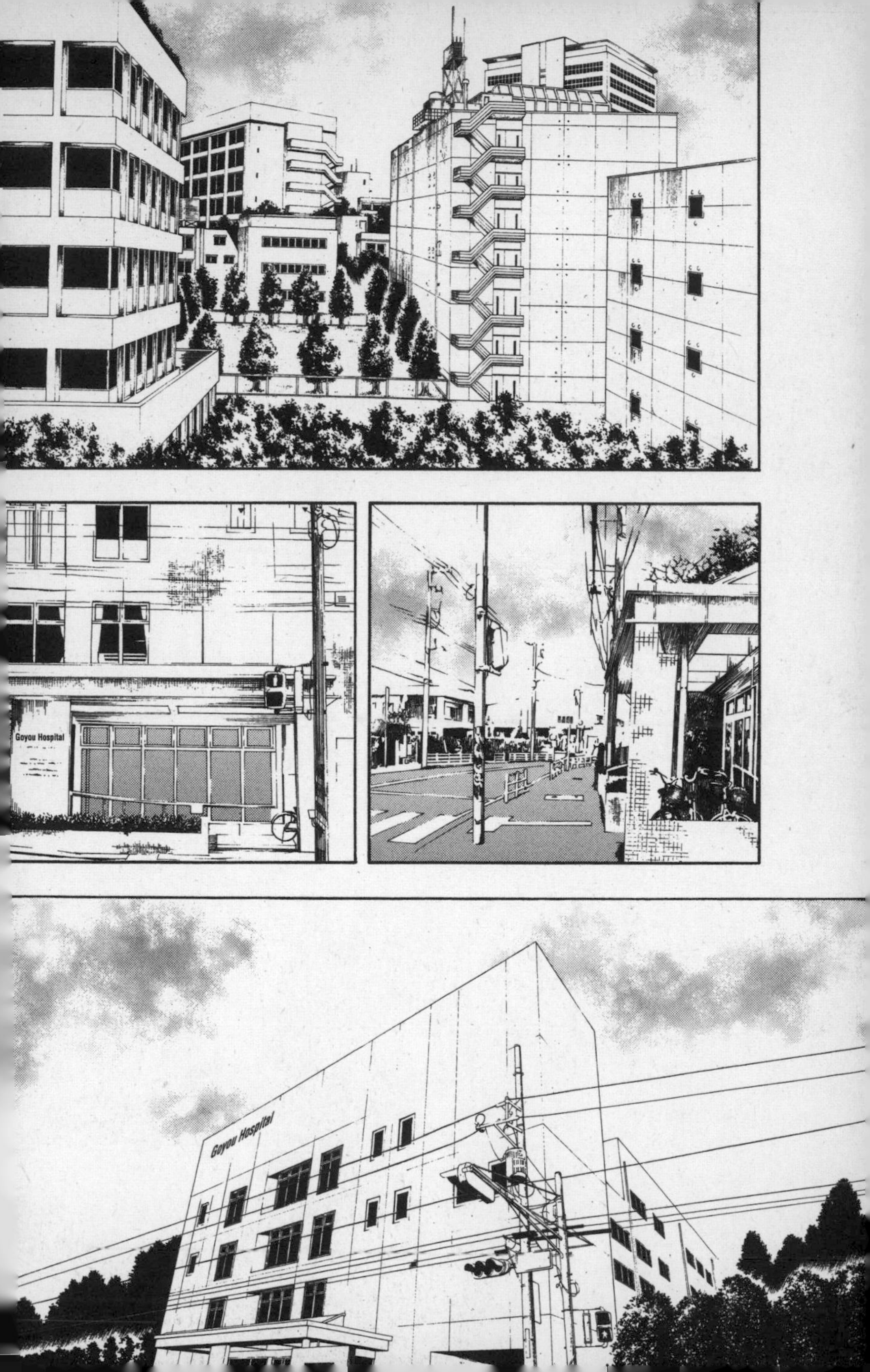
Goyou Hospital
Goyou Hospital

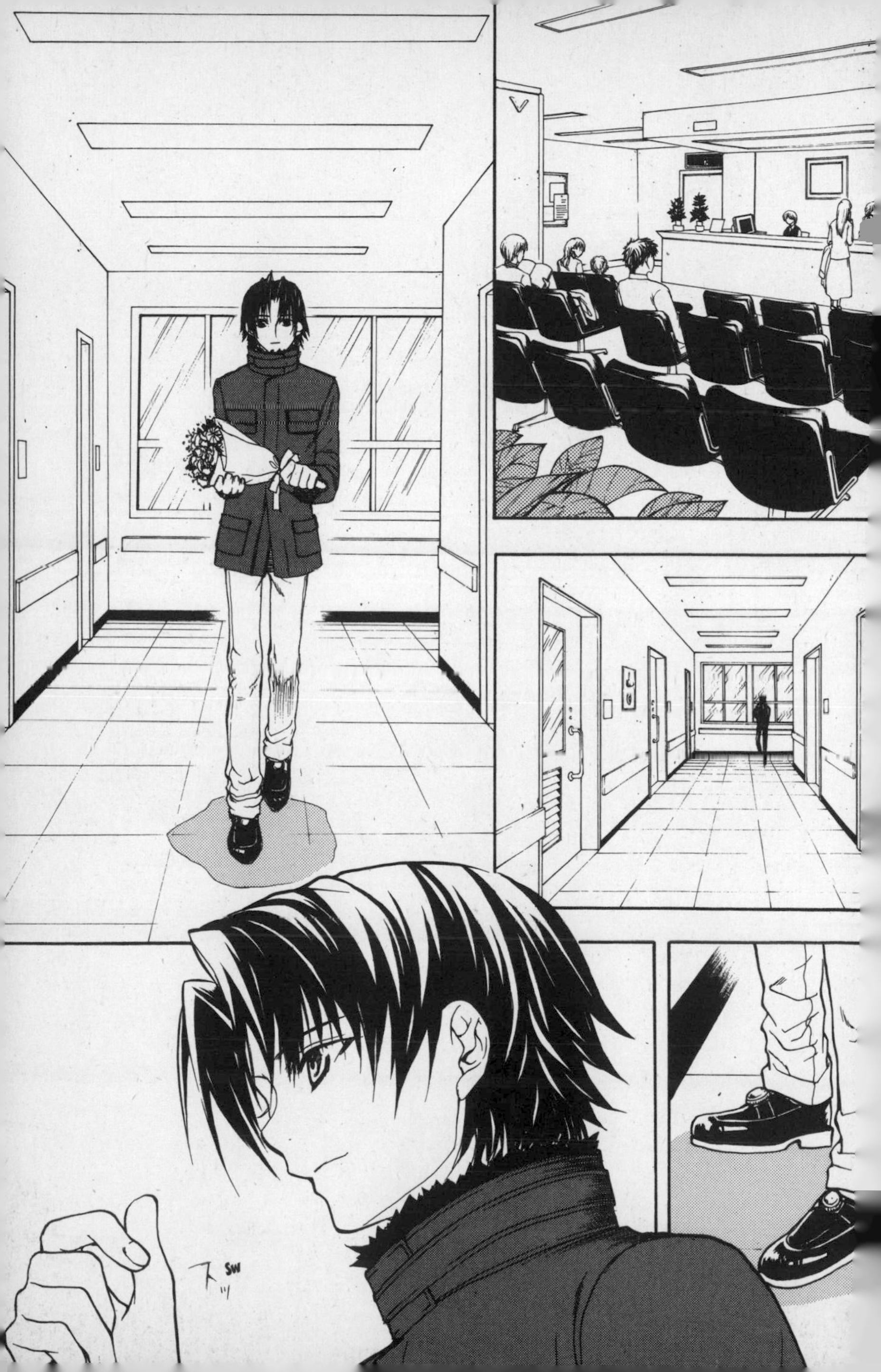
SW

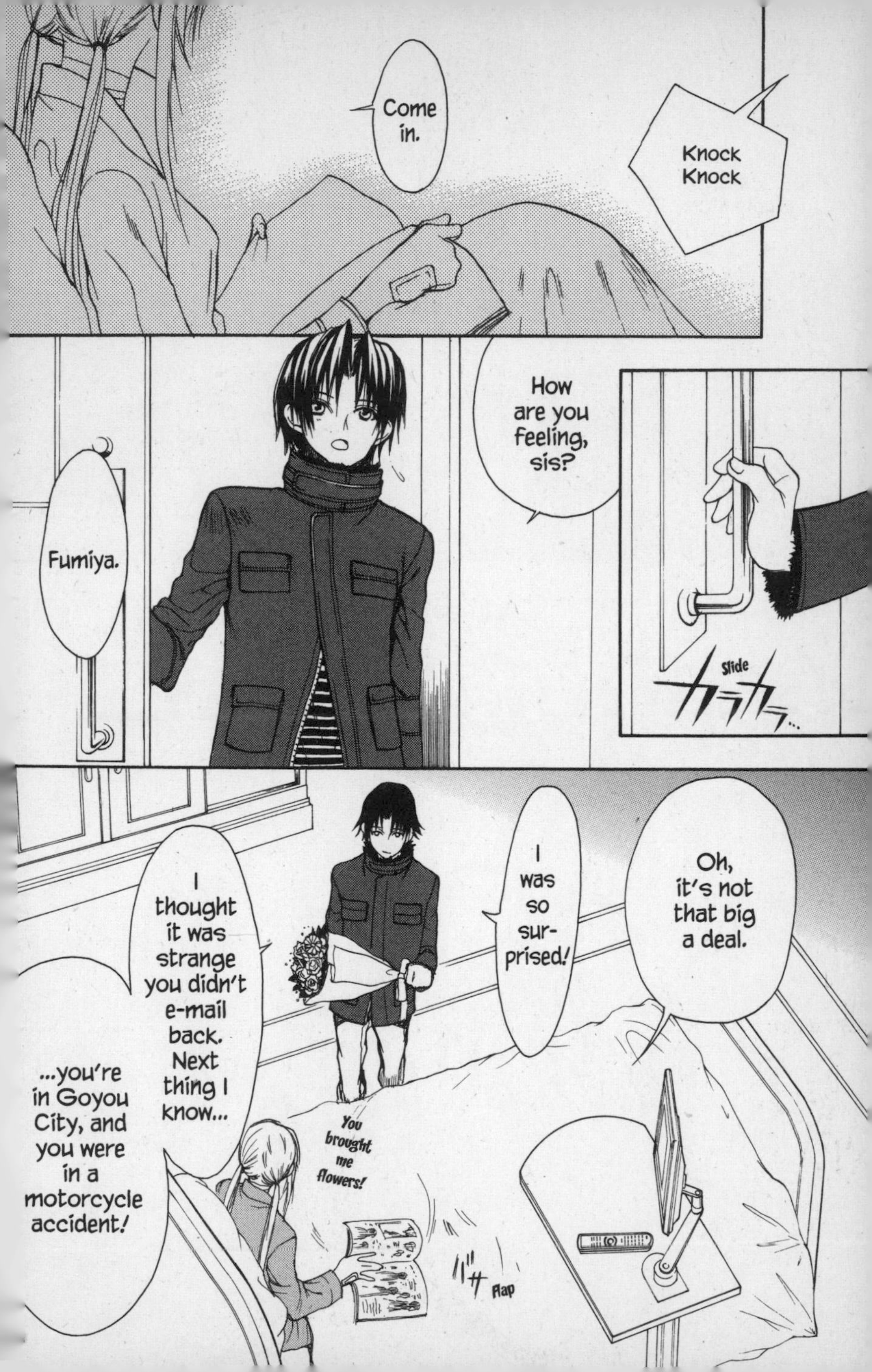
Knock Knock
Come in.
Slide
カラカラ...
How are you feeling, sis?
Fumiya.
Oh, it's not that big a deal.
I was so sur-prised!
I thought it was strange you didn't e-mail back. Next thing I know...
...you're in Goyou City, and you were in a motorcycle accident!
You brought me flowers!
Flap

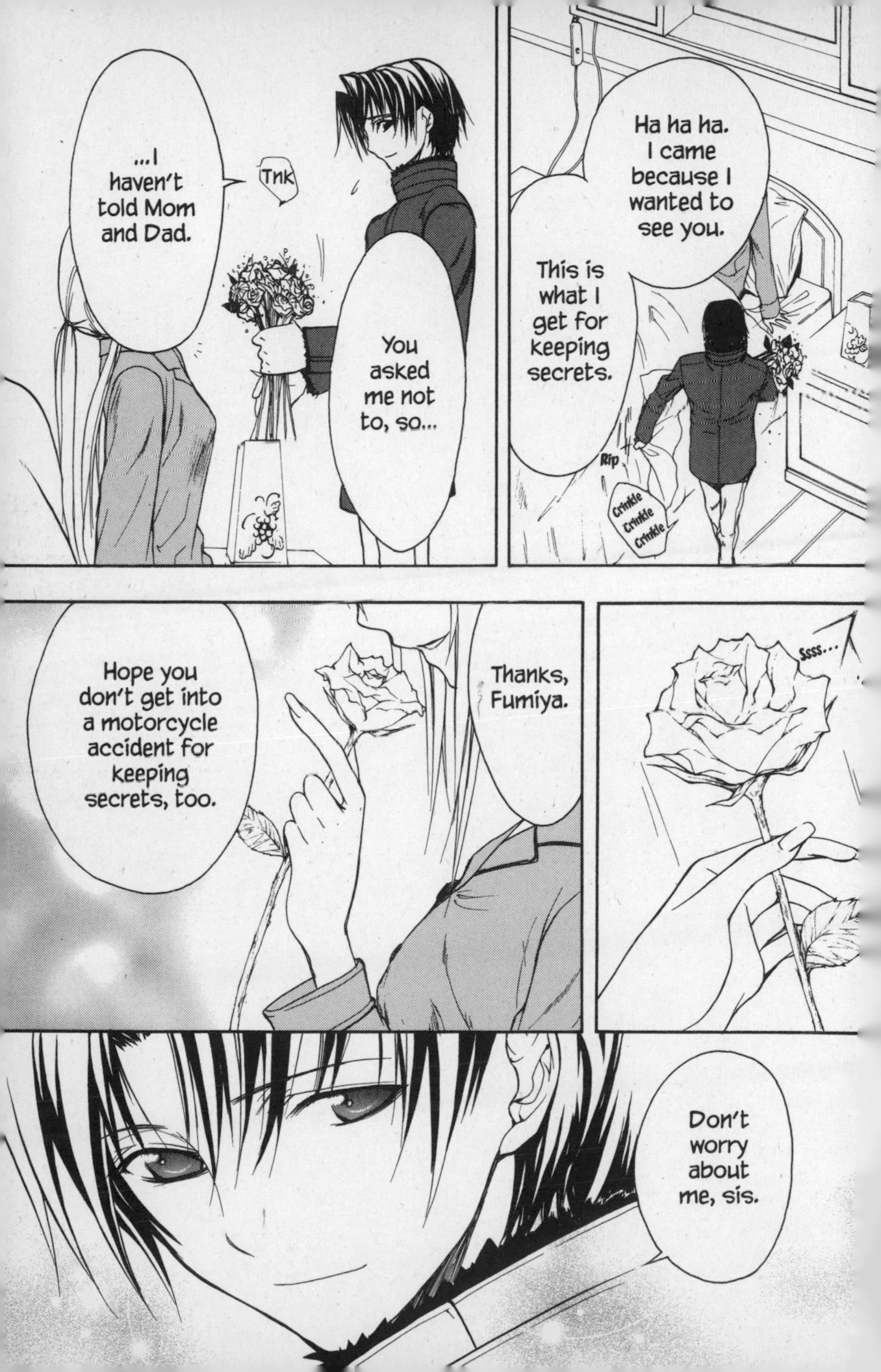
Ha ha ha. I came because I wanted to see you.
This is what I get for keeping secrets.
Rip
Crinkle Crinkle Crinkle
Tnk
...I haven't told Mom and Dad.
You asked me not to, so...
Ssss...
Thanks, Fumiya.
Hope you don't get into a motorcycle accident for keeping secrets, too.
Don't worry about me, sis.

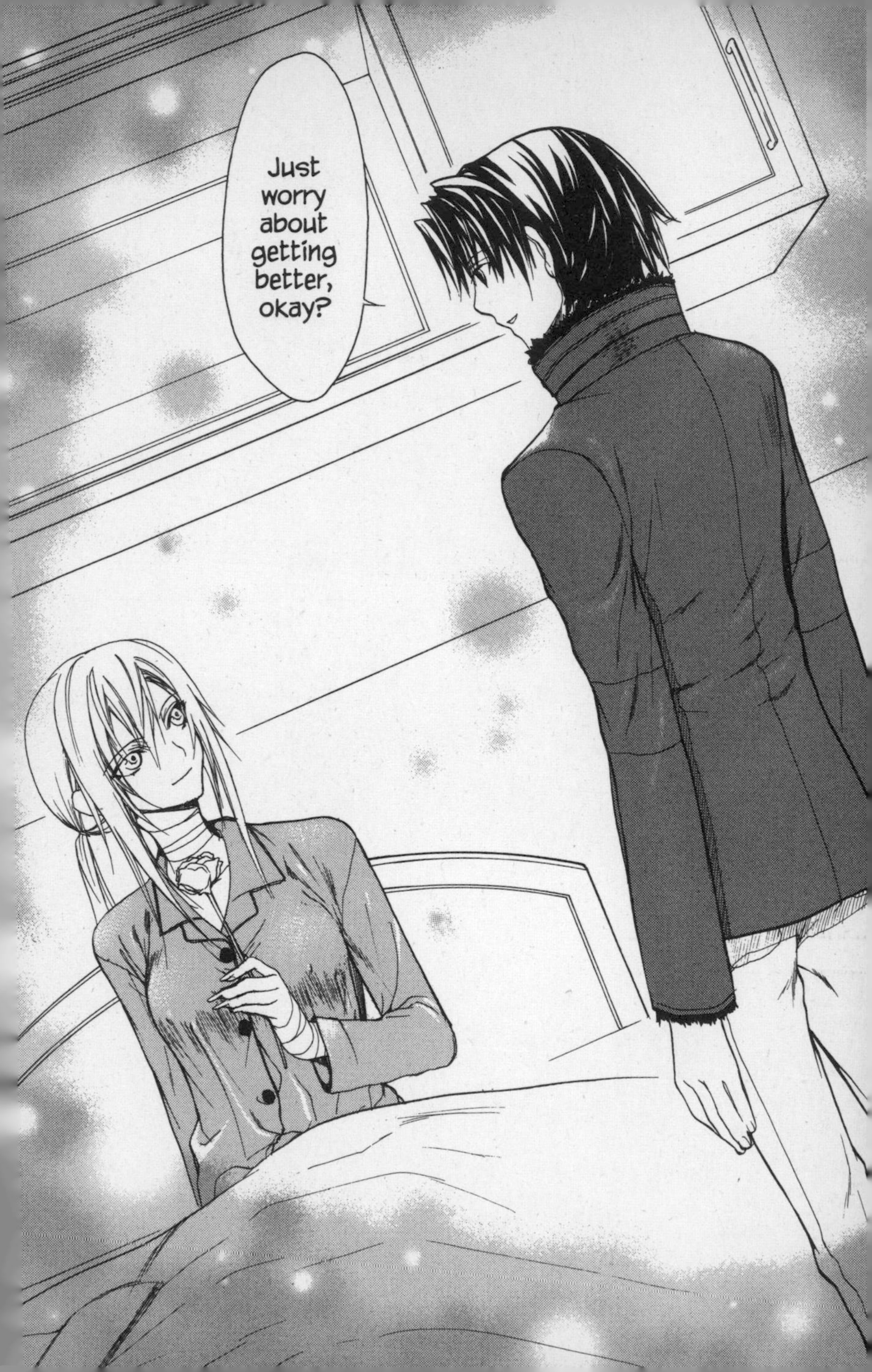
Just worry about getting better, okay?

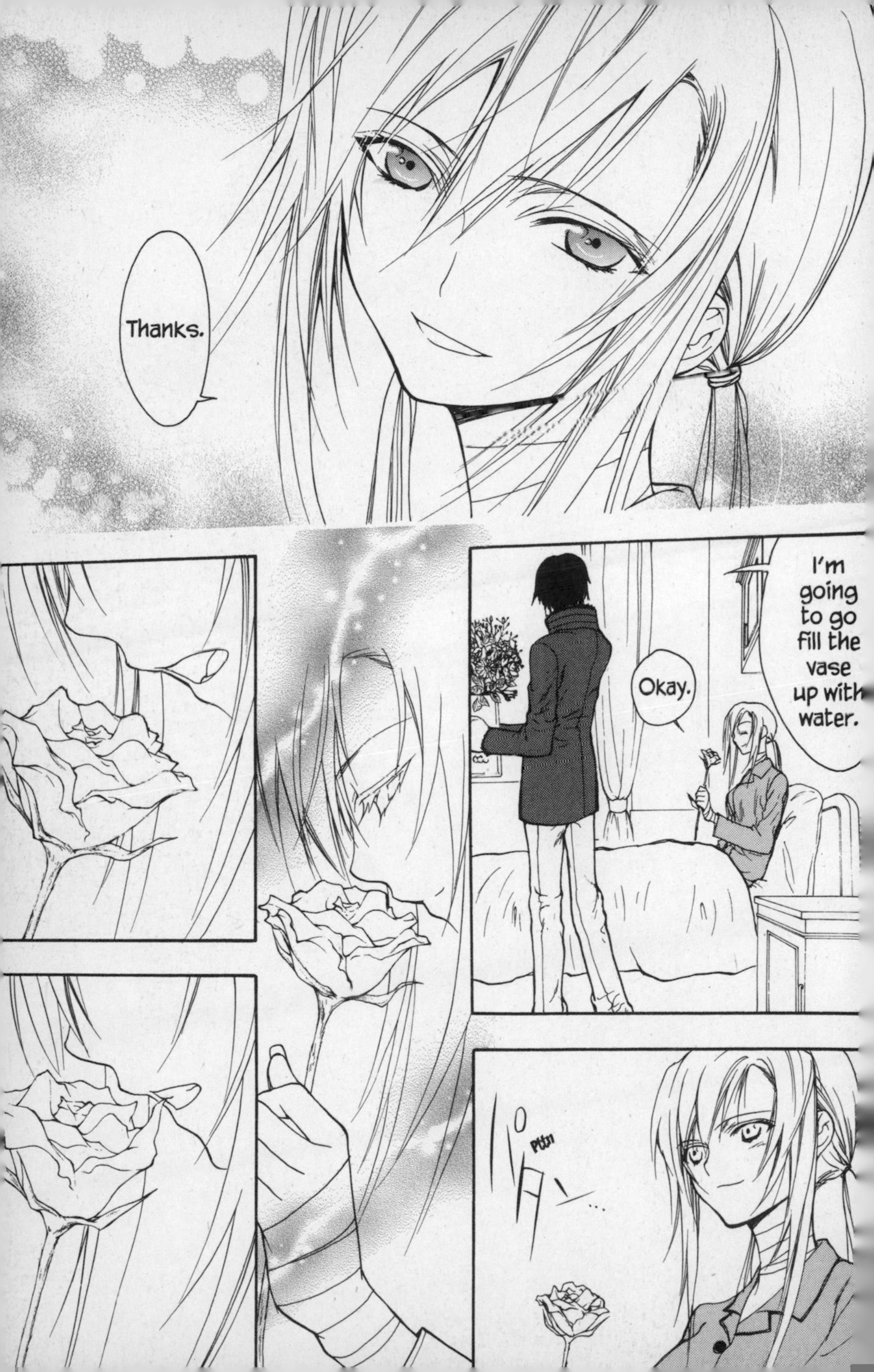
Thanks.
I'm going to go fill the vase up with water.
Okay.

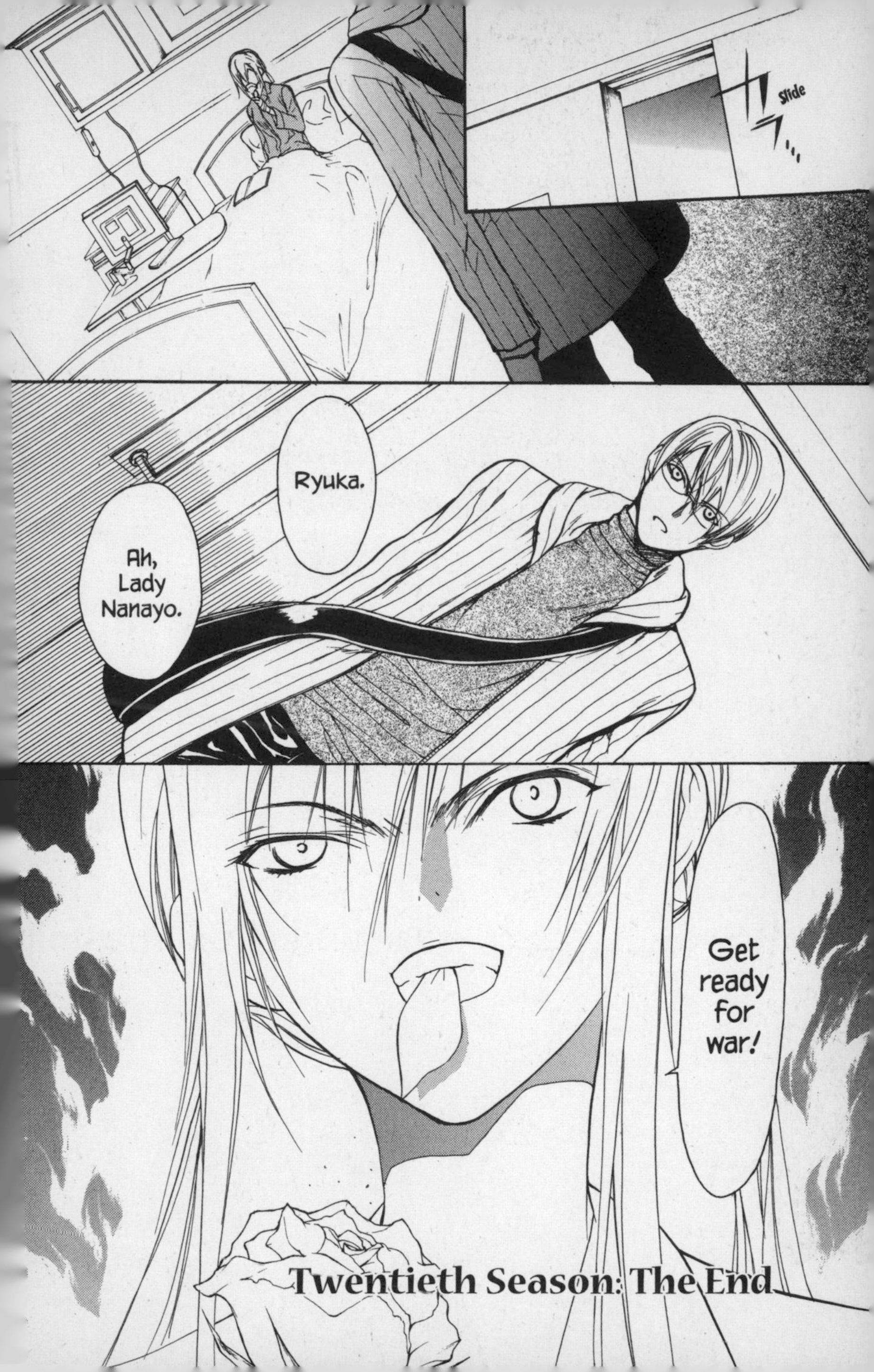
Slide
Ryuka.
Ah, Lady Nanayo.
Get ready for war!
Twentieth Season: The End

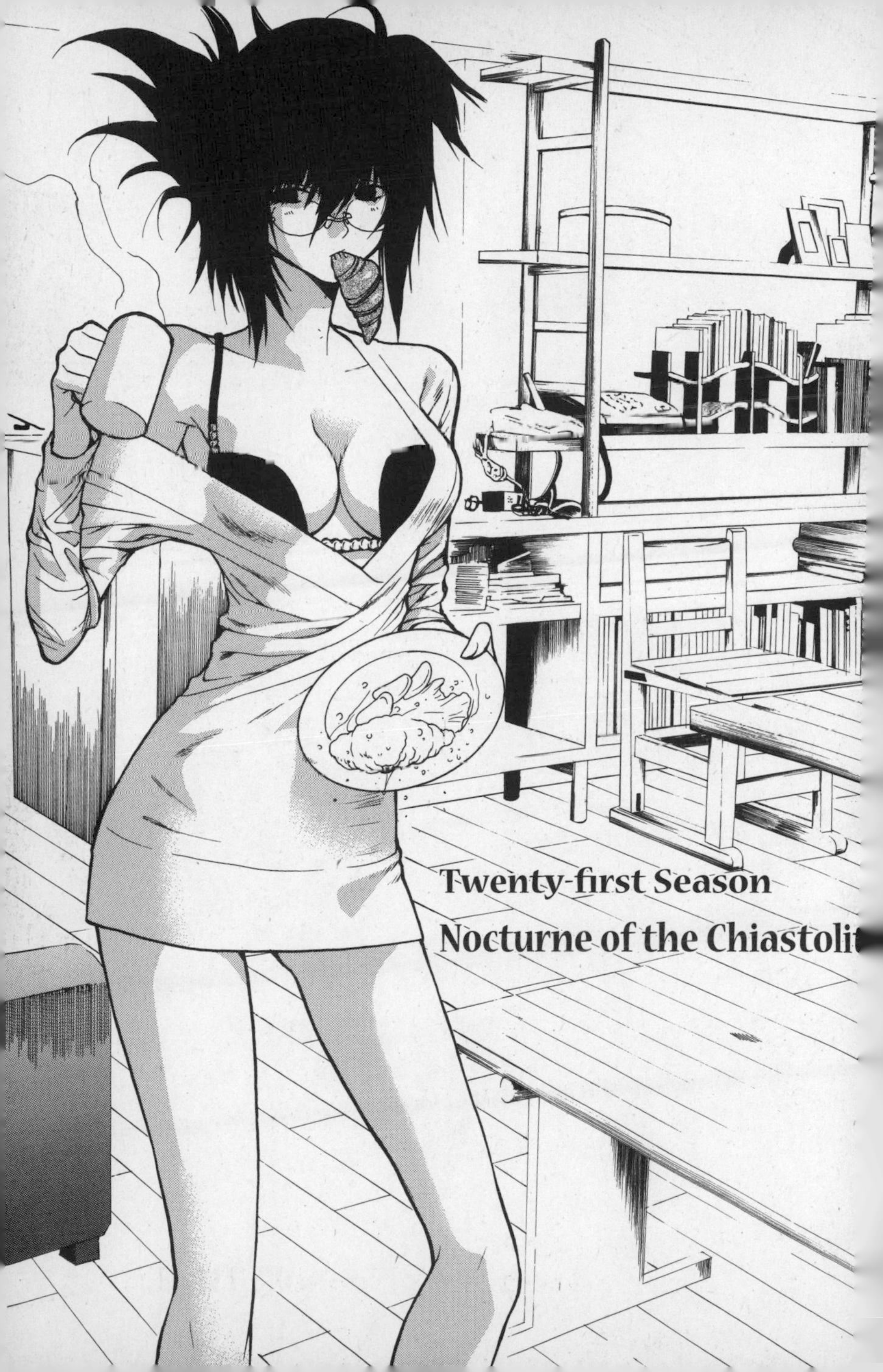
Twenty-first Season
Nocturne of the Chiastolit

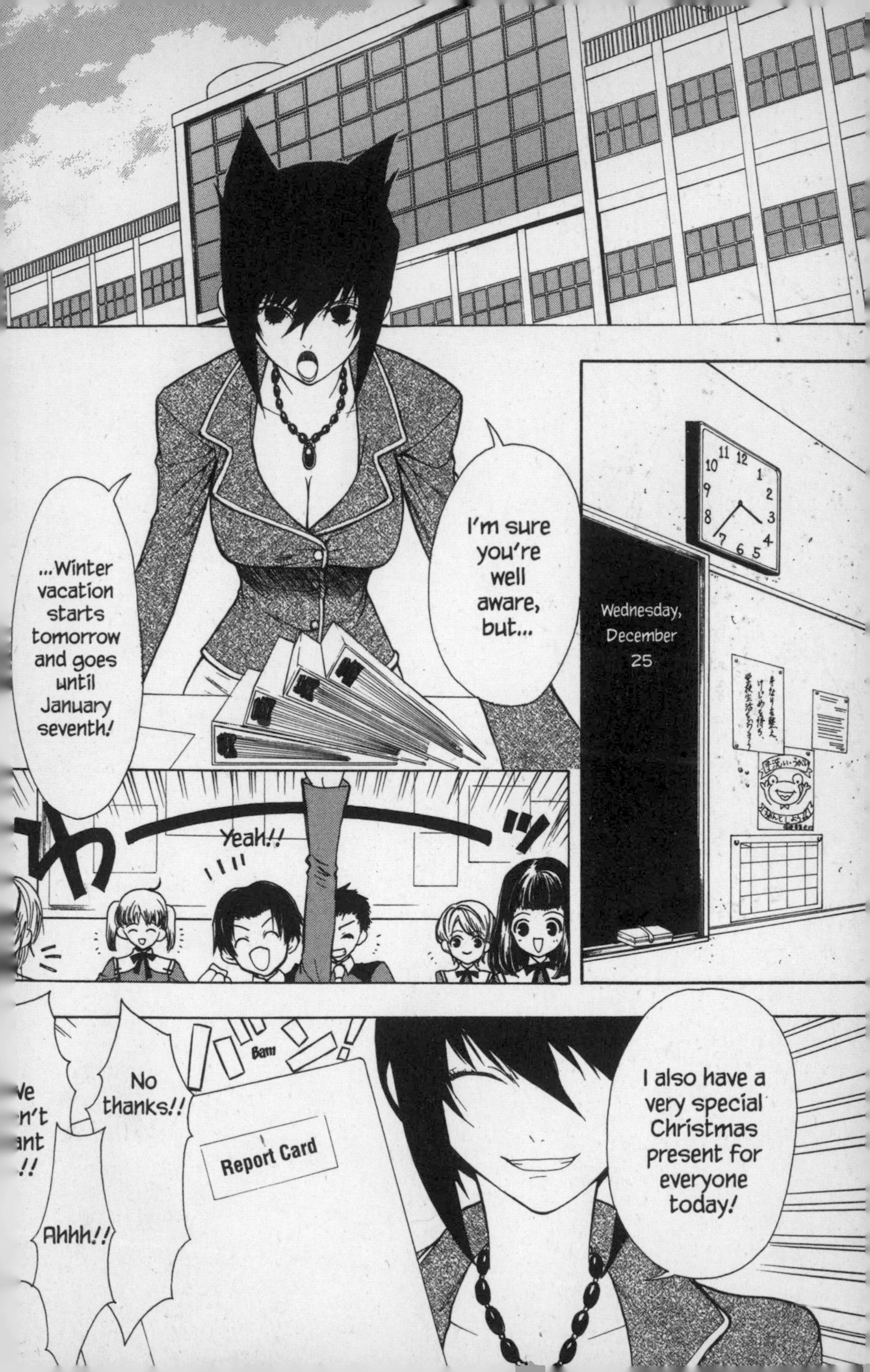
Wednesday, December 25
I'm sure you're well aware, but...
...Winter vacation starts tomorrow and goes until January seventh!
Yeah!!
I also have a very special Christmas present for everyone today!
Bam
Report Card
No thanks!!
Ahhh!!

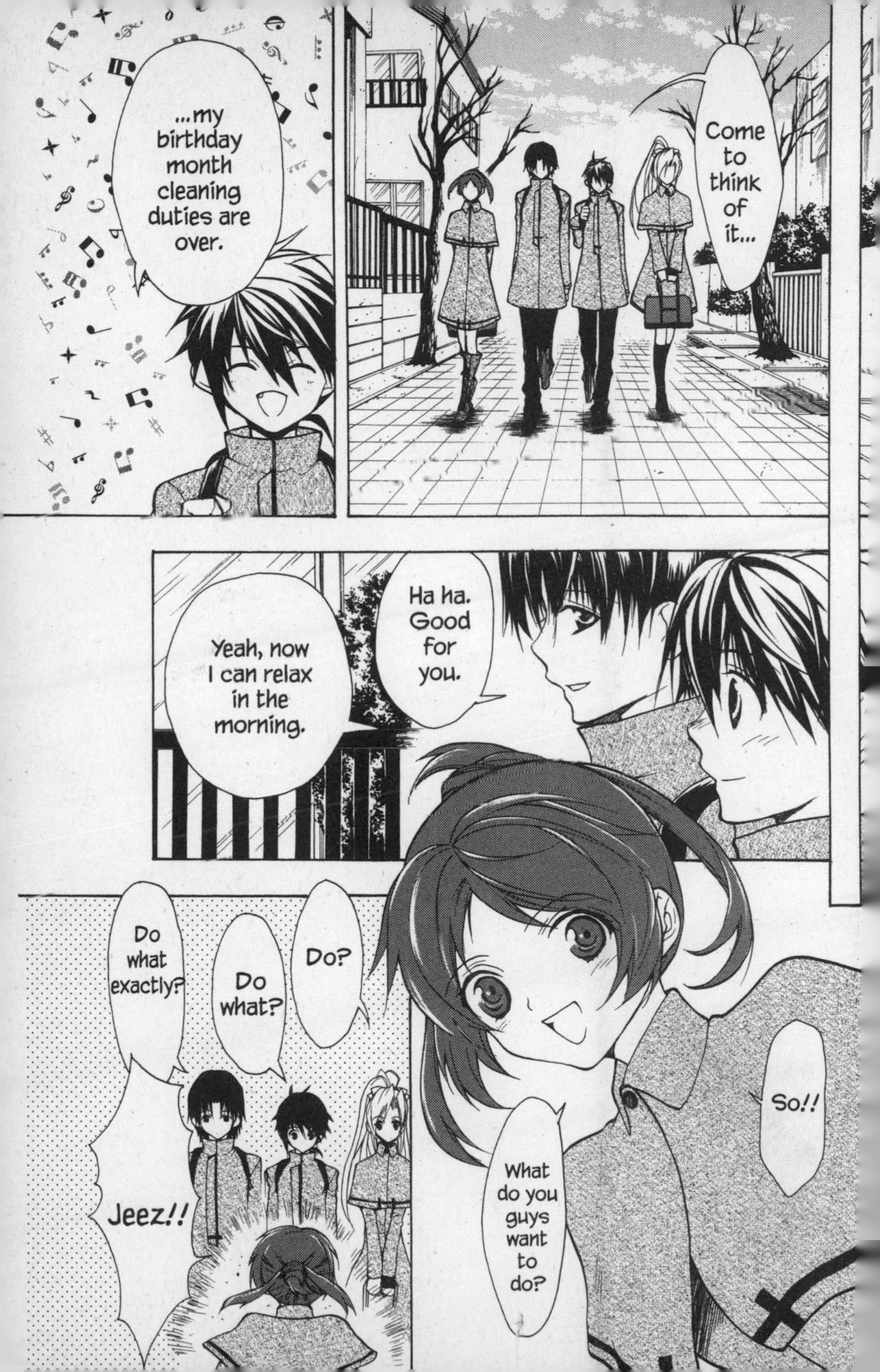
Come to think of it...
...my birthday month cleaning duties are over.
Ha ha. Good for you.
Yeah, now I can relax in the morning.
So!!
What do you guys want to do?
Do?
Do what?
Do what exactly?
Jeez!!

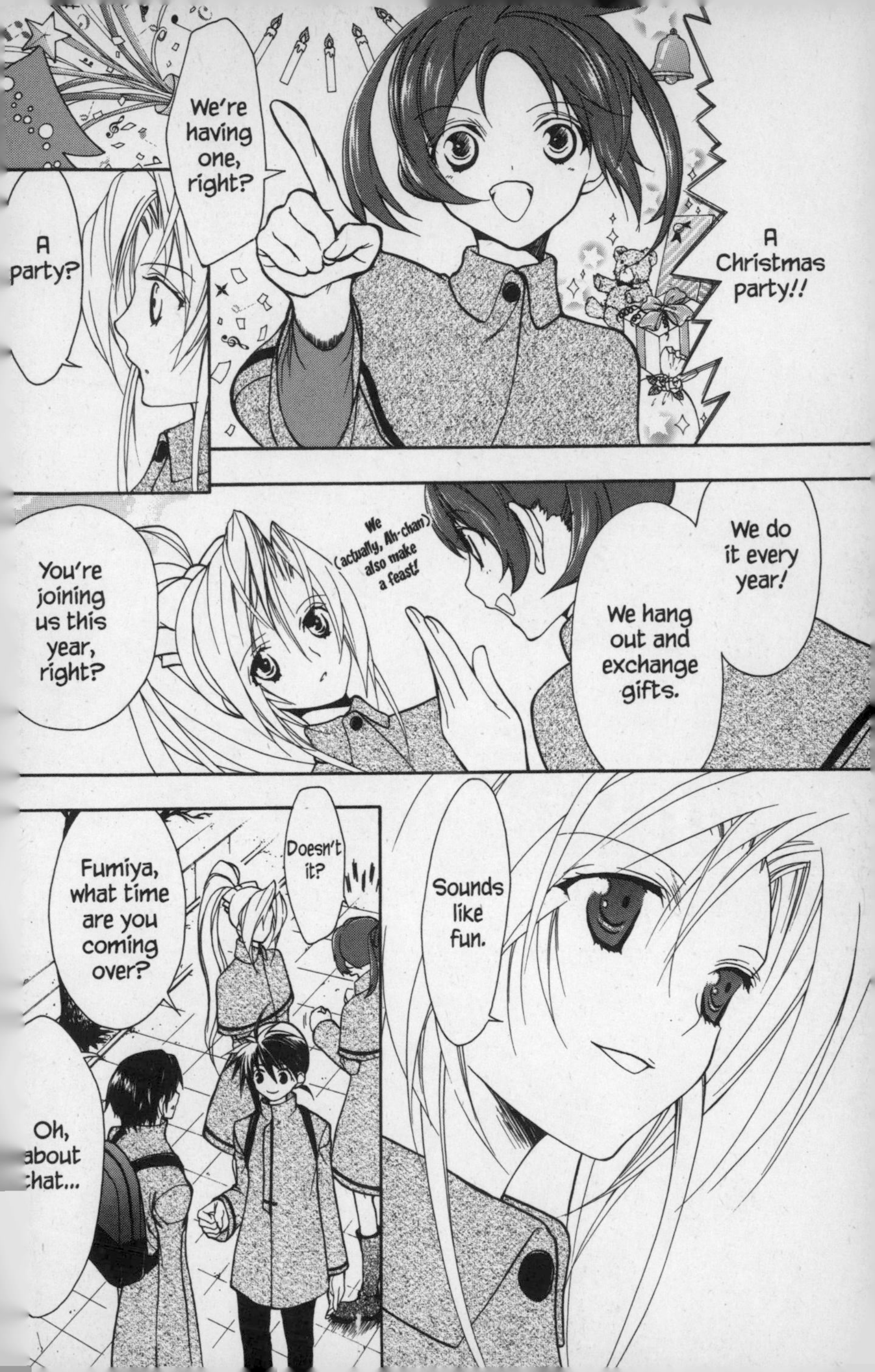
A Christmas party!!
We're having one, right?
A party?
We do it every year!
We hang out and exchange gifts.
We (actually, Ah-chan) also make a feast!
You're joining us this year, right?
Sounds like fun.
Doesn't it?
Fumiya, what time are you coming over?
Oh, about that...

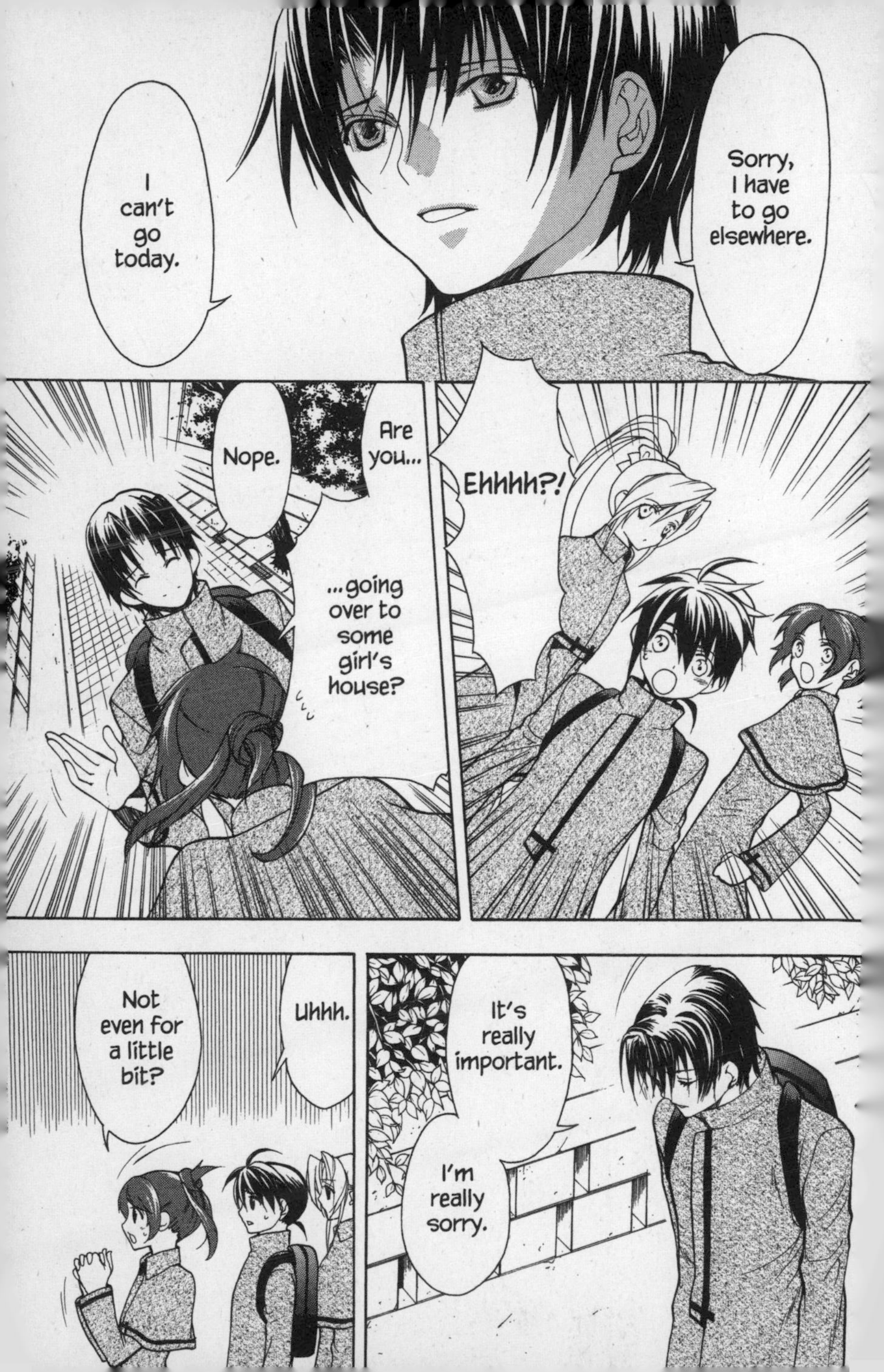
Sorry, I have to go elsewhere.
I can't go today.
Ehhhh?!
Are you...
...going over to some girl's house?
Nope.
It's really important.
I'm really sorry.
Uhhh.
Not even for a little bit?

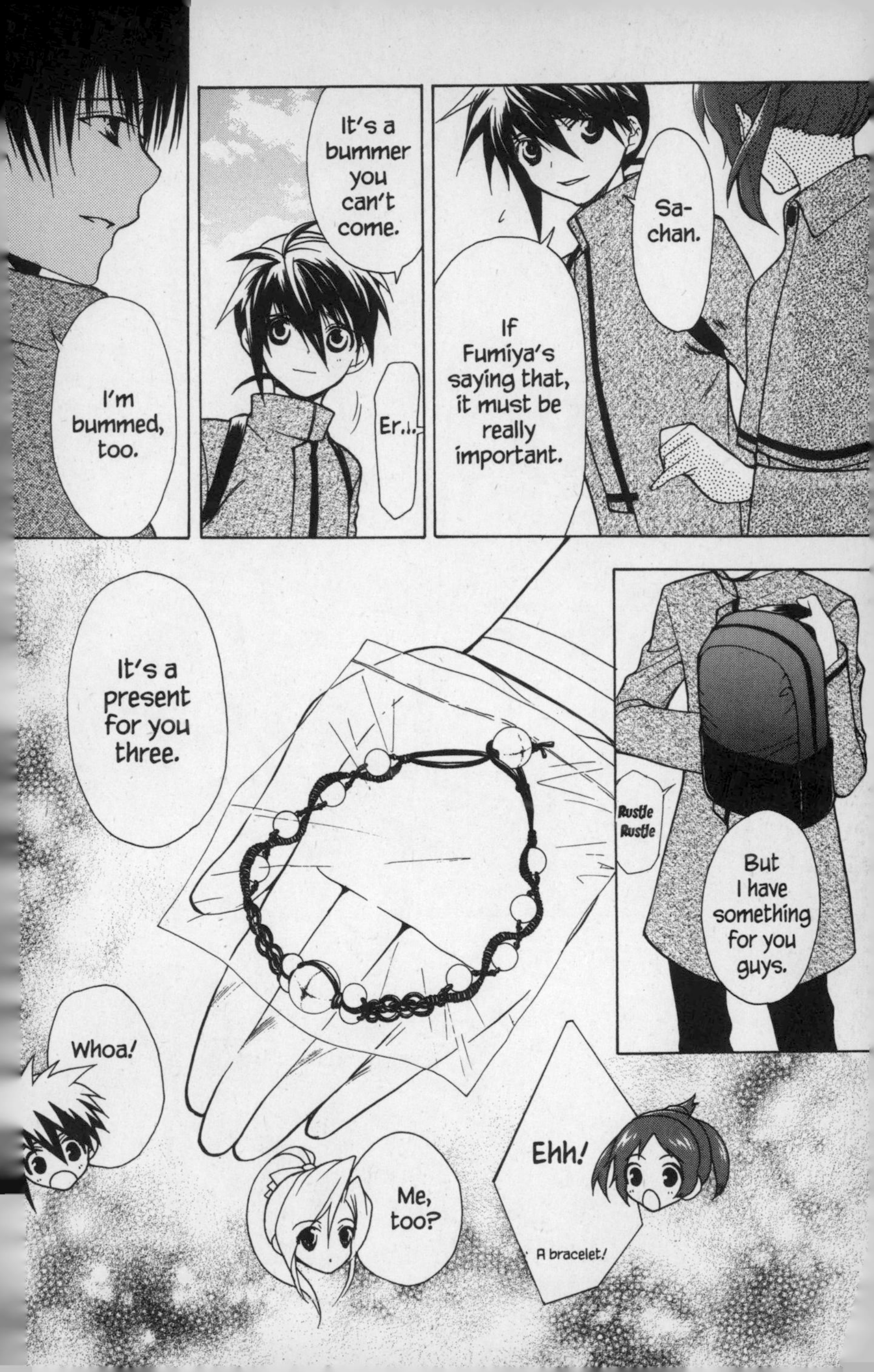
Sa-chan.
If Fumiya's saying that, it must be really important.
It's a bummer you can't come.
Er...
I'm bummed, too.
Rustle Rustle
But I have something for you guys.
It's a present for you three.
Ehh!
A bracelet!
Me, too?
Whoa!

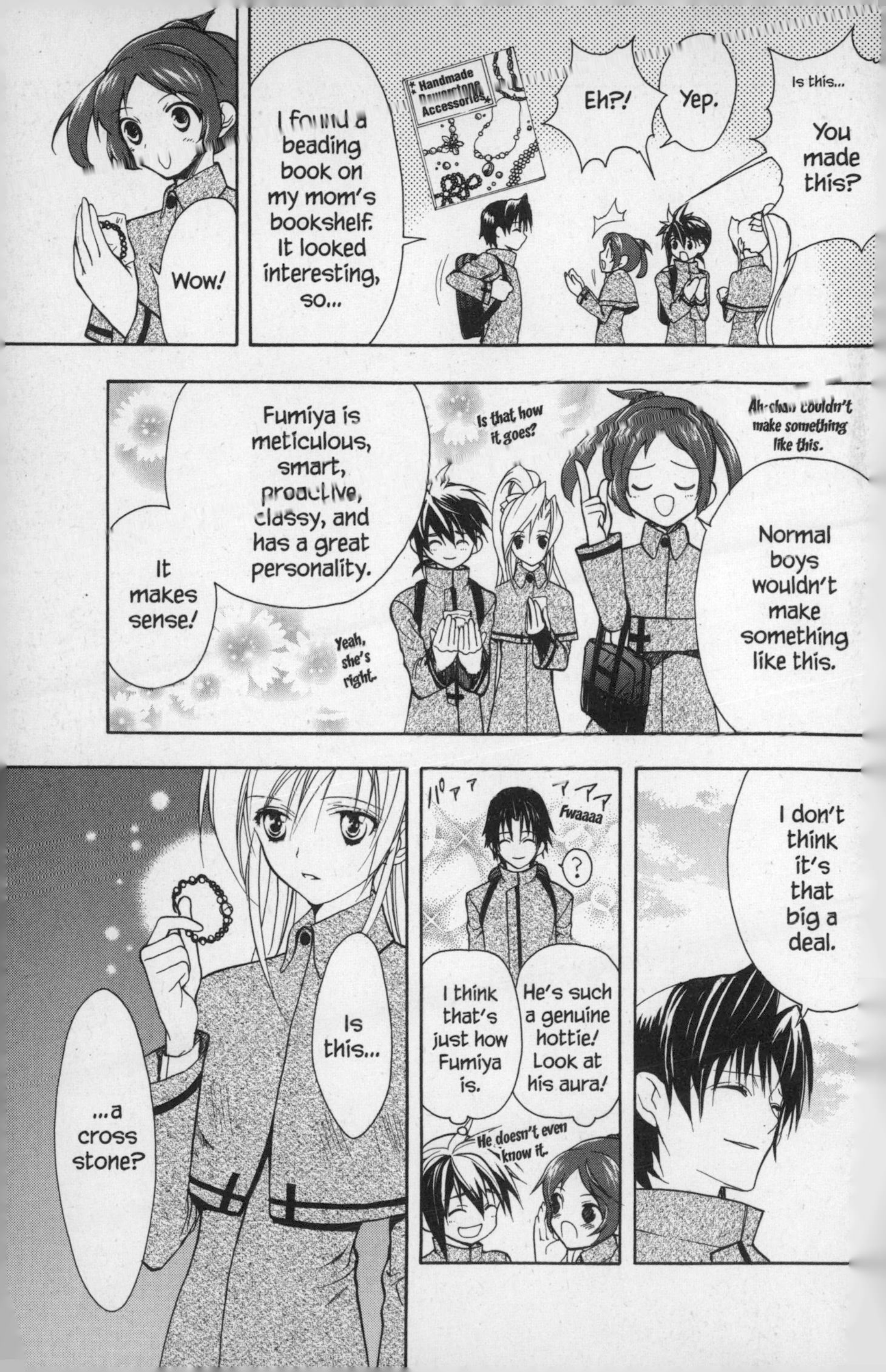
Is this...
You made this?
Yep.
Eh?!
Handmade Accessories
I found a beading book on my mom's bookshelf. It looked interesting, so...
Wow!
Ah-chan couldn't make something like this.
Normal boys wouldn't make something like this.
Is that how it goes?
Fumiya is meticulous, smart, proactive, classy, and has a great personality.
Yeah, she's right.
It makes sense!
I don't think it's that big a deal.
Fwaaaa
?
He's such a genuine hottie! Look at his aura!
I think that's just how Fumiya is.
He doesn't even know it.
Is this...
...a cross stone?

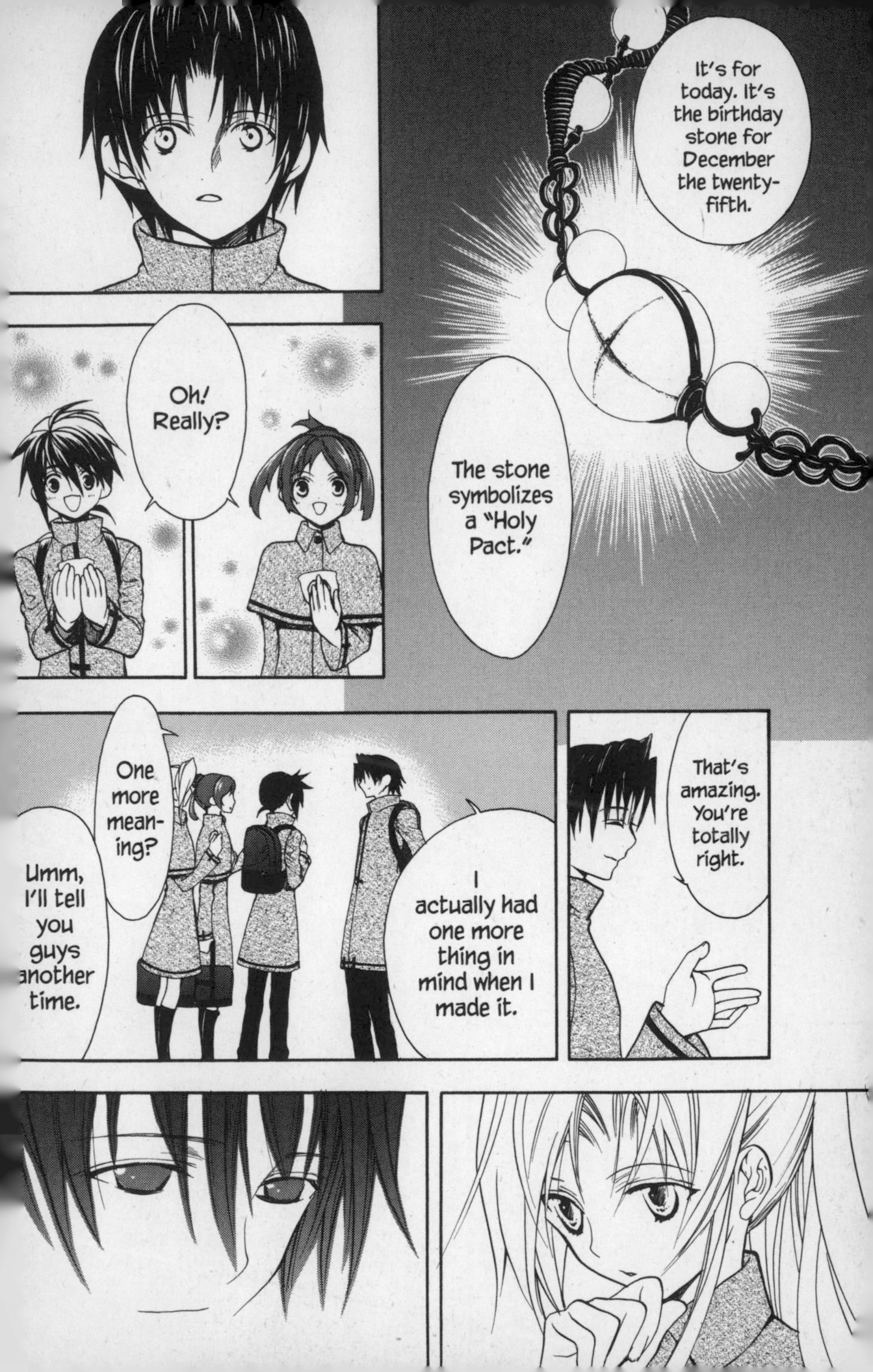
It's for today. It's the birthday stone for December the twenty-fifth.
The stone symbolizes a "Holy Pact."
Oh! Really?
That's amazing. You're totally right.
I actually had one more thing in mind when I made it.
One more meaning?
Umm, I'll tell you guys another time.

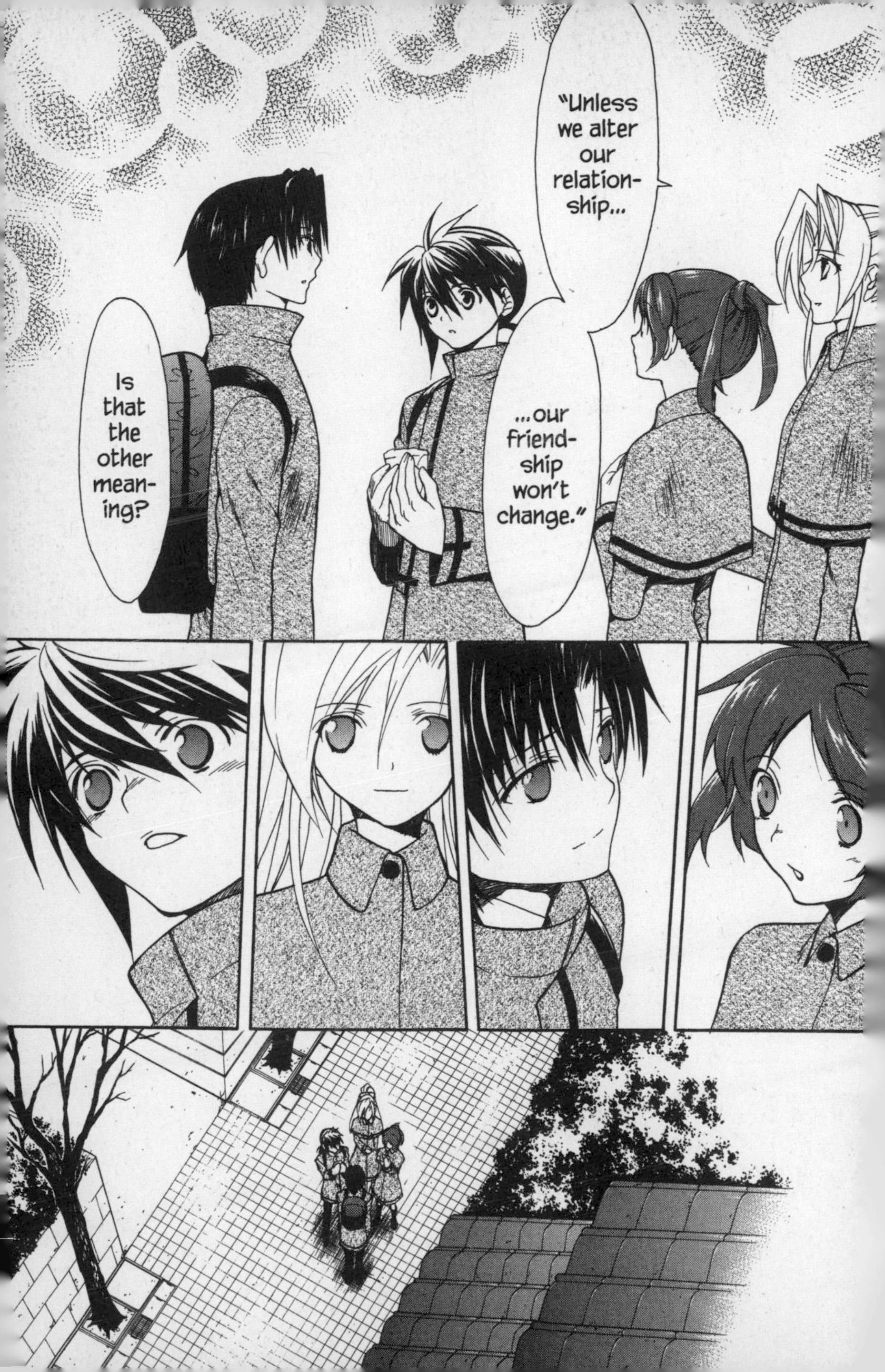
"Unless we alter our relation-ship...
...our friend-ship won't change."
Is that the other mean-ing?

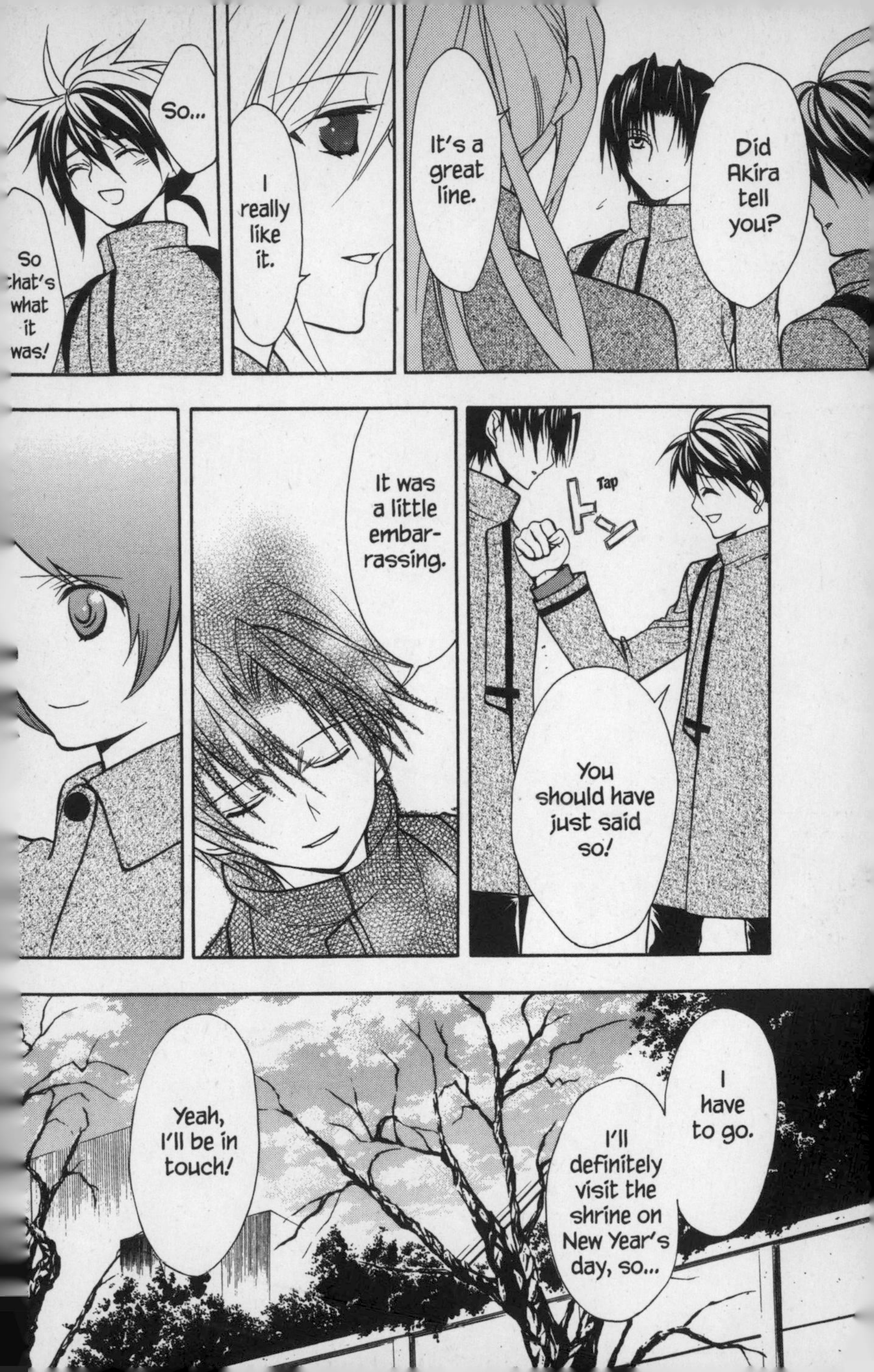
Did Akira tell you?
It's a great line.
I really like it.
So...
So that's what it was!
Tap
You should have just said so!
It was a little embarrassing.
I have to go.
I'll definitely visit the shrine on New Year's day, so...
Yeah, I'll be in touch!

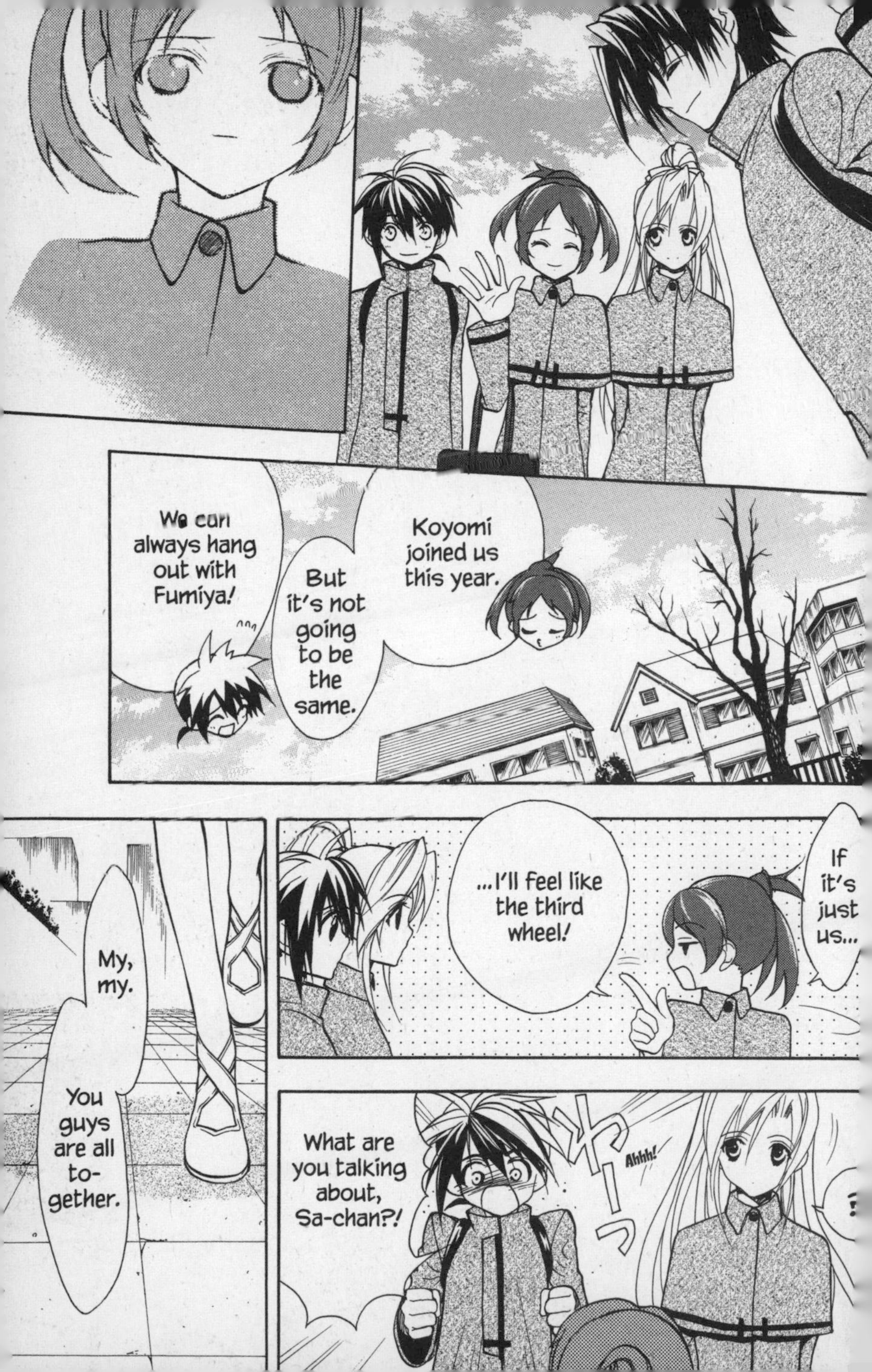
Koyomi joined us this year.
But it's not going to be the same.
We can always hang out with Fumiya!
If it's just us...
...I'll feel like the third wheel!
What are you talking about, Sa-chan?!
Ahhh!
My, my.
You guys are all to-gether.

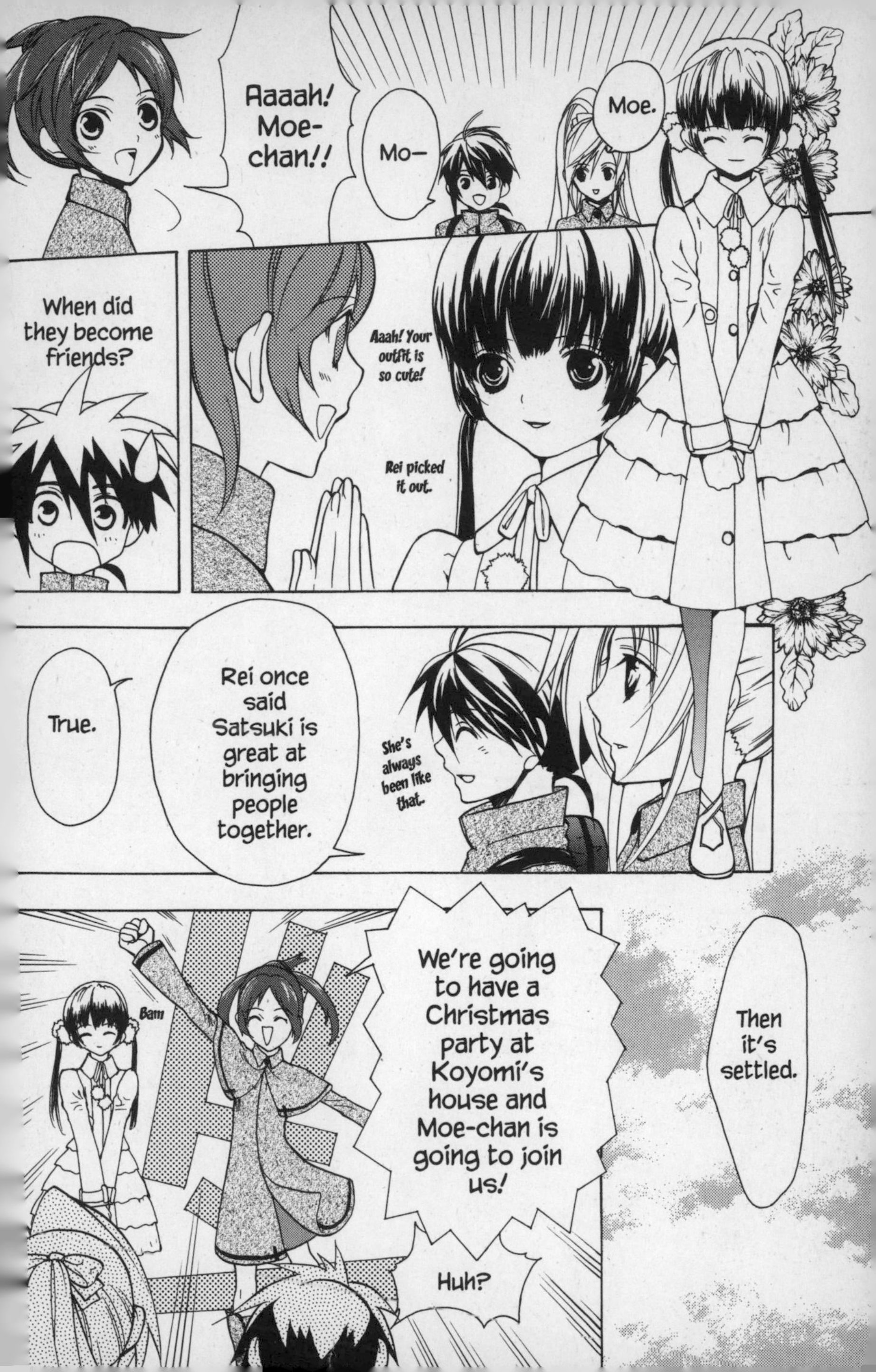

Moe.
Mo—
Aaaah! Moe-chan!!
Aaah! Your outfit is so cute!
Rei picked it out.
When did they become friends?
She's always been like that.
Rei once said Satsuki is great at bringing people together.
True.
Then it's settled.
We're going to have a Christmas party at Koyomi's house and Moe-chan is going to join us!
Bam
Huh?

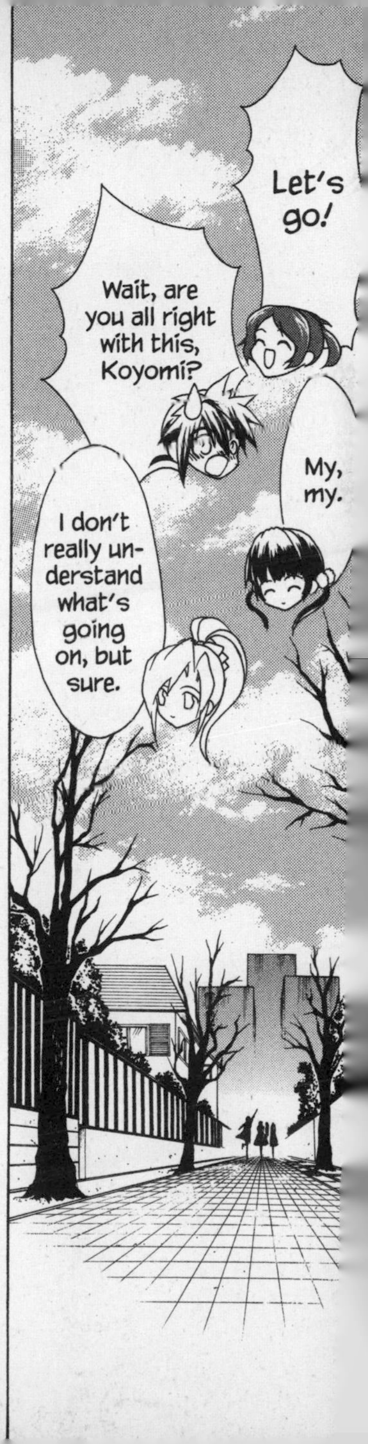
Let's go!
Wait, are you all right with this, Koyomi?
My, my.
I don't really understand what's going on, but sure.

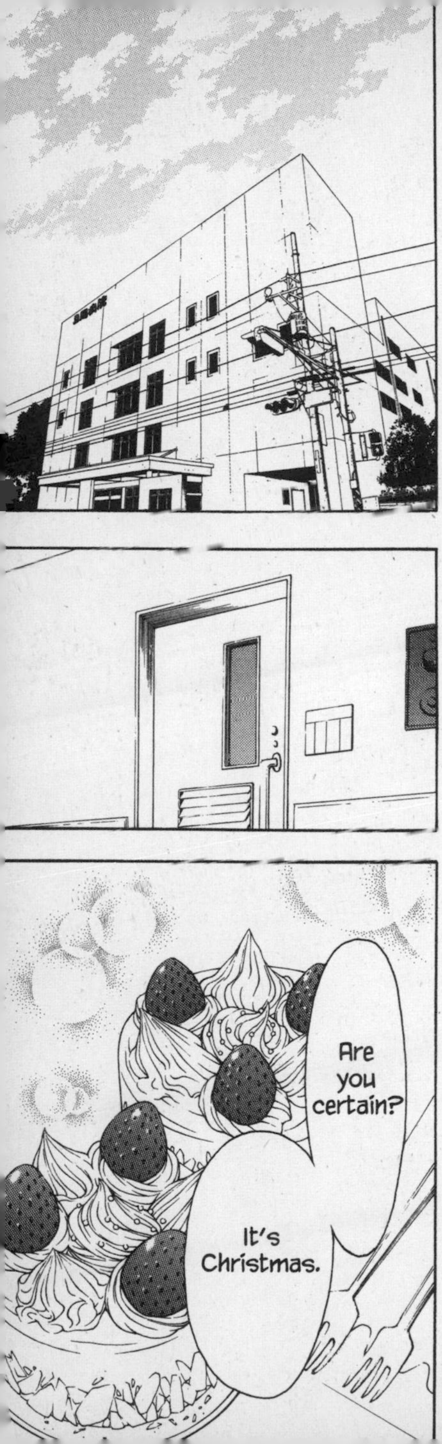
Are you certain?
It's Christmas.

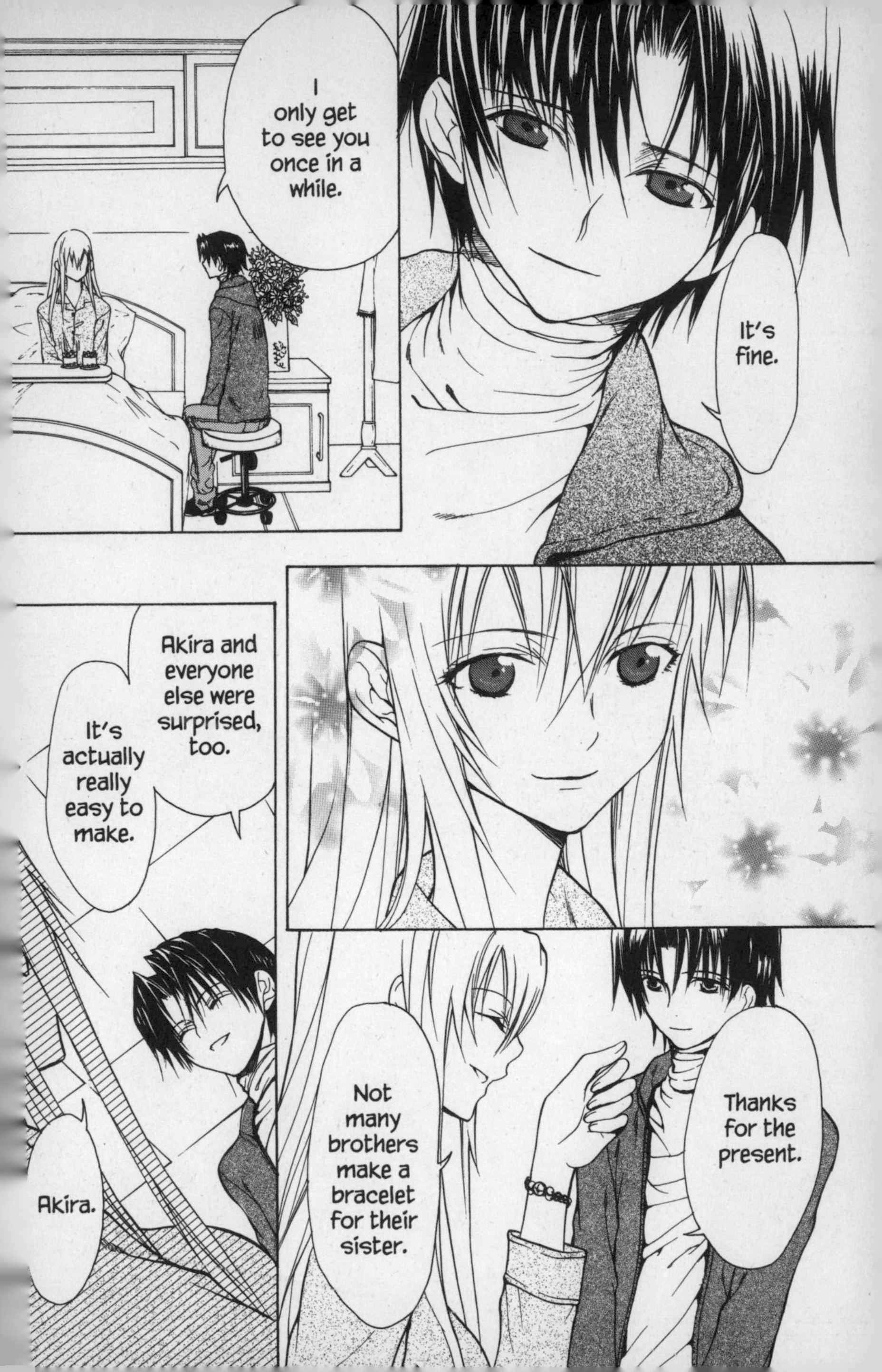
It's fine.
I only get to see you once in a while.
Thanks for the present.
Not many brothers make a bracelet for their sister.
Akira and everyone else were surprised, too.
It's actually really easy to make.
Akira.

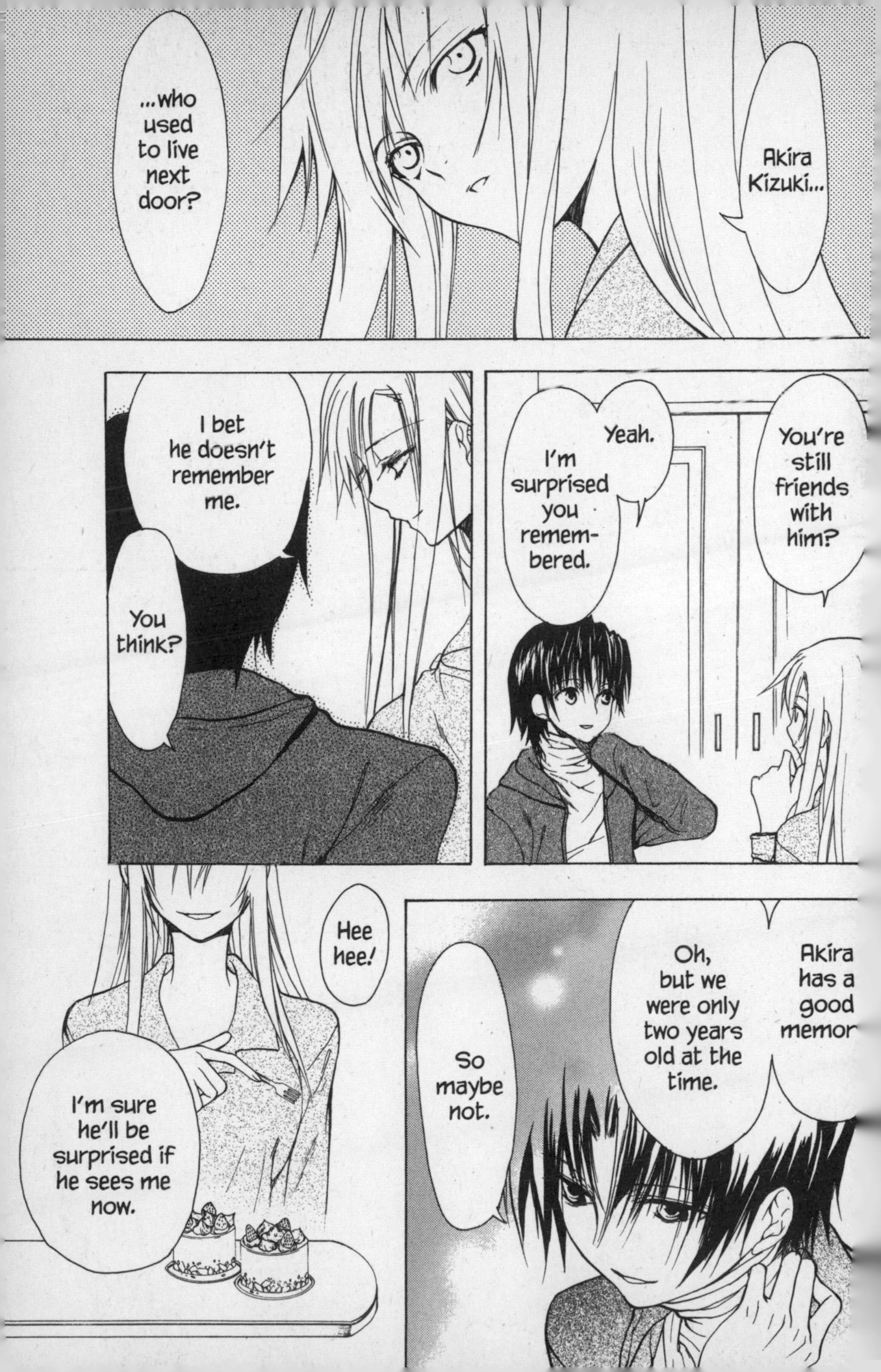
Akira Kizuki...
...who used to live next door?
You're still friends with him?
Yeah. I'm surprised you remembered.
I bet he doesn't remember me.
You think?
Akira has a good memor
Oh, but we were only two years old at the time.
So maybe not.
Hee hee!
I'm sure he'll be surprised if he sees me now.

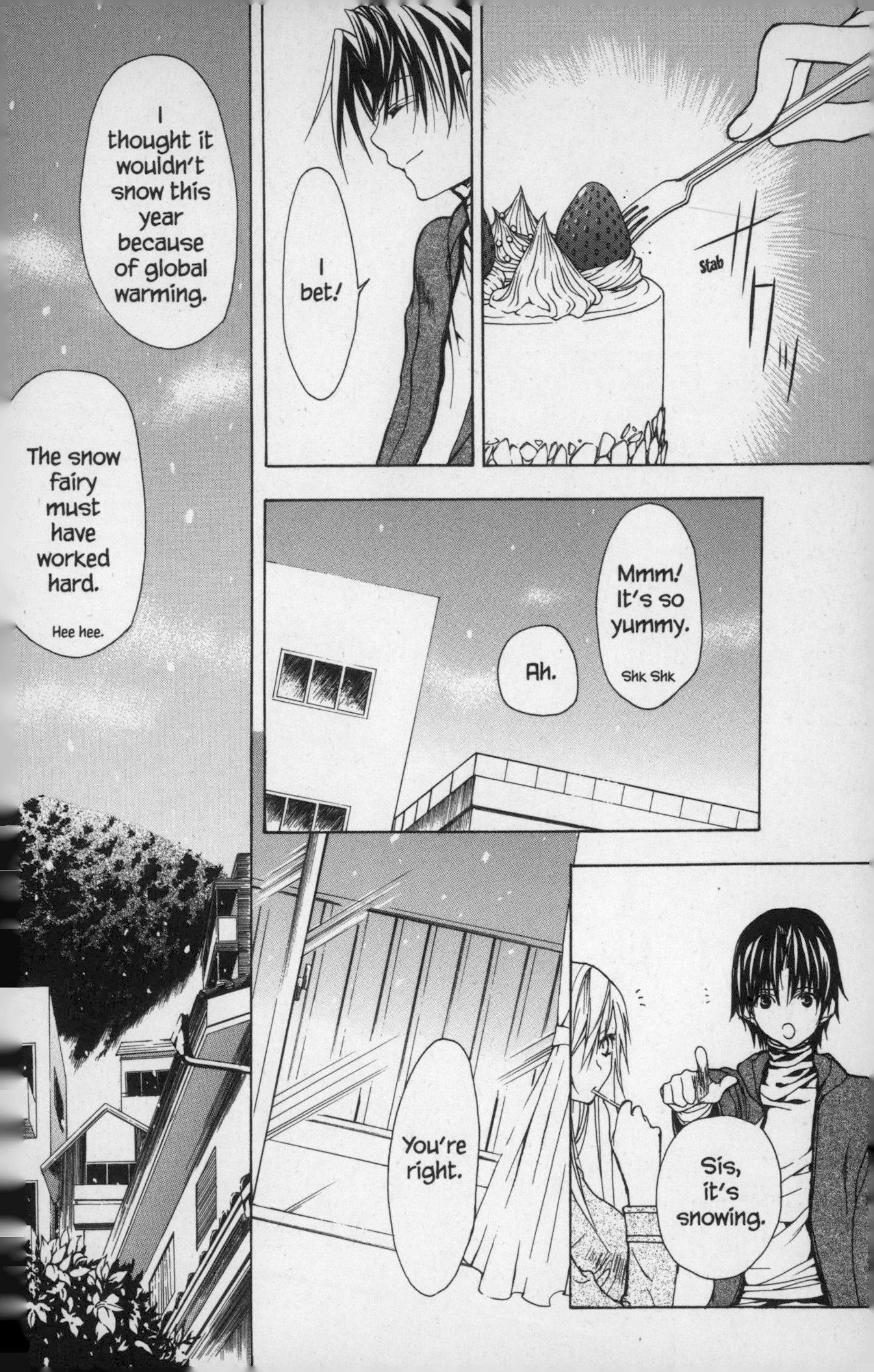
Stab
I bet!
Mmm! It's so yummy.
Shk Shk
Ah.
Sis, it's snowing.
You're right.
I thought it wouldn't snow this year because of global warming.
The snow fairy must have worked hard.
Hee hee.

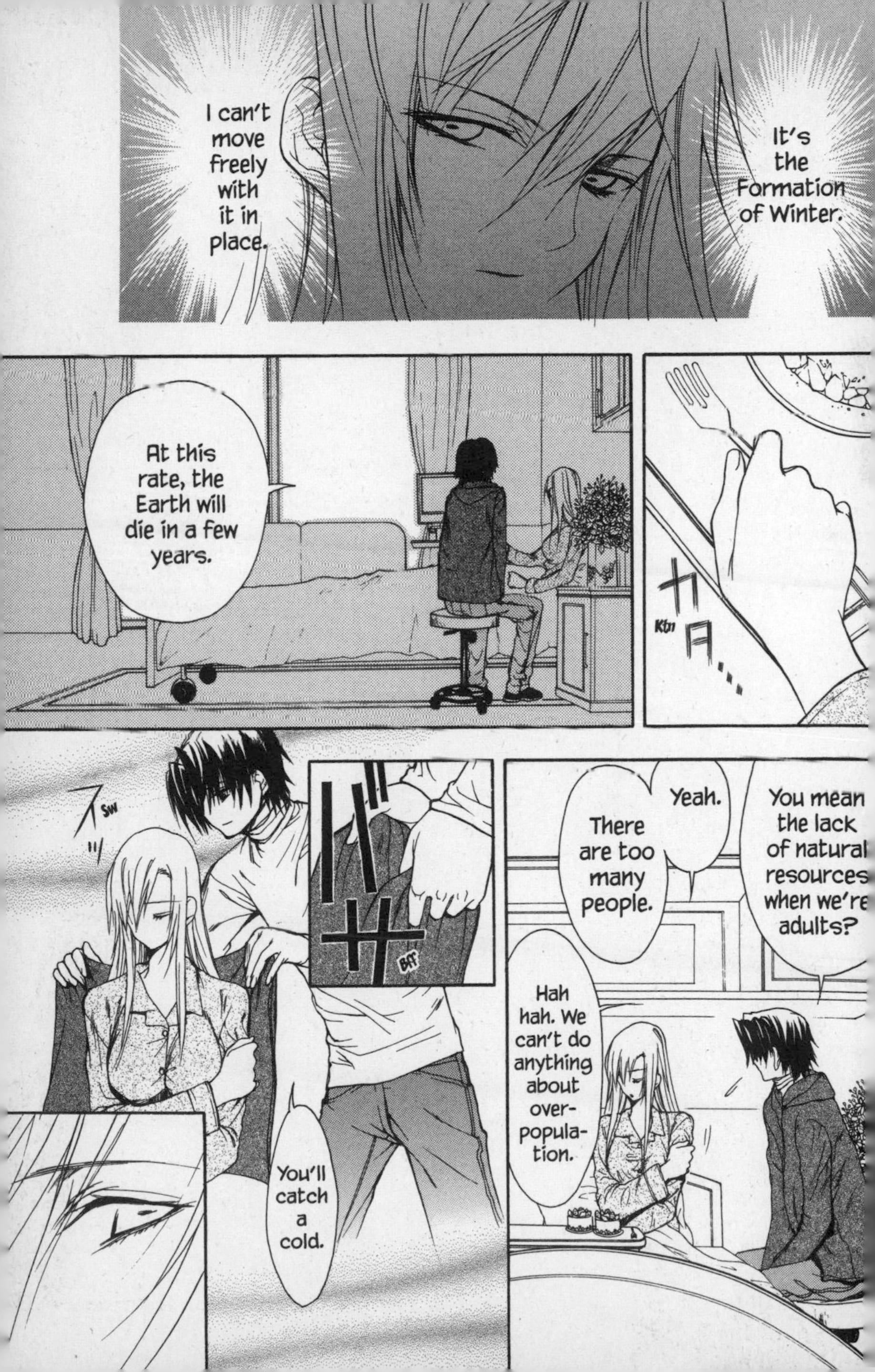
It's the Formation of Winter.
I can't move freely with it in place.
Ktn
At this rate, the Earth will die in a few years.
You mean the lack of natural resources when we're adults?
Yeah.
There are too many people.
Hah hah. We can't do anything about over-population.
BFF
SW
You'll catch a cold.

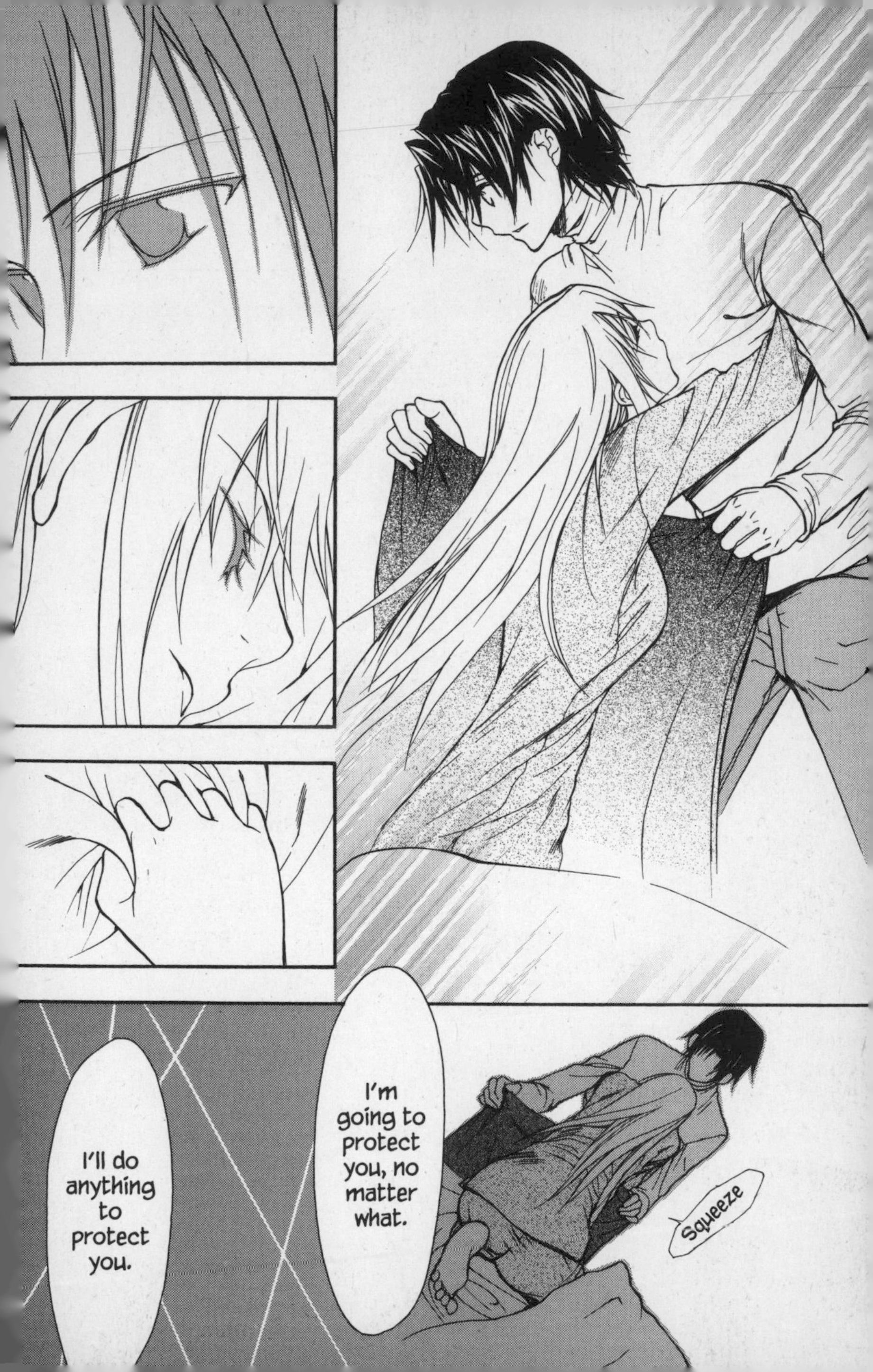
I'm going to protect you, no matter what.
Squeeze
I'll do anything to protect you.

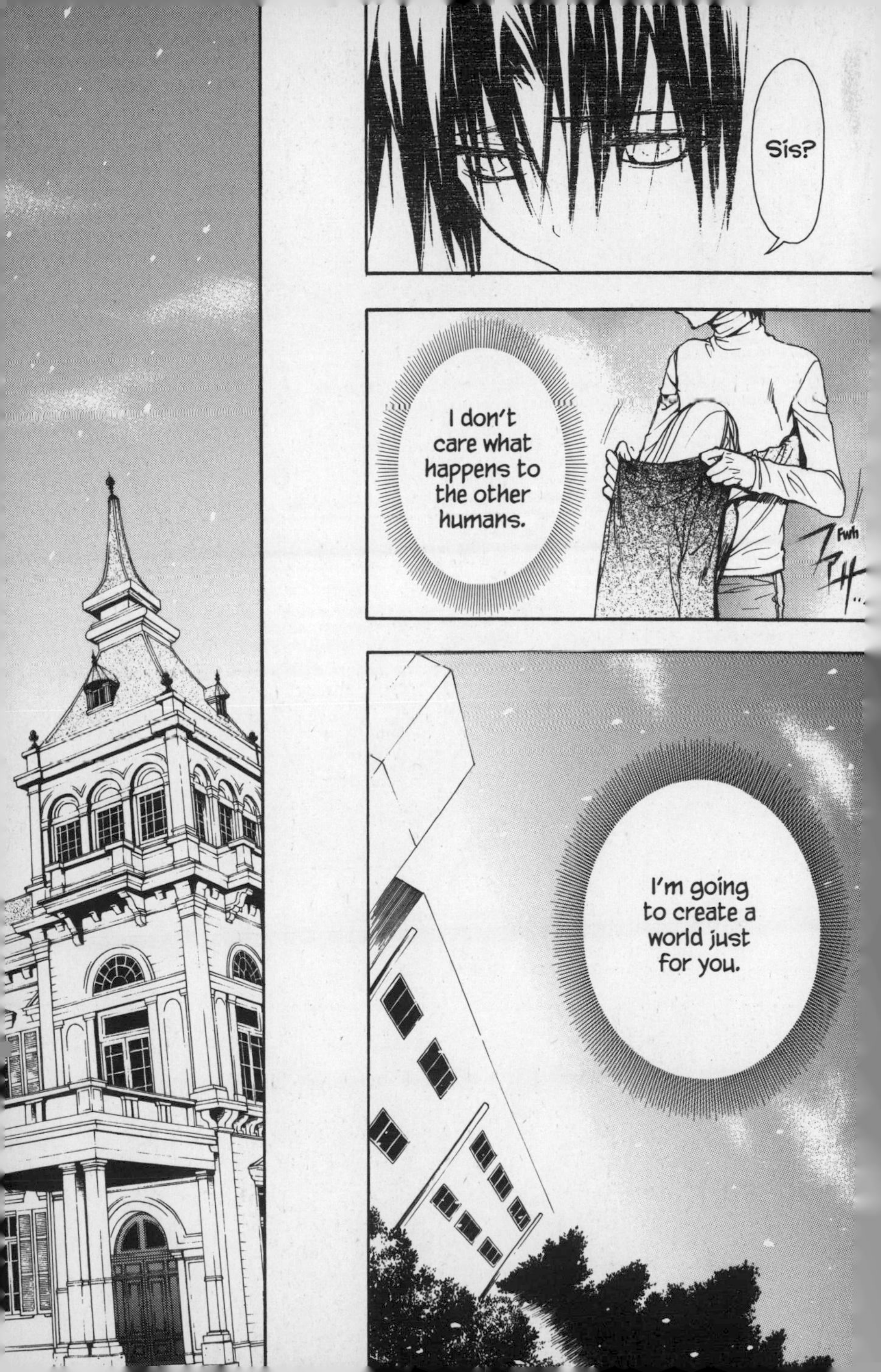
Sis?
I don't care what happens to the other humans.
Fwh
I'm going to create a world just for you.

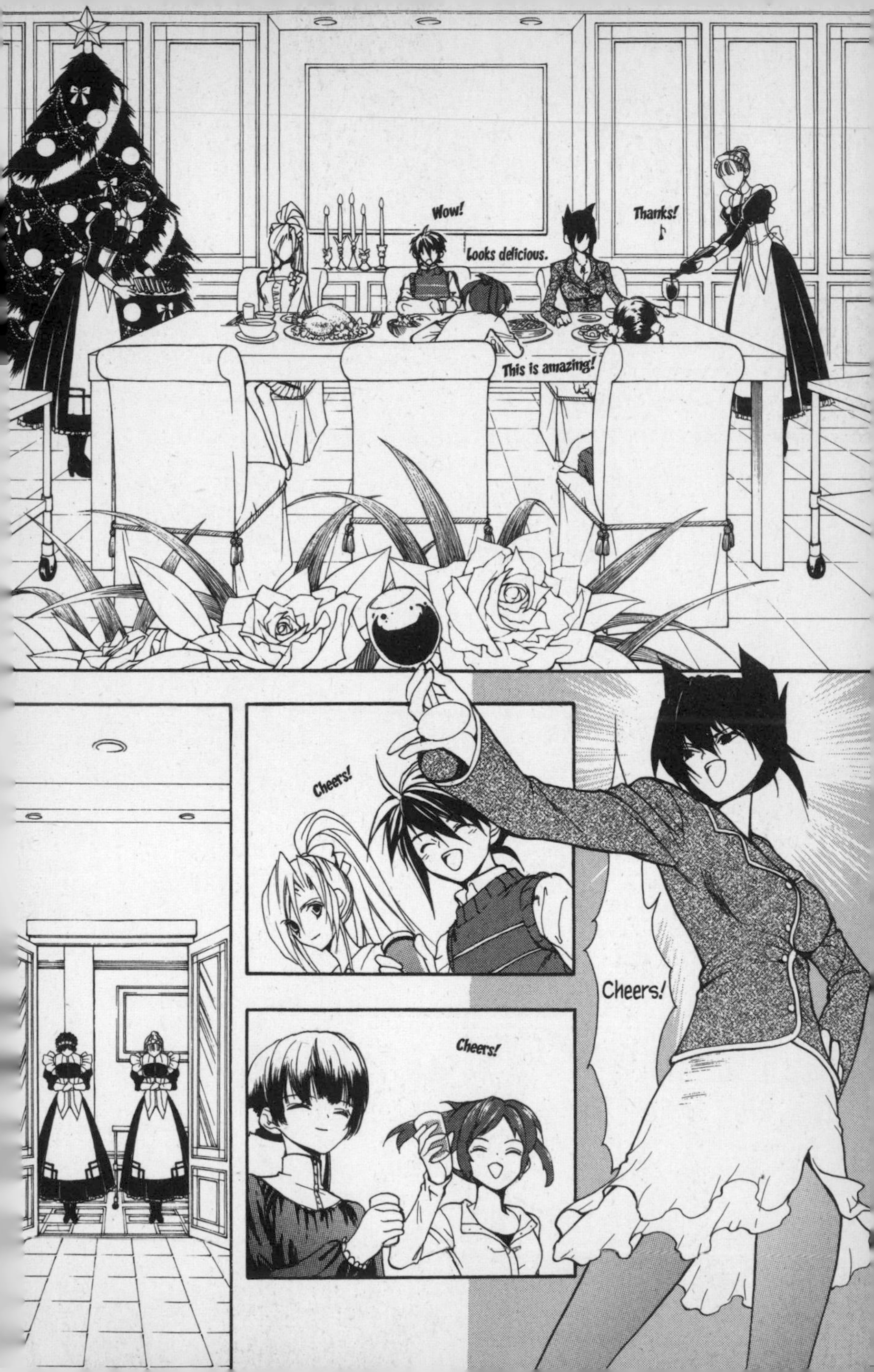
Thanks! ♪
Wow!
Looks delicious.
This is amazing!
Cheers!
Cheers!
Cheers!

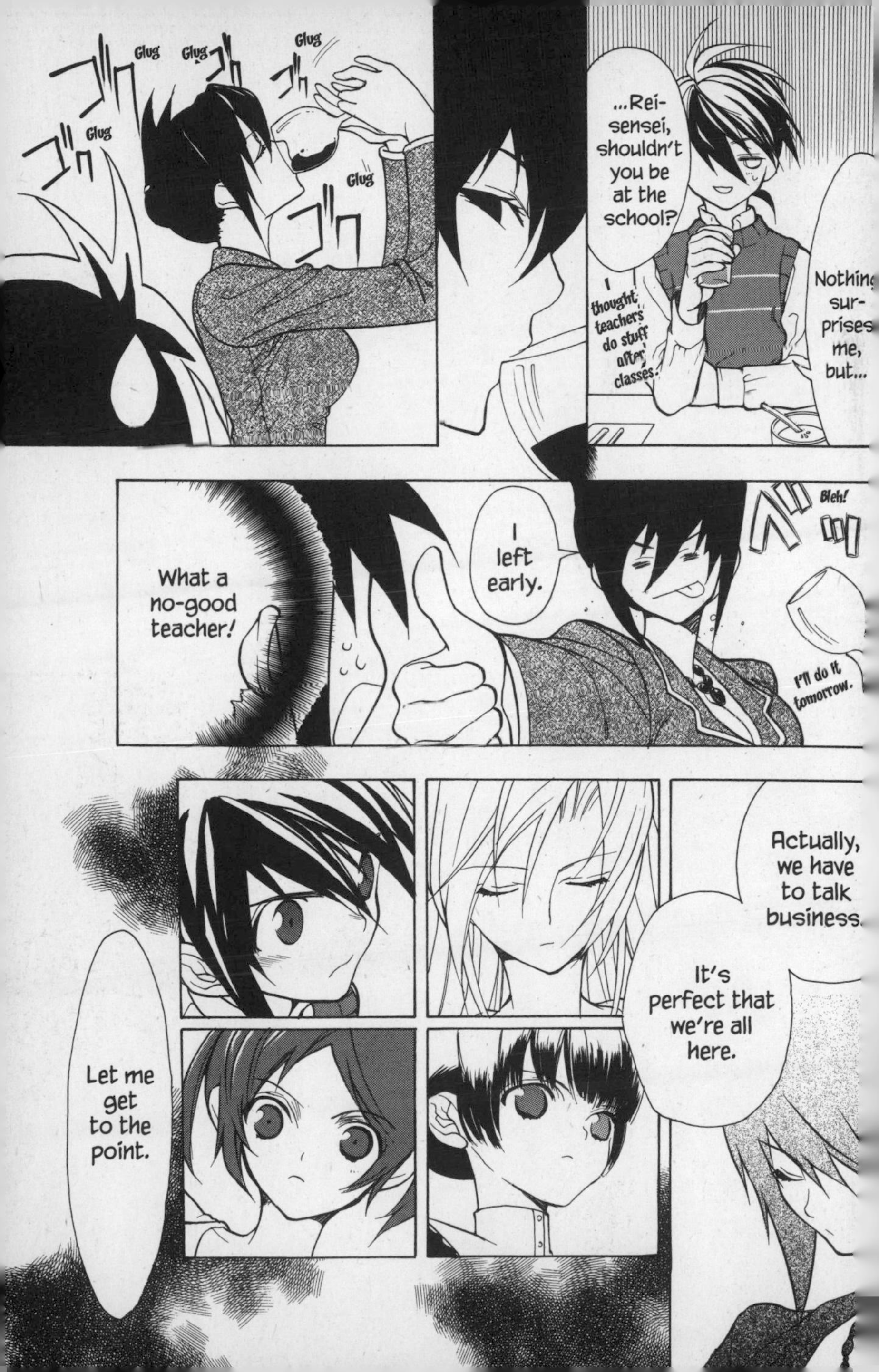
Nothing surprises me, but...
...Rei-sensei, shouldn't you be at the school?
I thought teachers do stuff after classes.
Glug
Glug
Glug
Glug
Glug
Bleh!
I'll do it tomorrow.
I left early.
What a no-good teacher!
Actually, we have to talk business.
It's perfect that we're all here.
Let me get to the point.

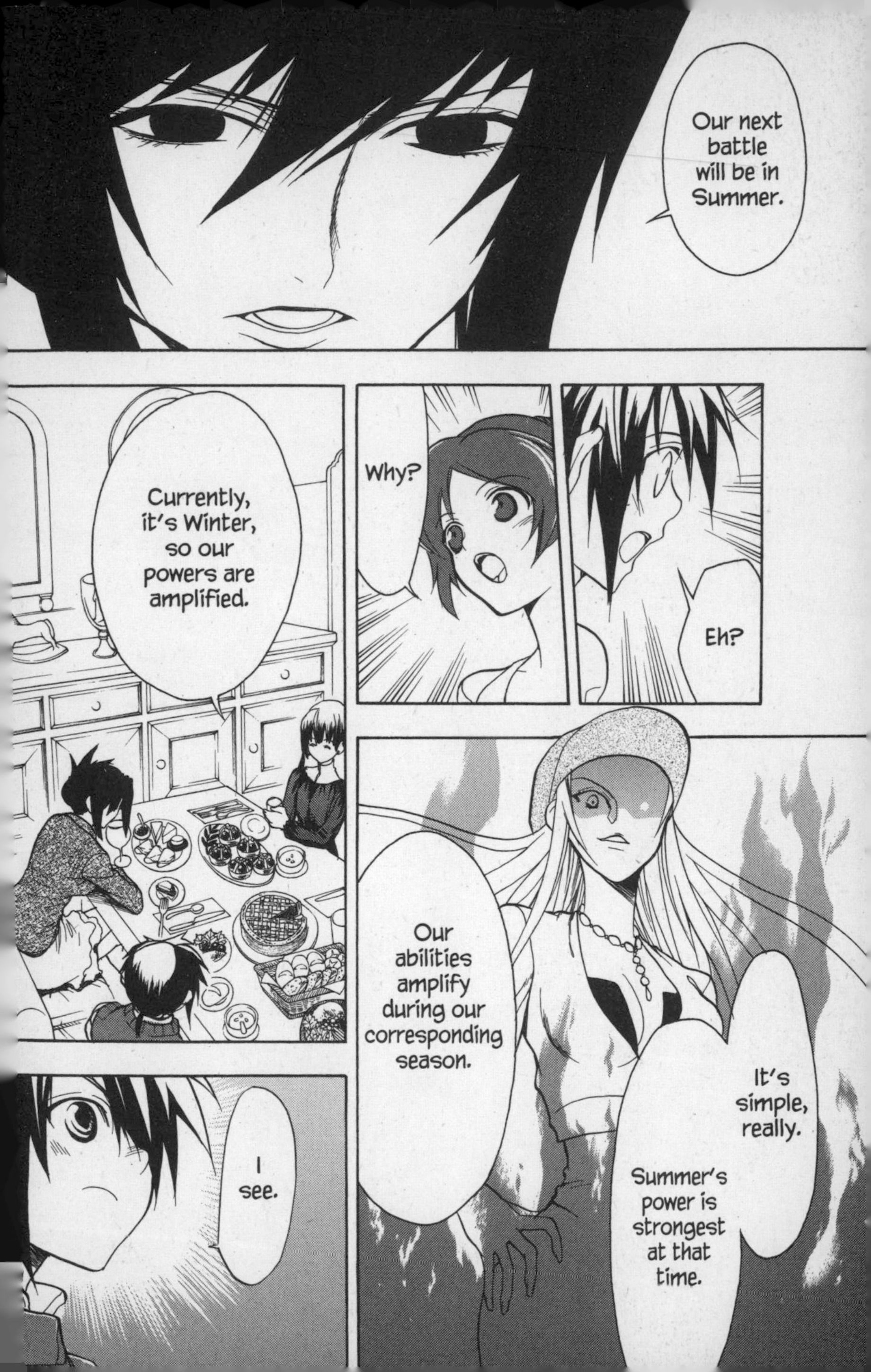

Our next battle will be in Summer.
Eh?
Why?
Currently, it's Winter, so our powers are amplified.
It's simple, really.
Summer's power is strongest at that time.
Our abilities amplify during our corresponding season.
I see.

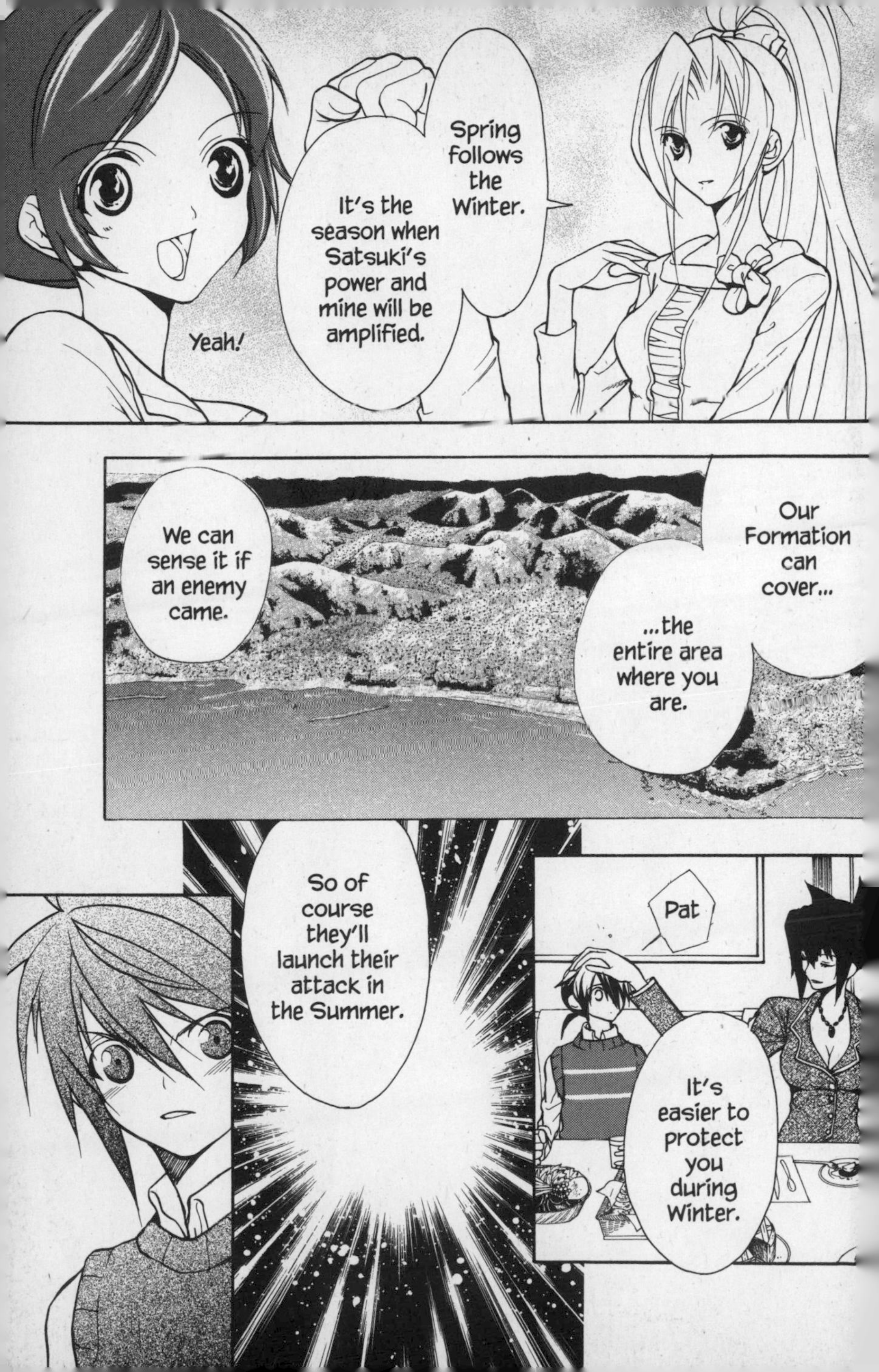
Spring follows the Winter.
It's the season when Satsuki's power and mine will be amplified.
Yeah!
Our Formation can cover...
...the entire area where you are.
We can sense it if an enemy came.
Pat
It's easier to protect you during Winter.
So of course they'll launch their attack in the Summer.

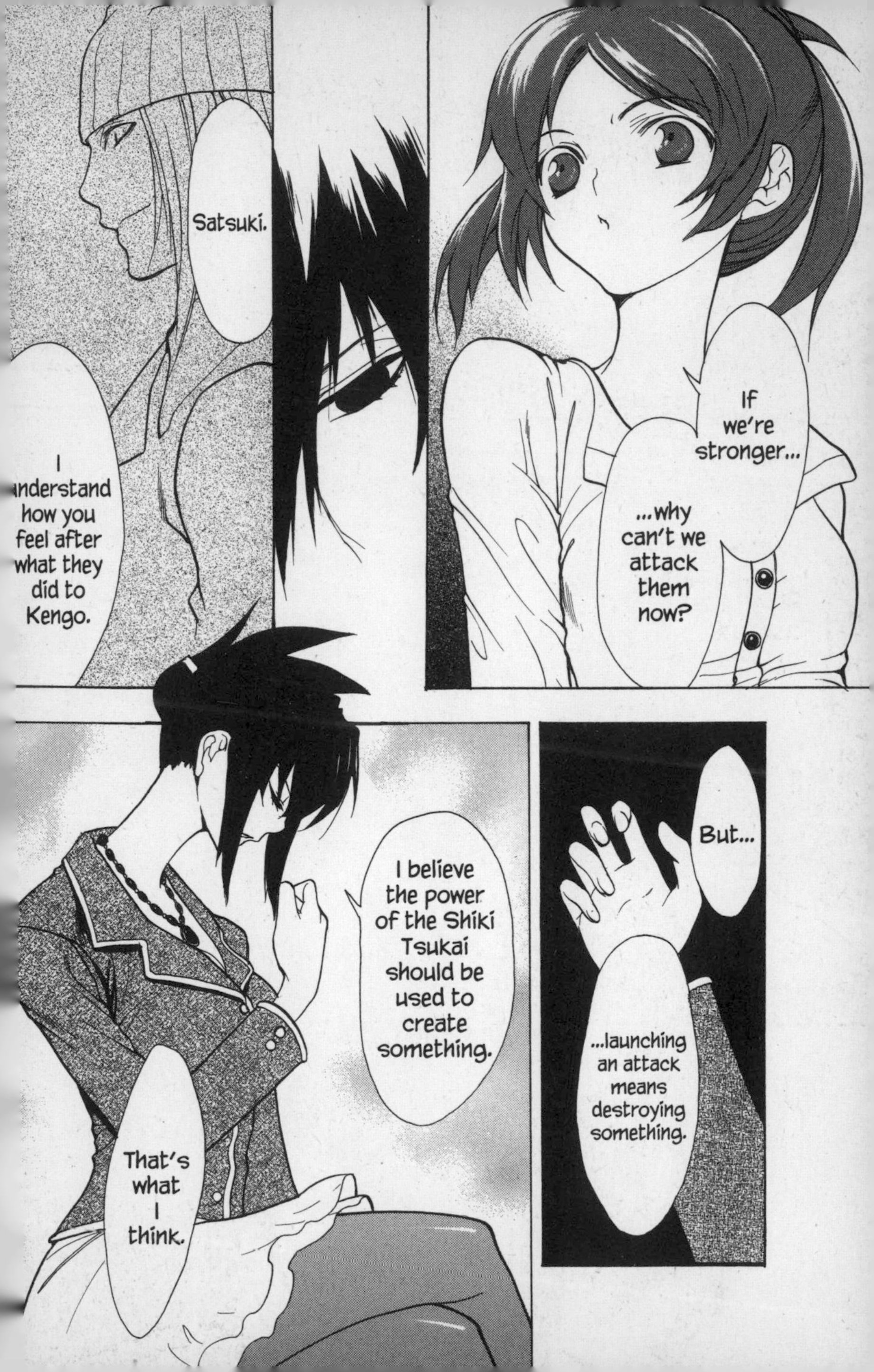
If we're stronger...
...why can't we attack them now?
Satsuki.
I understand how you feel after what they did to Kengo.
But...
...launching an attack means destroying something.
I believe the power of the Shiki Tsukai should be used to create something.
That's what I think.

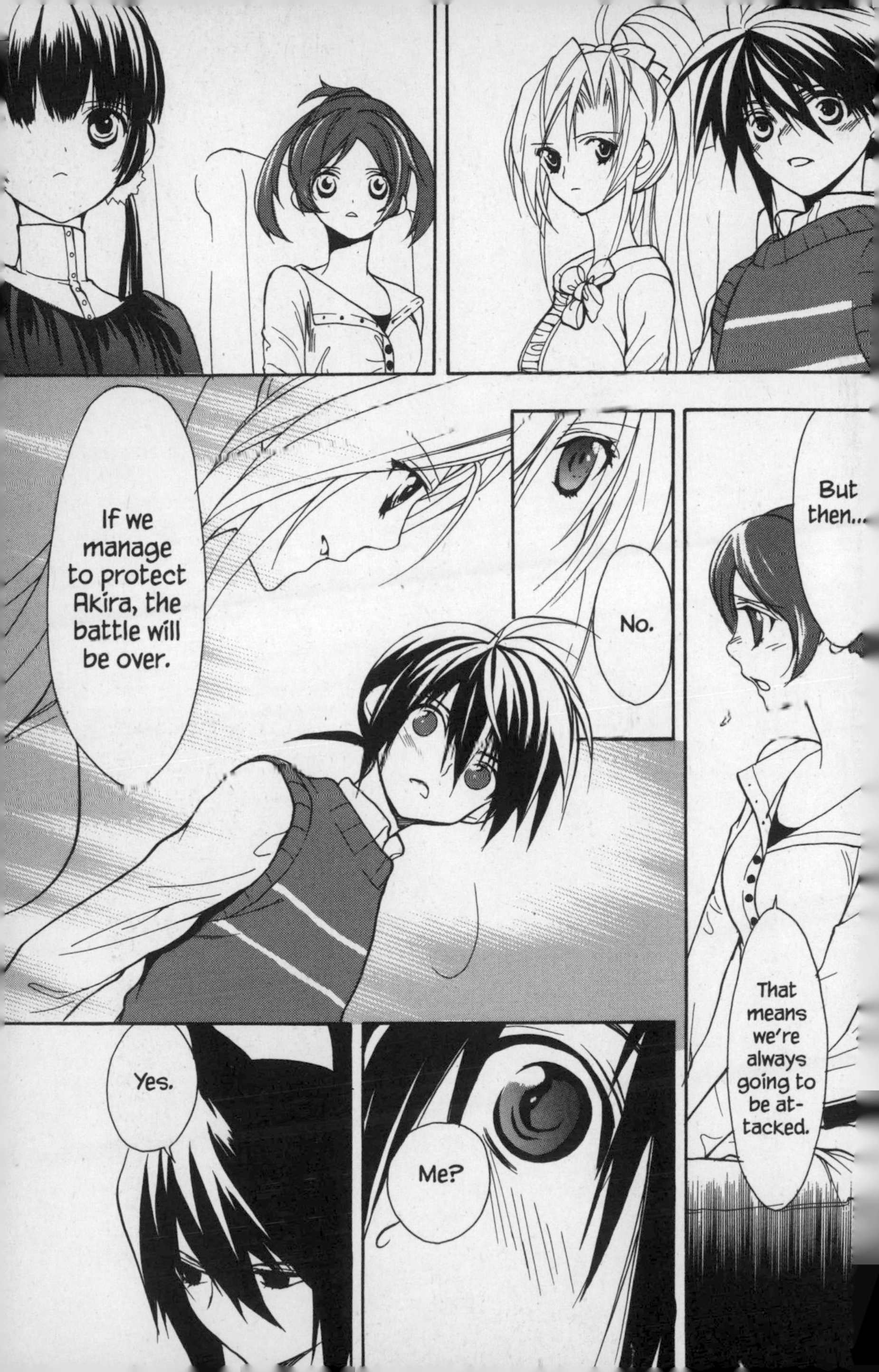
But then...
That means we're always going to be attacked.
No.
If we manage to protect Akira, the battle will be over.
Me?
Yes.

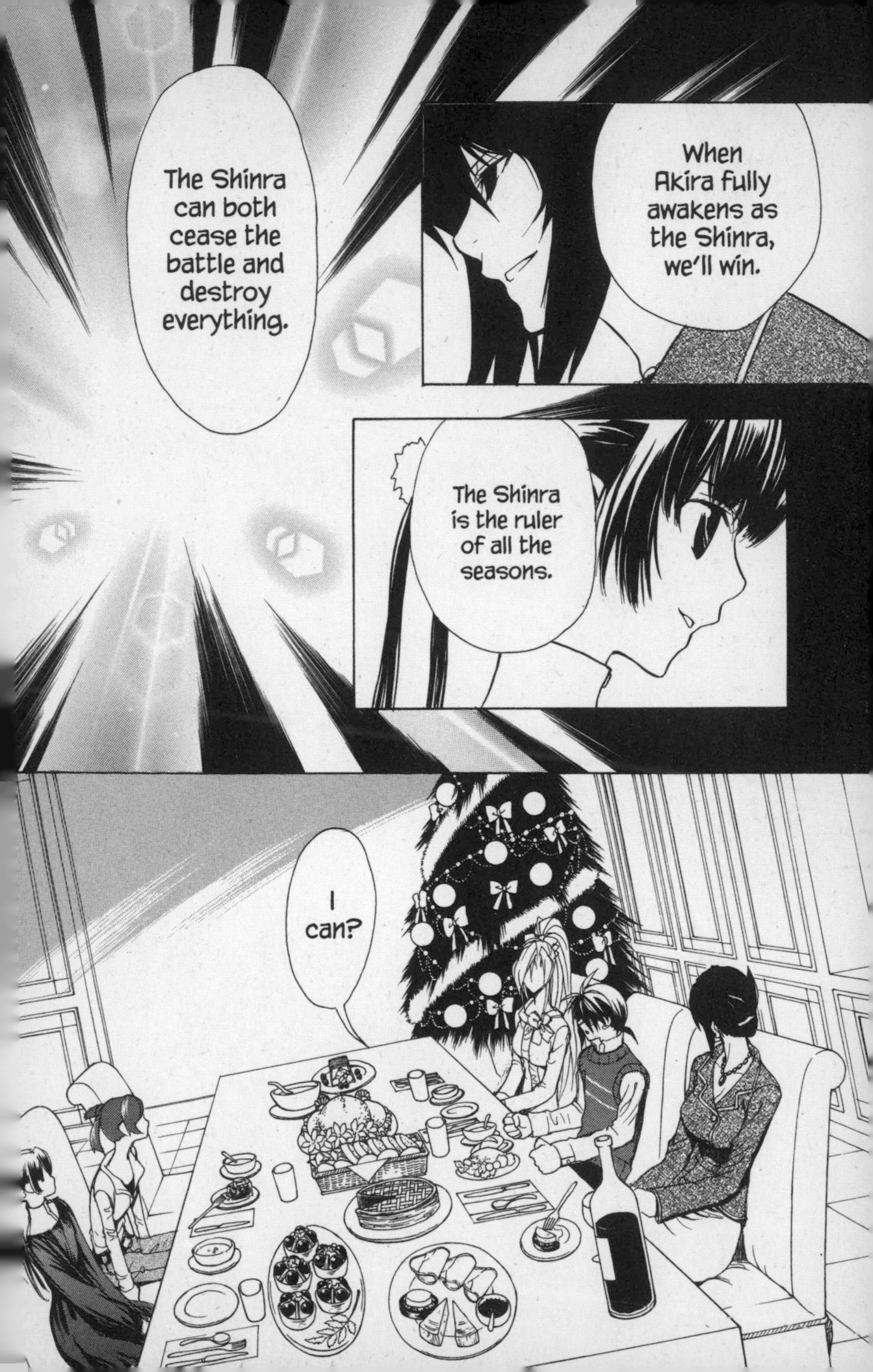
When Akira fully awakens as the Shinra, we'll win.
The Shinra is the ruler of all the seasons.
The Shinra can both cease the battle and destroy everything.
I can?

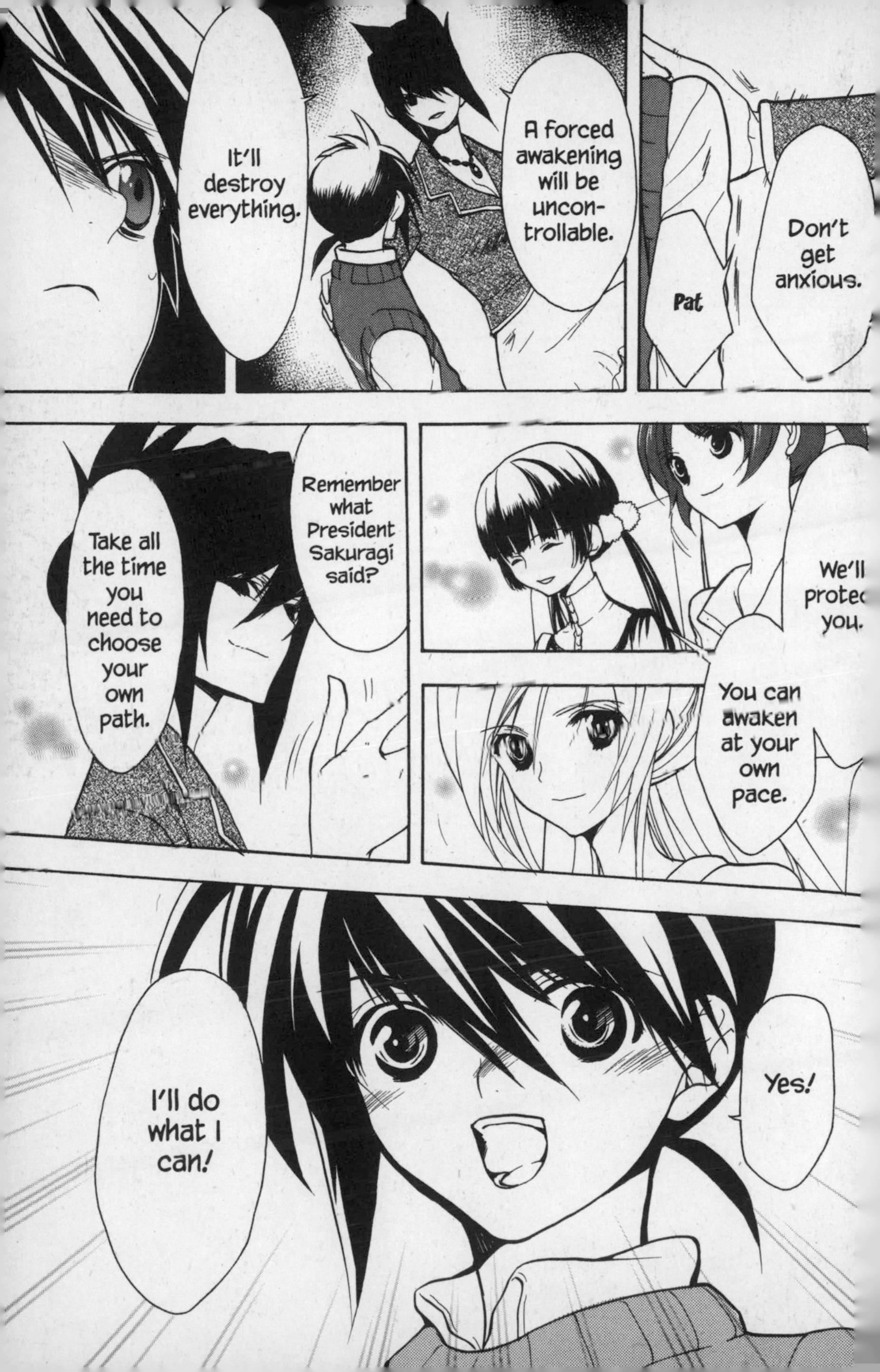
Don't get anxious.
Pat
A forced awakening will be uncontrollable.
It'll destroy everything.
We'll protec you.
You can awaken at your own pace.
Remember what President Sakuragi said?
Take all the time you need to choose your own path.
Yes!
I'll do what I can!

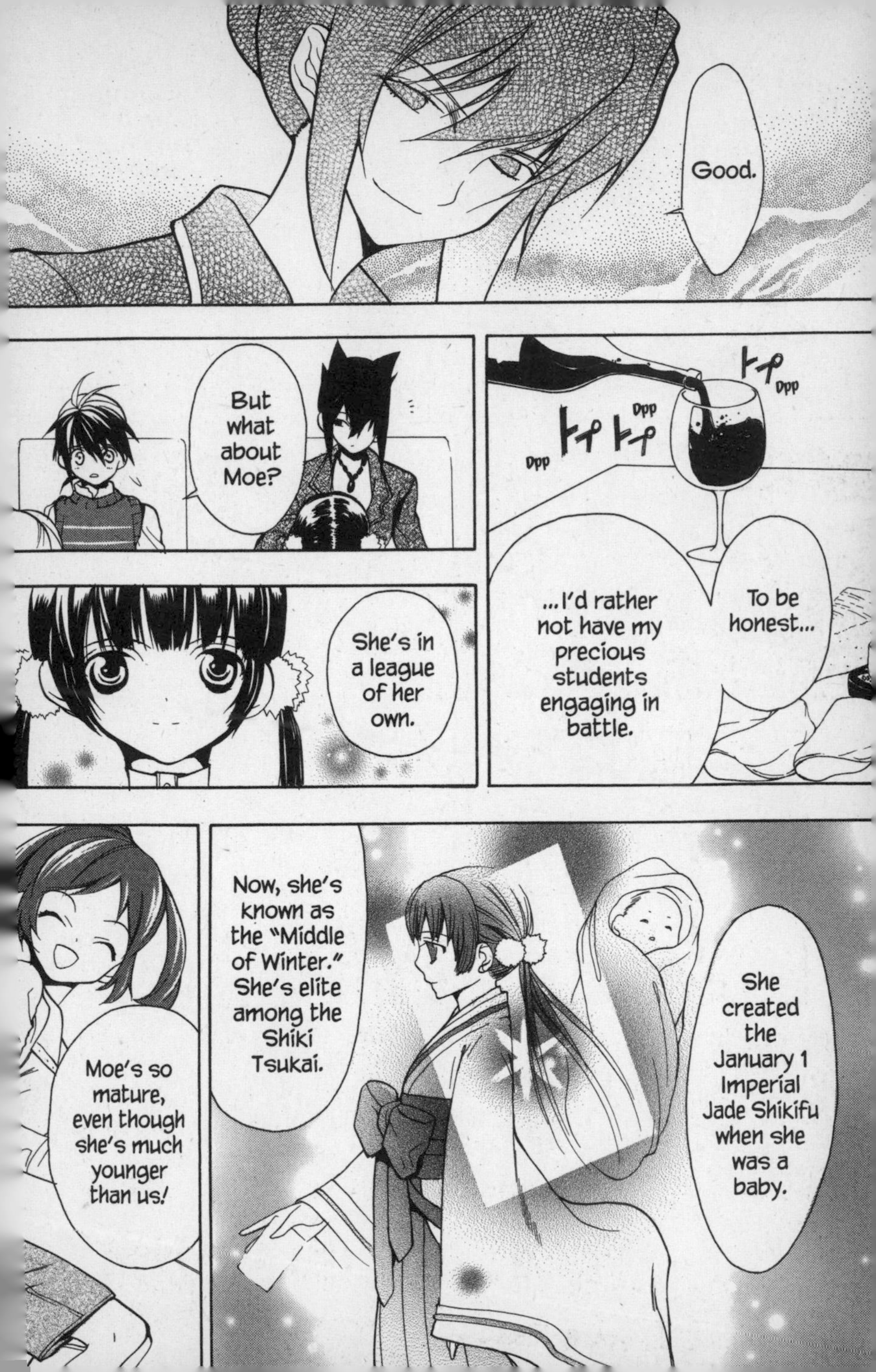
Good.
トプ Dpp
トプ トプ Dpp Dpp
To be honest...
...I'd rather not have my precious students engaging in battle.
But what about Moe?
She's in a league of her own.
She created the January 1 Imperial Jade Shikifu when she was a baby.
Now, she's known as the "Middle of Winter." She's elite among the Shiki Tsukai.
Moe's so mature, even though she's much younger than us!

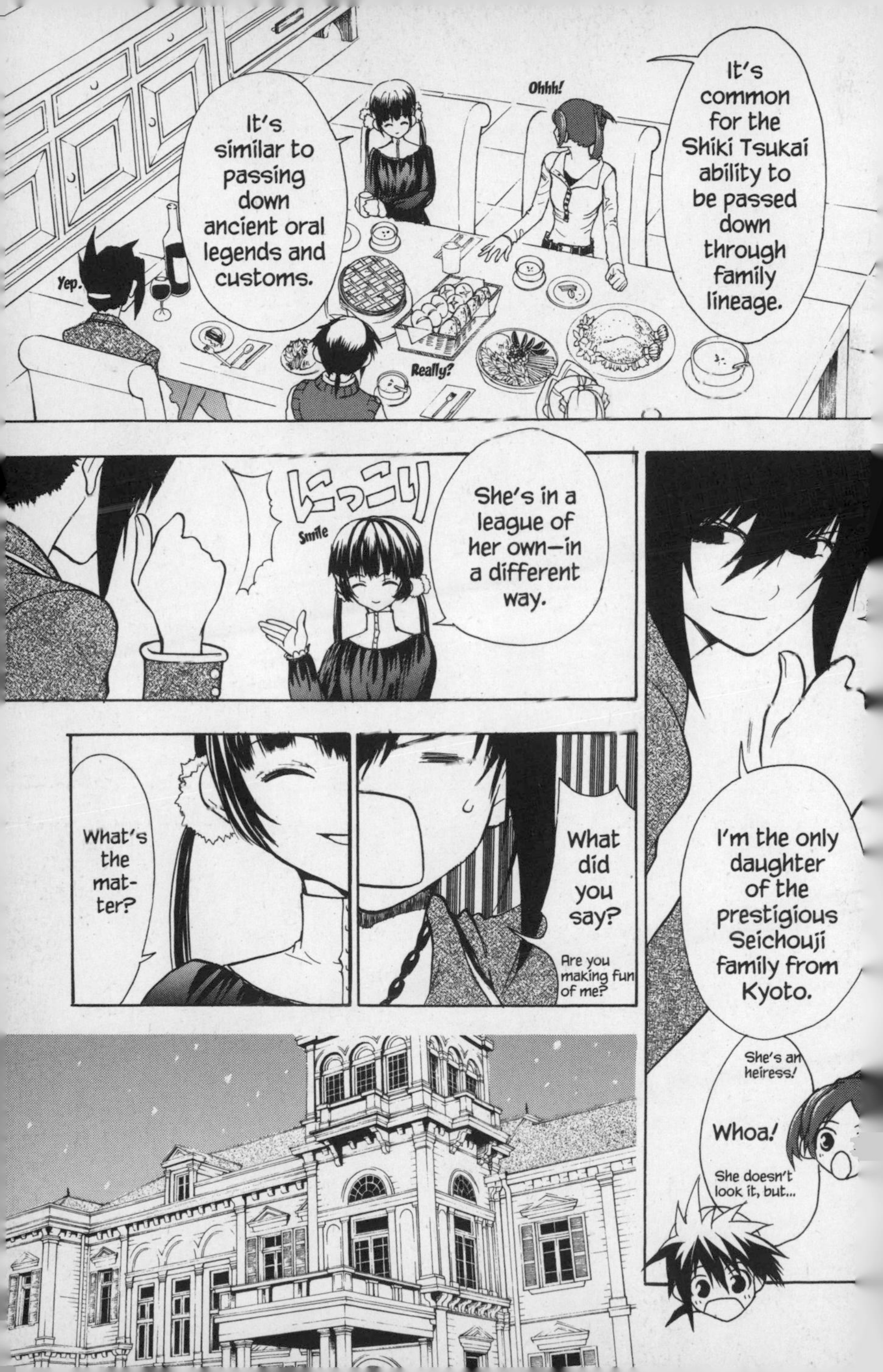

It's common for the Shiki Tsukai ability to be passed down through family lineage.
Ohhh!
It's similar to passing down ancient oral legends and customs.
Really?
Yep.
I'm the only daughter of the prestigious Seichouji family from Kyoto.
She's an heiress!
Whoa!
She doesn't look it, but...
She's in a league of her own—in a different way.
にっこり
Smile
What did you say?
Are you making fun of me?
What's the matter?

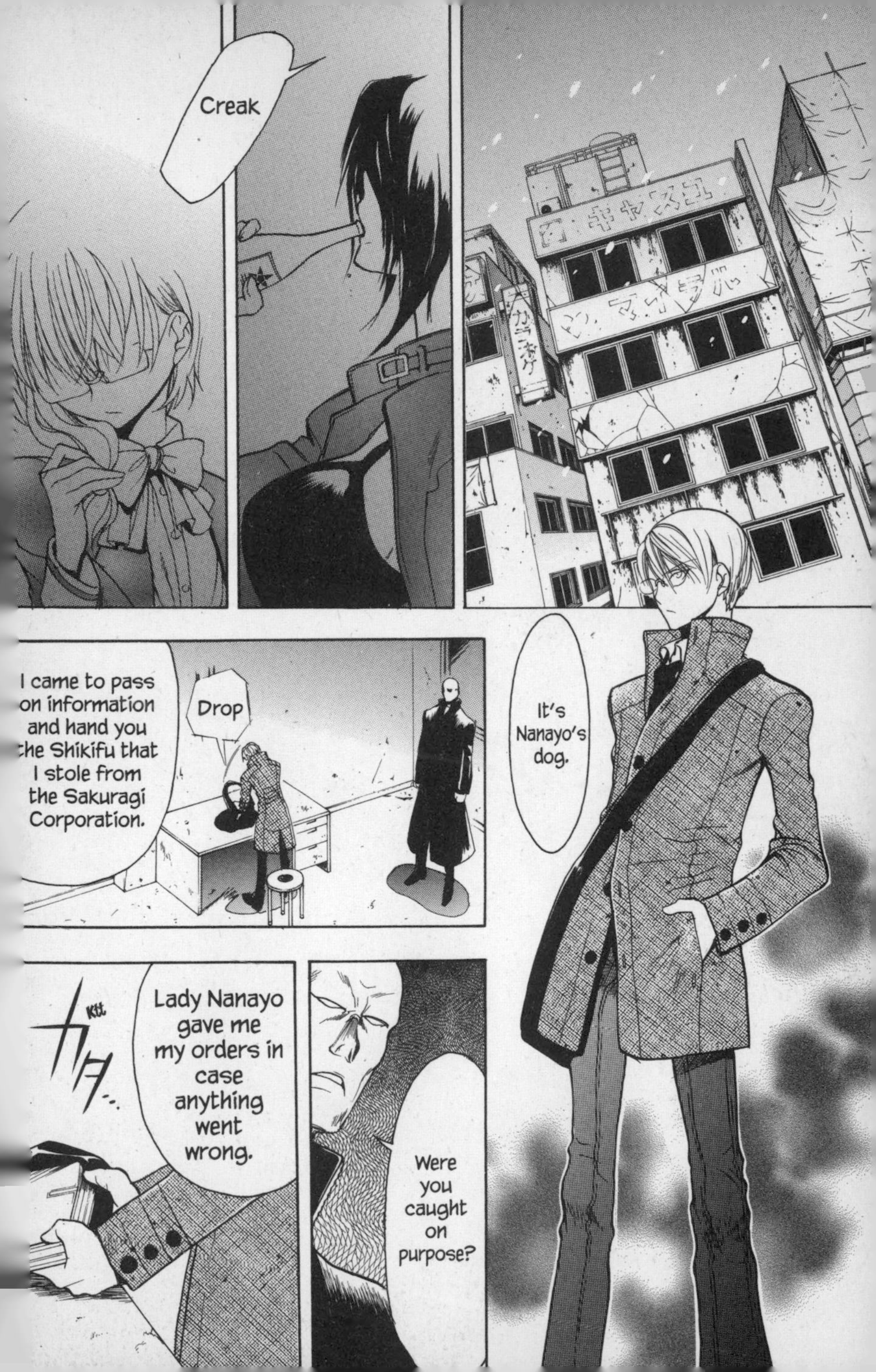
Creak
It's Nanayo's dog.
Drop
I came to pass on information and hand you the Shikifu that I stole from the Sakuragi Corporation.
Were you caught on purpose?
Lady Nanayo gave me my orders in case anything went wrong.
Ktt

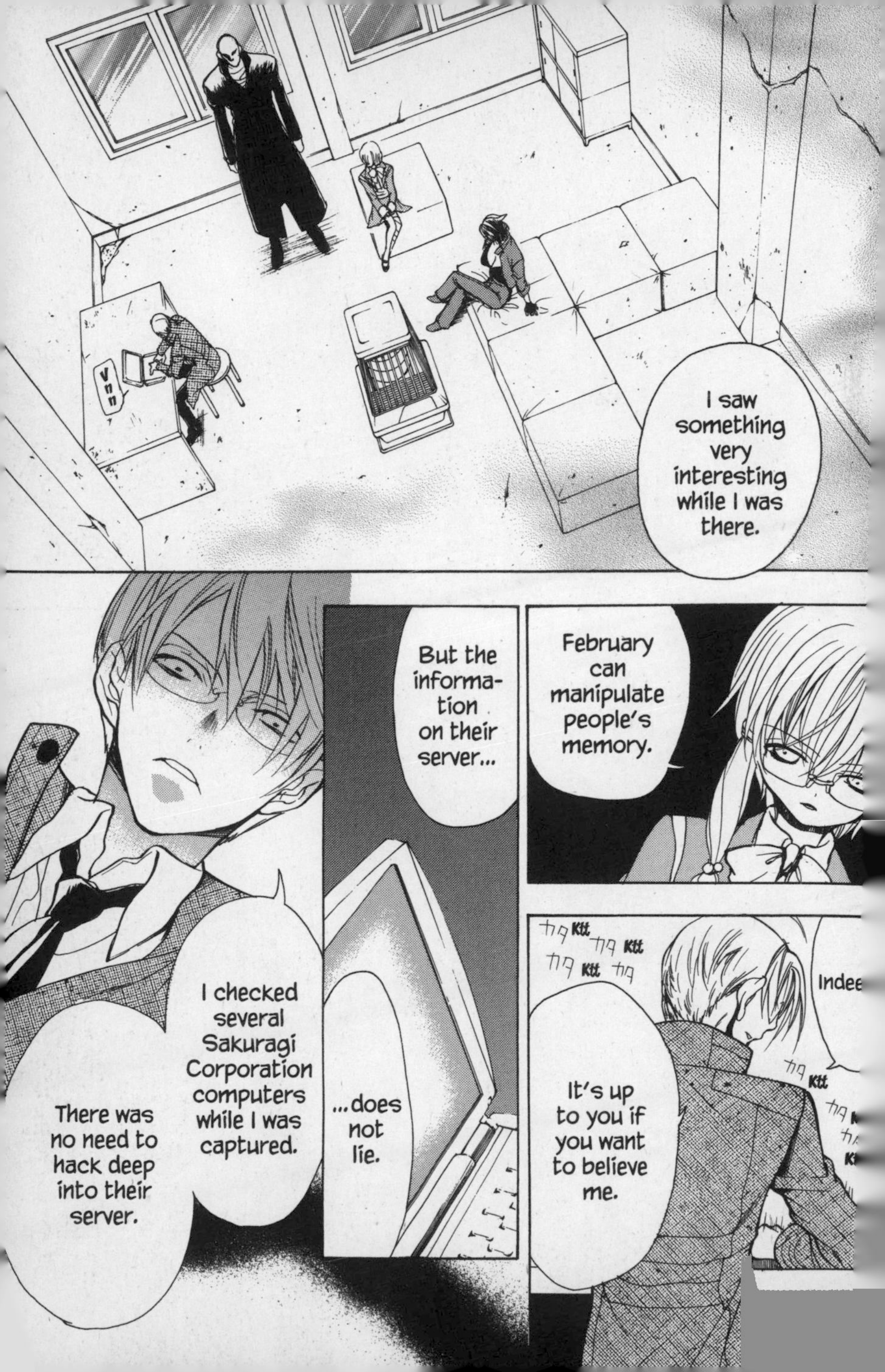
Vnn
I saw something very interesting while I was there.
February can manipulate people's memory.
カタ Ktt カタ Ktt カタ Ktt カタ
Indee
It's up to you if you want to believe me.
カタ Ktt
But the information on their server...
...does not lie.
I checked several Sakuragi Corporation computers while I was captured.
There was no need to hack deep into their server.

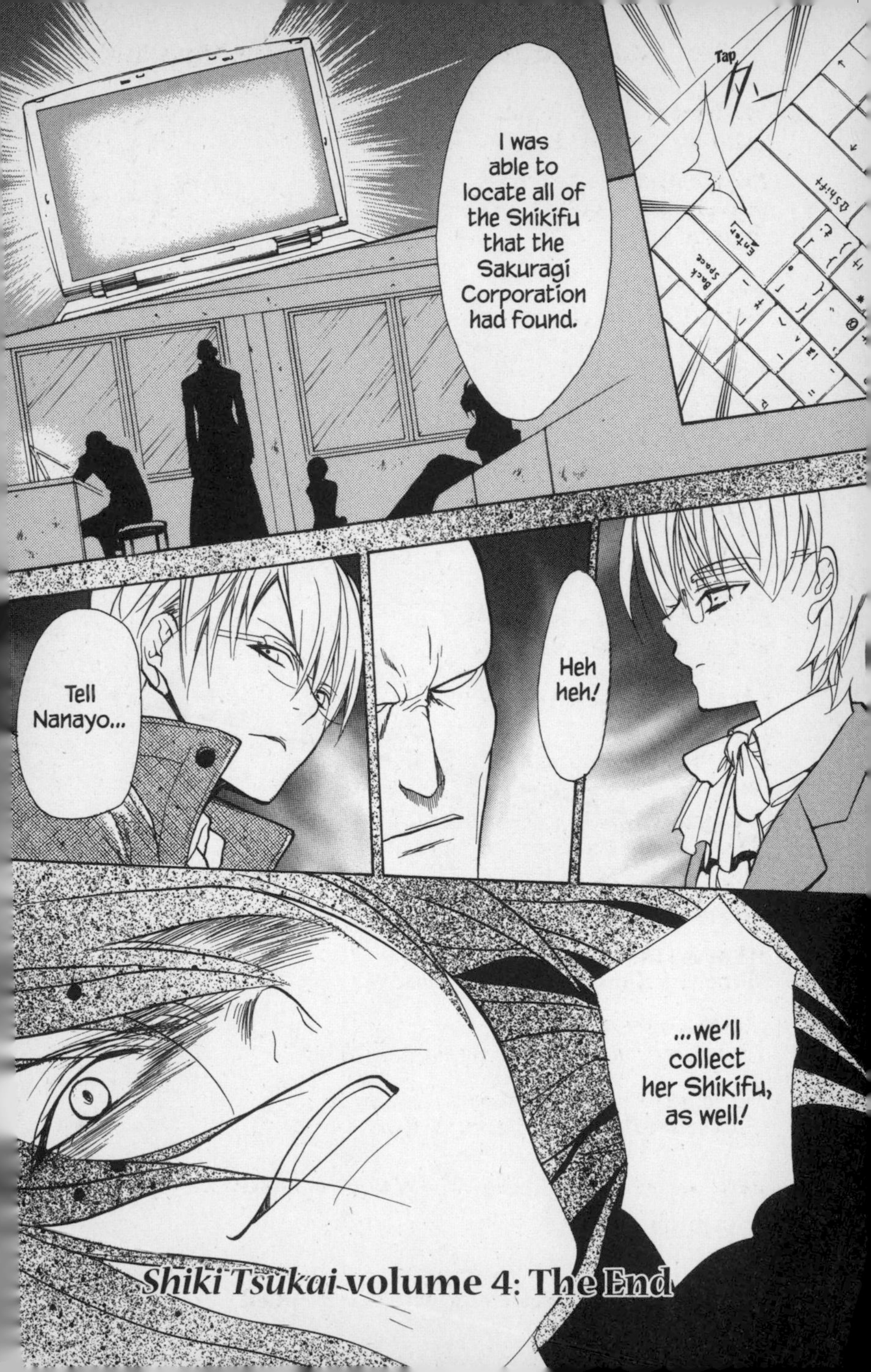
Tap
I was able to locate all of the Shikifu that the Sakuragi Corporation had found.
Heh heh!
Tell Nanayo...
...we'll collect her Shikifu, as well!
Shiki Tsukai volume 4: The End

Staff List (Birthday: Birthstone: Meaning)

Written by: To-ru Zekuu
(September 8: Akoya Pearl: Dignity)

Manga by: Yuna Takanagi
(November 24: Cobaltian Calcite: Anxiety Relief)

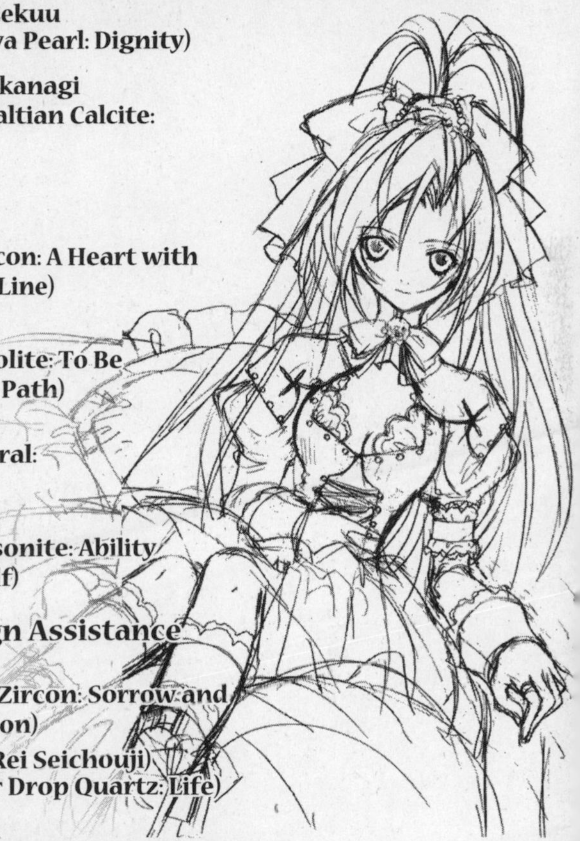

STAFF

Nemu Akatsuki
(April 10: White Zircon: A Heart with Everything on the Line)

Kira Ryuhi
(July 1: Bloodshot Iolite: To Be Directed Toward a Path)

Yu Hikawa
(August 28: Pink Coral: Cherishing Love)

Kouta Amatsuki
(November 20: Hessonite: Ability to Convince Oneself)

Character Design Assistance

Ouji
(January 5: Golden Zircon: Sorrow and Removal of Suspicion)

Takehiko Harada (Rei Seichouji)
(February 19: Water Drop Quartz: Life)

Okama
(May 25: Blue Amber: Quietly Burning Heart)

Hiroyuki Utatane (Mina Suzukure)
(June 15: Yellow Jasper: Safe Travel)

Yun Kouga (Nanayo Rangetsu)
(July 9: Brown Diamond: Unyielding Belief)

Kenichi Muraeda (Kureha Kazamatsuri)
(September 5: Golden Pearl: Mature)

Season Symbol & Shikifu Design Assistance

t-Design Lab

Naoki
(November 24: Cobaltian Calcite: Anxiety Relief)

■ We did it! It's volume 4. It's always great to see our books get published after all the work that gets put into them. Now, for the author's comments: For this volume, I'd like to discuss the character names. I'm sure there are many people who aren't familiar with Japanese calendar terms, but please enjoy.

Moe Mutsuki: January

Her last name is from "Mutsuki," the month name for January under the lunisolar calendar. Her first name was taken from "Moyutsuki," another name for January. I took the first kanji from "Moyutsuki," and the first kanji by itself is read as "Moe."

Rei Seichouji: February

Her last name comes from "Seichoutsuki," another name for February under the lunisolar calendar. Her family owns a temple, so I put the kanji for "temple" ("ji") at the end. Her first name comes from "Reigetsu"—another name for February. Actually, Rei's real name should be Rei Seichoutsuki.

Koyomi Sakuragi: March

Her last name comes from "Sakurazuki," another name for March under the lunisolar calendar. Her first name comes from "Koyomi," as in "calendar" in Japanese. (I once created a video game character with her last name as "Sakuragi." A lot of my heroines' names are Sakuragi.)

Shunten Ou

She's known as the "Middle of Spring." April symbolizes Spring and the heavens, but she has yet to appear.

Satsuki Inanae: May

Both her first and last name come from alternate names for May under the lunisolar calendar. "Inanaezuki" is a given, but how can I resist using "Satsuki" (another name for May under the lunisolar calendar) for her name in *Shiki Tsukai*?!

That's how I named all the characters! (Laugh)
Hope to see you in volume 5.

Drawn & Written by To-ru Zekuu

Shiki

Tsukai

Volume

Four

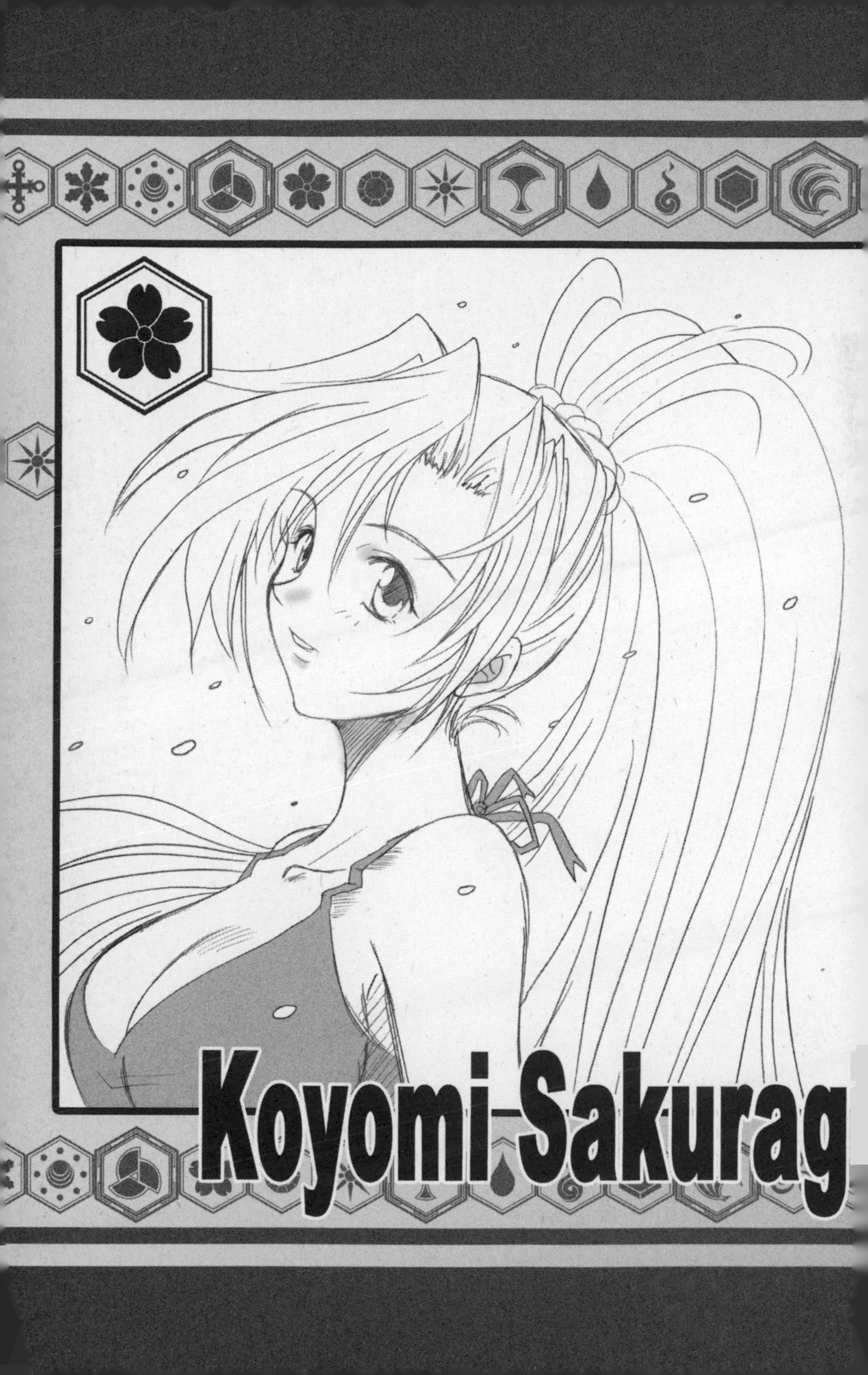
Koyomi Sakurag

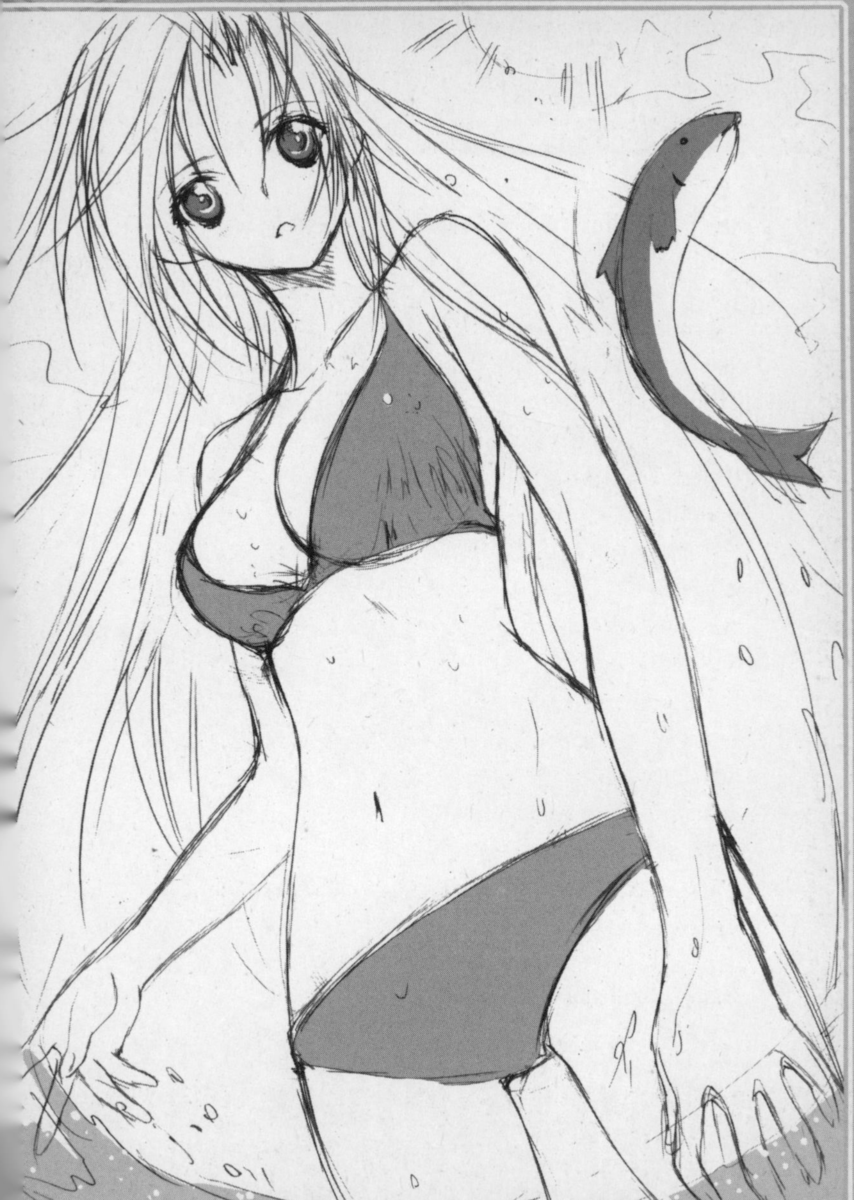

Shiki Tsukai *volume 4 has arrived!!*

Time flies. I've already drawn four volumes. Looking back, a lot of things have happened, but I realized no mechs have appeared! Like a giant robot! (Laugh) I doubt I would ever draw one for this series; if I have to, I'm going to be in trouble. ^ ^;;

I love mechs, robots, and battle-related machines, so I actually read and watch a lot of sci-fi stuff, but there's no way I can draw it myself!!

The story takes place in Winter, but for now, for all intents and purposes, this column is Summer. I drew a color page of Rei and Kureha in bathing suits. I'm sure those two are unstoppable together. I want to see them play beach volleyball!

Starting with Koyomi, I've drawn most of the female characters in bathing suits but… (Satsuki is in a bathing suit in an upcoming chapter!) Mina Suzukure is the only character I haven't drawn yet. What kind of bathing suit would she wear?? I couldn't think of anything, so I decided not to draw her. Come to think of it, she controls water, so maybe it makes sense that she doesn't wear anything.

Hope to see you in volume 5.

Yuna Takanagi

Shiki Tsukai

366-Day Calendar

Twelve-Month Ability Chart

Season Incantation Chart

Season Incantation Collection

Character Design Collection

366-Day Calendar

As long as time flows and the seasons change, everyone has the potential to become a Shiki Tsukai. What's your birthstone? Check it out!

1 JANUARY

Garnet – Chastity / Friendship / Loyalty / Perseverance

January 1	Imperial Jade	Immortality
January 2	Landscape Agate	Ability to avoid misfortune
January 3	Topazolite	Good news is on its way
January 4	Crisocola	Mentally sound
January 5	Golden Zircon	Sorrow and removal of suspicion
January 6	Star Garnet	Divine ability to make things happen
January 7	Ammolite	Memories of the past
January 8	Chrome Tourmaline	Strengthen one's inner self
January 9	Hydrogrossularite	Love becomes true
January 10	Gold	Helpful advice and strength
January 11	Specularite	Ability to recognize oneself
January 12	Obsidian	Eliminate distraction
January 13	Fowlerie	Binding love
January 14	Fresh Water Pearl	A harmonious love
January 15	Pigeon Blood	Eternalize
January 16	Blue Moonstone	Love between adults
January 17	Antimony	Defense against evil
January 18	Roselite	Symbol of hope
January 19	Amblygonite	Power that last an eternity
January 20	Snow Flake Obsidian	Sustained love
January 21	Peacock Color Opal	A feeling of a proposal
January 22	Star Beryl	Grace
January 23	Alexandrite-type Garnet	Change of night and day
January 24	Milky Quartz	Motherly love
January 25	Sardonyx	A happy marriage
January 26	Pyrope	Flames of love
January 27	Almandine	Being proactive leads to victory
January 28	Pink Topaz	Recovering strength and intelligence
January 29	Phantom Crystal	Ice fossil
January 30	Parti-Colored Fluorite	Past and future
January 31	Alexandrite Cat's Eye	Doubt, choice, and transformation

2 FEBRUARY

Amethyst – Ideal / Authority / Sincerity / Truth

February 1	Ulexite	Heart to see through all
February 2	Conch Pearl	Beloved
February 3	Melanite	War and victory
February 4	Bicolor Amethyst	Awakening
February 5	Prumusmume Stone	Overcome hardship
February 6	Grey Star Sapphire	Good news brought with dawn
February 7	Cairngorm	Rules and guardianship
February 8	Rutilated Quartz	Happy family
February 9	Red Jasper	Right decision
February 10	Red Tiger Eye	Fate of destruction and creation
February 11	Water Worn	Flow of time
February 12	Yellow Spinel	Self love, puberty
February 13	Bicolor Fluorite	Appeal of having two sides
February 14	Pink Opal	Encounter of love
February 15	Pink Zircon	Ease of pain
February 16	Dravite	Events in life
February 17	Tiger Iron	Courage, strong conviction
February 18	Orange Topaz	Knowledge and logic
February 19	Water Drop Quartz	Life
February 20	Brown Onyx	Chastity
February 21	Horn	Yearning of love
February 22	Cat's Eye Quartz	Prediction of the future
February 23	Cherry Pink Ruby	Love's distrust
February 24	White Pearl	Sincerity
February 25	Phantom Amethyst	Illusion
February 26	Gold Quartz	Eye to see the world
February 27	Cuprite	Multiple faces
February 28	Parasite Holed Coral	Perseverance
February 29	Pallasite	All things taking flight

3 MARCH

Aquamarine – Luminosity / Knowledge
Bloodstone – Devotion / Gallant

March 1	Fluorite	Secret Love
March 2	Shell Opal	Unite
March 3	Pink Beryl	Appeal of a sweet disposition
March 4	Silver	Symbol of youth
March 5	Royal Blue Sapphire	Happiness and Lifespan
March 6	Copal	Silence and movement
March 7	Shell Opal	Clarity
March 8	Smithsonite	Guardianship
March 9	Silver Pearl	Reverence of religion
March 10	Howlite	Symbol of something sublime
March 11	Inesite	Passion
March 12	Kyanite	Obedient and pure
March 13	Yellow Diamond	Changing peace
March 14	Colorless Spinel	Innocence
March 15	Orange Moonstone	Love moving fast
March 16	Rose Quartz	To convey love
March 17	Dioptase	Live free
March 18	Kaolinite	Caring heart
March 19	Bicolor Quartz	Arrival of Spring
March 20	Euclase	Well-considered plan
March 21	Iron	Amazing power
March 22	Sogdianite	Resurrection
March 23	Picture Jasper	Fantasize
March 24	Green Quartz	Calming the emotions
March 25	Peach Zircon	Relief from pain
March 26	Platinum	Susceptible heart
March 27	Purple Zircon	Too many conversations
March 28	Pink Diamond	Coming of love
March 29	Green Diamond	Graceful
March 30	Angel Skin Coral	Unchanging heart
March 31	Orthoclase	Attain one's goal

4 APRIL

Diamond – Innocence / Eternal Bond / Unyielding

April 1	Herkimer Diamond	Dream
April 2	Celestite	Cleansing of the Soul
April 3	Zeolite	Regeneration and harvest from the Earth
April 4	Gem Silica	Happiness and prosperity
April 5	Colorless Sapphire	Holy power and wisdom
April 6	Blue Diamond	Safety
April 7	Brazilianite	Intelligence
April 8	Padparadsha Sapphire	Flower of light
April 9	Cerasite	Mental beauty and purity
April 10	White Zircon	A heart with everything on the line
April 11	Bournite	Sense of aggression
April 12	Pink Fluorite	Mystical
April 13	Violet Pearl	Sense of pride
April 14	Colorless Topaz	Genius
April 15	Peacock Green Pearl	Love for nature
April 16	Hiddenite	Pure and modest
April 17	Green Spinel	Hope, faith, and happiness
April 18	Axinite	Continuation of effort
April 19	Violet Zircon	Earthliness and spirituality
April 20	Chloromelanite	Deceit and truth
April 21	Andalusite	Feeling of love
April 22	Astrophyllite	Trusting love
April 23	Desert Rose	Love and wisdom
April 24	Kunzite	Premonition of a future lover
April 25	Plasma	Binary decision
April 26	Sugilite	Eternal and unchanging love
April 27	Carnelian	Lucid love
April 28	Kimberlite	Guardian of love
April 29	Magnetite	Consistency
April 30	Sillimanite	Warning

7 JULY

Ruby – Passion / Freedom / Courage

Bloodshot Iolite	To be directed toward a path
Parisite	Law of nature
Rock Crystal	Heart that seeks pleasure
Diopside	Direction toward happiness
Anatase	Happiness toward the future
Apache Tears	Mystery
Star Rose Quartz	Rendezvous
Milky Opal	Excitement of love
Brown Diamond	Unyielding belief
Spodumene	Unlimited love
Cream Opal	New encounter
Red Beryl	Higher consciousness
Chrysoberyl	Brilliance
Three Color Fluorite	Multi-faced
Goethite	Spiritual power
Azurite	Ability to contemplate
Aventurine	Bright future
Labradorite Feldspar	Secret meeting
Hydro Rhodochrosite	Justice
Aquamarine Cat's Eye	Ray of light
Blue Jasper	Fine tuned emotions
Flower Obsidian	A new journey
Watermelon Tourmaline	Mounting happiness
Witherite	Poison and antidote
Shell	A beautiful vow
Fossil Coral	Conquer
Grey Diamond	To being from a minor role
Almandine Spinel	Strength and caring
Black Opal	Menace
Epidote	To be released from the past
Red Zircon	Time of peace

8 AUGUST

Peridot – Friendship / Harmony between husband and wife

1	Citrine	Sweet memory
2	Blue Quartz	Birth of life
3	Chrysoberyl Cat's Eye	Golden Eye
4	Marcasite	Memory and supposition
5	Cat's Eye Moonstone	Opportunity of love
6	Dark Green Zircon	Mental healing
7	Yellow Apatite	Suspicion
8	Rutile	Arrow of love
9	Chalcopyrite	Removal of oblivion
10	Iolite	To heighten one's spiritual power
11	Yellow Sapphire	Concentration
12	Concha Agate	Rules of nature
13	Yellow Zircon	Sorrows from birth
14	Fire Opal	Someone in love
15	Blue Lace Agate	To move one's soul
16	Labradorite	Longing
17	Pyrite	Ability to shelter
18	Orange Pearl	Recovery
19	Calcite	Splendor and prosperity
20	Star Ruby	Core
21	Jet	Oblivion
22	White Coral	Purify
23	Eosphorite	Offer one's unchanging love
24	Lava	Lover
25	Fire Agate	Belief
26	Turquoise Blue	Divine love
27	Apatite	Confuse
28	Pink Coral	Cherishing Love
29	Cactus Amethyst	Change
30	Rainbow Obsidian	Various sorts
31	Moss Agate	Nourishment for the soul

5 MAY

Emerald – Happiness / Integrity / Spousal Love / Noble / Health / Wisdom

May 1	Amazonite	Time has come
May 2	Yellow Beryl	Enduring love
May 3	Green Zircon	Wish for peace
May 4	Forsterite	Power of greatness
May 5	Red Coral	Child's heart
May 6	Idoclase	Promise
May 7	Creedite	Maturing of the heart
May 8	Emerald Cat's Eye	Imagination
May 9	Black Pearl	Silent strength
May 10	Robin's Egg Blue	Heart yearning for release
May 11	Lace Agate	Silent courage
May 12	Cacoxenite	Beginning of consciousness
May 13	Ivory	Pure, strength from reason
May 14	Blue Green Zircon	Disappearing strength
May 15	Red Jadeite	Ability to make decisions
May 16	Tektites	Freedom
May 17	Purple Sapphire	Memory of first love
May 18	Goshenite	Elegance
May 19	Noselite	Overçome a crisis
May 20	Zaratite	Inner strength
May 21	Opalized wood	Union and harmony
May 22	Dendritic Quartz	A satisfying growth
May 23	Andradite	Loyalty
May 24	Adularia	Plan
May 25	Blue Amber	Quietly burning heart
May 26	Copper	Prisoner of love
May 27	Verdelite	Perseverance
May 28	White Chalcedony	Gracefulness
May 29	Xalostocite	Victory of joy
May 30	Tsavolite	Influential
May 31	Smokey Quartz	Comforting peace

6 JUNE

Pearl – Wealth / Health
Moonstone – Anticipation of Love / A Fulfilling Love

June 1	Color Change Sapphire	Two-faced
June 2	Clear Amber	Fulfillment of a dream
June 3	Phenacite	Complete change in mood
June 4	Odontolite	Offence and defense
June 5	Alexandrite	Two-faced
June 6	Silicified Wood	Union and change
June 7	Pink Pearl	Persevering love
June 8	Sanidine	Fusion of supernatural powers
June 9	Ulexite	Brilliant mind
June 10	Quartz	Harmony, fusion and to strengthen
June 11	White Labradorite	Good rumor
June 12	Mabe Pearl	Allure
June 13	Uvarovite	Shy with a talent to steal hearts
June 14	Cyprine	Insight
June 15	Yellow Jasper	Safe travel
June 16	Blue Opal	A refreshing show of affection
June 17	Neptunite	Continuation of life
June 18	Argentite	Defense from evil
June 19	Black Star Sapphire	Soul of the dead
June 20	Green Fluorite	Secret virtue
June 21	Serpentine	Shelter
June 22	Sun Stone	Shine
June 23	Anyolite	Modest love
June 24	Water Opal	A maiden's love
June 25	Malachite	Perceptiveness and imagination
June 26	Spessartine	Loyalty and the will to obey
June 27	Liddicoatite	Various appeal
June 28	Blue Zircon	Illusion and dreaming heart
June 29	Jasper	Self-control
June 30	Ulexite	Insight

11 NOVEMBER

Topaz – Friendship / Loyalty / Prosperity

November 1	Cinnamon Stone	A chance for success
November 2	Black Onyx	Thinking based on religion
November 3	Golden Sapphire	Shining appeal and brilliance
November 4	Scepter Quartz	Joy of birth
November 5	Nephrite	Charming eyes
November 6	Sphalerite	Balance and moderation
November 7	Pit Amber	Embrace, a grand love
November 8	Red Topaz	Life and prosperity
November 9	Tortoise Shell	Long life and depth
November 10	Fossil	Ancestor's guardianship
November 11	Black Diamond	Beginning of happiness
November 12	Violet Sapphire	Graceful transformation
November 13	Crystal Opal	Strengthen of the inner self
November 14	Lavender Jade	A little rumor
November 15	Crimson Coral	A generous and silent love
November 16	Ammonite	Variations of thought
November 17	Green Rutile Quartz	Grab an opportunity
November 18	Anthophyllite	Generosity and plentiful love
November 19	Blue Topaz	Culture and learning
November 20	Hessonite	Ability to convince one's self
November 21	White Jadeite	Purified soul
November 22	Yellow Opal	Hidden instinct
November 23	Keshi Pearl	Momentary rest
November 24	Cobaltian Calcite	To be relieved from feeling anxious
November 25	Red Amber	Appeal of a little demon
November 26	Scapolite	Thinking towards the future
November 27	Petrified Wood	Fusion
November 28	Orangeish Brown Topaz	Guardianship and infinite patience
November 29	Alexandrite Tourmaline	Love and saga
November 30	Star Enstatite	Deep trust

12 DECEMBER

Lapis Lazuli – Health / Love and Harmony
Turquoise – Valor / Prosperity / Success / Life

December 1	Iron Opal	A caring gesture
December 2	Black Coral	A cool wit
December 3	Meteorite	A regeneration of the soul
December 4	Sodalite	Subconscious and manifestation
December 5	Angelite	Shining truth
December 6	Enstatite	Innocent justice
December 7	Gypsum	Furtile earth
December 8	Rubellite	Proactive action
December 9	Alabaster	To bring victory
December 10	Blue John Fluorite	A balanced heart
December 11	Cassiterite	A well planned strategy
December 12	Soft Pink Zircon	Aphrodisiac
December 13	Apophyllite	Clairvoyance
December 14	Pink Sapphire	Lovely
December 15	Trapiche Ruby	Transformation and challenge
December 16	Azuromalachite	Cooperativeness
December 17	Labradorite	Passionate and dangerous love
December 18	Tourmalinated Quartz	Oppositions unite
December 19	White Opal	Divine guardianship
December 20	Hemimorphite	Strange opposite
December 21	Black Moonstone	A new journey for two
December 22	Uvite	Creative thinking
December 23	Orange Jade	A heartwarming confession of love
December 24	Staurolite	Strong ability to shelter
December 25	Cross Stone	Holy pact
December 26	Purple Diamond	Hidden secret
December 27	Moldavite	Symbol of love
December 28	Rhodochrosite	Welcome a new love
December 29	Faustite	Regeneration and the power of life
December 30	Kosmochlor	Nature's knowledge
December 31	Ajoite	Purification of all

9 SEPTEMBE

Sapphire – Sincerity / Earnest

September 1	Tanzanite	Prideful
September 2	High Quartz	Victorious love
September 3	Red Diamond	Secret to creation
September 4	Sphene	Will of the universe
September 5	Golden Pearl	Mature
September 6	Zoisite	Symbol of spiritual pow
September 7	Jacinth	Relieved
September 8	Akoya Pearl	Dignity
September 9	Aragonite	Show one's ability
September 10	Danburite	Vast knowledge
September 11	Rainbow Fluorite	Wish come true
September 12	Fayalite	Fated bond
September 13	Golden Beryl	Bright [illegible] day
September 14	Iron Rose	Courage, power to save
September 15	Paraiba Tourmaline	Return to the starting
September 16	Prehnite	Natural beauty
September 17	Dioptase	Reunion
September 18	Mandarin Garnet	Wealth
September 19	Lazurite	Meditation
September 20	Blue Spinel	Spice of love
September 21	Selenite	Self consciousness
September 22	Zircon	Innocence
September 23	Ametrine	Light and shadow
September 24	Demantoid	To run
September 25	Bicolor Tourmaline	Symmetry and harmo
September 26	Orange Diamond	Promised love
September 27	Trapiche Sapphire	Living freely
September 28	Amethyst Quartz	Sound thinking
September 29	Imperial Topaz	Remarkable strength
September 30	Blue Star Sapphire	A guide to knowledge

10 OCTOB

Tourmaline – Wealth / Health
Opal – Anticipation of Love / A Fulfilling L

October 1	Elbaite	To re-create
October 2	High Quartz	To attain
October 3	Violet Diamond	Appealing relationshi
October 4	Opal Jasper	Precise intervals
October 5	Larimar	Silent observer
October 6	Chrysoprase	Fertility and happines
October 7	Rhodonite	Heighten one's self
October 8	Blue Chalcedony	Reminiscence
October 9	Blue Onyx	Good news
October 10	Tourmaline Cat's Eye	Eye opener
October 11	Rhodolite	Proactive love
October 12	Party Colored Sapphire	Calming the hatred
October 13	Hematite	Guide to victory
October 14	Trapiche Emerald	Rotation
October 15	Aventurine Quartz	Opportunity for love
October 16	White Onyx	A guide to success
October 17	Magnetite	To overcome fear
October 18	Blue Agate	Artistic
October 19	Scarab	Regeneration and eter
October 20	Chalcosiderite	Wish
October 21	Schorl	Recover one's streng
October 22	Lepidolite	Reform
October 23	Thulite	Mystical recovery
October 24	Indigolite	Artistic sense
October 25	Red Spinel	Curiosity
October 26	Tiger's Eye Quartz	Ability to see through t
October 27	Hauyne	Divine occupation
October 28	Cornflower Blue Sapphire	A straight line
October 29	Matrix Turquoise	Insight and imagina
October 30	Pin-Fire Opal	Correct direction
October 31	Hawk's Eye	Decision and to move

Knowledge

JANUARY

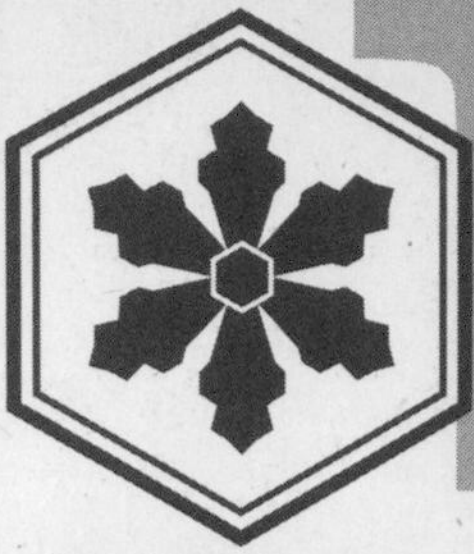

Mid-Winter month; has the ability to control "Ice." Can also use lightning and illusion incantations.

冬 *Winter*

FEBRUARY

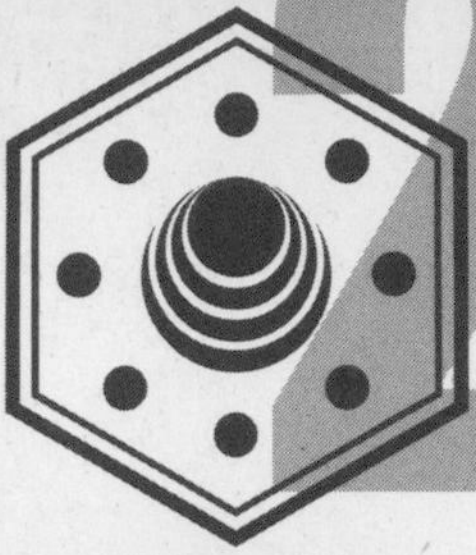

Has the ability to amplify, manipulate, and shoot "Chi." Can also use illusion incantations and has healing abilities.

冬 *Winter*

MARCH

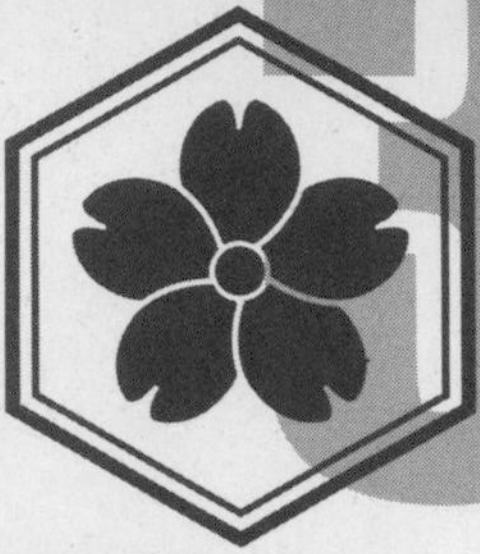

Has the ability to control "Plants." Has special power to control the wind and cherry blossoms. Can also use lightning incantations.

春 *Spring*

JULY

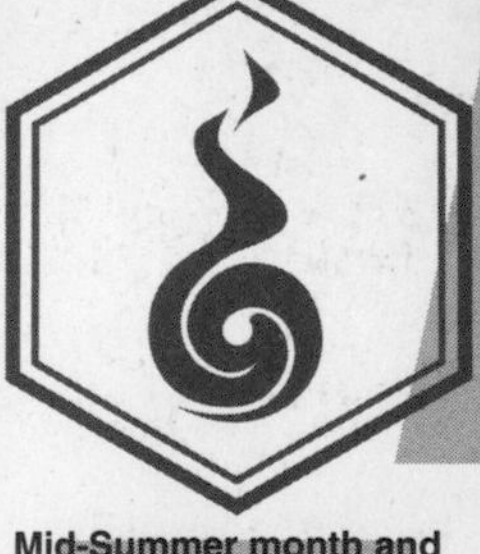

Mid-Summer month and has the ability to control "Heat." Can also use lightning incantations. The opposite of January and has many similar ability incantations.

夏 *Summer*

AUGUST

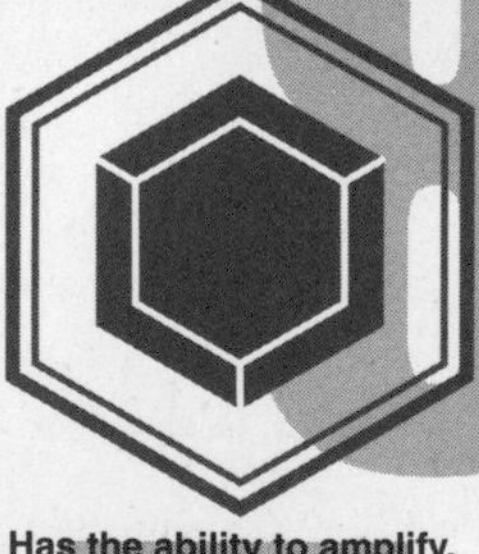

Has the ability to amplify, manipulate, and shoot "Spirit Power." Can also use healing and illusion incantations.

夏 *Summer*

SEPTEMBER

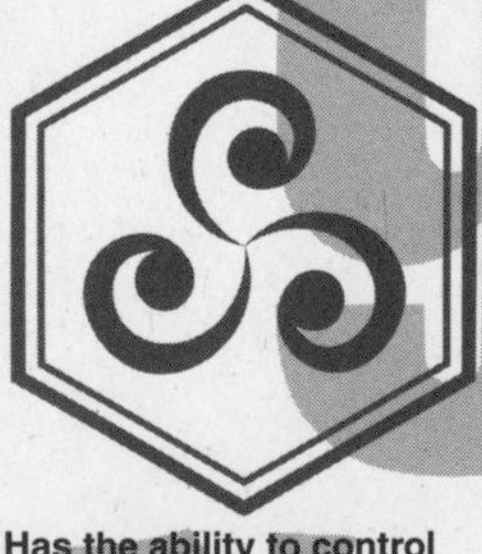

Has the ability to control "Air." Has special power to control gravity and typhoons. Can also control the wind and has strong offensive abilities.

秋 *Autumn*

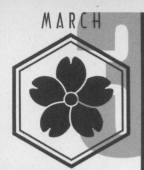

JUNE

Has the ability to control "Liquids." Has special power to control decay. Can also use defense incantations.

Summer

MAY

Has the ability to control "Light." Has special power to control heat. Can also use plant incantations.

Spring

APRIL

Mid-Spring month; has the ability to control the "Earth." Can also use lightning, plant, and magnetic incantations.

Spring

Twelve-Month Ability Chart

The Shiki Tsukai are divided into 12 different groups. Here are their abilities and the symbol of each month.

Shiki

DECEMBER

Has the ability to control and communicate with "Animals." Has incantations to arm people. Also has special abilities to control thought and has defense incantations.

Winter

NOVEMBER

Has the ability to control "Sound." Has special power to control colors. Can use cold temperature incantations. Has many abilities that affect the senses.

Autumn

OCTOBER

Mid-Fall month; has the ability to control "Metal." Can also use lightning incantations and has special defense abilities. The opposite of April and has similar ability incantations.

Autumn

Every season incantation that the Shiki Tsukai use is predetermined. It is thought the Shiki Tsukai learn the season incantations with guidance from their Shikifu.

The phrases needed to use the incantations.

Shows the incantation type.

72 Kou	Incantation Variety	Incantation Known name	Incantation Type
Grains begin to sprout under the snow. Water celery plants shall grow remarkably fast.	Silent Chill	Frost Pillar	Special: Snow
Water beneath the surface shall begin to flow. Male pheasants shall begin to twitter.	Ice Sin	Sinful Domain of Ice	Manipulate: Cold
	Ice Demon	Ice Demon Summon	Summon: Kijyuu
	Ice King	Silver Ice Flower	Weapon/Armor: Snow
Japanese butterbur plants begin to bud. Thick ice shall cover the mountain streams. Hens begin laying their eggs.	White Flower		Shoot: Snow
	White Cry		Special: Snow
	White Night		Special: Illusion
Hens begin laying their eggs. Eastern winds shall melt the ice.	White Night	Midnight Sun of Snow	Special: Illusion
Japanese nightingales begin to chirp in the mountain villages. Fish shall jump through the cracks in the ice.	Chi Bullets	Ice Storm Bullets / Rime Snow Bullets	Shoot: Chi
	Chi Beast	Sleeting Snow Bullets	Summon: Kijyuu
	Chi Weapon/Armor	Frost Wind Bullets	Weapon/Armor: Chi
Rain shall fall and the Earth will soak up the water. The mist shall begin to flow.	Sacred Ground	Ice Crane	Manipulate: Chi
	Holy Heal	Divine Healing	Special: Healing
The grass and the trees shall lay their roots. Hibernating insects shall appear from their burrows.	Holy Eye		Special: Plant
Peach tree flowers begin to blossom. Caterpillars become small white butterflies.	Tree Shadow		Manipulate: Bugs
	Tree Banish	Tree Summon, Peach Wall	Weapon/Armor: Plants
	Tree God	Tree God Summon	Summon: Kijyuu
Sparrows shall begin to build their nests. Cherry trees shall begin to blossom. Thunder can be heard from the distance.	Blue Sky	Spring Storm	
	Blue Heaven	Blue Sky Gust	
	Clear Blue Sky	Blue Winds of Conflict	Shoot: Wind
Thunder can be heard from the distance. Swallows arrive from the south.	Clear Blue Sky	Blue Heaven Adazakura	Special: Cherry Blossom
The geese shall migrate north. Rainbows appear after the rain. Reed plants begin to flower.	Stiffness		Special: Lightning
	Great Strength		Shoot: Minerals
	Strong Mind		Weapon/Armor: Minerals
The frost shall cease and the grains shall grow. Peony flowers begin to bloom.	Earthquake	Gates of Tremor	Manipulate: Earth
	Earth Dust		Special: Magnetic
	Earth Flower		Special: Plant

Season Incantation Chart

SHI	KI
TSU	KAI

The four Shiki Tsukai groups: shows which months belong to which season.

The Shiki Tsukai can use only the incantations corresponding to the Sigil dates on their Shikifu.

SHIKI TSUKAI

Season	Month	Sigil Dates	Month Name & 24 Sekki		Meaning of 24 Sekki
			Month Name	24 Sekki	
Winter	January	1/1–1/4	Mutsuki	Touji	The Dark Emperor takes the throne and the sun shall not rise.
		1/5–1/9			
		1/10–1/14		Shoukan	Cold air shall encase all as we enter the dead of Winter.
		1/15–1/19			
		1/20–1/24			
		1/25–1/29		Daikan	A feast to the arctic cold begins and the cold shall find its light
		1/30–1/31			
Winter	February	2/1–2/3	Kisaragi	Daikan	A feast to the arctic cold begins and the cold shall find its light.
		2/4–2/8			
		2/9–2/13		Risshun	Spring arrives from the North in search of its Zassetsu.
		2/14–2/18			
		2/19–2/23		Usui	Snow shall cease, thus turning into rain, and the Blue Emperor shall weave his water.
		2/24–2/28			
Spring	March	3/1–3/5	Yayoi	Usui	Snow shall cease, thus turning into rain, and the Blue Emperor shall weave his water.
		3/6–3/10			
		3/11–3/15		Keichitsu	Those who hide in the earth shall rise with the light.
		3/16–3/20			
		3/21–3/25		Shunbun	Days and nights have split and celebrate the coming of Spring.
		3/26–3/30			
		3/31			
Spring	April	4/1–4/4	Uzuki	Shunbun	Days and nights have split and celebrate the coming of Spring.
		4/5–4/9			
		4/10–4/14		Seimei	A time when all is full of life and the flowers begin to bloom.
		4/15–4/19			
		4/20–4/24		Kokuu	The tears of Heaven shall wet the crop lands.
		4/25–4/29			
		4/30			

72 Kou	Incantation Variety	Incantation Known name	Incantation Type
Peony flowers begin to bloom. Frogs begin to croak.	Earth Flower		Special: Plant
Worms come out of the ground. Bamboo shoots will begin to appear.	Light Waves	Mirage of Light	Shoot: Light
	Light Wings	Wings of Light/ Lovebird of Light	Manipulate: Light
	Light Fangs	Light Fang Summon	Summon: Kijyuu
Tree worms will begin to eat the mulberry leaves. Safflowers are all in full bloom.	Sudden Sun		Weapon/Armor: Light
	Silent Sun	Silent Spring Light	Special: Sun
	Sun Cease	Dancing Spring Light	Special: Defense
Grains shall grow ripe for the autumn harvest. Mantis birth.	Sun Cease	Shadow Cicada Shell	Special: Defense
Fireflies shall appear from the marshes. Plums shall ripen and turn yellow.	Water Ogre	Water Ogre Summon	Summon: Kijyuu
	Water Fowl	Waterfowl Flying Rain/Waterfowl Fog Rain	Manipulate: Liquid
	Water Dragon	Fleeting Rain Water/Dragon's Rain	Weapon/Armor: Water
The Spica prunellae shall wither. Iris flowers begin to bloom.	Striking Beast	Claws of Rain/Beasts of Rain	Shoot: Water
	Burial	Beasts of the Ocean Fog/ Decaying Rain	Special: Decay
Crowdipper plants begin to grow. Warm winds shall blow.	Silent Attack	Decaying Blossom	Special: Flame
Lotus flowers begin to bloom. Falcons shall take flight.	Fiery Sin		Manipulate: Heat
	Fiery Cry	Inferno Demon Summon	Summon: Kijyuu
	Enou (Fire King)	Enou Blaze	Weapon/Armor: Flame
The tung tree shall bear fruit. The ground shall sweat and the air shall become humid.	Fire Flower	Flowering Blaze of Wind Fire Flower Ring	Shoot: Flames
	Fire Cry	Fire Lighting of Screams	Special: Lightning
The ground shall sweat and the air shall become humid. Heavy rain shall fall at times.	Fire Cry	Scream of the Gods	Special: Lightning
	Fire Night		Special: Illusion
A cool breeze sets in. Cicadas begin to sing their songs. Thick mists shall settle in.	Bullets of darkness		Shoot: Spirit
	Beast of darkness		Summon: Kijyuu
	Dark Cloak		Weapon/Armor: Spirit
The boll covering the cotton fiber shall open. The summer heat finally eases.	Divine land		Manipulate: Spirit
	Divine restoration		Special: Heal
The summer heat finally eases. Crops are ready for harvest.	Divine restoration		Special: Heal
	Divine Eyes		Special: Air
The frost on the grass shines white. The gray wagtail bird begins to chirp.	Wind shadow	Winds of Darkness	Manipulate: Gravity
	Banished Wind	Forbidden Autumn Winds	Weapon/Armor: Air
	Wind God		Summon: Kijyuu
Swallows begin their journey home south. The roars of thunder ceases. Insects seal the entrance of their burrows.	Fierce Blast	Fierce Blasting Winds	Shoot: Wind
	Fierce Heaven	Fierce Heavenly Winds Heavenly Winds of Fire	Special: Storm
Insects seal the entrance of their burrows. It is the time to dry out the fields.	Fierce Heaven		Special: Storm
	Fierce Sky		Special: Lightning
The geese arrive from their migratory journey. Chrysanthemum flowers begin to bloom.	Mineral Character		Shoot: Metal
	Mineral Strength		Weapon/Armor: Metal
	Mineral Beast		Summon: Kijyuu
Crickets chirp by the entranceway. Frost begins to fall. Light rain falls quietly.	Lightening Tremor		Manipulate: Lightning
	Lightening Dust		Special: Defense
Light rain falls quietly. Japanese maple trees and vines begin to turn yellow.	Lightening Dust		Special: Defense
	Lightening Flower		Special: Color
Sasanqua flowers begin to bloom. The Earth shall begin to freeze. Daffodils begin to bloom.	Sound waves		Shoot: Sound
	Wings of Sound		Manipulate: Sound
	Fangs of Sound		Summon: Kijyuu
Rainbows can no longer be seen. The northern winds shall carry away the leaves.	Bright Moment		Weapon/Armor: Sound
	Bright Silence		Special: Freeze
The northern winds shall carry away the leaves. The mandarin tree leaves begin to turn yellow.	Bright Silence		Special: Freeze
	Bright Closure		Special: Defense
The Heavens close their gates and winter settles in. Bears burrow themselves for hibernation. Salmon begin to group and rise upstream.	Mind Ogre		Summon: Kijyuu
	Mind Fowl		Manipulate: Animals
	Mind Dragon		Weapon/Armor: Life
The Prunella vulgaris plant shall reveal itself. Deer shall lose their horns.	Silent Beast		Shoot: Kijyuu
	Silent Burial		Special: Thought

Season	Month	Sigil Dates	Month Name & 24 Sekki		Meaning of 24 Sekki
			Month Name	24 Sekki	
Spring	May	5/1–5/4	Satsuki	Kokuu	The tears of Heaven shall wet the crop lands.
		5/5–5/9			
		5/10–5/14		Rikka	The Blue Emperor shall bring summer and all plants shall rejoice.
		5/15–5/20			
		5/21–5/25		Shouman	A time when all life shall reach maturity.
		5/26–5/30			
		5/31			
Summer	June	6/1–6/5	Minazuki	Shouman	A time when all life shall reach maturity.
		6/6–6/10			
		6/11–6/15		Boushu	A time when all life shall reach maturity. Bearded grains shall flow with the summer stream.
		6/16–6/20			
		6/21–6/25		Geshi	The Fire Emperor shall take his throne and the sun shall remain in the heavens.
		6/26–6/30			
Summer	July	7/1–7/6	Fumizuki	Taisho	The Fire Emperor shall take his throne and the sun shall remain in the heavens.
		7/7–7/11			
		7/12–7/16		Rishuu	Heat rises and dances in the seventh evening sky.
		7/17–7/22			
		7/23–7/27		Shosho	A feast to the sweltering heat begins and thus it shall reach the temperature of the sun.
		7/28–7/31			
Summer	August	8/1	Hazuki	Taisho	A feast to the sweltering heat begins and thus it shall reach the temperature of the sun.
		8/2–8/6			
		8/7–8/11		Rishuu	The Fire Emperor will take his leave but his fiery will shall linger.
		8/12–8/16			
		8/17–8/22			
		8/23–8/27		Shosho	The heat subsides and the winds shall carry it away.
		8/28–8/31			
Fall	September	9/1	Nagazuki	Shosho	The heat subsides and the winds shall carry it away.
		9/2–9/7			
		9/8–9/12		Hakuro	The White Emperor descends and creates a trail of frost.
		9/13–9/17			
		9/18–9/22			
		9/23–9/27		Shuubun	Days and nights have split and celebrate the coming of fall.
		9/28–9/30			
Fall	October	10/1–10/2	Kannazuki	Shuubun	Days and nights have split and celebrate the coming of fall.
		10/3–10/7			
		10/8–10/12		Kanro	The dew shall embrace the cold and solidify.
		10/13–10/17			
		10/18–10/22			
		10/23–10/27		Soukou	Starry frost shall fall and begin to silence all.
		10/28–10/31			
Fall	November	11/1	Shimotsuki	Soukou	Starry frost shall fall and begin to silence all.
		11/2–11/6			
		11/7–11/11		Rittou	The White Emperor shall bring winter and thus bring rain.
		11/12–11/16			
		11/17–11/21			
		11/22–11/26		Shousetsu	Rain turns into snow and all will be blanketed in white.
		11/27–11/30			
Winter	December	12/1	Shiwasu	Shousetsu	Rain turns into snow and all will be blanketed in white.
		12/2–12/6			
		12/7–12/11		Taisetsu	Snow continues to fall and all life shall fall into slumber.
		12/12–12/16			
		12/17–12/21			
		12/22–12/26		Touji	The Dark Emperor takes the throne and the sun shall not rise.
		12/27–12/31			

Shiki Tsukai

Season Incantation Collection

Volume 3 & 4

Here we will explain the Incantations used in Volume 3 & 4.

◆ Name of Incantation ▼ User ● Season Incantation and Phrases ■ Explanation

First Incantation: Eleventh Season

◆ Winds of Darkness

▼ September: Kureha Kazamatsuri

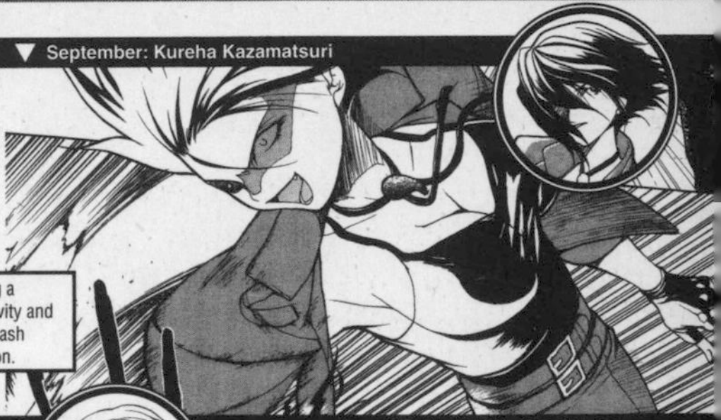

- First Phrase: Nagazuki Hakuro.
- Second Phrase: The White Emperor descends and creates a trail of frost.
- Third Phrase: The frost on the grass shines white.
- Fourth Phrase: Winds of Darkness.

■ A "Manipulate: Gravity" incantation that can be used by acquiring a September 8–12 sigil date. It's an incantation that manipulates gravity and can change the weight of an object at will. It's typically used to squash something. It's the opposite of the "March Tree Shadow" incantation.

Second Incantation: Eleventh Season

◆ Waterfowl's Flying Rain

▼ June: Mina Suzukure

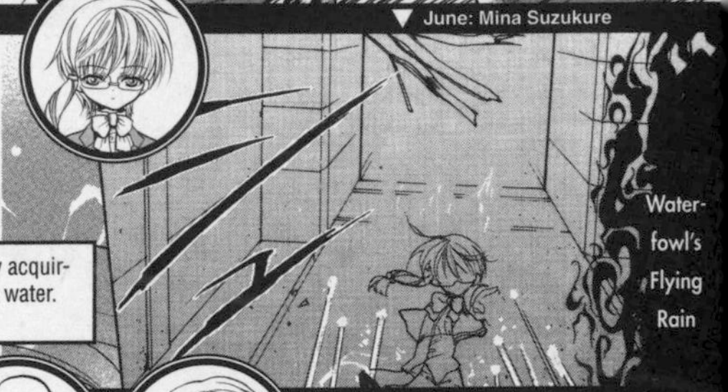
Water-fowl's Flying Rain

- First Phrase: Minazuki Boushu.
- Second Phrase: Bearded grains shall flow with the Summer stream.
- Third Phrase: Fireflies shall appear from the marshes.
- Fourth Phrase: Waterfowl's flying rain.

■ A "Manipulate: Liquid" incantation that can be used by acquiring a June 11–15 sigil date. It's an incantation that shoots water. Most liquids can be manipulated by this incantation.

Third Incantation: Sixth, Eleventh, Fifteenth Season

◆ Shadow Cicada Shell

▼ June: Rinsho Matsukaze/Mina Suzukure, May: Kengo Inanae

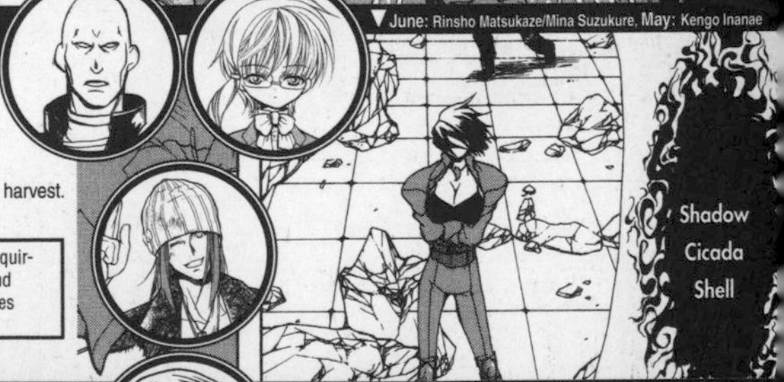
Shadow Cicada Shell

- First Phrase: Minazuki Shouman
- Second Phrase: A time when all life shall reach maturity.
- Third Phrase: Grains shall grow ripe for the Autumn harvest.
- Fourth Phrase: Shadow Cicada Shell.

■ A "Special: Defense" incantation that can be used by acquiring a May 31 / June 1–5 sigil date. It's mainly used to defend and teleport things. It was used without chanting the phrases in the book.

Fourth Incantation: Eleventh Season

◆ Fierce Heavenly Winds

▼ September: Kureha Kazamatsuri

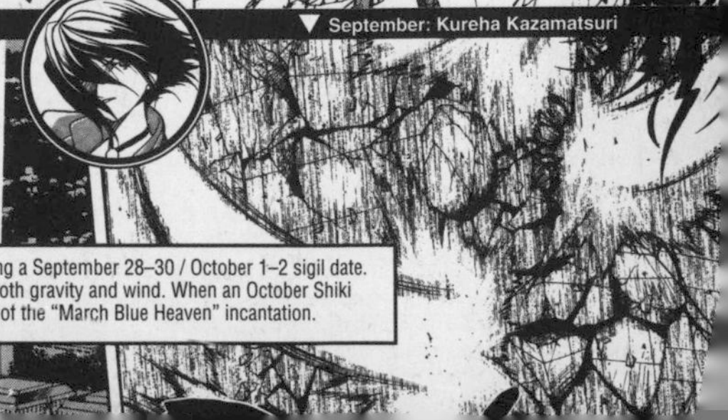

- First Phrase: Nagazuki Shunbun.
- Second Phrase: Days and nights have split and celebrate the coming of Fall.
- Third Phrase: Insects seal the entrance of their burrows.
- Fourth Phrase: Fierce Heavenly Winds.

■ A "Special: Typhoon" incantation that can be used by acquiring a September 28–30 / October 1–2 sigil date. It's a very symbolic incantation of September, as it manipulates both gravity and wind. When an October Shiki Tsukai uses this incantation, it isn't as powerful. It's the opposite of the "March Blue Heaven" incantation.

Fifth Incantation: Twelfth Season

◆ Fleeting Rain

- First Phrase: Minazuki Boushu.
- Second Phrase: Bearded grains shall flow with the Summer stream.
- Third Phrase: Fireflies shall appear from the marshes.
- Fourth Phrase: Fleeting Rain.

■ A "Manipulate: Liquid" incantation that can be used by acquiring a June 11–15 sigil date. This incantation allows the designated water to move from one location to the other.

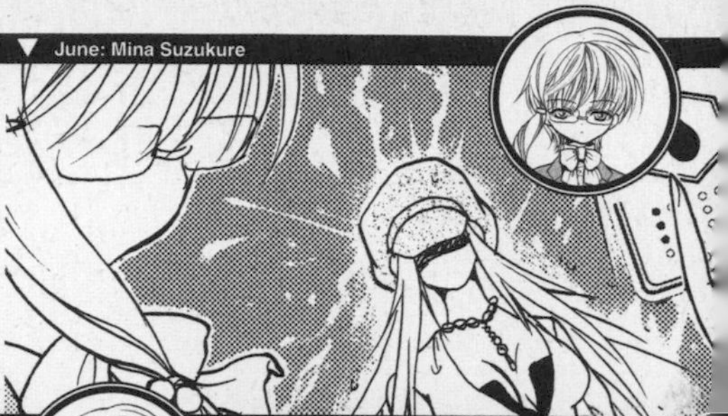

▼ June: Mina Suzukure

Sixth Incantation: Fourteenth Season

◆ Waterfowl's Foggy Rain

- First Phrase: Minazuki Boushu.
- Second Phrase: Bearded grains shall flow with the Summer stream.
- Third Phrase: Fireflies shall appear from the marshes.
- Fourth Phrase: Waterfowl's Foggy Rain.

■ A "Maniuplate: Liquid" incantation that can be used by acquiring a June 11–15 sigil date. It's an incantation that creates fog. It's a type of illusion incantation. It was used without chanting the phrases in the book.

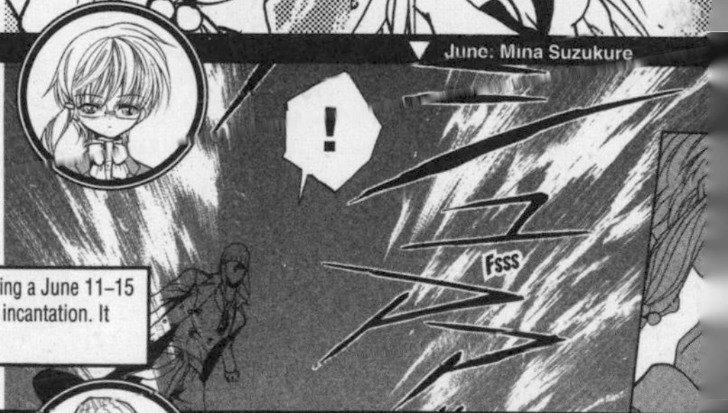
!
Fsss

▼ June: Mina Suzukure

Seventh Incantation: Fifteenth Season

◆ Light Fang Summon

- First Phrase: Satsuki Rikka.
- Second Phrase: The Blue Emperor shall bring Summer and all plants shall rejoice.
- Third Phrase: Bamboo shoots will begin to appear.
- Fourth Phrase: Light Fang Summon.

■ A "Summon: Kijyuu" incantation that can be used by acquiring a May 5–20 sigil date. There is a different Kijyuu for each sigil date. Kengo has the 15, 18, and 19 sigil dates so he can summon up to three Kijyuu, but he seems to be using all his powers on one flying dragon Kijyuu. The Kijyuu's name was Kilurian, but Satsuki didn't think it was cute, so she renamed it Ryula.

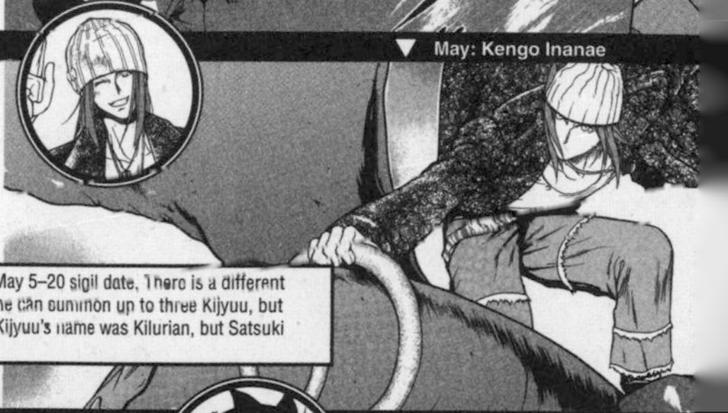

▼ May: Kengo Inanae

Eighth Incantation: Fifteenth Season

◆ Rime Snow Bullets

- First Phrase: Kisaragi Risshun.
- Second Phrase: Spring arrives from the north in search of its Zassetsu.
- Third Phrase: Eastern winds shall melt the ice.
- Fourth Phrase: Rime Snow Bullets.

■ A "Bullet: Chi" incantation that can be used by acquiring a February 4–8 sigil date. Ice forms around the chi bullets, so sleeting snow bullets are more effective than the ice storm bullets. It's a type of incantation that changes, depending on the Shiki Tsukai's ability.

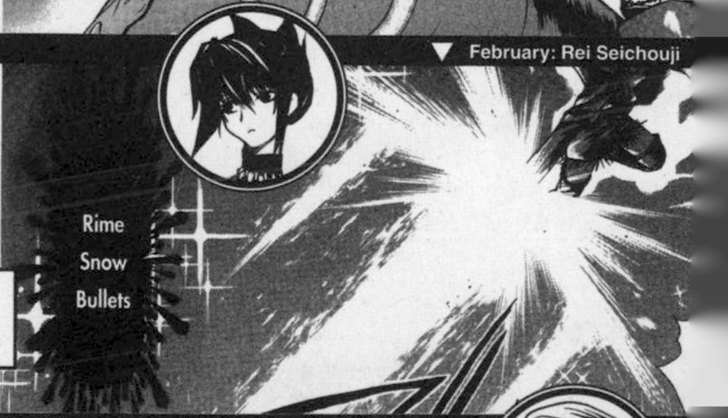
Rime
Snow
Bullets

▼ February: Rei Seichouji

Ninth Incantation: Fifteenth, Eighteenth Season

◆ Fierce Blasting Winds

- First Phrase: Nagazuki Shuubun.
- Second Phrase: Days and nights have split and celebrate the coming of Fall.
- Third Phrase: The roars of thunder shall cease.
- Fourth Phrase: Fierce Blasting Winds.

■ A "Launch: Wind" incantation that can be used by acquiring a September 23-27 sigil date. This incantation launches a piercing blast of wind. It's the opposite of the "March Blue Sky" incantation.

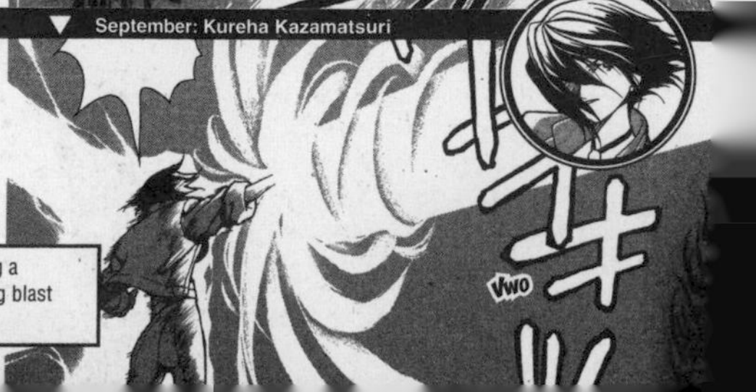
Vwo

▼ September: Kureha Kazamatsuri

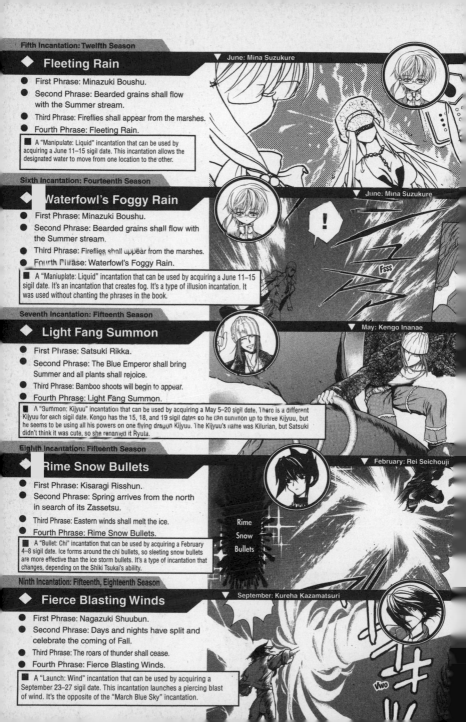

Tenth Incantation: Fifteenth Season

◆ Beasts of Rain

▼ June: Mina Suzukure

- First Phrase: Minazuki Geshi.
- Second Phrase: The Fire Emperor shall take his throne and the sun shall remain in the heavens.
- Third Phrase: The *Spica prunellae* shall wither.
- Fourth Phrase: Beasts of Rain.

■ A "Launch: Water" incantation that can be used by acquiring a June 21–25 sigil date. The point is always rotating, so it pierces through its target. It was used without chanting the phrases in the book.

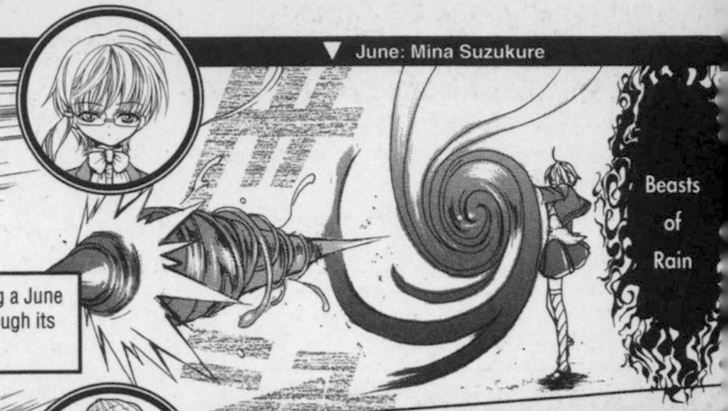
Beasts of Rain

Eleventh Incantation: Fifteenth Season

◆ Mirage of Light

▼ May: Kengo Inanae

- First Phrase: Satsuki Rikka.
- Second Phrase: The Blue Emperor shall bring Summer and all plants shall rejoice.
- Third Phrase: Frogs begin to croak.
- Fourth Phrase: Mirage of Light.

■ A "Launch: Light" incantation that can be used by acquiring a May 5–9 sigil date. This incantation creates a fast-traveling blade of light. Light incantations are one of the sharpest blade incantations. It was used without chanting the phrases in the book.

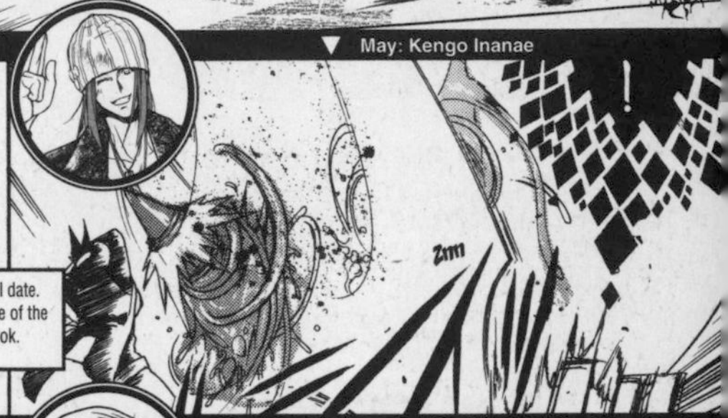
!
Zm

Twelfth Incantation: Fifteenth Season

◆ Heavenly Winds of Fire

▼ September: Kureha Kazamatsuri

- First Phrase: Nagazuki Shuubun.
- Second Phrase: Days and nights have split and celebrate the coming of Fall.
- Third Phrase: Insects seal the entrance of their burrows.
- Fourth Phrase: Heavenly Winds of Fire.

■ A "Special: Typhoon" incantation that can be used by acquiring a September 28–30/ October 1–2 sigil date. This incantation creates a small typhoon. When an October Shiki Tsukai uses this incantation, it isn't as powerful. It was used without chanting the phrases in the book.

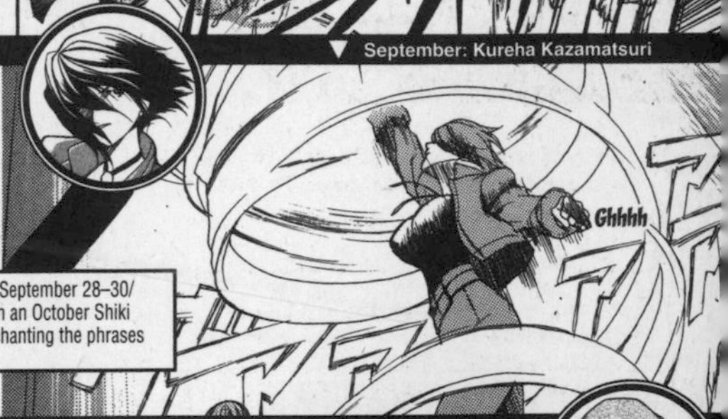
Ghhhh

Thirteenth Incantation: Ninth, Fifteenth Season

◆ Inferno Demon Summon

▼ July: Nanayo Rangetsu

- First Phrase: Fumizuki Shousho.
- Second Phrase: Heat rises and dances in the seventh evening sky.
- Third Phrase: Lotus flowers begin to bloom.
- Fourth Phrase: Inferno Demon Summon.

■ A "Summon: Kijyuu" incantation that can be used by acquiring a July 12–16 sigil date. There is a different Kijyuu for each sigil date. Nanayo has the 12, 13, and 16 sigil dates, so she can summon up to three Kijyuu. Her Kijyuu's name is Hien.

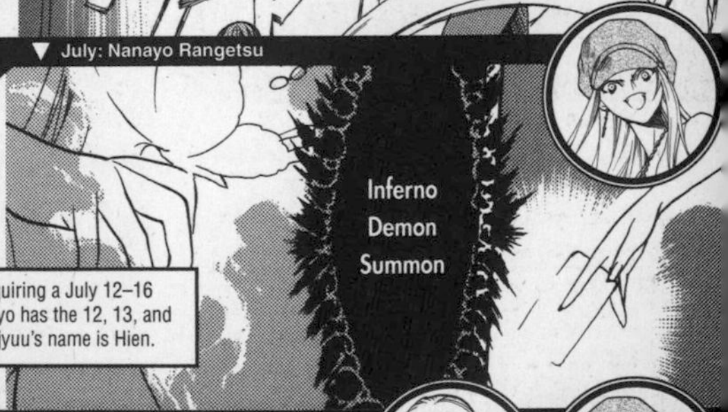
Inferno Demon Summon

Fourteenth Incantation: Sixth, Fifteenth Season

◆ Flowering Blaze of Wind

▼ July: Nanayo Rangetsu

- First Phrase: Fumizuki Taisho.
- Second Phrase: A feast to the sweltering heat begins, and thus it shall reach the temperature of the sun.
- Third Phrase: The tung tree shall bear fruit.
- Fourth Phrase: Flowering Blaze of Wind.

■ A "Launch: Fire" incantation that can be used by acquiring a July 23–27 sigil date. It's an incantation that shoots fire and flames in bullet form. Depending on the Shiki Tsukai's ability, the flames can reach far.

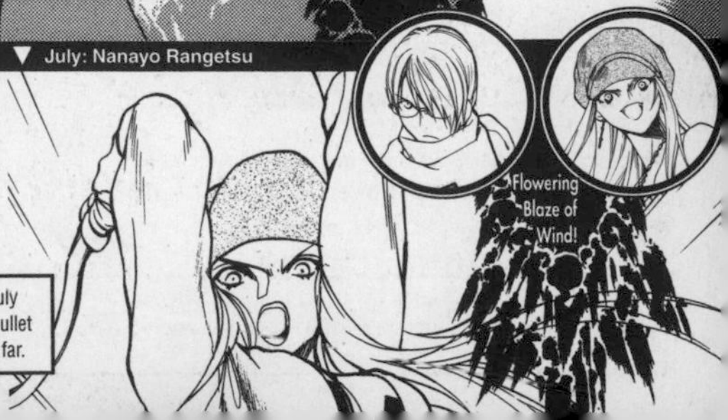
Flowering Blaze of Wind!

Fifteenth Incantation: Sixteenth Season

Blue Sky Gust

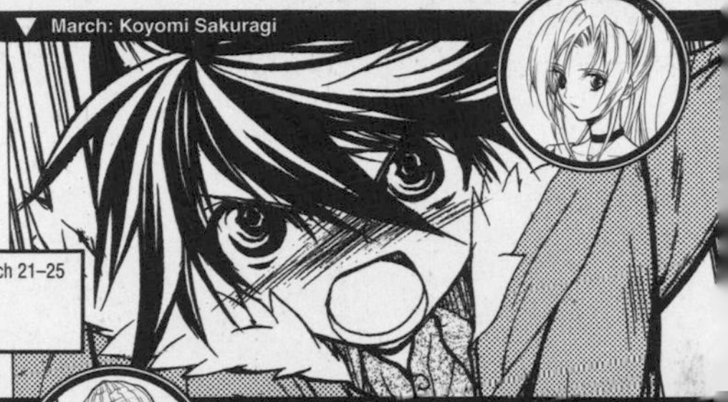
March: Koyomi Sakuragi

- First Phrase: Yayoi Shunbun.
- Second Phrase: Days and nights have split and celebrate the coming of spring.
- Third Phrase: Sparrows shall begin to build their nests.
- Fourth Phrase: Blue Sky Gust.

■ A "Launch: Wind" incantation that can be used by acquiring a March 21–25 sigil date. This incantation releases a powerful wind that will cause a blunt-force injury to its target.

Sixteenth Incantation: Sixteenth Season

Silent Spring Light

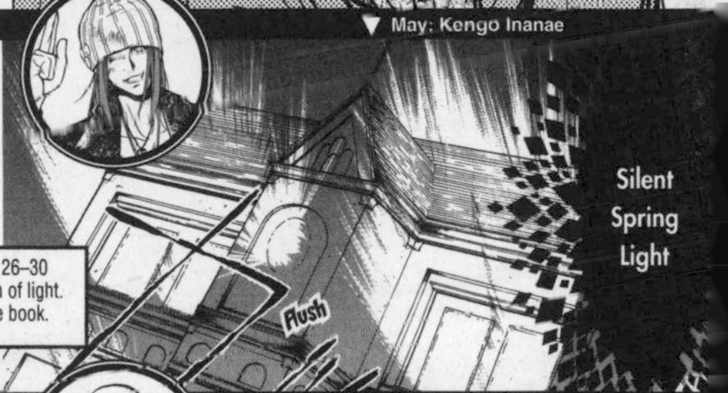
May: Kengo Inanae
Silent Spring Light
Flush

- First Phrase: Satsuki Shouman.
- Second Phrase: A time when all life shall reach maturity.
- Third Phrase: Safflowers are all in full bloom.
- Fourth Phrase: Silent Spring Light.

■ A "Special: Sun" incantation that can be used by acquiring a May 26–30 sigil date. It is a sun incantation that blinds the opponent with a flash of light. It can be very useful. It was used without chanting the phrases in the book.

Seventeenth Incantation: Sixteenth Season

Decaying Rain

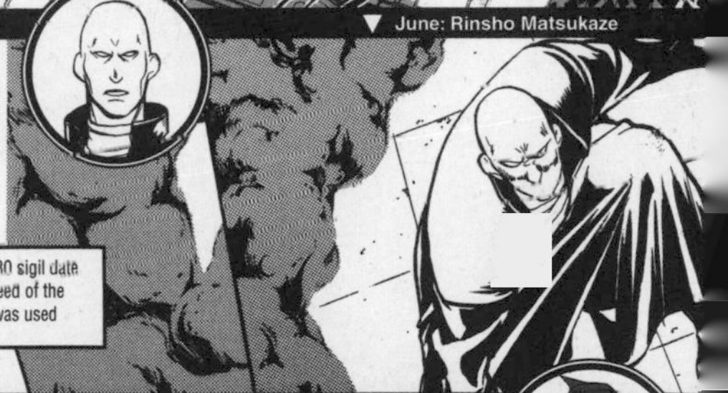
June: Rinsho Matsukaze

- First Phrase: Minazuki Geshi.
- Second Phrase: The Fire Emperor shall take his throne and the sun shall remain in the heavens.
- Third Phrase: Iris flowers begin to bloom.
- Fourth Phrase: Decaying Rain.

■ A "Special: Decay" incantation that can be used by acquiring a June 26–30 sigil date. It's a special type of incantation that only a July Shiki Tsukai can use. The speed of the decay is slow, but it also emits a poisonous gas while the decay spreads. It was used without chanting the phrases in the book.

Eighteenth Incantation: Sixteenth Season

Wings of Light

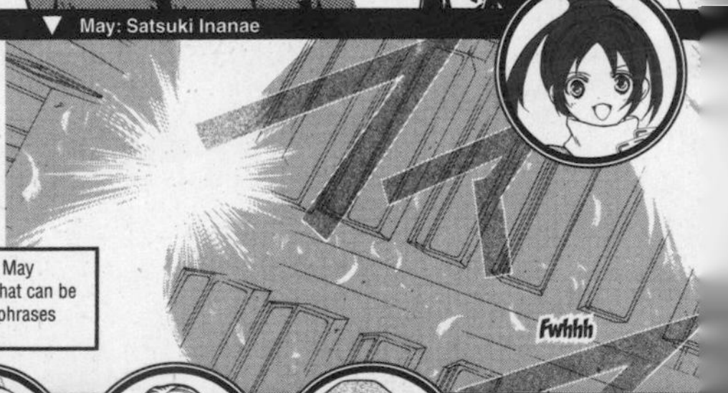
May: Satsuki Inanae
Fwhhh

- First Phrase: Satsuki Rikka.
- Second Phrase: The Blue Emperor shall bring Summer and all plants shall rejoice.
- Third Phrase: Worms come out of the ground.
- Fourth Phrase: Wings of Light.

■ A "Manipulate: Light" incantation that can be used by acquiring a May 10–14 sigil date. The incantation gives the user wings made of light that can be used for both offense and defense. It was used without chanting the phrases in the book.

Nineteenth Incantation: Sixth, Sixteenth, Seventeenth Season

Flowering Blaze of Wind

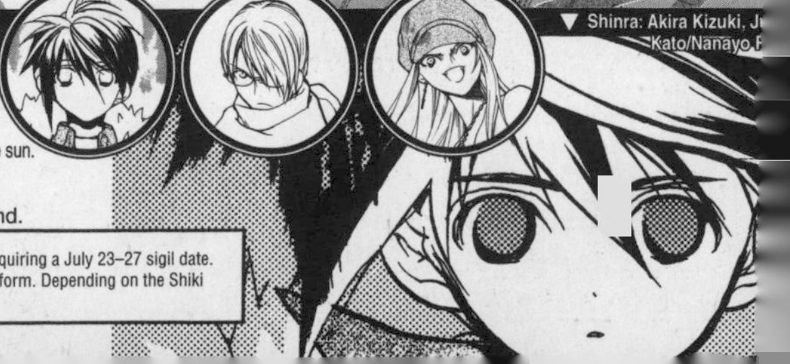
Shinra: Akira Kizuki, J
Kato/Nanayo F

- First Phrase: Fumizuki Taisho.
- Second Phrase: A feast of the sweltering heat begins, and thus it shall reach the temperature of the sun.
- Third Phrase: The tung tree shall bear fruit.
- Fourth Phrase: Flowering Blaze of Wind.

■ A "Launch: Fire" incantation that can be used by acquiring a July 23–27 sigil date. It's an incantation that shoots fire and flames in bullet form. Depending on the Shiki Tsukai's ability, the flames can reach far.

Twentieth Incantation: Seventeenth Season

◆ Gates of Tremor

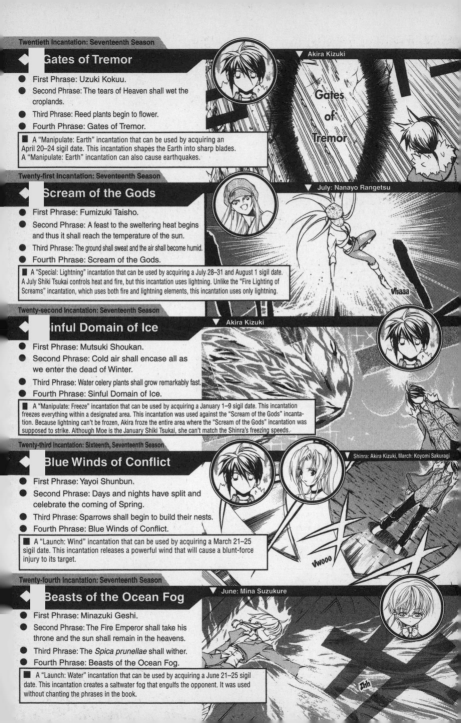

- First Phrase: Uzuki Kokuu.
- Second Phrase: The tears of Heaven shall wet the croplands.
- Third Phrase: Reed plants begin to flower.
- Fourth Phrase: Gates of Tremor.

■ A "Manipulate: Earth" incantation that can be used by acquiring an April 20–24 sigil date. This incantation shapes the Earth into sharp blades. A "Manipulate: Earth" incantation can also cause earthquakes.

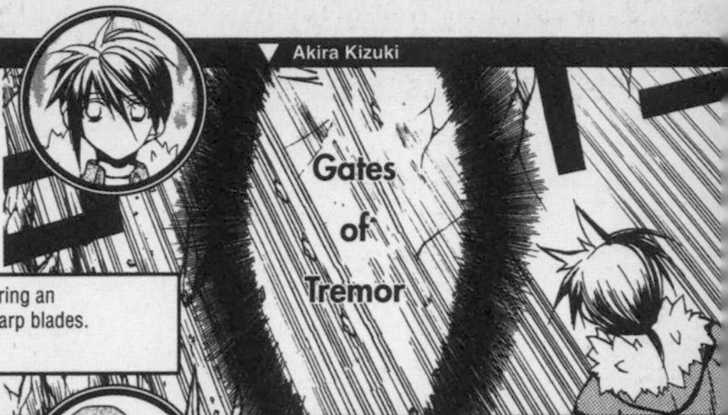

Gates of Tremor

▼ Akira Kizuki

Twenty-first Incantation: Seventeenth Season

◆ Scream of the Gods

- First Phrase: Fumizuki Taisho.
- Second Phrase: A feast to the sweltering heat begins and thus it shall reach the temperature of the sun.
- Third Phrase: The ground shall sweat and the air shall become humid.
- Fourth Phrase: Scream of the Gods.

■ A "Special: Lightning" incantation that can be used by acquiring a July 28–31 and August 1 sigil date. A July Shiki Tsukai controls heat and fire, but this incantation uses lightning. Unlike the "Fire Lighting of Screams" incantation, which uses both fire and lightning elements, this incantation uses only lightning.

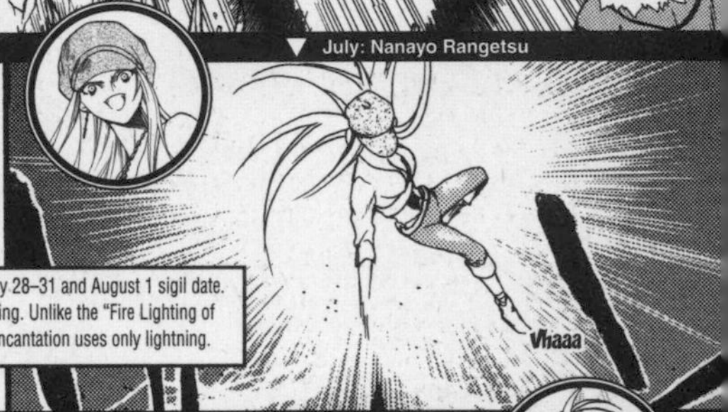

Vhaaa

▼ July: Nanayo Rangetsu

Twenty-second Incantation: Seventeenth Season

◆ Sinful Domain of Ice

- First Phrase: Mutsuki Shoukan.
- Second Phrase: Cold air shall encase all as we enter the dead of Winter.
- Third Phrase: Water celery plants shall grow remarkably fast.
- Fourth Phrase: Sinful Domain of Ice.

■ A "Manipulate: Freeze" incantation that can be used by acquiring a January 1–9 sigil date. This incantation freezes everything within a designated area. This incantation was used against the "Scream of the Gods" incantation. Because lightning can't be frozen, Akira froze the entire area where the "Scream of the Gods" incantation was supposed to strike. Although Moe is the January Shiki Tsukai, she can't match the Shinra's freezing speeds.

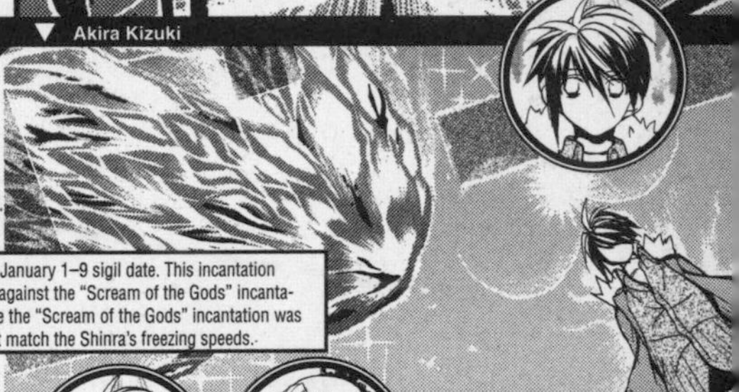
▼ Akira Kizuki

Twenty-third Incantation: Sixteenth, Seventeenth Season

◆ Blue Winds of Conflict

- First Phrase: Yayoi Shunbun.
- Second Phrase: Days and nights have split and celebrate the coming of Spring.
- Third Phrase: Sparrows shall begin to build their nests.
- Fourth Phrase: Blue Winds of Conflict.

■ A "Launch: Wind" incantation that can be used by acquiring a March 21–25 sigil date. This incantation releases a powerful wind that will cause a blunt-force injury to its target.

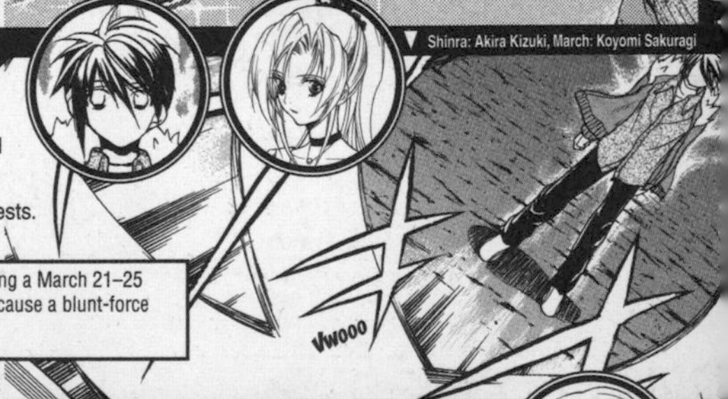

Vwooo

▼ Shinra: Akira Kizuki, March: Koyomi Sakuragi

Twenty-fourth Incantation: Seventeenth Season

◆ Beasts of the Ocean Fog

- First Phrase: Minazuki Geshi.
- Second Phrase: The Fire Emperor shall take his throne and the sun shall remain in the heavens.
- Third Phrase: The *Spica prunellae* shall wither.
- Fourth Phrase: Beasts of the Ocean Fog.

■ A "Launch: Water" incantation that can be used by acquiring a June 21–25 sigil date. This incantation creates a saltwater fog that engulfs the opponent. It was used without chanting the phrases in the book.

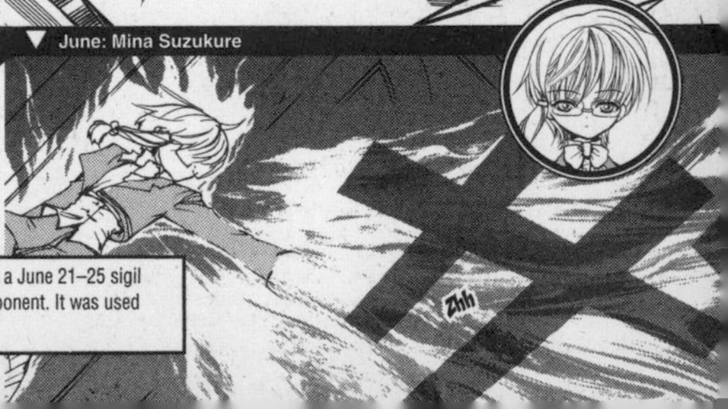

Zhh

▼ June: Mina Suzukure

Twenty-fifth Incantation: Eighteenth Season

◆ Lovebird of Light

- First Phrase: Satsuki Rikka.
- Second Phrase: The Blue Emperor shall bring Summer and all plants shall rejoice.
- Third Phrase: Worms come out of the ground.
- Fourth Phrase: Lovebird of Light.

■ A "Manipulate: Light" incantation that can be used by acquiring a May 10–14 sigil date. It's both an offensive and defensive incantation that creates wings made of bright light. It's a simpler version of the "Wings of Light" incantation and increases agility. It was used without chanting the phrases in the book.

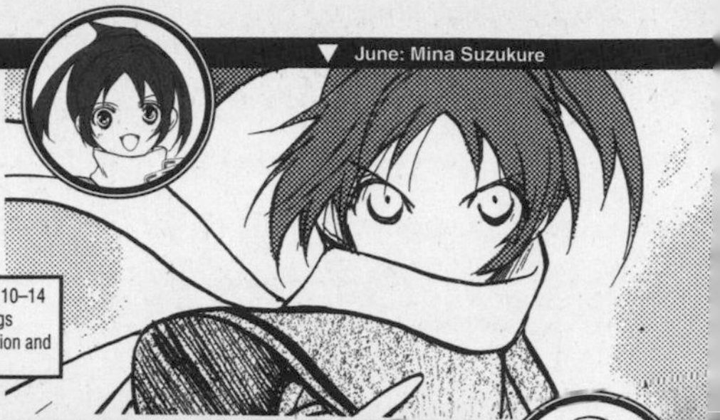

▼ June: Mina Suzukure

Twenty-sixth Incantation: Eighteenth Season

◆ Decaying Blossom

- First Phrase: Minazuki Geshi.
- Second Phrase: The Fire Emperor shall take his throne and the sun shall remain in the heavens.
- Third Phrase: Iris flowers begin to bloom.
- Fourth Phrase: Decaying Blossom.

■ A "Special: Decay" incantation that can be used by acquiring a June 26–30 sigil date. It's a special type of incantation that only a July Shiki Tsukai can use. The movement of the decaying blossom is slow, but the blossoms create a deadly virus. It was used without chanting the phrases in the book.

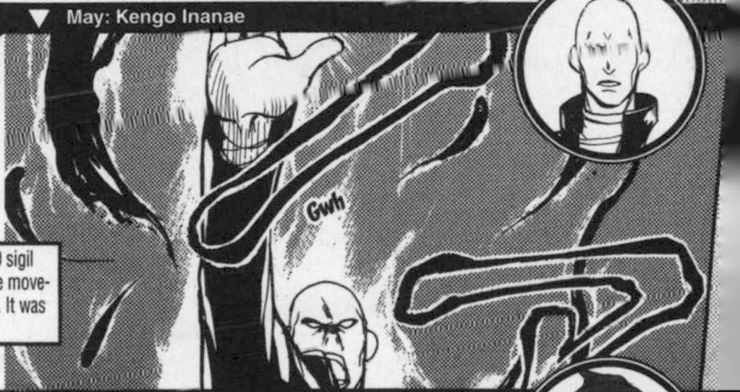
Gwh

▼ May: Kengo Inanae

Twenty-seventh Incantation: Eighteenth Season

◆ Dancing Spring Light

- First Phrase: Satsuki Shouman.
- Second Phrase: A time when all life shall reach maturity.
- Third Phrase: Safflowers are all in full bloom.
- Fourth Phrase: Dancing Spring Light.

■ A "Special: Sun" incantation that can be used by acquiring a May 26–30 sigil date It's an incantation that manipulates the rays of the sun. Many sun incantations greatly benefit speed and defense. The "Dancing Spring Light" incantation boosts speed. It was used without chanting the phrases in the book.

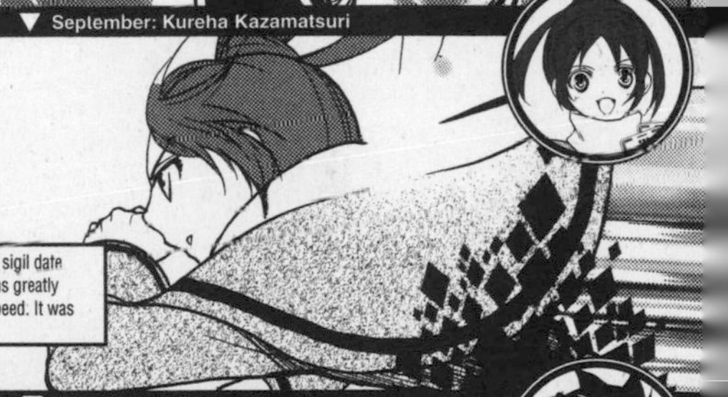

▼ September: Kureha Kazamatsuri

Twenty-eighth Incantation: Fifteenth, Eighteenth Season

◆ Sleeting Snow Bullets

- First Phrase: Kisaragi Risshun.
- Second Phrase: Spring arrives from the north in search of its Zassetsu.
- Third Phrase: Eastern winds shall melt the ice.
- Fourth Phrase: Sleeting Snow Bullets.

■ A "Bullet: Chi" incantation that can be used by acquiring a February 4–8 sigil date. Ice forms around the chi bullets, so sleeting snow bullets are more effective than the ice storm bullets. It's a type of incantation that changes, depending on the Shiki Tsukai's ability.

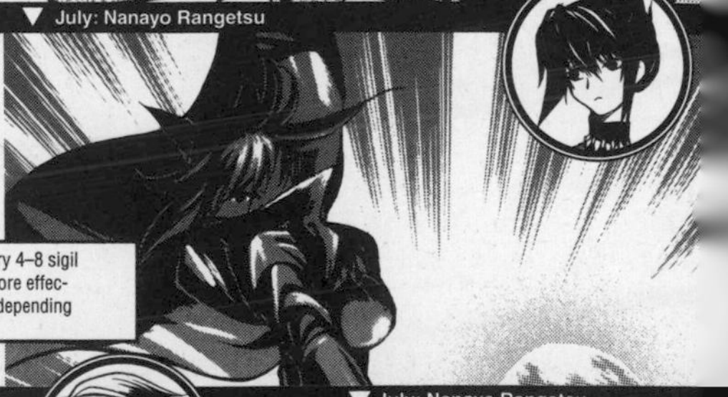

▼ July: Nanayo Rangetsu

Twenty-ninth Incantation: Eighteenth Season

◆ Forbidden Autumn Winds

- First Phrase: Nagazuki Hakuro.
- Second Phrase: The White Emperor descends and creates a trail of frost.
- Third Phrase: The Grey Wagtail bird begins to chirp.
- Fourth Phrase: Forbidden Autumn Winds.

■ An "Armor: Air" incantation that can be used by acquiring a September 13–17 sigil date. A storm surrounds the user and unleashes an attack, but this incantation can also be used to travel. It's the opposite of the "March Tree Banish" incantation.

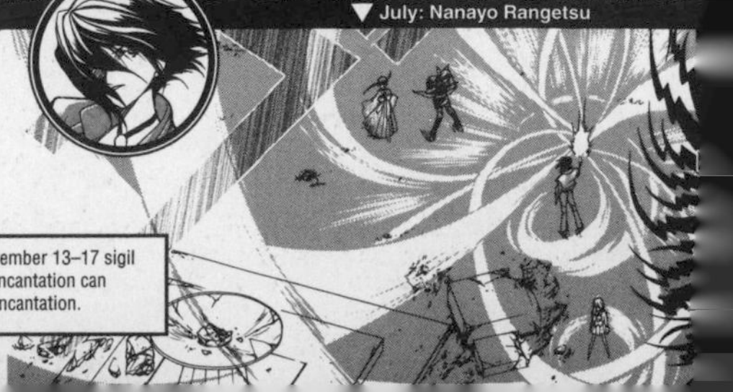

▼ July: Nanayo Rangetsu

Looks a bit childish

Kengo Inanae

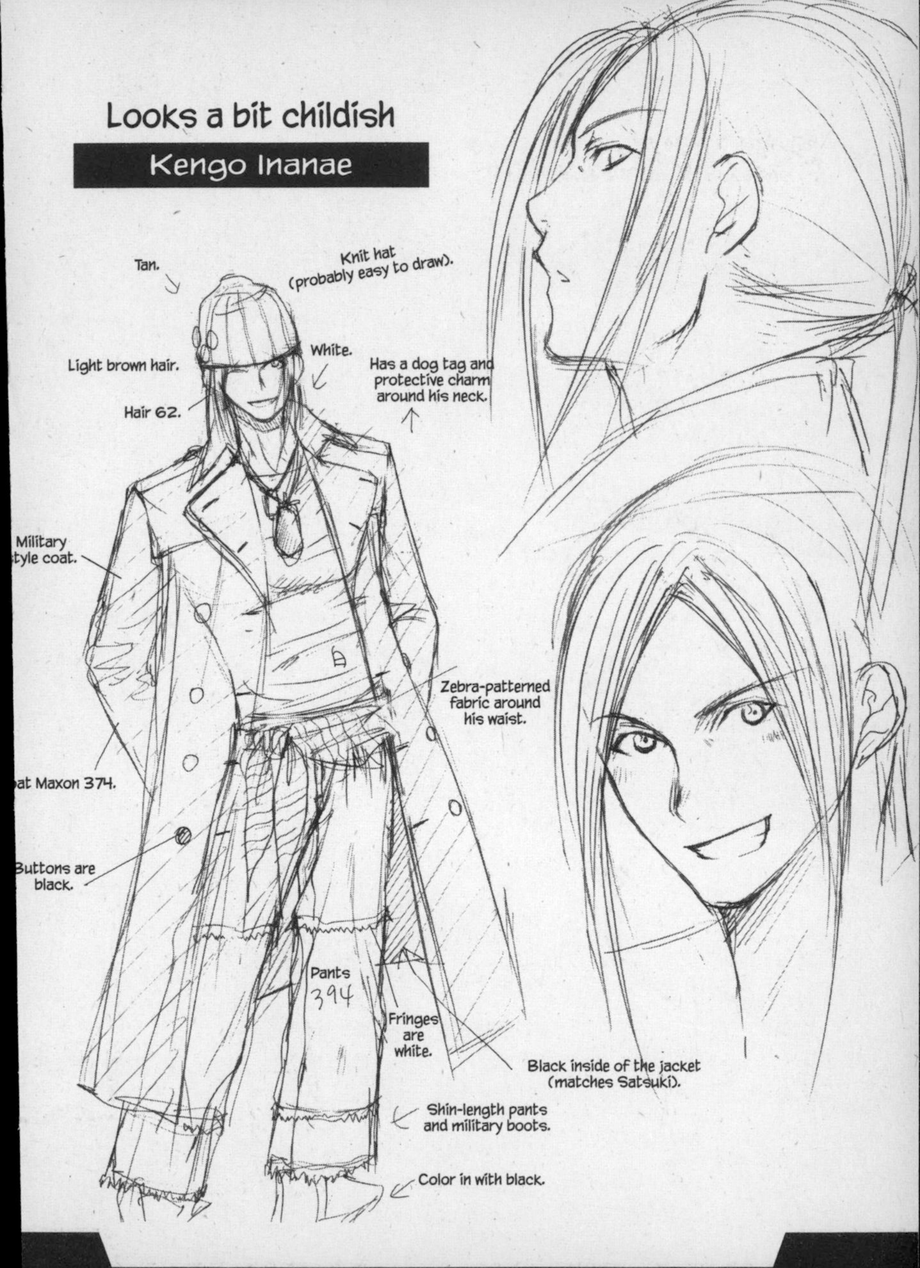
Tan.
Knit hat (probably easy to draw).
White.
Light brown hair.
Has a dog tag and protective charm around his neck.
Hair 62.
Military
tyle coat.
Zebra-patterned fabric around his waist.
at Maxon 374.
uttons are black.
Pants 394
Fringes are white.
Black inside of the jacket (matches Satsuki).
Shin-length pants and military boots.
Color in with black.

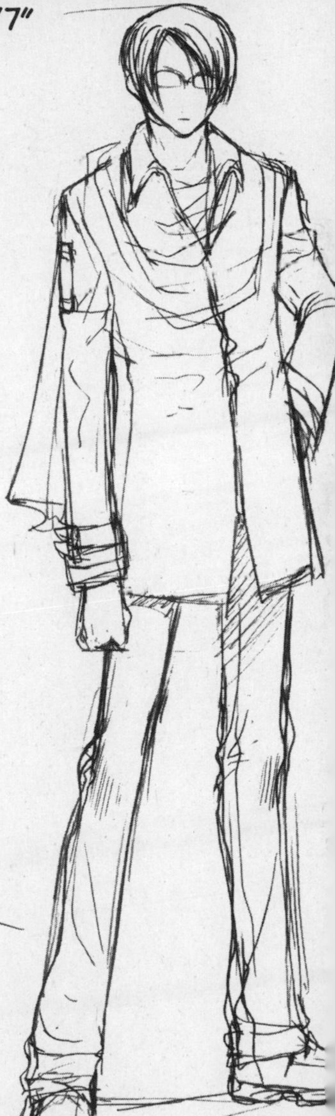
5'7"

Ryuka Kato

He's sarcastic.

He's smart, but because of that, he's very apathetic toward the world.

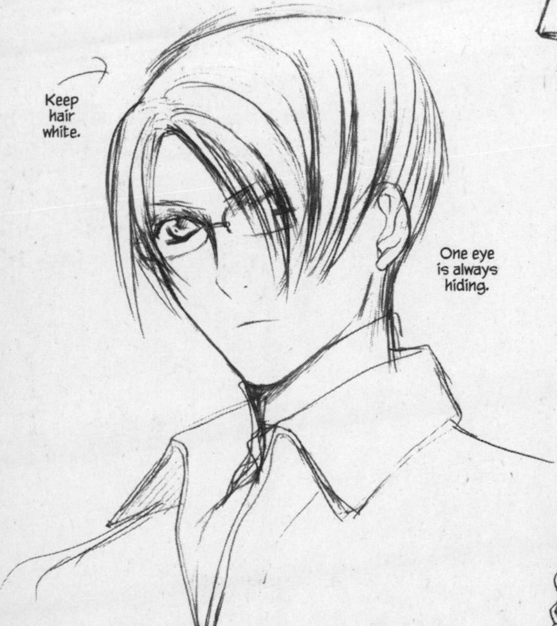
Keep hair white.
One eye is always hiding.

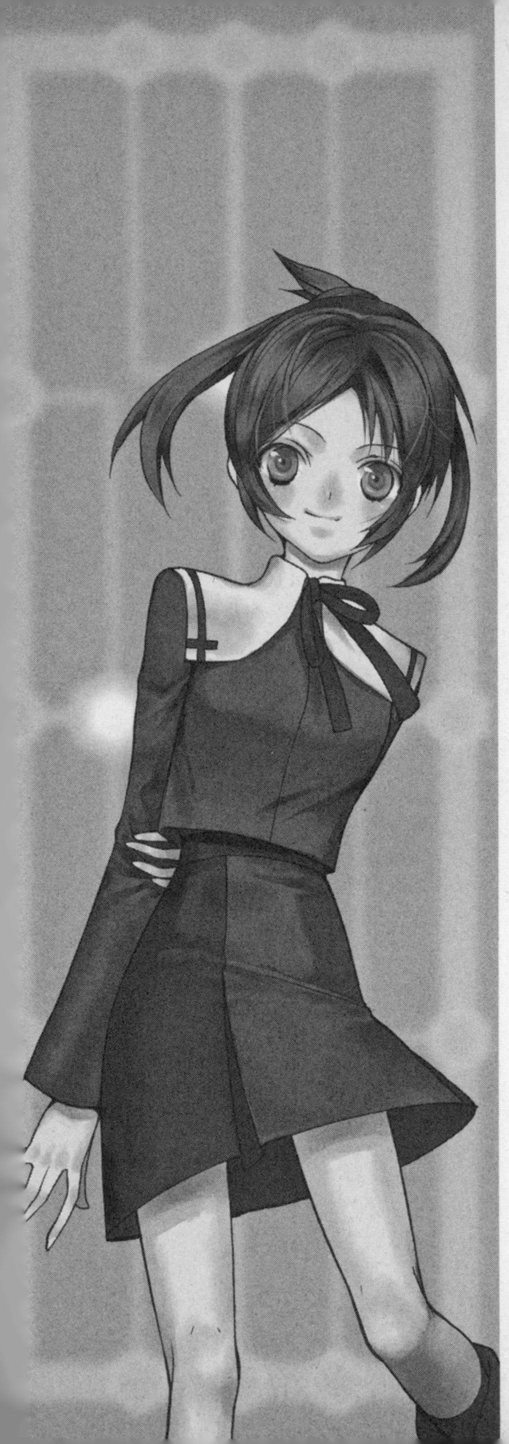

Satsuki Inanae

Shikifu: Red Coral

Shiki Tsukai of May

Birthday: May 5, 1999
Age: 14 years old
Blood Type: O
Height: 5′
Weight: 95 lb.
Three Sizes: Bust 30″ / Waist 22″ / Hip 31.5″

- Best friends with Akira Kizuki and Fumiya Kirihara.
- Considers herself Akira's older sister figure.
- A food junkie; likes ice cream and *konyaku*.
- Likes dogs but also likes things to be clean, so she doesn't own one.
- Always happy. Doesn't like people who are underhanded.
- *Data is based on December 2013.

Kengo Inanae

Shikifu:

Former Shiki Tsukai of May

Birthday: May 5, 1973
Age: 29+ (give or take)
Blood Type: O
Height: 6'1"
Weight: 203 lb.

- One of the "Jyuuni Getsu Ken," the last generation of Shiki Tsukai.
- An acclaimed geologist.
- Loves to go on adventures. He collects Shikifu as if he's a treasure hunter.
- Kengo inherited his Shikifu from his late wife.
- *Data is based on December 2013.

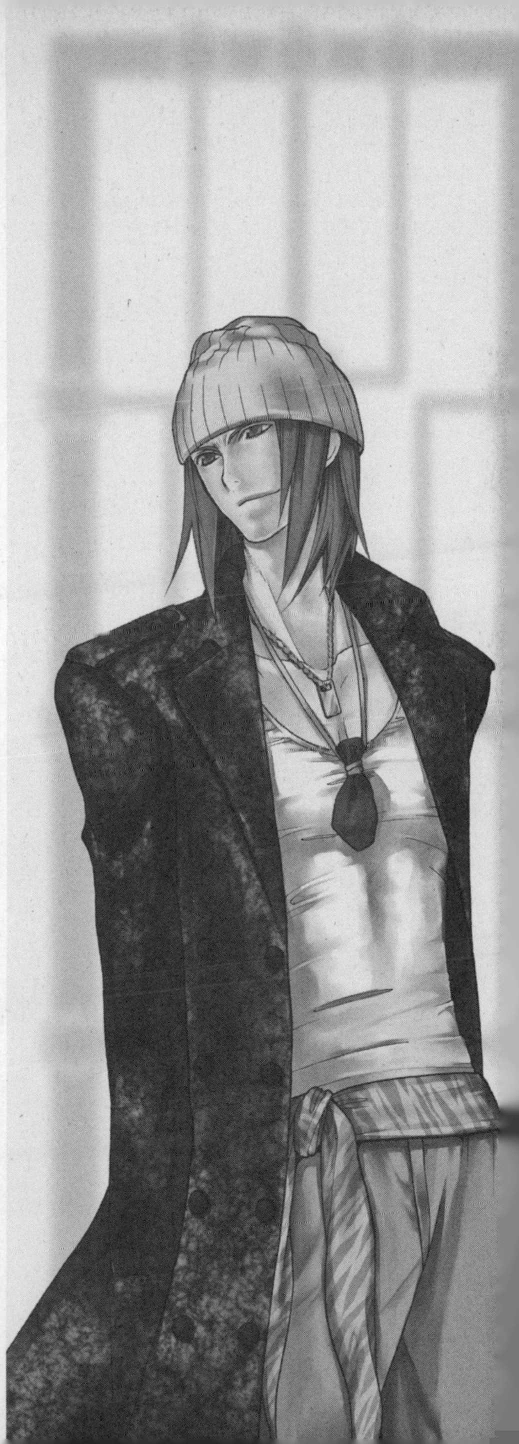

Translation Notes

Japanese is a tricky language for most Westerners, and translation is often more art than science. For your edification and reading pleasure, here are notes on some of the places where we could have gone in a different direction with our translation of the work, or where a Japanese cultural reference is used.

Shiki Tsukai, page 3
One who possesses the power of the seasons. *Shiki* means the "four seasons" and *Tsukai* literally means "someone who uses" (in this case the seasons).

Shikifu, page 3
Shikifu is a card that the Shiki Tsukai possess. It is the source of the Shiki Tsukai's power.

Shinra, page 3
A Shiki Tsukai that has the ability to control all the seasons.

A Shiki Tsukai wields the seasons using a Shikifu. As the Shiki Tsukai of March, Koyomi's mission is to protect Akira (the boy who has the possibility of becoming the Shinra who can wield all the seasons) from the Shiki Tsukai of Summer.

Shinra Banshou, page 13

Shinra Banshou means "all creation" or "universe."

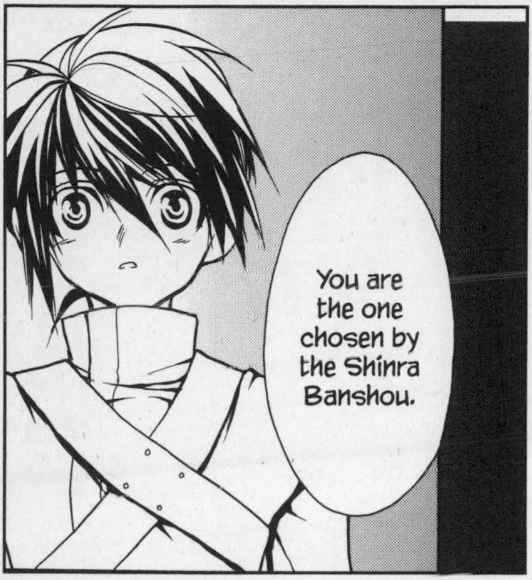
You are the one chosen by the Shinra Banshou.

Inclusion, page 55

In mineralogical terms, an inclusion is any material trapped inside a mineral during its formation. In *Shiki Tsukai* terms, it is the act of a Shikifu absorbing another Shikifu.

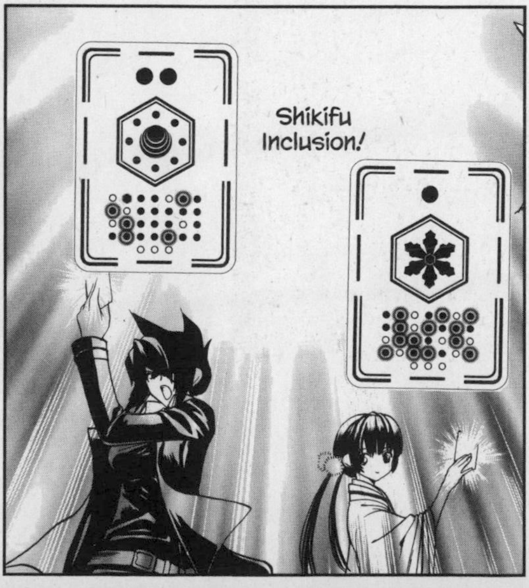
Shikifu Inclusion!

Kijyuu, page 74

Kijyuu is an elemental beast that's born from the seasons. *Ki* means "seasons" and *jyuu* is the character for "beast."

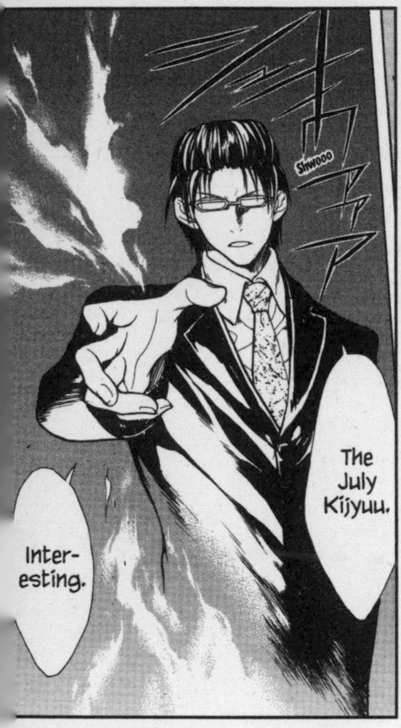
Shwooo
The July Kijyuu.
Inter-esting.

Formation, page 151

A special "sealed dimension" that a Shiki Tsukai can create.

It's the Formation of Winter.
I can't move freely with it in place.

Konyaku, page 190

Konyaku is a traditional Japanese jelly-like health food made from an elephant yam.

Jyuuni Getsu Ken, page 191

The previous generation of Shiki Tsukai.

Akira's adventures continue in *Shiki Tsukai,* volume 5! Check out the Del Rey Manga website [www.delreymanga.com] to find out when it will be available in English!

FROM HIRO MASHIMA, CREATOR OF *RAVE MASTER*

Lucy has always dreamed of joining the Fairy Tail, a club for the most powerful sorcerers in the land. But once she becomes a member, the fun really starts!

Special extras in each volume! Read them all!

RATING T AGES 13+

VISIT WWW.DELREYMANGA.COM TO:
• Read sample pages
• View release date calendars for upcoming volumes
• Sign up for Del Rey's free manga e-newsletter
• Find out the latest about new Del Rey Manga series

DEL REY MANGA
The Otaku's Choice.™

Fairy Tail © 2006 Hiro Mashima / KODANSHA LTD. All rights reserved.

STORY BY SURT LIM
ART BY HIROFUMI SUGIMOTO

A DEL REY MANGA ORIGINAL

Exploring the woods, young Kasumi encounters an ancient tree god, who bestows upon her the power of invisibility. Together with classmates who have had similar experiences, Kasumi forms the Magic Play Club, dedicated to using their powers for good while avoiding sinister forces that would exploit them.

Special extras in each volume! Read them all!

VISIT WWW.DELREYMANGA.COM TO:
• Read sample pages
• View release date calendars for upcoming volumes
• Sign up for Del Rey's free manga e-newsletter
• Find out the latest about new Del Rey Manga series

RATING   T AGES 13+

DEL REY MANGA
The Otaku's Choice™

Kasumi © 2008 Monkey Square Productions. All rights reserved.

KITCHEN PRINCESS

STORY BY MIYUKI KOBAYASHI
MANGA BY NATSUMI ANDO
CREATOR OF ZODIAC P.I.

HUNGRY HEART

Najika is a great cook and likes to make meals for the people she loves. But something is missing from her life. When she was a child, she met a boy who touched her heart—and now Najika is determined to find him. The only clue she has is a silver spoon that leads her to the prestigious Seika Academy.

Attending Seika will be a challenge. Every kid at the school has a special talent, and the girls in Najika's class think she doesn't deserve to be there. But Sora and Daichi, two popular brothers who barely speak to each other, recognize Najika's cooking for what it is—magical. Could one of the boys be Najika's mysterious prince?

Special extras in each volume! Read them all!

VISIT WWW.DELREYMANGA.COM TO:
- Read sample pages
- View release date calendars for upcoming volumes
- Sign up for Del Rey's free manga e-newsletter
- Find out the latest about new Del Rey Manga series

RATING T AGES 13+

DEL REY MANGA デルレイ

The Otaku's Choice

Kitchen Princess © 2005 Natsumi Ando and Miyuki Kobayashi / KODANSHA LTD. All rights reserved.

Subscribe to

DEL REY'S MANGA
e-newsletter—

and receive all these
exciting exclusives directly
in your e-mail inbox:

• Schedules and announcements about
the newest books on sale

• Exclusive interviews and exciting
behind-the-scenes news

• Previews of upcoming material

• A manga reader's forum, featuring a
cool question-and-answer section

For more information and to sign up
for Del Rey's manga e-newsletter,
visit www.delreymanga.com

DETROIT PUBLIC LIBRARY

3 5674 05075879 7

YOUNG ADULT
GRAPHIC NOVEL

TOMARE!

止まれ

[STOP!]

You're going the wrong way!

Manga is a completely different type of reading experience.

To start at the *beginning*, go to the *end*!

That's right! Authentic manga is read the traditional Japanese way—from right to left. Exactly the opposite of how American books are read. It's easy to follow: Just go to the other end of the book, and read each page—and each panel—from right side to left side, starting at the top right. Now you're experiencing manga as it was meant to be!

JUN 2010

WILDER BRANCH LIBRARY
7140 E. SEVEN MILE RD.
DETROIT, MI 48234

WL

W9-DFV-428

the game we play
is let's pretend
and pretend
we're not pretending

we choose to forget
who we are
and then forget
that we've forgotten

who are we
really

the center
that watches
and runs the show
that can choose
which way
it will go

the I AM
consciousness
that powerful
loving perfect
reflection
of the cosmos

but in our attempt
to cope with
early situations
we chose or were
hypnotized into
a passive position

to avoid punishment
or the loss of love
we choose to deny
our response/ability
pretending that
things just happened
or that we were
being controlled
taken over

we put ourselves
down
and have become
used to this
masochistic posture
this weakness
this unsureness
this indecisiveness

but we are
in reality
free
a center
of cosmic
energy

your will
is your power

don't pretend
you don't have it

or you won't

stop playing
poor me

either you will
or you won't

be willing
to express
your will power
in a skillful
loving manner

remember
by saying
to your SELF
I will
not be
swallowed up by
undesirable thoughts
feelings
or circumstances

I refuse
to identify with them
I AM
not these thoughts
feelings or circumstances
I will not let them
dominate me

I AM
now always
in each situation
as fully free
as I allow myself
to be

you are the sun
not the moon
nor the clouds

no matter what
the weather
you are always
shining

the new age
is now

it's about time
bliss
timelessness

balance
energy

infinite consciousness

moving through
to a deeper source

leaving our
preoccupation
with the past
our fear
of the future
our overstressing
the rational mind
superficial sex
excessive competition
consuming material
power games
our bitching
and negativity

to realize

who we are
and what it is
we want

the quest

the question
the questionnaire

who are you

a body

a mind

a role

a goal

you are
consciousness

a loving powerful
eternal soul

with the quality
of an observer
who has
thoughts
emotions
sensations

you have
a physical body
but you are not
that everchanging
form

you have
feelings and
emotions
but you are not
these
fluctuating patterns

you have
a mind
but you are not
this panorama
of ideas
pictures and thoughts

the body
feelings and thoughts
are all impermanent
changing instruments
of experience
perception
action and reaction

you are
an always
constant center
of pure radiant
energy consciousness

I AM
SATORI

all else
is trans/satori

for
all you are
you see

is energy

different degrees
of speed
density
intensity

chains of linking
atoms in space
patterns
in the delight dance
of everchanging matter

go look
somewhere else
for subject matter
for what does
the subject matter
for all matter
is subject to
other matter

and it

really

doesn't

matter

or it
only matters
for a while

for energy
is the sun
earth air sea
you me

chemistry
electricity
your body
breathing
circulation
sensation
impulses
thoughts
words
images
sounds
colors

this paper
book
chair
floor
to ceiling

unlimited life

consciousness

vibrating
everywhere

in various
states
solid
liquid
gas jewels
invisible molecules
finding their
temporary place
in endless
space

you are
a series
of energy fields
in a field of energy
the eternal play
of the gross subtle
shadow light
night and day

exchanging
interchanging
rearranging
itself
in the evolution
dream called
life

formless free
the cosmic energy
delightfully
created form
and will continue
to reform
in subtler
and subtler form
until it
again returns
to its former
formless form

the following
ancient/modern
energy system
to be presented
in this book
is a model
a guide map
that can assist you
to enhance

your awareness

being

creative
spirit

mind
body
dance

sit down,
close your eyes
and imagine
a white light sun
6 inches
above the
top of your head.
see the bottom
of the sun open
pouring white
light energy
down toward
the top of your head.

open your head
and let this
soothing light come
slowly into
and through
every space,
muscle, nerve,
bone, organ, cell,
atom and molecule
of your head.
now, let this
warm nourishing energy
flow through
every inch of you;
into your neck, shoulders,
down your arms
and out your hands.
let it pour down into
your torso: chest,
stomach and back;
through your hips,
lower legs, feet
and out your toes.

let the energy move through
every inch of you.
then , close
your fingers and toes
and let your body being
be filled to overflowing
with this soft,
bright, soothing light.
let it completely saturate
the inside and cover
the outside of you.
take your time,
as much as you need.
then, let the image
of the light fade;
experience how you feel
and open your eyes.

6

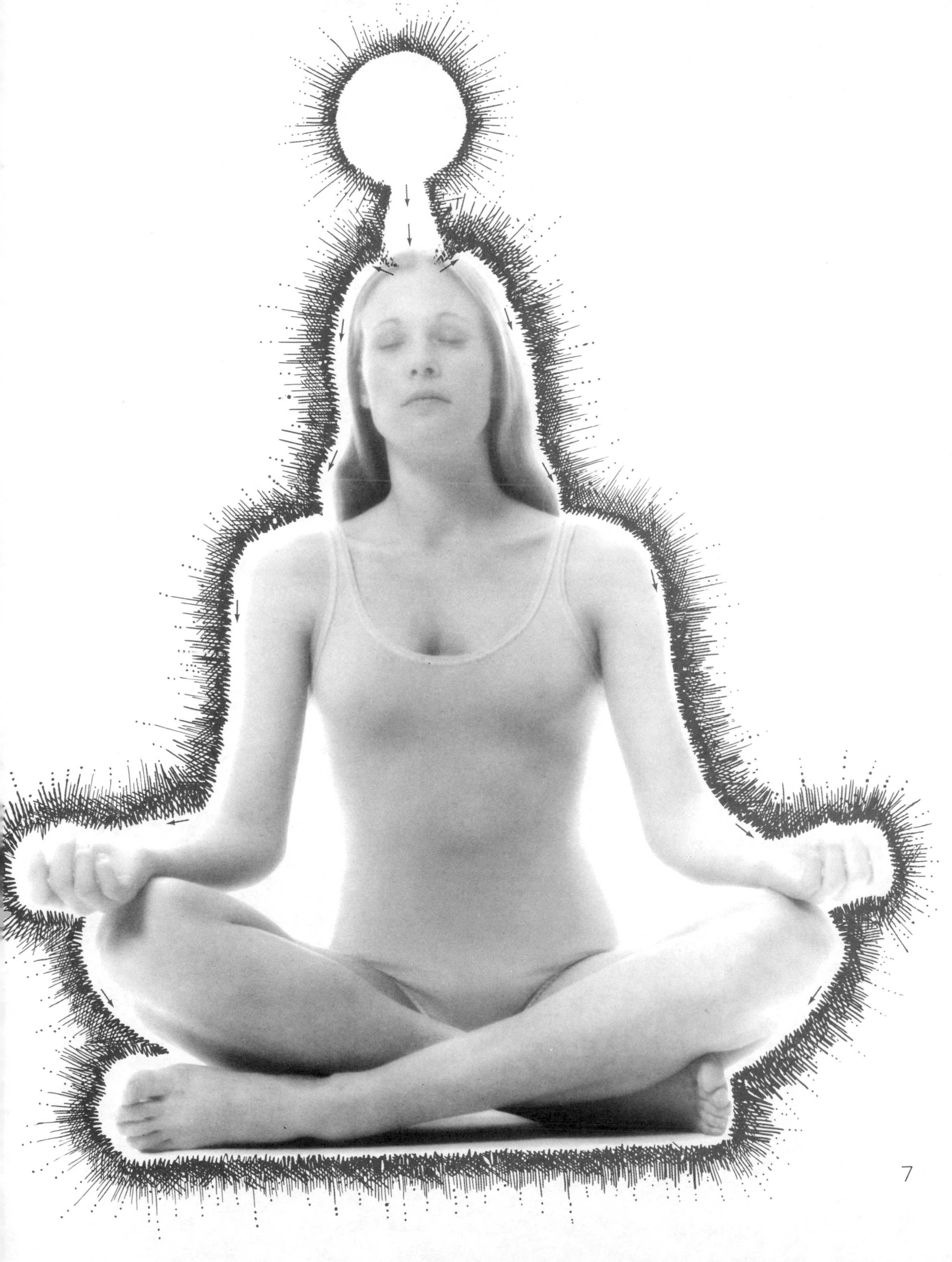

energy ecstasy

and your seven vital chakras

by bernard gunther

chakra paintings by
philip kirkland

newcastle publishing company, inc.
north hollywood, california
1983

9

copyright © 1978, 1979
by bernard gunther
all rights reserved, including
the right of reproduction
in whole or in part in any form.

ISBN 0-87877-066-6
library of congress
catalog card number
77-87416

a newcastle book
  12 13 14 15 93 92
printed in united states of america

contents

to
the ultimate
supreme
infinite
love
bliss
peace
that is
bhagwan
shree
rajneesh

acknowledgment
heart
full
felt
feeling
thanks

for the inspiration of
Bhagwan Rajneesh

for the dedication of
Jack Schwartz*
Philip Kirkland
Phyllis Lathers
Barbara Nash
and Dede Smith

*i wish to extend
special credit
appreciation
to my friend
colleague
Jack Schwartz
for teaching me
some of the theory
and exercises
found in this book

ENERGY CENTERS

there is
a series
of fine,
subtle
energy bodies
within,
permeating
and emanating
outside of
the dense
observable
physical body.

according to psychics
with extrasensory perception,
the physical,
emotional,
mental organism
gets most of its
primary energy
from invisible rays
which come down
into the organism
through minute openings
in the top
of the head.

these rays
entering the head
may be single colored
or dual in nature.

each color,
its quantity
and positon,
whether it forms
the inside
or outside
of the ray,
will affect
the unique talent,
vitality,
disposition, personality
character,
and behavior pattern
of the individual.

as this energy
comes into the head,
it is filtered
and reflected
downward
through seven etheric
energy centers
called chakras.
these energy wheels,
or lotuses,
are located
just in front
of the spinal column
at the following locations:

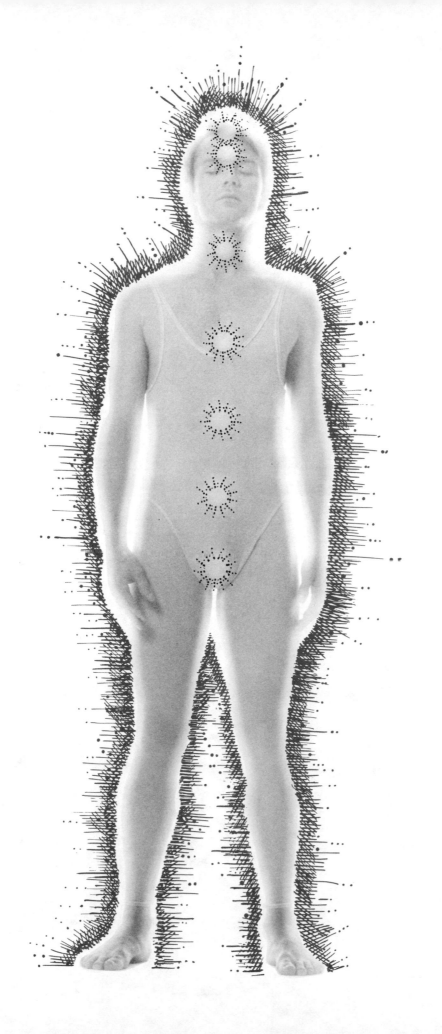

the crown center
at the top
of the head
is to be found
at an intersection
created by two lines,
one coming down the head
through the fontanel
at the upper back
of the head,
the other
through the middle
of the forehead.

the brow center
is found
at the first
cervical vertebra.

the throat center is
at the third cervical,
and the heart center
at the first thoracic.

the solar plexus is
at the eighth thoracic,
the spleen center
at the first lumbar,
and the sacrum
just above the coccyx.

as this suble energy
comes into the head,
it moves down
an extremely fine
invisible stem
located in the center
of the spinal cord.

as it filters down
through each center,
it becomes more
and more dense
so that when it
reaches the chakra
at the base of the spine.
it is relatively heavy,
very low,
slow frequency.

here it mixes with
a dense, dormant
earth energy
known in yoga as
kundalini (serpent power).

according to many different
eastern and western,
ancient and modern
ways of liberation,
it is the task
of the individual consciousness
to mix, raise,
balance, and refine
this energy force
and direct it upward.

as this ascent occurs,
the various energies
are blended and transmuted,
creating a variety
of experiences
and profound changes
in awareness.

the ultimate goal
is not only
to raise this
vertical energy,
but to appropriately open
and balance
each of these
horizontal centers fully
in a flowing harmony
up, down, in, throughout
the whole
total mind/body/soul
our system.

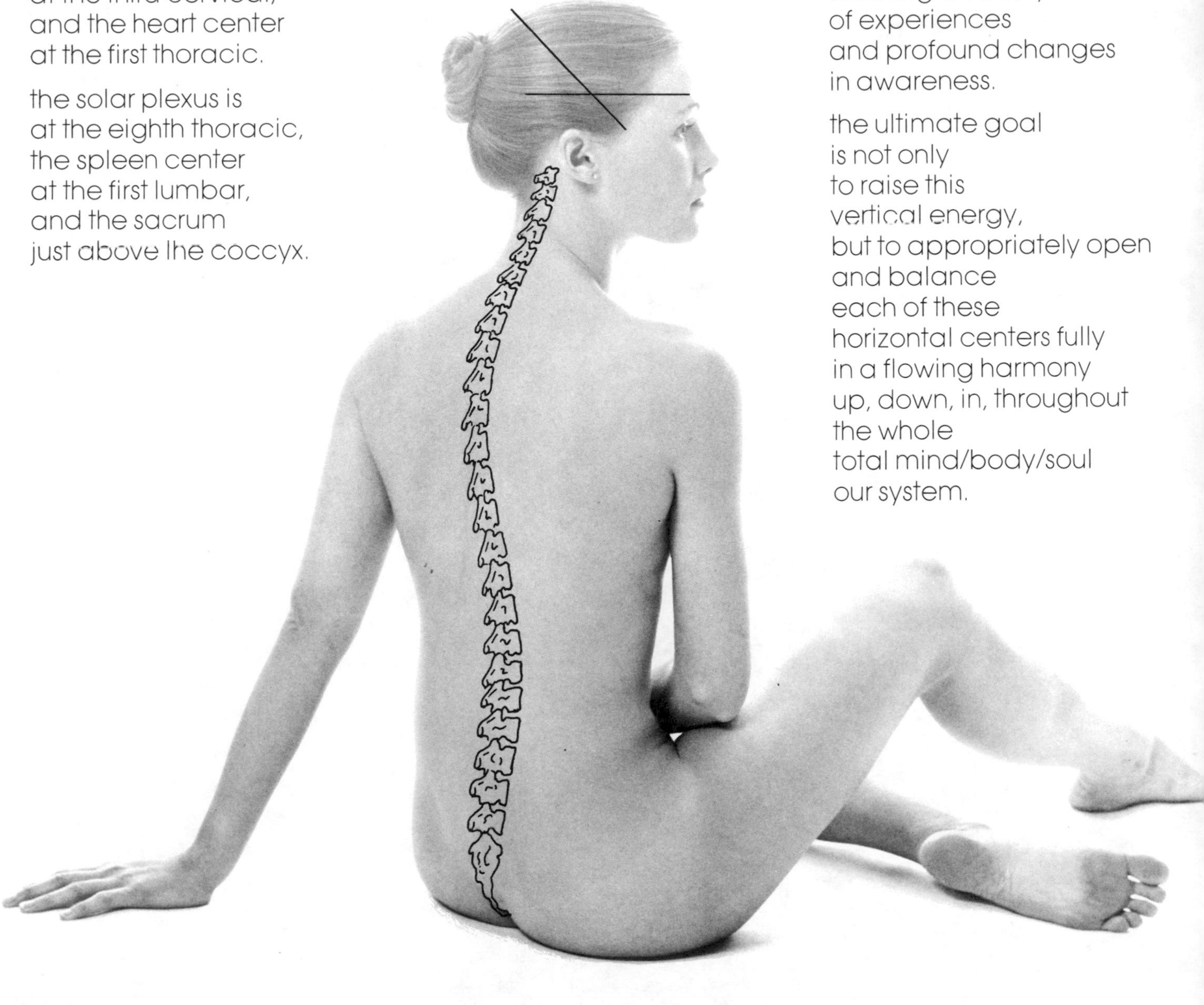

these seven centers
are related to
and have a significant
effect on
the endocrine glands.

and these
ductless glands
ultimately affect
the whole organism.

if the flow
through these
energy wheels
is excessive,
blocked,
or disrupted
by inadequate
or undue activity,
the corresponding
endocrine
will be affected.

these glands
of internal secretion
along with
the nervous system
are the master
internal
controlling,
balancing,
and self-regulating
system
of the unified
mind/body.

the slightest imbalance
in these areas
can cause fluctuations
in minute
but extremely

powerful hormone secretions
that enter directly
into the blood stream
creating subtle
instantaneous changes
in mood,
appearance,
relaxation, respiration,
digestion,
initiative, and intelligence.

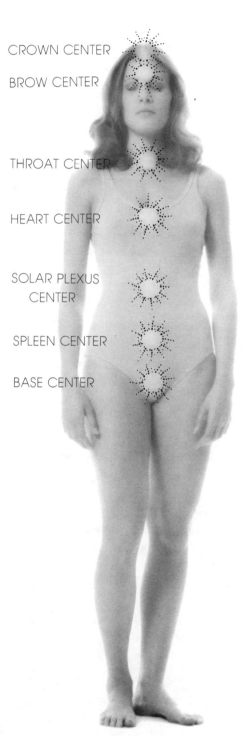

CROWN CENTER

BROW CENTER

THROAT CENTER

HEART CENTER

SOLAR PLEXUS
CENTER

SPLEEN CENTER

BASE CENTER

17

the power of this
internal energy system
can be related
to the chi energy
in t'ai chi
and the ki force
in akido and karate
as well as to
the basic principles
of acupuncture.

the acupuncture points
and their meridians
can be thought of
as the tributaries
flowing from
these seven rivers
of light.
if these centers
become blocked
or disharmonized,
these subtle estuaries
become unbalanced
causing symptoms
and malfunctions
in weak
or symbolic areas
within the organism.

according to chinese
and occult medicine,
all physical, emotional,
and psychological illness
is the result of
an improper balance
or an interruption
of this vital energy flow.
if this delicate
natural balance is restored,
the person once again
becomes a unified center
of well-being
bliss, health, harmony,
wholeness.

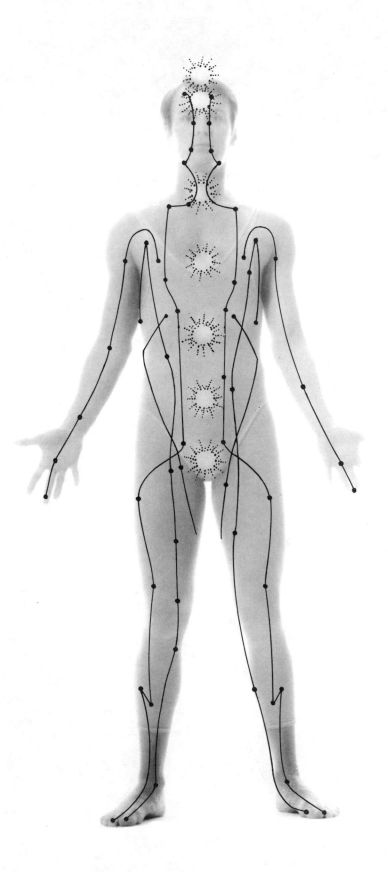

each of these centers
has its own
function, color, sound,
and symbolic form.
by understanding
these forms
of condensed energy,
each of these wheels
can be
appropriately
cleansed, opened,
and balanced.

basic exercises
for this purpose
will be found
throughout this book.

various systems differ
in the number,
location, function,
symbol, sound,
and color
of the centers.

the method
used in this book
is based less on tradition
and more on actual
visual, experimental,
and experiential evidence.

the first center,
the root chakra
located at
the base of the spine,
is the seat
of the physical life force,
kundalini.
classically
the function
of this center
is said to be
concerned with
basic existence
and survival.

for us, the function
of the base center
is to influence
sexual activity,
regeneration, and creativity.
this chakra
affects the sex glands,
ovaries and testes.
It is responsible for
the sex drive,
reproduction, and the
secondary sex characteristics.

the transmutation
of this procreative energy
can be used
to enhance all forms
of creative activity,
personal growth,
health, healing,
intuition,
and intelligence.

influenced by
the planet saturn,
earth is the element
of the first lotus,
the square
its symbolic form,
and lead its metal.

smell is the dominant
sense of the base chakra,
its color is red-orange,
and the sound vibration
of the root center is
LA.

19

the second center
or spleen chakra,
located halfway between
the pubis and the navel,
is usually considered
the center of
sexual activity.

in our system
it is the center
for cleansing,
purification,
and health.
its endocrine function
is connected with
the liver, pancreas,
and spleen,
glands that influence
metabolism,
digestion,
the detoxifications
of poisons,
immunity to disease,
and the balance
of blood sugar.

influenced by the
planet jupiter,
water is the element
of the second center,
tin its metal,
and taste
its dominant sense.

the symbolic form
of the spleen chakra
is a pyramid
with the capstone removed;
its color is pink,
and the sound
of the second lotus is
BA.

the third center,
the solar plexus,
located just
above the navel,
is the center of
emotion and power.
this third chakra
influences the adrenal glands
which profoundly affect
the sympathetic nervous system,
muscular energy,
heartbeat,
digestion,
circulation, and mood.

excessive use
and overabuse
of adrenalin
due to constant stress
produces various physical
and psychological symptoms
including ulcers,
nervous disorders,
and chronic fatigue.

influenced by
the planet mars,
fire is the element
of the power chakra,
iron its metal,
and sight
its dominant sense.

the symbolic form
of the third center
is a circle,
its color is kelly green,
and the sound
of this lotus
is like the emotional cheer
at a football game,
RA.

the heart chakra
is the center center,
the source of boundless
love and compassion,
rather than
one dimensional
sexual or
sentimental romantic passion.

located in the center
of the chest,
the heart lotus
when fully opened
expresses unconditional love
for spirit,
consciousness,
and every
level manifestation
of creation.

the fourth chakra
influences the thymus gland
located in the center of the chest
just behind
the upper breast bone.
the main function
of the thymus
in adults
is the proper utilization
of the
amino-competence factor,
that aspect
of the body
which helps create
immunity to disease.

it is interesting to note
how open, loving people
are usually hearty,
and how our culture's
competitive emphasis
makes people hardhearted,
susceptible to
heart disease.

influenced by
the planet venus,
air is the element
of the love lotus,
copper its metal,
and touch
the dominant sense.

the symbolic form
of this chakra
is the equilateral cross,
its color is yellow-gold,
and the sound vibration
of the fourth chakra
is the two-syllable sound
YM (Ya-Mm).

the fifth chakra
is located
in the throat.
it is the center
for creativity
and self-expression.

the throat center
influences
the thyroid gland
which affects the balance
of the entire
nervous system,
metabolism,
muscular control,
and body heat production.

this center is called
the gateway to liberation
because it leads
beyond the physical/
emotional planes
and into the astral spaces.

influenced by
the planet mercury,
ether is its element,
and hearing,
the dominant sense
of this lotus,
with mercury as its metal.

the symbolic form
of this chakra
is a chalice
(the integrated
physical/emotional body
becomes the holy grail).

its color is sky blue,
and its sound vibration
is the joyous delight
expressed in
the act of creation
HA.

the sixth chakra,
the all seeing
third eye,
is located
just above and between
the brows,
in the center
of the forehead.

here is the source of ecstasy,
extrasensory perception,
clairvoyance, clairaudience,
heightened intuition,
and the paranormal powers.
in ancient egyptian paintings
and statues,
one sometimes sees
a pharoah or initiate
with a snake figure
coming out at this point
in the forehead.
this is symbolic
of that person having raised
the latent serpent energy
to this level
which is also known as
christ consciousness.

classically,
the sixth center
is said to influence
the pineal gland,
but in our system,
it relates to the pituitary
which in sequential order
is located below the pineal.

the pituitary gland
is the master control center
of the mind/body
affecting to some degree
all of the other endocrines.

beyond the senses
and the five elements,
the sixth center
is influenced by
the sun and the moon;
its metals are gold
and silver,
and its symbolic form
is a six-pointed star.

indigo, a pure midnight blue,
is the color
of the brow center,
while the sound vibration
of the third eye
is related to the utterance
one makes when finally
reaching a deep insight
or experiencing the solution
to a baffling problem;
that sound is
AH.

the crown chakra,
or thousand-petaled lotus,
is located in and around
the upper skull.

in mystic lore,
when the lower energies
are balanced,
refined, and raised
to this region
known as cosmic consciousness,
unconditional enlightenment
beyond name,
form,
thought,
or rational experience
takes place.
it is this
highest frequency
that is the source
of the halo
that surrounds the head
of spiritually evolved beings.

the seventh center
influences the pineal gland
which medically
seems to have no function,
though the ancients
thought it was
the seat of the soul.

beyond the five elements,
mind, senses, and form,
the inexplicable state

realized at this center
is unmitigated
bliss/rapture.

total unity
with the source,
the mystical,
transcendental,
timeless,
changeless
experience of I AM,
pure being,
without subject or object
(i and my father are one).

the color
of the crown chakra
is purple,
and its symbolic form
is a lotus flower
(with its roots in the mud,
the dense energies
of the base center,
its stem in the water,
the emotional energies
of the torso,
but its blossom,
untouched by the water,
fully open
to the energy
of the sun).

the sound vibration
of this center
is the total amalgamation
of all sounds,
OM.

the human aura
is the energy field
that surrounds the
material body.
it is the sum total
of the energy given off
by the centers;
it is the glow
of part of the aura
that is pictured in
kirlian photography.

the aura has been mapped
into seven bands
or layers by observers
and is distinguished
as follows:

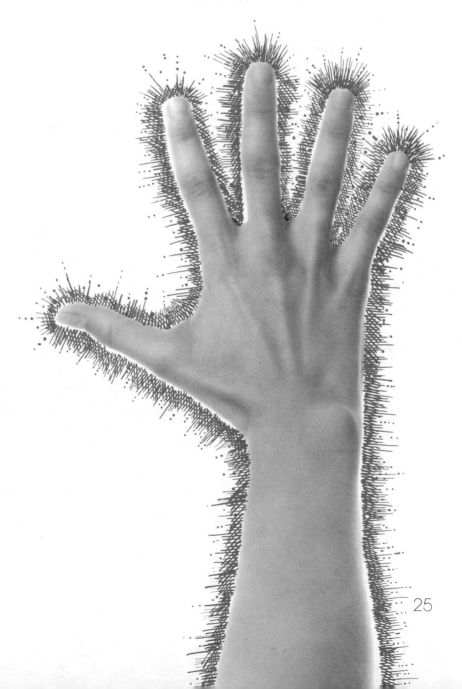

the ovum is
a one-eighth inch
blank space
between the physical body
and the first color emanation.

the first layer,
the health band,
radiates bluish white
under most normal conditions.
if a person
has a health problem,
there will be localized dark spots
related to
the origin of the problem
or there may be
a color change
in the whole aura.

the next space is
the emotional band
which reflects
the feeling level
of that person's experience.

next we find
the mental band
that deals with
the individual's
thought patterns.

the fourth
or para-conscious band
has to do with
intuition and
extrasensory power,
(most people are
totally unconscious
of the fact
that they have
these outer layers).

the fifth or
causal layer
corresponds to personal karma
(previous action).

the sixth layer,
or spiritual band,
is related to soul evolution.

the seventh,
or cosmic band,
connects with
universal consciousness.

each of these bands
radiates different colors
of varying intensity.
these emanations
can be seen
and read
by sensitives
who can tell
a person's personality makeup,
state of health,
emotional disposition,
mental attitudes,
abilities, and aptitudes,
as well as past problems,
difficulties,
and tendencies.

through the use
of this sensitive vision,
individuals can be advised
of future directions
and trends
in personal,
interpersonal,
and transpersonal
development.

(my own experience
is that i feel
rather than see the centers
and can,
with this ability,
tell which of the chakras
are open
and which are
partially blocked.)

by experiencing
the condition of the centers
and knowing their functions,
it is possible
to get a relatively
clear idea
of what a person
is holding back;
for example,
people with power problems
will be somewhat closed
in the solar plexus,
while a person
with congestion
in the throat center
will often not be
expressing himself
or his creativity.

the implications
of this sensitive sight
for health, creativity,
and optimal functioning,
as well as for
therapeutic diagnosis
and treatment,
are obvious.

according to practitioners,
a great many people
have this gift
and can be trained
to see and feel
in this way.

and so we move
out of the nineteenth century
piscean materialism
and into twentieth century
aquarian energy space,
entering a new age
where individual progress
is directly related
to group evolution,
a time when what has been
esoteric
will become exoteric;
the invisible
will become visible
in the age-old rediscovery
of the subtle,
indivisible truth
that radiates out
from within.

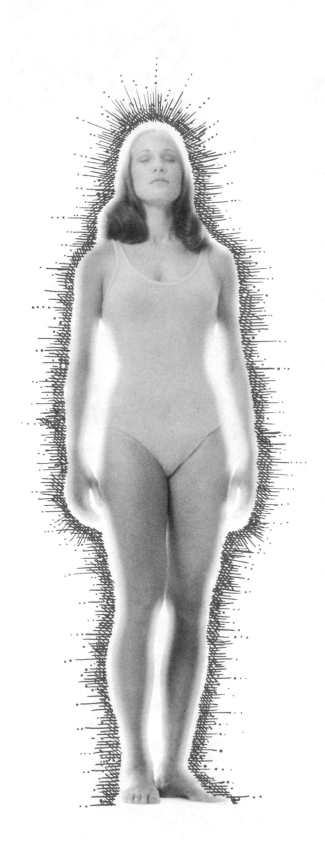

we are all
points of light
and as we link
light up
we are

turning the world
into a star.

chapter 1
ENERGY MEDITATIONS

the universe,
your existence,
is a vast whole,
a hologram.
every energy,
feeling, thought,
quality, desire,
and its opposite,
time and no time,
is there
around you.

all any being/
situation
can do
is to
touch/stimulate
that place
that is always there,
an aspect
of that
which is
all around you.

for every thing,
past, present, future,
person, possibility,
is going on,
all existing
at the same time.

your being,
moving through
every simple/
complex plane,
joy, bliss, pain,
with and against
the grain.

but our conditioned
ego identification
and our biological
social filters

organize and linearly
distort our awareness
so that we
are usually
only conscious of
one or some
aspects at a time.

the figure or figures
that are
most homeostatically
or symbolically rewarding
emerge from the
background of totality.
for example,
when you are feeling
very depressed,
low down,
discouraged,
courage exists
within you.
it is there,
but you are only
narrowly aware
so that you don't
experience it.

in this
constricted situation,
your consciousness
is largely
identified with
the negative side,
and you are not
in contact
with your being,
that deep,
centered perspective
which is beyond
any limited association
and which has
the power to
encourage you.

now drugs,
of course,
provide one way
to open more doors,
to become more open,
to perceive more,
but you come
to depend on them,
and the price
is too often
inconsistent motivation,
concentration,
and functional preciseness.

so the direction
we are looking for
is to be more
perennially centered,
accepting and observing
who/what/where
we are at each moment,
to be
loose, natural, and easy,
more meditatively,
attentively alive.

fully aware,
totally there,
for every activity
or quiet space,
as much as possible,
in touch/harmony
with our
full perspective.

this kind of
wholesomeness
can be realized
through continuous
self remembering
and by moving
out of the hole
where the identification
perspective
is deceptively shallow,
narrow, one-sided,
and limited,
and into wider,
higher states of energy,
consciousness,
where the ability
to see/experience/feel
expands
until you are
able to fuse
with the whole.

this process
can be accelerated
through constantly
witnessing your behavior
and using
the exercises
and meditations
found in this book
to keep your
energy universe
cleansed, harmonious,
vital, and balanced.

by gradually quieting
and disidentifying
with desires,
wonderings, and distractions,
this focused force
can keep you
continuously aware,
and through the building
of this identification
with the self,
you can learn to
merge/be
compassionately

nonattached,
unified,
and disidentified.

like the open sky,
not getting carried away
by passing clouds,
thoughts, feelings,
and pictures.

but clearly
able to be,
to watch,
and enjoy your movie
without getting caught
in it
so that you can
transform,
transcend, and end
the illusory,
partial
point of view
which is the cause
of almost all
of your suffering.

energy at your fingertips

first clap your hands
at various speeds
for about 30 seconds,
then put your hands
facing palms up
on your knees.
close your eyes
and experience what's happening
in your hands,
not just the slight stinging
on the surface,
but what's happening
in the center of the hands.
let that feeling
flow up your arms into your body.
let it flow
wherever it wants to go.

now open your eyes.
place your hands
in front of you,
two or three inches apart,
then very slowly
move them back and forth,
closer and farther apart.
the motion is like
playing an accordian.
don't go too close together
or too far apart.
feel what's happening.

in most cases
you will be aware
of warmth
or a feeling of
magnetic attraction
or resistance
between the hands.
you might feel any
one, two, or all three
of the above.

your body is a battery
of water cells.
your arms are the
positive and negative cables.

psychic energy
_____

to increase
the energy between
your hands
use thought power.
with your hands facing
each other,
feel the energy
and then think warm.
imagine a red hot force
between your hands.
after you feel the heat,
change that force
between your hands to resistance
by imagining
a powerful current
that keeps your hands
from coming together.
then experiment:
use light or sound
between your hands,
and experience
the results.

this is a simple experiment
in mind over matter.

in tibet, initiates were taught
to use their mental concentration
to the point
where they could
sit outside naked
in the middle of winter
and melt snow.

energy in/hand/sir
_____

to balance and harmonize
the emotional energy
in the solar plexus,
place the left hand
flat on the area
just above the navel,
the right hand on top
of the left.

to balance, stimulate
and harmonize the energy
in the heart center,
place the right hand
flat over the center of the chest,
the left hand
on top of the right.

to balance and harmonize
the relationship between
the solar plexus and heart,
place the left hand
over the solar plexus,
the right hand over the heart.

to balance and enhance
the energy within the spinal cord,
sit on your left hand;
make sure the center of the hand
is under the bottom
of the spine.
the right hand
goes over the back top
of the head.
try switching hands
and experience the difference.

keep each of these positions
for 30 to 60 seconds,
or as long as desired.

these hand positions
are especially useful
when you are upset,
over-emotional, or under
excessive tension.

increasing energy
_____

sit comfortably with your
back and neck straight,
eyes closed.

create a glowing pink light
at the level
of your heart center.
hold it there
for a slow count of 9.
next, see a glowing pink light
just above the top of the head.
hold it there for a
slow count of 15.
then visualize a pink light
surrounding your entire body.
you are sitting
in the middle of that light.
hold that image around you
for a slow count of 12.

then create a radiating blue light
at the level of your throat
and hold it there
for a slow count of 9.
next see a radiating blue light
just above the top of the head.
hold it there for a
slow count of 15.
then visualize a blue light
surrounding your entire body.
you are sitting
in the middle of that light.
hold the image around you
for a slow count of 12.

now create a glowing white light
at the level of your forehead
and hold it there
for a slow count of 9.
next see a glowing white light
just above the top of your head.
hold it there
for a slow count of 15.
then visualize a white light
surrounding your entire body.
you are sitting
in the middle of that light.
hold the image
of that glowing light
for a slow count of 12.

after, experience how you feel
and open your eyes.

this process can calm
as well as energize.

cleansing meditation

---

sit comfortably
with your back
and neck straight,
eyes closed.

imagine a 6-inch sun
6 inches above your head.
this sun is radiating
warm, white-light energy.
see the bottom of the sun open
pouring this purifying
white light down
to the top of your head.
now visualize at the upper head
a closed lotus flower
which slowly and fully opens
as the sun energy
pours in and downward,
saturating, purifying, balancing,
harmonizing and energizing
the crown center.
repeat this process of
slowly opening the closed flower
and allowing the light
to permeate through
the brow, throat,
heart, solar plexus, spleen
and base center.

next, connect and combine
these centers
one to the other
by seeing and feeling
a stream of light energy
flowing from one to the other;
from the base to the spleen,
spleen to solar plexus,
solar plexus to heart,
heart to throat,
throat to brow center,
brow to crown center.
then take a moment or two
to experience how you feel.

next visualize your physical body
as a closed flower.
slowly it opens fully
to the light
which pours in and downward
cleansing and balancing,
energizing and harmonizing.

next, within the open
physical form,
see a closed flower
that represents the emotional body.
feel that flower slowly opening fully
to the cleansing white light.

now see a closed flower
that represents your mental body
and experience it opening
to the purifying light.

then open the closed flower
that represents your spiritual body
and let it be saturated
by the sun light.

next blend and fuse these bodies
one to the other:
the physical to the emotional,
the emotional with the mental,
the mental with the spiritual
take a moment to experience this.

then see in your mind's eye
a closed flower
that represents your
unconscious mind.
let the light pour in and
and downward
clearing, cleansing,
balancing and harmonizing.

next see a closed flower
that represents your
conscious mind
and allow it to open
to the incoming light.

next see a closed flower
that represents your
superconscious mind
and watch it open
to the healing light.

now blend these aspects
of the mind
one to the other:
the unconscious to the conscious,
the conscious
to the superconscious.

after, take a few moments
to experience the effects
and then open your eyes.

become free of the
psychophysical/emotional fatigue
toxins and debris
that accumulate
during the day.

forehead/solar plexus/heart

---

sit comfortably
with your back
and neck straight,
eyes closed.

focus your consciousness
on your forehead.
keep it there
for a few moments
until you experience
that area warm and alive.
now move down
to your solar plexus
and hold
your awareness there.
next bring it up
to your heart
and spend some time there.
then move back
to your forehead,
again, back to the solar plexus,
and up to your heart;
forehead, solar plexus, heart.
repeat this cycle slowly
at least 3 times.

then, if you wish,
continue at the same speed,
increase the speed,
or reverse the order
for a period of time
until the heat/energy
is strongly felt
in these centers.

balancing and enhancing
the connection
between the mind,
love and emotions.

energy charge

lie on your back on the floor,
take a deep breath
and make the sound AH
as loud as possible.
continue to make the sound
as long as your breath lasts.
repeat this process
2 more times.

next undulate your belly
sucking your belly
in and out for 30 to 60 seconds,
allowing your upper body
to move as much as it can
while still lying
flat on the floor.

now, take a
deep breath
and make the sound OH.
do this over a cycle
of 3 breaths.

then do the
belly/upper body undulations
again for 30 to 60 seconds.

repeat this entire process
3 to 9 times
and experience the results.

a practical way to get
the energy moving at the
start of the day or when you
experience tension
and fatigue.

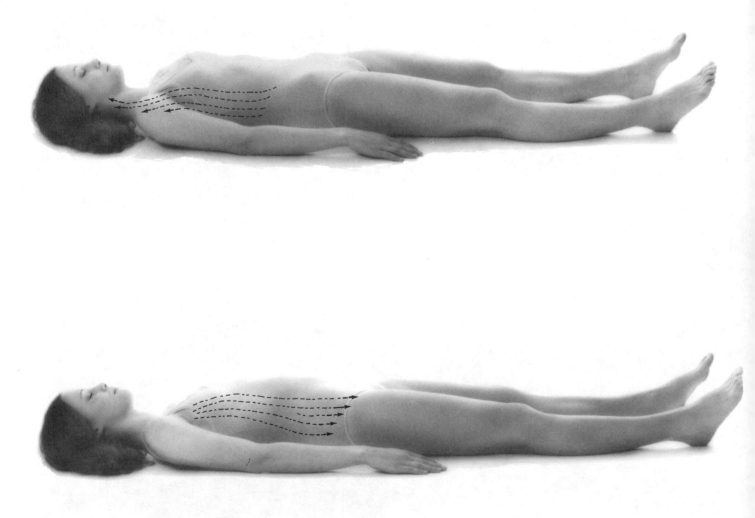

universal light
_____

close your eyes
and create a 6-inch
white-light sun
6 inches above your head.

see the bottom
of the sun open,
pouring liquid-like
white-light energy
into you.
fill and feel
your entire body aglow
with this flowing,
soothing, bright-light energy.

now see that glow grow
so that it encompasses
the room you're sitting in.
next let that emanation
move out to include
the neighborhood around you.
then let it open up
to include the city
you're living in,
expanding even more
throughout the entire state,
opening up even wider
to include the entire country,
then the whole hemisphere,
the entire world,
the solar system,
the galaxy,
the universe.

see yourself as a dynamo
of light
in a universe of light.
as long as it feels right.

then let go,
experience how you feel,
and open your eyes.

the more you
open up to
and share the light,
the more it will
move through you.

be light
head
heart
id

39

chapter 2
ENERGY BALANCING CENTERS

balance
is flexibility,
steadiness,
stability,
the ability
to flow
back and forth
with agility
in unlimited possibility.

without falling
too far off,
dis/ability.

for balance is
a basic key
to being·
bliss/health/harmony.

the difficulty
is that
most of us
live as if balance
is jumping
from one extreme
to the other.

like riding the ends
of a teeter-totter,
we become involved
in excessive binges,
hopping
back and forth
from depression
to elation,
boredom to excitation,
love/hate/frustration,
forgetting
that real lasting balance
is within,
an alive neutral point
at the fulcrum
of your being,
and that

extreme
extremes
are extremely

painful.

the central, nervous system,
brain and spinal cord
offer us
a profound perspective.
for this self-balancing system
and can be divided
into two polar parts:
the sympathetic
and the parasympathetic.
the first of these halves
operates during emergencies,
contracting in readiness
for fight or flight,
while the latter is
related to dilation,
expansive regeneration.

at their extremes
these poles can
analogously represent
the hyperactivity
of the united states
and the inertia
to be found in india.

like india and america,
they are symbolic
of both a personal
and world-wide excess
that creates chronic
physiological/psychological/
ecological imbalance,
tension, irritation,
dissatisfaction, and disease.

these behavioral extremes
are further confused
and compounded
by the use and abuse
of language.

our verbal symbolic systems
take over and run us,
and we get lost.

instead of identifying
and cultivating
our conscious,
our being,
we become attached to
and identified with
our roles, desires,
fantasies, concepts,
and beliefs,
associating and
reacting to them
as if they were real.

like pavlov's dogs,
we salivate to a bell
even when no food
is around.

we become nervous,
tense, and angry
al imaginary dangers,
mentally creating
physical, psychological,
and eventually
depression,
fear and rejection,
the need for protection.

our minds
tyranically rule
and deceive us
to the degree
that we are unable
to tell the difference
between actual
and symbolic reality.

most of the time,
thoughts, emotions,
the past, future,
dominate our consciousness,
disrupting and dissipating
our energies
so that we miss
the unique
reality satisfaction
of simply being
with what is
now.

we seldom allow time
to stop,
to expand,
to transform,
to care for ourselves
and one another.

even sexual intimacy
has become an
ego status game,
turning a gentle
love, playful,
regenerative,
biological pleasure
into a tense,
orgasm-oriented,
goal orientation,
with all the frustrations,
malfunctions,
and seeming threats
of an actual
survival situation.

the alternative
we can choose
is to consciously be
accepting, centered
aware, natural, and easy,
compassionately
nonattached,
and totally involved
in discipline
and spontaneity.

learning to constantly
observe and experience
with sensitivity.

not going
too far off balance
so that we can regain
our own balance.

like a tightrope walker,
if we don't go
too far off
in any direction,
we won't fall down
and need
someone else
to pick us up.

using observation,
skillfull will,
focused energy,
constructive thought,
visualizations,
and chakra meditations
to continually
reestablish
and keep balance.

feeling and experiencing
the active/quiet,
passive/expressive cycles
that move
through the mind/body.

continually allowing
new ideas,
feelings,
and patterns that
let us be
appropriately
open,
clear, and easy,
in rest
and activity,
acting with the center
rather than
stereotype reacting
from the periphery,
responding totally
to the everchanging flow
to that
which actually is.

sound centering

sit comfortably with your
back and neck straight,
eyes closed.

take a deep breath
and make a low
deep OM sound.
let this vibration
encompass the entire area
from the base of the spine
to the solar plexus
including the belly.
repeat 2 more times.
experience the effects.

next make a
medium range OM sound
vibrating in the area
of the etheric heart in
the center of the chest.
repeat 2 more times.
experience the results.

then make a
loud, high-pitched OM sound
vibrating throughout the head.
repeat 2 more times.
experience how you feel.

this simple exercise
is most rewarding
when you are feeling scattered
and are willing to
take the energy/time
to return to center.

chakra breathing

sit comfortably
with your back
and neck straight,
eyes closed.

inhale white light energy
through your mouth
to an 8 count
into the base center.
hold it there
for a count of 4.
as you exhale
through your nose
to a count of 8,
see the center glow.
hold the glow
without breathing
for a count of 4.

again, draw white light energy
through your mouth
to a count of 8
into the base center.
hold it there
for a count of 4.
now, as you exhale
through your nose
to an 8 count,
send the energy
up the spine
to the spleen center
and see it glow there
without breathing
for a count of 4.

next, inhale white light energy
through your mouth
to a count of 8
into the base center.
hold it there for 4.
as you exhale
through your nose,
raise the energy
1 count
to the spleen center
and 7 counts
to the solar plexus center.
hold for 4
without breathing
and see the
solar plexus glow.

now, draw white light energy
through your mouth
to a count of 8
into the base center.
hold it there
for a count of 4.
exhale through your nose,
and raise the energy
1 count
to the spleen center,
1 count
to the solar plexus center,
1 count
to the spleen center,
and 6 counts
to the heart center.
hold for 4
and see the heart glow.

43

inhale white light energy
through your mouth
to an 8 count
into the base center.
hold it there for 4.
exhale through your nose
and raise the energy
1 count
to the spleen center,
1 count
to the solar plexus center,
1 count
to the heart center,
and 5 counts
to the throat center.
hold for 4
and see the throat glow.

inhale white light energy
through your mouth
to the count of 8
into the base center.
hold it there for 4.
exhale through your nose
and raise the energy
1 count
to the spleen center,
1 count
to the solar plexus center,
1 count
to the heart center,
1 count
to the throat center.
and 4 counts
to the brow.
hold for 4 without breathing
and see the brow glow.

inhale white light energy
through your mouth
to the count of 8
into the base center.
hold it there for 4.
exhale through your nose
and raise the energy
1 count
to the spleen center,
1 count
to the solar plexus center,
1 count
to the heart center,
1 count
to the throat center,
1 count
to the brow center,
and 3 counts
to the crown center.
hold for 4
without breathing
and see the crown glow.

repeat this exercise
a total of 3 times
and experience
how you feel.

this activity
raises the level and amount
of energy in the body
as it balances the centers.

44

colors through centers

sit comfortably
with your back
and neck straight,
eyes closed.

visualize
the color red-orange
radiating in the
base center.
after 15 seconds,
see it as a
red-orange searchlight beam
radiating light beams
forward from the body,
radiating from the
back of the body,
radiating to the
right from the body,
radiating to the
left from the body,
radiating downward
into the floor,
radiating upward
to the sky.
see it shine
in all 6 directions
at once.
now let that
emanating light
become white,
and hold this image
for 10 to 20 seconds.

repeat this sequence
in each of the other
6 centers
using these specific
colors in each center:

spleen	pink
solar plexus	kelly green
heart	yellow-gold
throat	sky blue
brow	indigo
crown	purple

each time, after radiating
the specific color
in all 6 directions,
let that color
become white light.

sounds of centers

take a deep breath
through the mouth
and make the sound
LA
as you make this sound
let it vibrate
at the base of the spine.
on the next breath
as you make the sound
LA
see a red orange light
radiating/vibrating
at the base center.
on the third breath
make the sound
LA
and see a white light
as you vibrate the sound
in the base center.

repeat this sequence
changing the sound
color and location
that is appropriate
for each chakra:

spleen
sound BA
color pink

solar plexus
sound RA
color kelly green

heart
sound YM (Ya Mm)
color yellow-gold

throat
sound HA
color sky blue

brow
sound AH
color indigo

crown
sound OM
color purple

always end each procedure
with white light in
the chakra you are working.

this exercise is for cleansing
the lungs, expansion of
the breath, balancing
and energizing the centers.

a less complicated version
of this exercise
is just to make
the designated sound
in the individual center
3 times
without the color.

this simple form
can easily be done
while performing
an activity,
even driving a car.

draw the energy centers

meditate on each center
one by one.
try to feel, smell,
taste, experience
each in turn.
then, using colored
felt pens,
paints or crayons
draw that center.
examine the drawing
and move on
to the next center.

when you have drawn
all 7 of your centers
place them on the floor,
in order,
one above the other.
then meditate on the whole.
experience the energy
you feel from them.

periodically
repeat this exercise
to make contact
with growth changes.

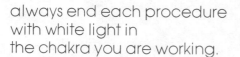

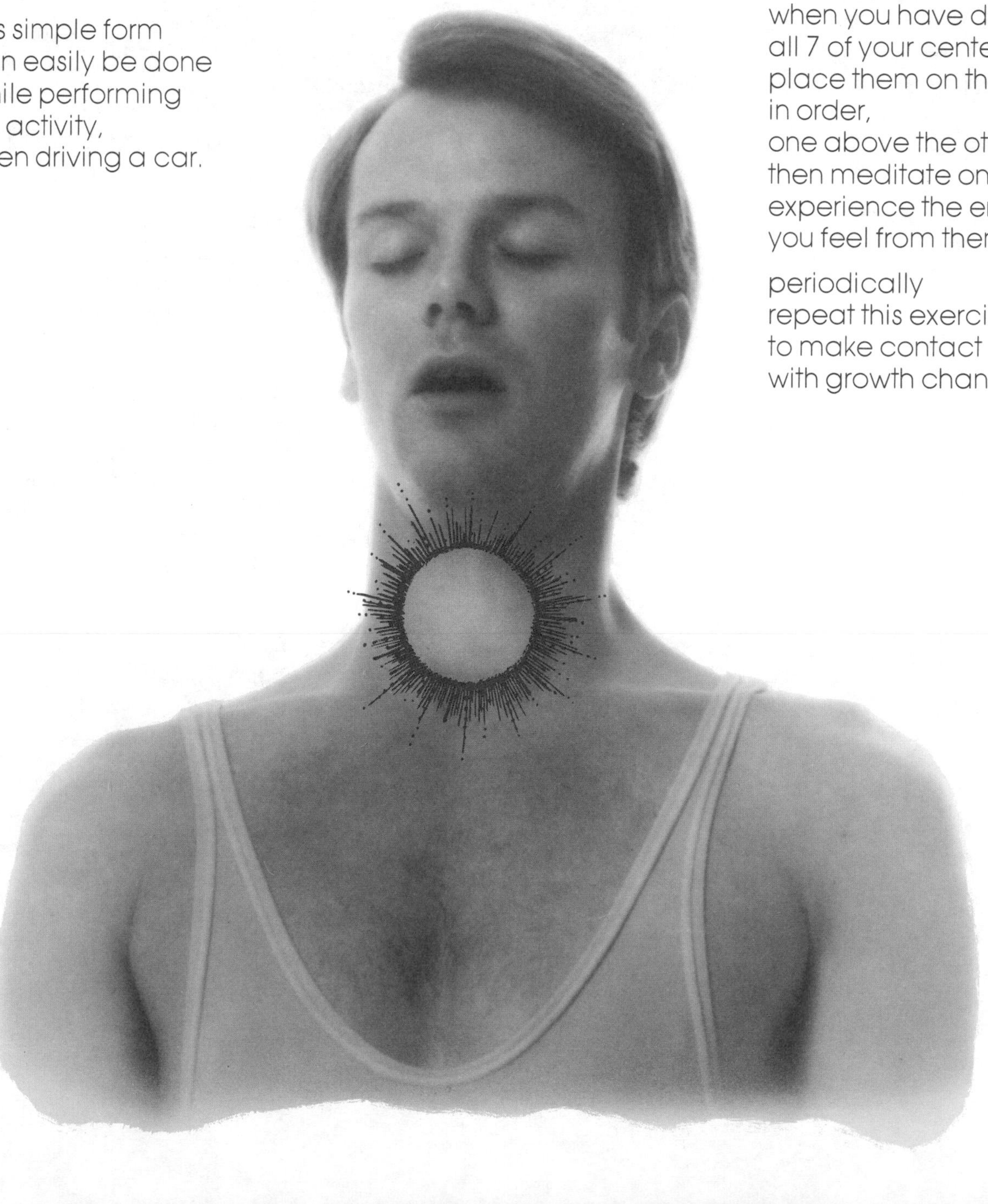

all of these
chakra exercises
can have
a powerful effect
on you.
be aware
of your reactions
and do not
overdo.

the following
symbolic chakra exercises
are some of the
most powerful
this writer has
ever experienced.
they involve the integrated
use of color, breathing
and symbols
to cleanse and rebalance
all of the centers.

as you do the process
the colors and feelings
you have
are an indication
of the state
your centers are in
at that specific time.
black or dark browns
are usually indicative
of blockage and disharmony,
while bright colors
suggest some congestion
and lack of balance.
soft, whitish colors,
(bluish-white, greenish-white,)
mean clearing and flow
while gray, white or opaque
are signals that
the center is clear.

the idea of these exercises
is not to make
the lighter or whiter
colors appear,
but to accept what emerges,
and then, if necessary,
work with the center
until that clarity
appears on its own.

how you feel
after each sequence
is as important
as the color you get.

in fact,
in the final analysis
when trying to diagnose
whether a center
is clear,
let your feelings
take precedence
over the color.

if a center does not clear
after doing the exercise
3 times,
repeat the sequence
or work on it
at another time
during the day.

it is not advisable
to do these practices
late at night
unless you want to
stay awake.

it is desirable
that you familiarize
yourself with these
exercises before you
actually do them
so that you can
perform them
in a relaxed state
with your eyes closed.

symbolic chakra exercise
BASE CENTER

sit comfortably
with your back
and neck straight,
eyes closed.

visualize at the level
of your forehead
a 2-inch by 4-inch box
full of red-orange energy.

as you inhale
through your mouth
to an 8 count,
draw the red-orange energy
down the vertebral column
to the base center.
hold it there
for a count of 16.
then exhale it
through your mouth
to an 8 count
blowing the energy
back up the vertebral column
and into the box.
observe the color
of the energy
in the box.

inhale that color
through your mouth
to an 8 count
down to the base center.
hold it there for 16.
then exhale
through your mouth
to an 8 count
blowing the energy
back into the box.
observe the color.

on the third inhalation,
draw whatever color
you found in the box
down to the base center
to an 8 count.
hold it there for 16.

then blow it out
through your mouth
to a count of 8
all around
the outside of the box
in a clockwise direction.
observe the color
around and in the box.
experience how you feel.

if the center is not clear,
repeat the sequence 3 times
and move on to
the spleen center.

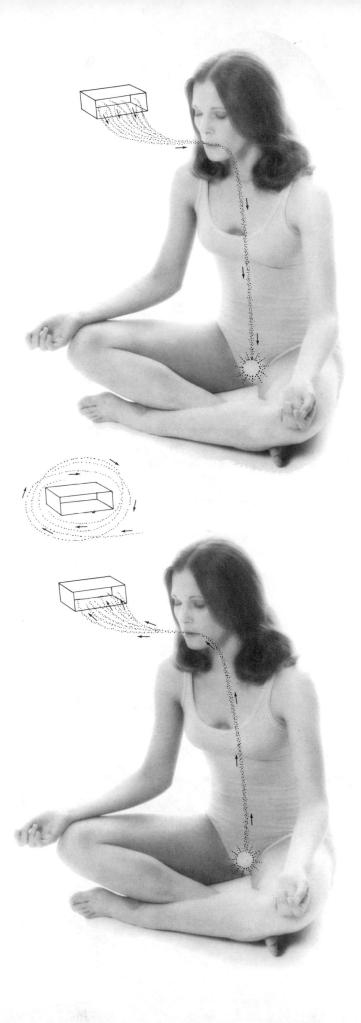

49

symbolic chakra exercise
SPLEEN CENTER

sit comfortably
with your back
and neck straight,
eyes closed.

visualize a glass pyramid
at the level
of your chest.
the capstone
of the pyramid
has been removed
and you can see
the four corners
that comprise the base
of the structure.
the pyramid is full
of pink energy.

draw that pink energy
through your mouth
to an 8 count
raising it up
from the four corners
and walls of the pyramid
and down
the vertebral column
to the base center.
raise this energy
to the level
of the spleen
and hold it there
for 16.
then exhale it
through your mouth
to an 8 count
blowing it up
the vertebral column,
out your mouth
and into the pyramid,
down the walls
of the pyramid
to the four corners
of the foundation.
observe the color.

inhale that color
through your mouth
to an 8 count
down to the base center.
raise it to the
level of the spleen
and hold for 16.
then, blow that energy
through your mouth
into the pyramid
to a count of 8.
observe the color

again draw that color
through your mouth
to an 8 count
down to the base center.
raise it to the level
of the spleen
and hold for 16.
then blow that energy
through your mouth
with force
to a count of 8
back into the pyramid.
as the energy comes down
into the pyramid,
the walls collapse.
observe the color, and
experience how you feel.

if the center is not clear,
repeat the sequence 3 times
and move on to the
solar plexus center.

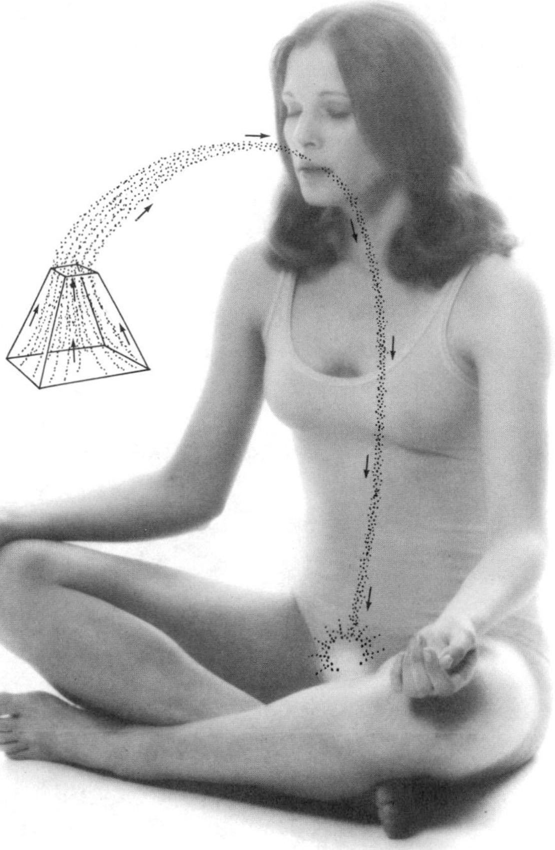

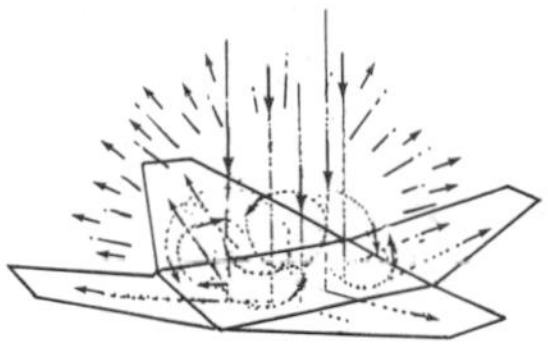

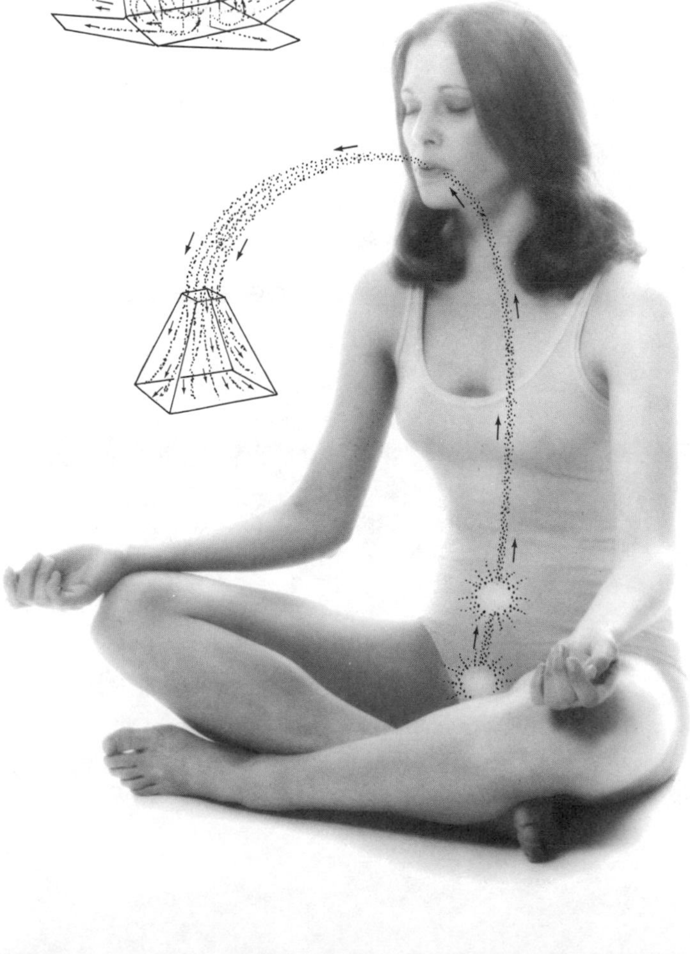

symbolic chakra exercise
SOLAR PLEXUS CENTER

───────────────

sit comfortably
with your back
and neck straight,
eyes closed.

visualize an image of yourself
standing in a kelly green
disc/pool of energy.
see yourself
bend your knees
and as you start
to inhale through your mouth
to a count of 4
imagine yourself raising
this green pool
up over your head.
from this position
to a 4 count
let it turn inward
coming down the body
to the base center.
from the base center
raise this pool
to the level
of the solar plexus
and hold for 16.
then, exhale
through your mouth
to a count of 8
blowing the energy
back over your head
and down to your feet.
observe the color.

inhale that color
through your mouth
to a count of 4
bringing the pool up
over your head
and inward again
to a count of 4
down to the base center.
raise it
to the solar plexus
and hold for 16.

inhale through your mouth
to an 8 count
blowing the pool
up over your head
and back down
to your feet.
observe the color.

again, see yourself
bend down
and pick up
the color pool
as you inhale
through your mouth
raising it up
over your head
to a 4 count,
and down to
the base center
to a 4 count.
raise it to
the solar plexus
and hold for 16.
exhale
through your mouth
to an 8 count
and blow the pool
with force
straight up
over your head
into the sky.
observe the color.
experience how you feel.

if the center is not clear,
repeat the sequence 3 times,
and move on
to the heart center.

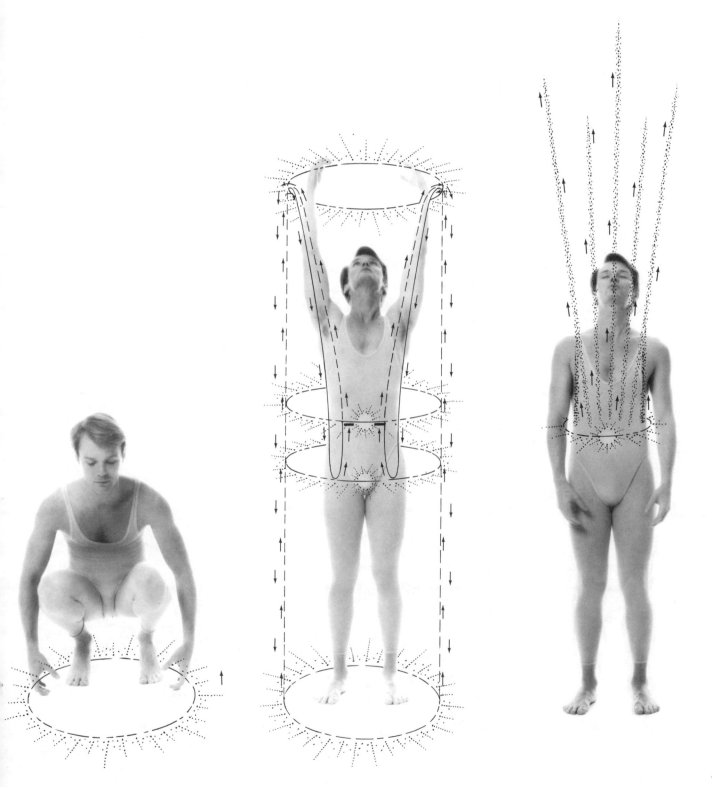

symbolic chakra exercise
HEART CENTER
————————————————

sit comfortably
with your back
and neck straight,
eyes closed.

visualize in front of you
an equilateral cross
full of yellow-golden energy.
the cross is
about the size
of your seated body.

a straw comes out
of the cross
and into your mouth.
as you inhale
through your mouth
to an 8 count,
draw all the golden energy
out of the cross
down all the vertebral column
to the base center.
raise it to the level
of the heart center.
hold it there
for a count of 16,
then blow it
through your mouth
to a count of 7
out the straw
and back into the cross.
observe the color.

again, draw that color
down to the base center
through the straw
while inhaling
through your mouth
to an 8 count.
raise it to the level
of the heart
and hold for 16.
now, with force
blow it through your mouth
to an 8 count
through the straw
back into the cross

as the energy
goes into the cross,
it hits the bottom
and that pressure
forces it up
out the two
horizontal sides
and the top
like a gushing fountain.
observe the color.
experience how you feel.

if the center is not clear,
repeat the sequence 3 times
and move on
to the throat center.

54

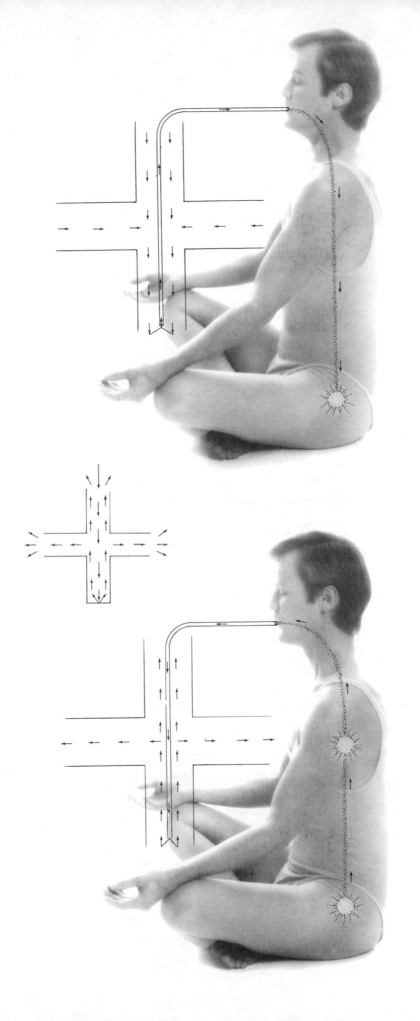

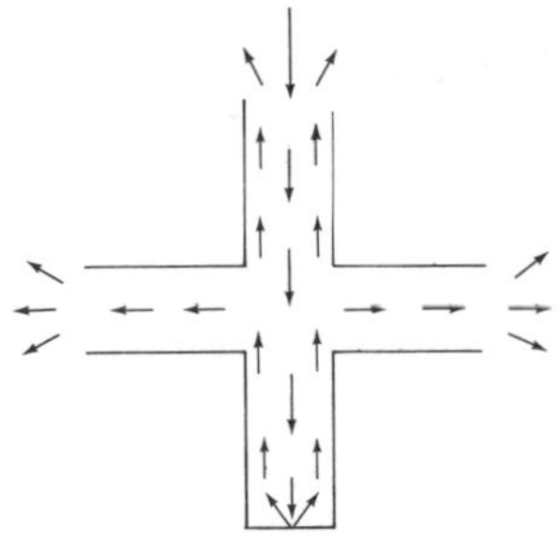

55

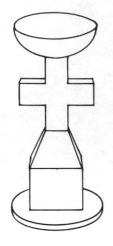

symbolic chakra exercise
THROAT CENTER

_____

sit comfortably
with your back
and neck straight,
eyes closed.

visualize a golden chalice
composed of a circle,
a square,
a triangle,
an equilateral cross
and a crescent moon.
it is filled with
sky blue liquid light.

take hold of the chalice
above the horizontal bars
of the cross
and gently drink
the sky blue liquid,
inhaling through your mouth
to a count of 8.
gently suck it down
the vertebral column
to the base center.
raise it to the level
of the throat center
and hold it there
for a count of 16.
then regurgitate
the substance back
into the cup
while exhaling
through your mouth
to an 8 count.
observe the color.

again, gently drink
that color in and down
to the base center
while inhaling
to an 8 count.
raise it to the level
of the throat
and hold for 16
while gagging slightly.
then, regurgitate it
back into the cup
while exhaling.
observe the color.

this time, inhale
and draw that color
through your mouth
to a count of 8.
drink in the liquid energy
with gusto
and suck it down
to the base center.
raise it to the level
of the throat
where you gently
but intensely
gag on it
for a count of 16.
then regurgitate
it back into the cup
while exhaling
through your mouth
to a count of 8.
observe its color.
experience how you feel.

if the center is not clear,
repeat the sequence 3 times
and move on
to the brow center.

symbolic chakra exercise
BROW CENTER
———————————————

sit comfortably
with your back
and neck straight,
eyes closed.

in front of your forehead
at the level of a brow
visualize a 6-pointed star
lying on its side.
it is filled with
an indigo energy.

as you inhale
through your mouth
to an 8 count,
draw this indigo energy
counterclockwise
from the 6 points
of the star
down the vertebral column
to the base center.
raise it to the level
of the brow
and hold
for a count of 16.
then, exhale
through your mouth
to an 8 count
blowing the energy clockwise
back into the 6 points
of the star.
observe the color.

again, inhale this energy
through your mouth
to an 8 count
from the 6 points
of the star
counterclockwise.
bring it down
to the base center.
raise it to the brow
and hold for 16.
blow it through your mouth
to a count of 8

back into the
6 points of the star.
observe the color.

inhale that color
through your mouth
to a count of 8
counterclockwise
from the 6 points
of the star
and draw it down
to the base center.
raise it to the brow
and hold
for a count of 16.
then, blow it
with force
clockwise
to an 8 count
into the 6 points
of the star.
as the energy is blown
into these points
and they fill,
the energy leaps
into the air
observe the color.
experience how you feel.

if the center is not clear,
repeat the sequence 3 times
and move on
to the crown center.

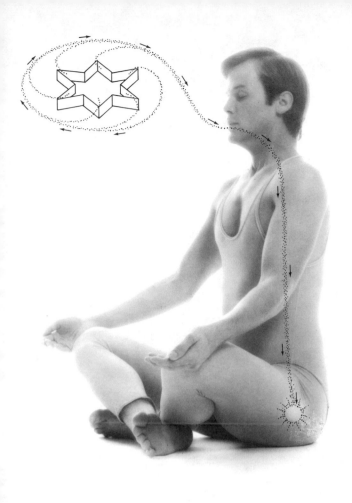

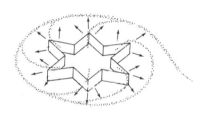

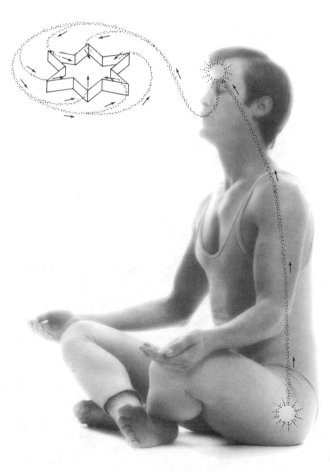

59

symbolic chakra exercise
CROWN CENTER
———————————

sit comfortably
with your back and neck
straight, eyes closed.

visualize
at the top
of your head
a closed lotus flower
filled with purple energy.

as you inhale
through your mouth
to an 8 count,
draw the purple energy
from the lotus
down through your body
and into your feet.
as the energy
is drained from it
the lotus opens completely
and remains open
until the energy returns.

now, raise the energy
from your feet
in a clockwise spiral
up your body
to the crown
and hold it there
for a count of 16.
then blow the energy
through your mouth
back into the lotus
to an 8 count
and close the lotus.
observe the color.

inhale the energy
from the lotus
through your mouth
to an 8 count
and draw it
down to your feet.
as the color is drained
the lotus opens fully.
now raise the energy
from your feet
in a clockwise spiral
up your body

to the crown
and hold it there
for a count of 16.

then close
the center of the lotus
and blow the energy
through your mouth
back into it
at a count of 8.
observe the color.

again, inhale
through your mouth
to a count of 8
drawing that color
down to your feet
as the center
of the lotus opens.
spiral the energy
clockwise up your body
to the crown.
hold it there
for a count of 16.
then, leaving the center
of the lotus open,
blow the energy
with force to an 8 count
through the open center
of the lotus
straight up
into the sky.
observe the color
and then take plenty
of time
to digest the entire
experience.

if the center
is not clear,
repeat the sequence
3 times.

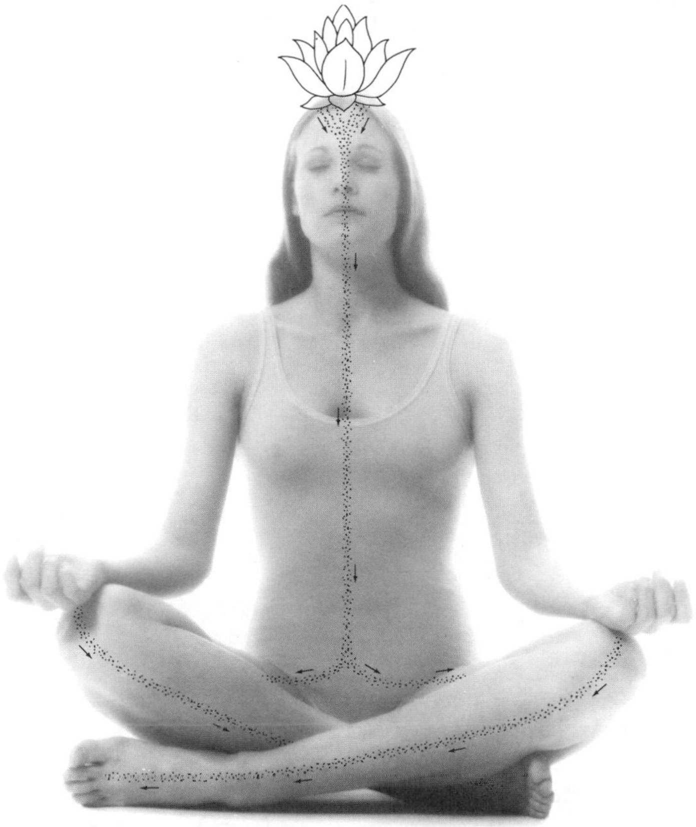

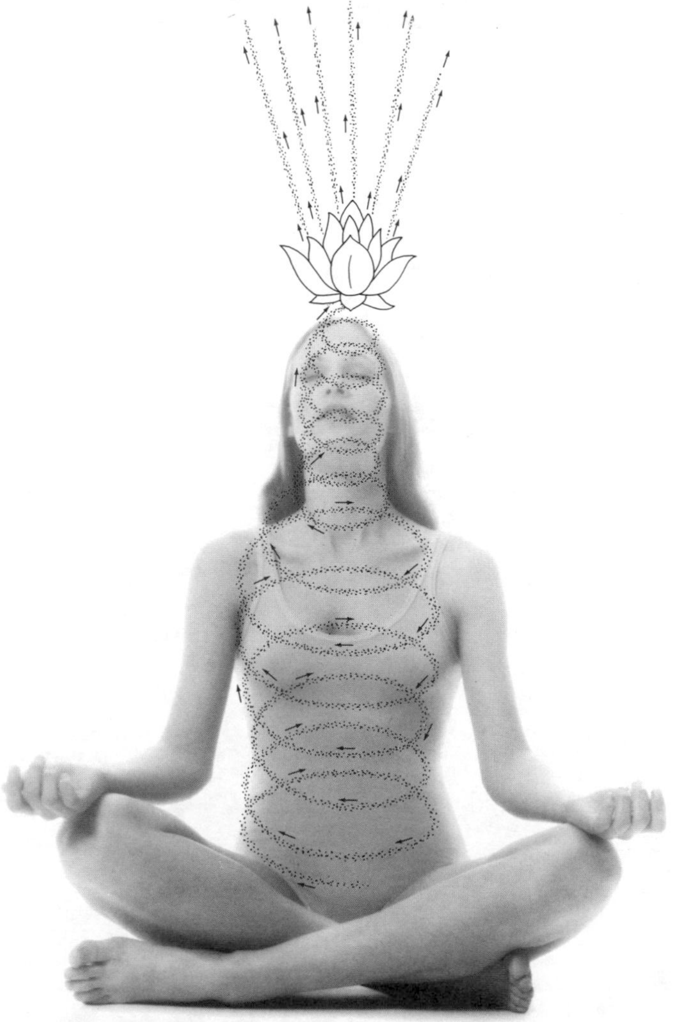

heart meditation

sitting in
meditation position
imagine a closed
golden-petaled lotus flower
at the level
of the heart.

this flower is composed
of 12 petals which
very gradually
begin to separate.
as this opening
slowly occurs,
a blue light emerges
radiating out
from the center of the flower.
as the lotus
continues to open,
the blue light expands.
take 1 to 5 minutes
for the flower
to open completely.

experience the center
totally open
emanating electric blue light.

now see a beam of white light
coming from the sky
pouring directly into
the center of the
open heart flower.

after 30 seconds
let the image go,
experience how you feel
and open your eyes.

it is important
to fuse the love energy
of the heart
with the spiritual
wisdom light.

awaken
your
sleeping
beauty

the vital root
red orange center
of procreative energy
dense latent
potent serpent power
ready to shoot
grow love
create
transmute

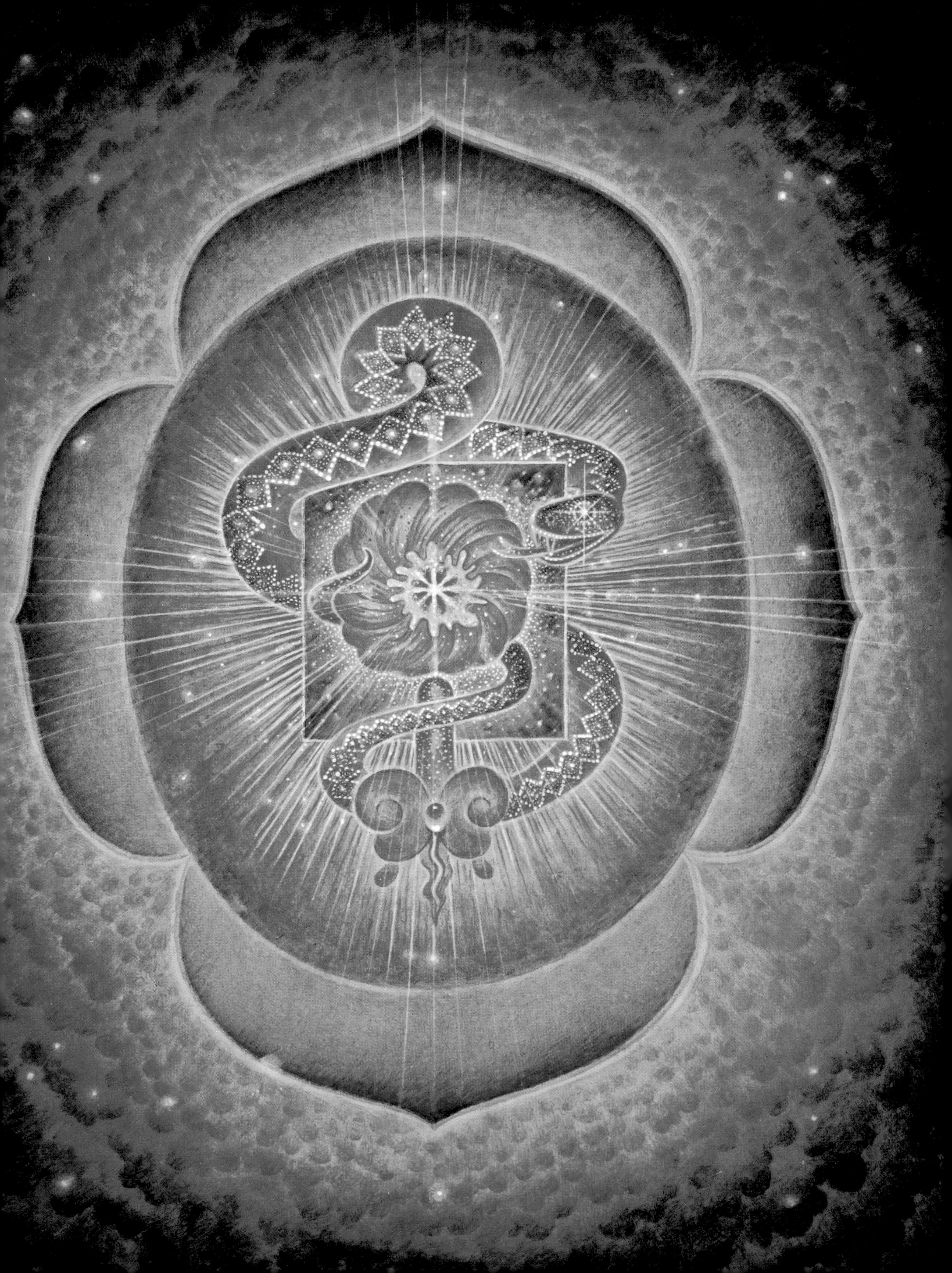

in the pink
spleen center
for purification
and health
the deep sea serpent's
rejection or protection
from anxiety
toxicity and infection

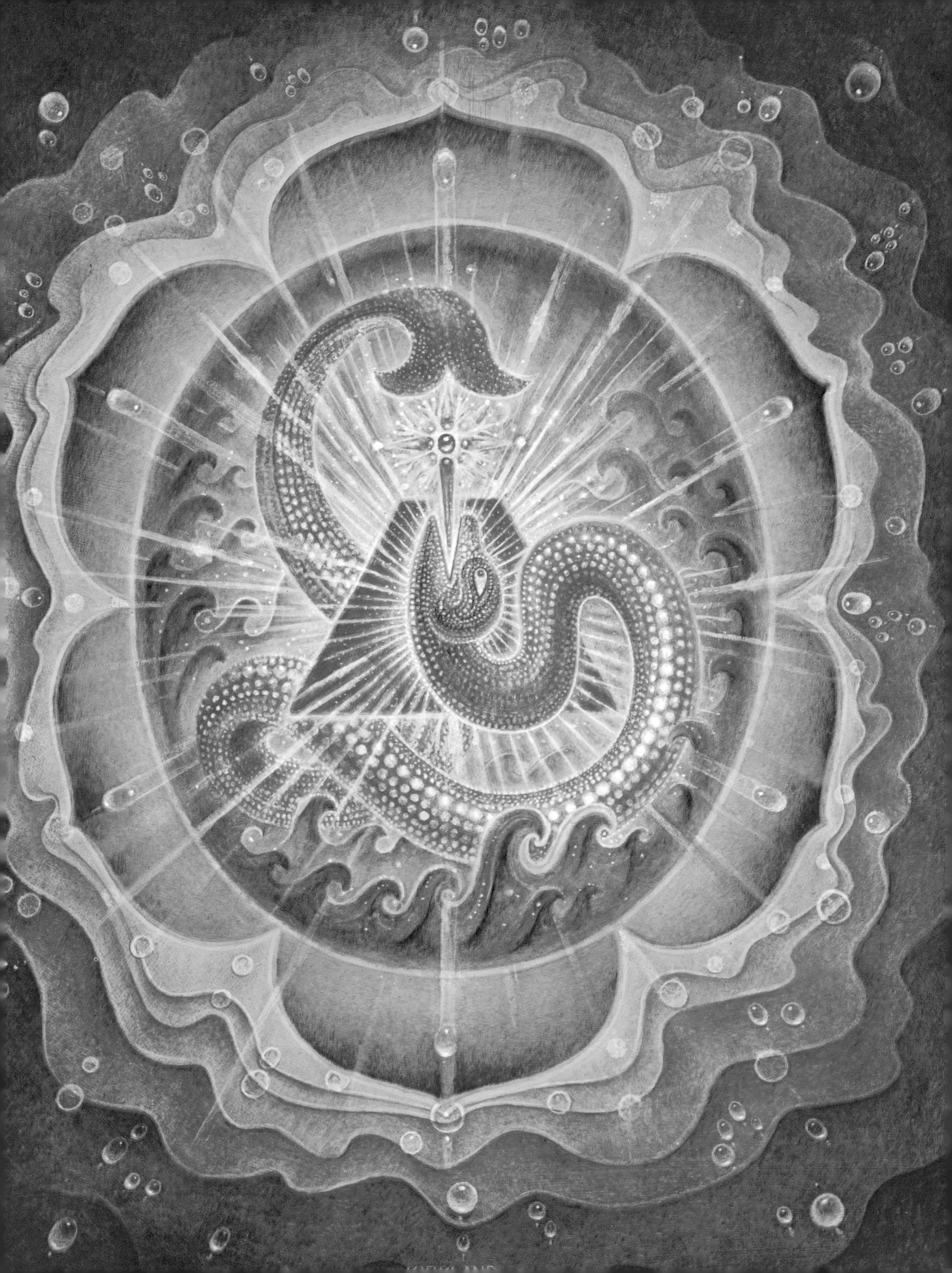

the solar plexus
fire center
for emotion and power
the green dragon
of ambition inhibition
ready to devour
or focus
open
flower

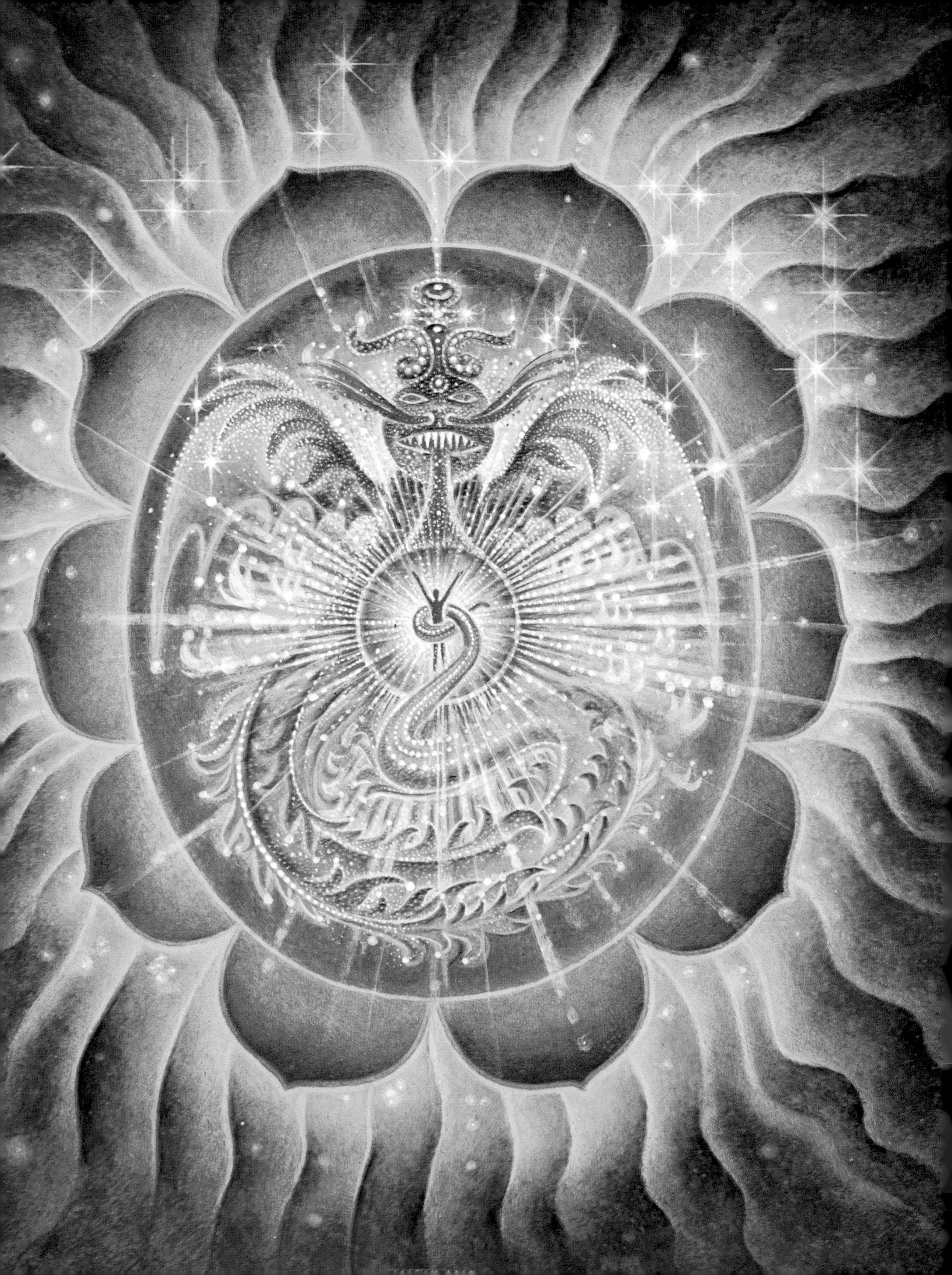

the heart
air center
for giving compassion
the snake serpent dragon
transforms
satin soft
light warms
into one
love connecting
golden sun

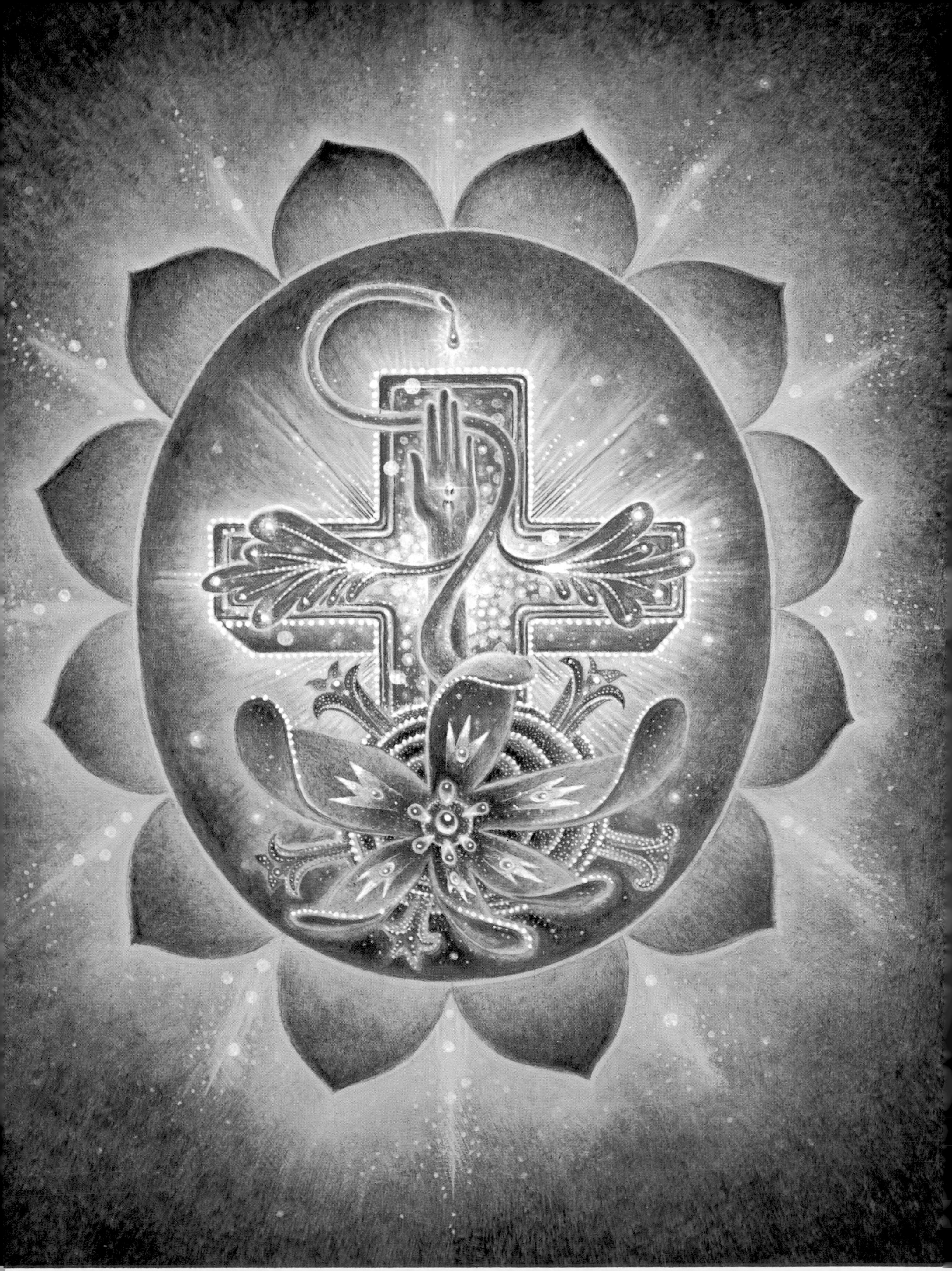

the sky blue
throat center for
creativity and
self expression
the unified
balanced
gossamer body
of elation
becomes the overflowing
cup of divine communication

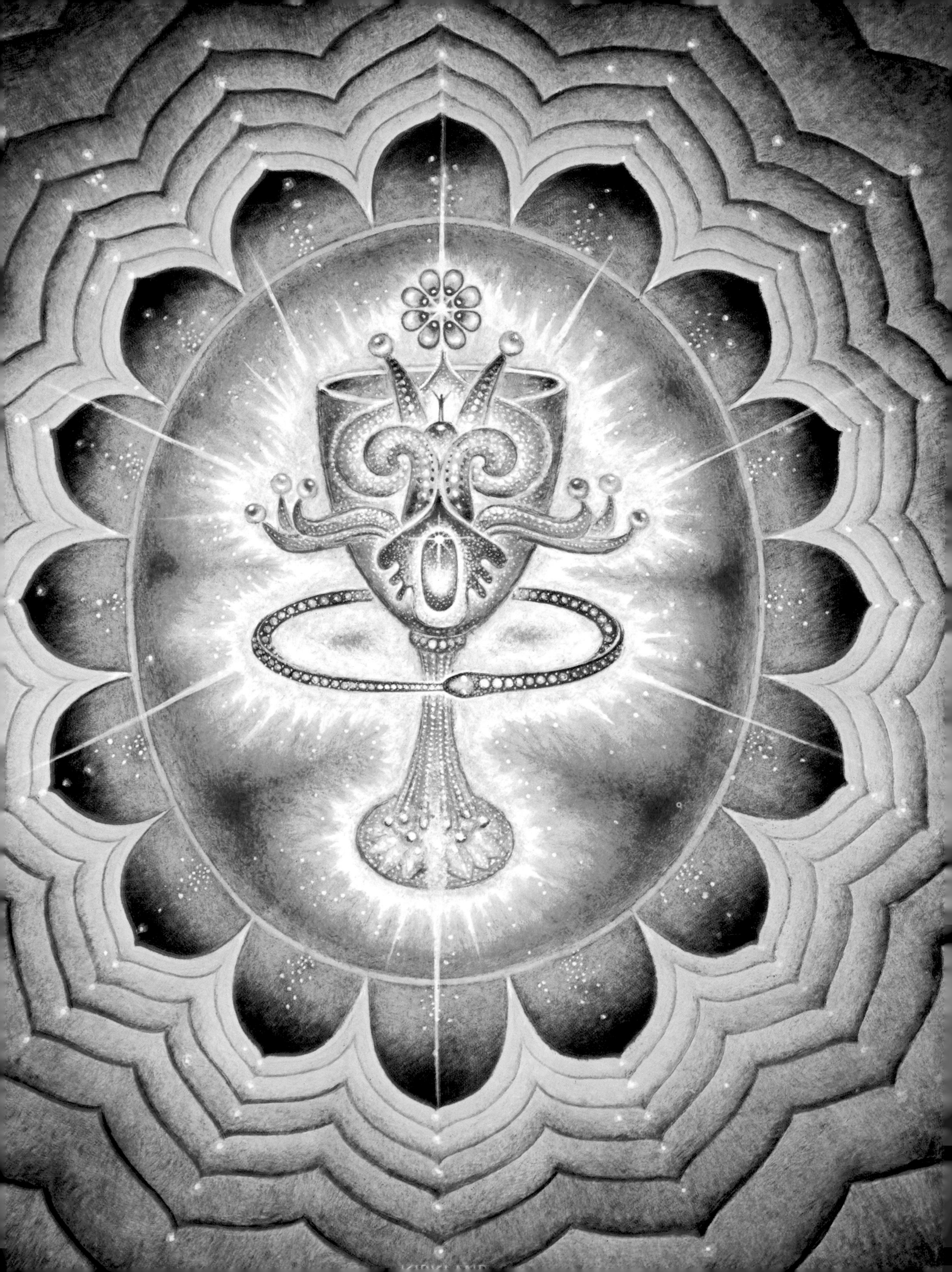

the indigo
brow center
of extrasensory
perception and
intuition
the third eye opens
in integration
ecstatic vision
and soul realization

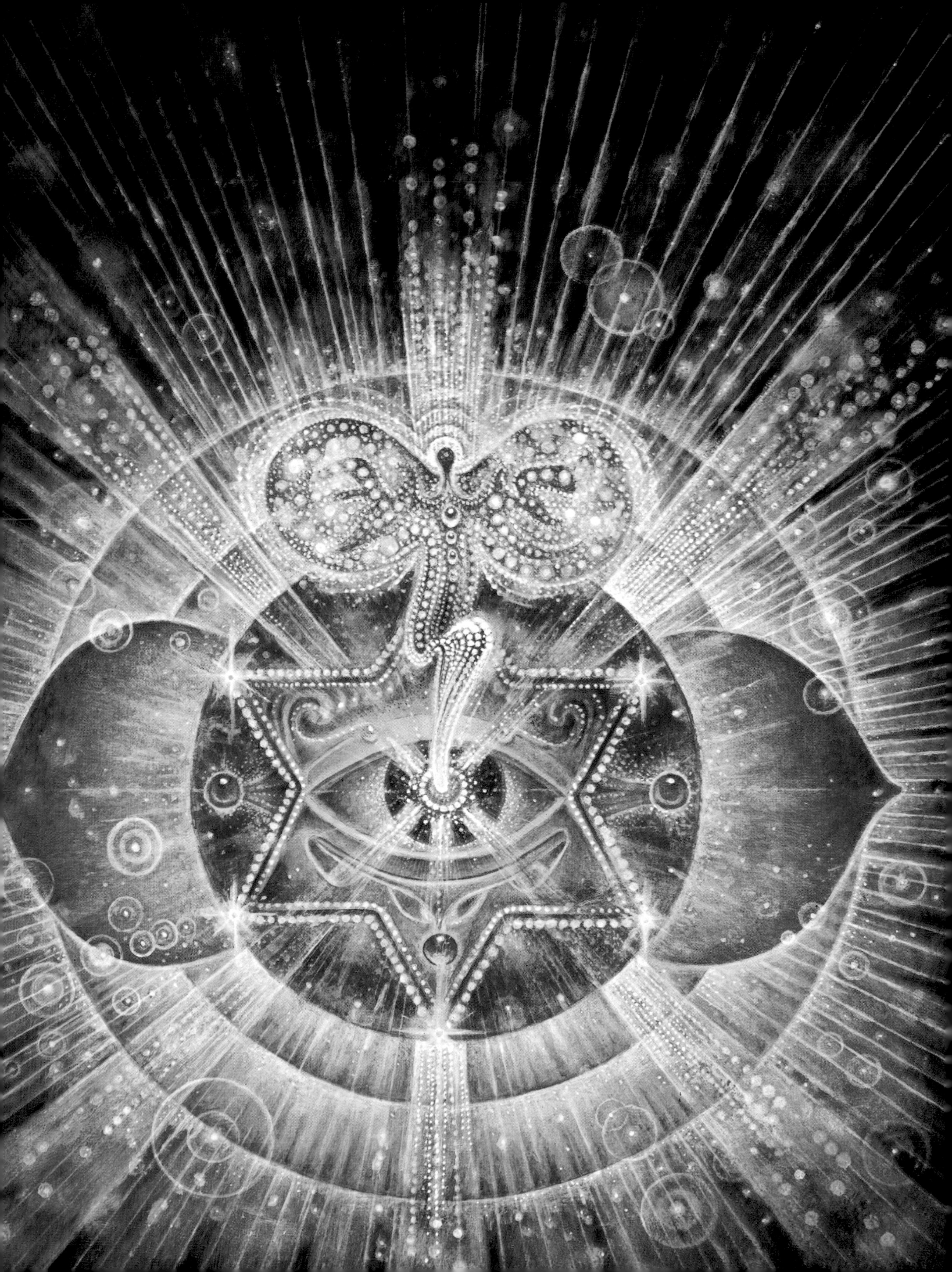

the purple
crown center
of absolute unity
silence and bliss
reality beyond duality
space
eternal

knowoneness

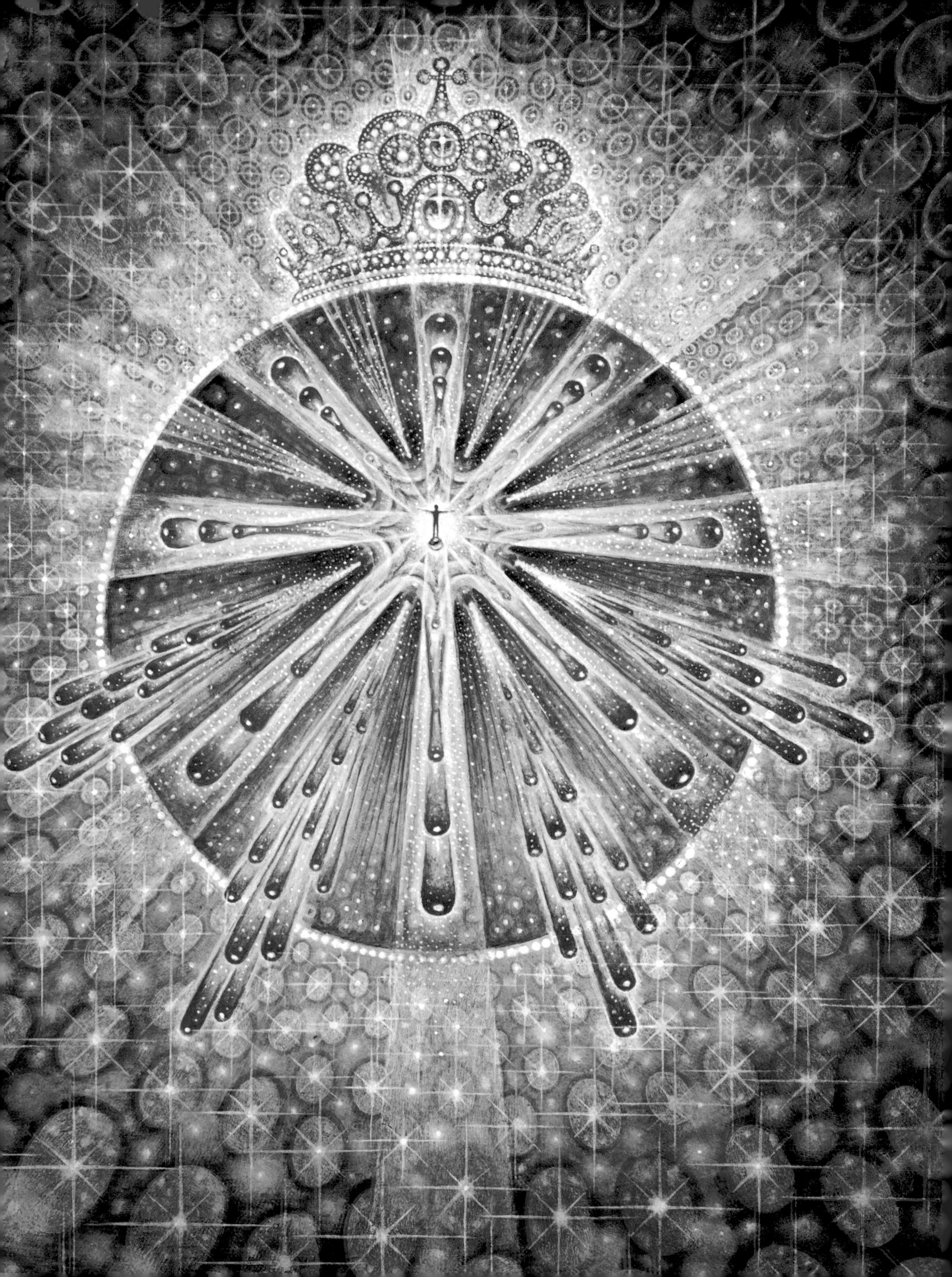

CHART OF THE SEVEN CHAKRAS

name	base center	spleen center	solar plexus	heart center	throat center	brow center	crown center
location	base of the spine	half way between pubis & navel	just above navel	center of the chest	middle of the throat	middle of the forehead	top of the head
function	sex	health	power	com-passion	creativity & self-expression	para-normal powers	libera-tion
endrocine influence	ovaries gonads	liver pancreas spleen	adrenal gland	thymus gland	thyroid gland	pitui-tary gland	pineal gland
color	red-orange	pink	kelly green	yellow gold	sky blue	indigo	purple
symbol	square	pyramid with cap-stone off	circle	cross	chalice	6-pointed star	lotus
sound	LA	BA	RA	YM	HA	AH	OM
element	earth	water	fire	air	ether		
dominant sense	smell	taste	sight	touch	hearing		
planetary influence	saturn	jupiter	mars	venus	mercury	sun & moon	
emotion	frustra-tion rage passion	anxiety well be-ing	power desire fear guilt doubt	joy grief	inspira-tion repres-sion	obses-sion ecstasy	bliss
related illness	hemorrhoids sciatica prostate ovarian uterine	diabetes cancer	ulcers gall-stones	stroke angina arthritis	thyroid flu	schizo-phrenia kidneys	psychosis

chapter 3
ENERGY BREATHING

breath is life
and change.

a basic connection
between the
inner/outer,
conscious/unconscious
ego and perfection.

a flowing bridge
between life
and death,
every breath
is rebirth,
inspiration,
for integration,
growth,
and re-creation.

a non-with-hold,
a letting go
of the old.
breathing is
a constant source
of energy prana
(the life force),
spirit's regeneration,
a continuous affirmation
of process,
flowing through,
weightless,
it can
in-lighten-you.

change your breathing
and you will
think/feel differently.

and this change
can be created by choice,
because breathing
is one of the few
bodily functions
that can be
voluntary
or automatic.

depression
is a deep pressing
against breathing.

it is almost impossible
to be depressed
when you are breathing
naturally.

the problem is
that most people
don't breathe normally,
that they
only half breathe,
and therefore
allow themselves
to be only half alive.

this is especially true
in a culture
which suppresses excitement
during sex and anger,
minimizing pleasure,
and maximizing anxiety.

play it cool
is the rule,
and so like a fool
we misrule.

know
your
inner
kingdom

rather
than
acting
like a
dumb king

for breathing is power,
full/love/health,
and well being,
freeing
vitality,
giving the ability
to use your
every facility.

reverse abdominal breathing

in the reverse procedure,
the opposite
of yoga breathing.
you bring your
diaphragm in
on the inhalation,
and let the diaphragm out
on the exhalation.
it may take
a short while
to coordinate this movement,
but the results
are worth it.

temporarily
breathing through the mouth
creates more energy,
while breathing
through the nose
brings tranquility.

slow, rhythmic breathing,
facilitates
quiet and calm,
stilling the mind,
soothing the nerves,
balancing the energy
so that
in this very moment,
the inner/outer
can be experienced
as one.

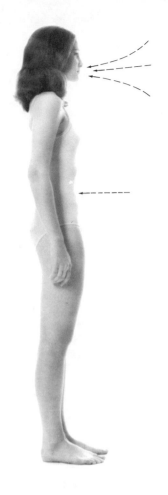

counting the breath

inhale
through your nose
to a slow
count of 8
(diaphragm comes in
on the inhalation).
hold the breath
for 4 counts.
then exhale
through your nose
to a count of 8
(diaphragm comes out
on the exhalation).
repeat this process
6 to 10 times.

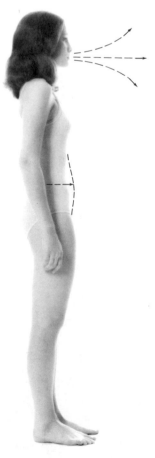

regeneration breath

above your head see
a cloud of blue energy.
as you inhale
through your nose
(your diaphragm goes in),
fill your lungs
with this blue energy.
then, as you exhale
through your nose
(your diaphragm comes out),
see a gray substance
coming out of you
and let it go into the
empty cloud.

experience
how you feel

turn the cloud blue
and repeat the process
6 to 10 times.

expansion breath

as you inhale
through your nose
(diaphragm comes in),
imagine every cell/pore
of your body expanding.
as you exhale
through your nose
(diaphragm comes out),
imagine every cell/pore
in your body contracting.

repeat this process
6 to 10 times.

and experience
how you feel

radiating breath

fix your concentration
in the middle
of the forehead.
see a radiant jewel there.
watch and observe
what happens
as you inhale
through your nose
(diaphragm comes in),
exhale through your nose
(diaphragm comes out).
repeat this process
6 to 10 times.

raising sexual energy

sit or stand
with your back straight,
both feet
squarely on the ground.
one of your nostrils
should be closed
with your finger;
(for men,
the right nostril,
for women, the left.)

inhale through
the open nostril
and retain the air;
contract the
abdominal region
several times,
then exhale
and repeat the process
3 or 4 times.

next, inhale
through the open nostril,
and this time,
contract your anus.
while the anus is held
in a gentle,
contracted state,
imagine the energy
rising from the
base center,
and see it moving up
to the heart, throat, or
brow center.
after a
comfortable retention,
relax the anus
and exhale
through the open nostril.
repeat this part
of the process
up to 12 times.

this exercise
is a precise way
to raise and transform
emotional and
excessive reproductive
energy.

so ham

_____

inhale
as you subvocally
say SO.
exhale
as you subvocally
say HAM.

so = that
ham = i am

repeat over and over
for an extended
period of time.

this mantra
is going on within you
all the time
as you breathe.

between breath

_____

sit in a
comfortable position.
allow your breathng
to take over
and watch each breath.
for a while
just observe your breathing
and allow it to
regulate itself.
pay special attention
to the pauses
between the inhalation
and the exhalation,
between the exhalation
and the inhalation.
allow yourself
to deeply experience
these pauses.

these pauses
can become
experiences
of divine,
infinite space.

you are a figment
of your figment

chapter 4
ENERGY
CHANTING

the brain,
it appears,
has two
functionally distinct
hemispheres,
each with its own
kind of process.

the left is
rational, linear,
dualistic,
verbal,
analytical.

while the right
is holistic,
intuitive,
symbolic,
synthetic.

literally branching out
of the spinal cord,
the brain's hemispheres
can be conceived of
as the tree of knowledge,
the apple of separation
in the mind/garden of eden.

another way
of seeing
these two halves
is as yin and yang
or male and female,
the primal opposites
usually unwilling or
unable to listen
to one another
because they don't
speak the same language.

the individuation process
starts to occur,
mature,
when these two sections
begin to really
listen
to one another,
start to become sensitive
to each other,
to appreciate
that they both are
part of the same organism,
that one doesn't have to be
either rational or intuitive,
hard or soft,
passive or aggressive,
separated or united,
but that they can exist
as a whole
mind/body/soul
at the same time.

this is the
inner mystical marriage.

but the ultimate goal
is beyond
even this harmonious duality
for it is the point
at the top
of the triangle.

the totality
above the two,
the three,
the absolute unity
symbolized by
the holy trinity,
kabalistically
the tree of life.

for within the spine
and the brain
is the subtle energy body
and at its core,
the chakra system,
with its roots
in the base center,
moving up the trunk,
middle of the spine-brain,
and blossoming fully
into the
thousand-petaled lotus.

here bliss sits
forever beyond all opposites

one
with
the source sun

in the peace
that passes all understanding

pure being

without thinking
just being
radiant light love,
without
a shadow of a doubt

left
right

now

the continuous
chanting of songs
focuses the mind,
elevates
the emotions,
opens the heart,
creating,
cultivating,
the relaxed delight
of well-being.

in india
it is recognized
that the supreme
manifests
in all forms,
so songs are sung
to different manifestations
as a way
of re-identifying oneself
with the divine
within,

to be

in chanting.

shri ram
jay ram
jay jay
ram om
shari ram
jay ram
jay jay
ram ommm

sing in a
joyous tempo
repeat over and over,
eventually lower
and lower
until it disappears.

sri — great master
ram — the divine inner
aspect which pervades
all beings
jay — hail
om — essence of all

i am the peace within
i am the peace within
i am i am
i am i am
i am the peace within

this song
is a way
to reinforce
your desirable
attributes
which always exist
along with their
opposites.
it's a matter of which
you choose
to continue to
cultivate
in thought, action
and deed.

i am the _____ within
i am the _____ within
i am i am
i am i am
i am the _____ within

in each verse
put in the attitude
you wish to develop
(joy-love-bliss-
courage-harmony-strength-
humanness)
each time you sing it
you may come up
with new aspects
you wish to add/encourage.

85

rama rama rama
rama rama rama
rama rama rama
rama rama
ram

rama rama rama
rama rama rama
rama rama rama
rama rama
ram

repeat slowly over
and over again.

RAMA — the absolute
which pervades all beings
within and without.

thou art that
thou art that
thou art
thou art
thou art that

i am that
i am that
i am
i am
i am that

repeat over and over
at your own rhythm
and tempo.

(tat tuam asi)
that thou art
is the basic
concept/realization
behind all
yogic practices.

govinda jaya jaya
gopalala jaya jaya
govinda jaya jaya
gopalala jaya jaya
radha
ramana hari
govinda jaya jaya
radha
ramana hari
govinda jaya jaya

repeat going progressively
faster and faster.
in the end slow down
and repeat it
very slowly.

govinda — that divine aspect
which is the observer.

jaya — hail.

gopalala — another name
for krishna the joyous
irresistible aspect
of the divine within.

rada — krishna lady love
his shakti (divine energy).

radharamana — one who loves
rada and delights in
his own pure energy.

hari — one who takes
away sorrow.

listen listen listen
to my heart song
listen listen listen
to my heart song
i will never forget you
i will never forsake you
i will never forget you
i will never forsake you

repeat over and over,
fast or slow,
loud or soft.

may the long-time sun
shine upon you,
all love
surround you
and the clear light
within you
guide your way home.

remember
you are
singing
these songs
to yourself,
your own inner being.

slow down

let up
and realize

your deeper self
is there
already

chapter 5
ENERGY SOUNDS

the universe,
your mind,
is an energy generator
or degenerator.

thoughts are energy,
sounds are energy,
images are energy,
energy follows thought.

words,
sounds, and pictures
hypnotically
create your world.

how you think
affects your body,
feelings, health,
creativity,
relationships,
conflicts,
harmony, wealth.

thinking
you are a separate i,
forms your i/dentity.
believing
you are your body,
your feelings,
thoughts, possessions,
desires,
creates a restricting
i/dentification.

you are
the master
of your mind,
but you have
let the mind
master you.

you are dominated
by all of the mind clouds
with which you identify

you are free
as the sky
when you dis/identify

for example,
the idea that you
are a certain way,
that you have
all kinds of habits,
patterns and limitations,
creates
and perpetuates
this behavior.

understand that
under hypnosis,
if someone tells you
that your finger
is badly burned,
a blister will appear.

realize
in the beginning
was the word.
words are sounds,
sound is
a condensed form
of energy.
the whole world show
is a matter of energy,
every thought
an atom
constructing
your universe.

it is as if
you are not only
the actor,
but the writer,
director,
producer,
the creator
of your drama,
creating harmonious verse
or adverse reactions
to what you experience.

it's not
what happens

but what
you tell yourself

that makes it

awful

good

or bad

but ultimately,
to use another analogy,
you are
not the screen,
the motion picture projector,
or the film,
but the light, energy,
consciousness, electricity
that has a mind
and that can
watch/run the show.

you can
keep from getting lost
by constantly
remembering
who you are,
and reminding yourself
and others
that words and ideas
are models,
relative,
relatively
incomplete concepts
rather than absolute
levels of reality.

thoughts are ultimately
just noises
in your head,
a convenient, partial map,
a finger
pointing at the moon,
but not the moon.

so watch your mind;
realize that it
is the source
of all problems,
suffering, and separation,
duality, and frustration.

observe what it tells you,
what you tell yourself,
how you react,
how these thoughts move,
creating sunny spaces
or clouds
and emotional storms.

study your mind
for a brief period
and you will realize
that if anyone else
talked to you
the way your mind does,
you probably would
break the relationship
and never speak
to him again.

so then
when you get stuck
in an inner verbal pattern,
"nobody loves me,"
"i'm no good,"
"nothing ever works out,"
"god damn me,"
objectively
hear these
negative mantras,
these destructive commercials,
without reacting
to them.

in a nonattached manner,
understand
when/where
you first heard
these thoughts,
who said them,
how limited,
distorted, momentary,
and one-sided they are.

observe how
these old tapes
affect you,
and then,
if you're willing
from a
disidentified place
acknowledge their existence,
accept them,
but refuse to
go along
or be ruled by them.

then,
if you choose,
use
one of the mantras,
affirmations, or chants
in this book
to transform
the direction
of your
thought/
feelings.

for mantras are
affirmations and chants,
words, phrases,
or sometimes
sacred sounds
that evoke
a deep reaction
in, through, out
the organism.

since sound is
a highly laser-like
form of energy,
the repetition of
these vibratory patterns
can and will affect
your inner programming.

choose/use
any or all
of the following
mantras and affirmations,
repeat them out loud
or subvocally
over and over again
as you go about
your daily activity.

be sensitive as to how
each affects you.
some will be
more rewarding
than others.
use those you find
most meaningful,
and remember
in the last analysis,
you are the
final authority.

try writing them
numerous times
on a piece of paper
or in your mind's eye,
and if you
feel like it,
make up your own mantra.

so you can,
when you wish,
learn to
leave your mind
and move
into process/
experience:

a vast open space,
and ever new place
where your total being
can be.

love wisdom power
_____

i invoke the love
wisdom and power
of my higher
consciousness
to guide me
to the right activity
in the plan

to illuminate inspire
and clarify my mind
to transform transmute
and stabilize my feelings
and emotions
to energize vitalize
and heal
my physical
and vital body
so there is a normal
flow of energy
through my being
today and everyday

to attract to me
all those i can truly help
and to attract to me
all those
who can help me
in any way

this affirmation
is best used
in the morning
or before
retiring at night.

GURU OM

gu—darkness and impermanence
ru—light and permanence
om—totality

this mantra moves you
through darkness
into the light
of all totality.

repeat aloud 6 times
then subvocally
12 times
or for
as long as you like.

OM NAMAH SIVAYA

om—all
namah—i bow
sivaya—that aspect
of the divine
who promotes
the well being
of all creatures

to be sung
or spoken aloud
slowly
and then
repeated subvocally
for an extended
period of time.

cleansing affirmation

father mother consciousness
i ask
that i be cleared and cleansed
within the pure white light
the green healing light
and the purple transmuting flame

within your will
and for my highest good
i ask
that any and all disharmony
be totally removed from me
and be encapsulated
within the ultraviolet
(black) light
and cut off
and removed from me

impersonally
with neither love nor hate
i return all disharmony
to its source of emanation
decreeing that it never again
be allowed to reestablish
within me
or anyone else
in any form

now i ask
that i be placed
within a capsule of
the pure white light
and protection
and for this gift
i give thanks

use in the morning,
before retiring
or any time
during the day
when you are feeling low
or in need of
cleansing or protection.

OM MANI PUDME HUM

om—the all
mani—jeweled essence
pudme—center of the lotus
hum—everyday level of reality

this mantra
is to bring
the supreme
into this everyday level
of fully functioning
consciousness.

repeat this chant
aloud or subvocally
for an extended
period of time.

PEACE JOY PLENTY
PEACE JOY PLENTY
THE BEING WITHIN ME
IS PEACE JOY PLENTY

repeat this chant
aloud or subvocally
for as long
as you like.

unification blessing

the sons of men are one
and i am one with them
i seek to love not hate
i seek to serve
and not exact due service
i seek to heal not hurt
let pain bring due reward
of light and love
let the soul control
the outer form
and life and all events
and bring to light the love
which underlies
the happenings of the time
let vision come and insight
let the future stand revealed
let inner union demonstrate
the outer cleavages be gone
let love prevail
let all beings love

can be used
during meditation,
as an invocation,
or validation
of your relationship
to the whole.

use the name
of divine beings

SHIVA
RAM
JESUS
BUDDHA

or attributes like

LOVE
COURAGE
BLISS

and repeat
these or any sounds
you wish
over and over
for from 5
to 20 minutes.

BE STILL

AND KNOW

I AM

repeat aloud
or subvocally
as long as you wish
with an emphasis on
still, know
and I AM.

then sit in silence
and experience
your I AM.

everything's
all
light

chapter 6
ENERGY CONTACTING OTHERS

energy is continually
created and exchanged
through contact.

beings who are open,
interact, intersect,
interfuse, interlace,
interchange, interest
more than people
are who closed/
tight/isolated.

for healthy relationship
is an inter/relationship,
verbal or nonverbal
commun/i/cation.

vitality in a flow,
to and fro,
an invisible, feelable,
connecting intercourse
between energy beings,
in various ways,
on a multitude of levels.

or for that matter,
openness can become
direct contact
with any
external/internal source,
thoughts,
feelings,
food,
flowers,
work, play.
any way,
it all depends
on the degree
of separation and unity.

at the opposite extreme,
contracted,
subject/object relationships
are unconscious,
automatic, and defensive,

closed off.

not really alive
or real
because the current,
the ongoing,
ingoing, outgoing
experience/energy/feeling
is blocked off.

the excessively
defensive individual
is buying
safety and security
at the expense
of minimizing vitality
and life.

only letting
experience be
partially
or hardly at all,
continuous contraction,
suppression, and inhibition,
a trickling expenditure
of energy
with little or no return.

contact on the other hand,
for example,
between two or more
sensitive, aware,
interconnecting beings
is stimulating,
recharging, regenerating.

a perpetual,
perpetuating glow,
a flow that moves
back and forth,
that recycles,
that nourishes.
when this exchange
becomes more fully open,
there is
less and less
sense of separation.

in stillness, activity,
or conversation,
the other ultimately
becomes the self,
and the self
becomes the other,
and what is,
is.
extra/ordinary
and zen's
nothing special.

this is the symbolism
behind tantric yoga,
for the tantric sexual union
is symbolic
of this kind
of complete intimacy.

but meditative love
is only one
of many ways,
openings, to ultimately
join with
any/every/no/thing
to become,
to be,
unity,
consciousness, energy,
fully
with one's self.

in an i-thou
flowing union,
boundaries dissolve,
and you-it are one.
whether it is contact
with the sun,
the ground,
the sea,
breathing, touching,
people, emotions,
contemplation, or action,
it's all energy.

contact is some degree
of totality,
and ultimately
it can be
at/one/ment,
communion.

you become the flow.
this point is meditation,
the experience, essence,
is tantra,
realization
that you are
love, wisdom,
all.

the perfection
that is,
aways was
and always will be.

the following
meditations
on energy relationship
in this chapter
will assist you
to move
in this direction.

until at last
there is
no ego,
no other,
just energy,
consciousness, being,
the infinite
love play
of eternal delight.

energy handshake
_____

face your partner.
put your hands out
to each other
left palm up
right palm down
below and above
your partner's hands
without making physical contact,
your hands an inch or two apart.
close your eyes and feel
the energy between you.
move your hands
up and down,
closer and farther apart
and experience the
inner/outer limits
of your energy fields.
open your eyes and explore
all the possibilities
open to you.
after, discuss the experience.

energy embrace
_____

without touching,
physically
embrace each other
face to face
and remain silent
in this position
for a comfortable
period of time.
then separate
and share your experience.

feeling/calming
the energy body
_____

have your partner
stand up
and close his eyes.
now with your hands
about one inch
from your partner's body,
explore the outline
of his energy field.
start at the head
and slowly move down,
up, and around
the neck, shoulders,
and arms,
then the torso and
upper back.
be sensitive to temperatures
and open spaces
or different kinds of
vibrations
in the field.
next do a thorough job
over the hips
and legs.
afterwards, go over
the entire body
from head down to toes,
back, front, and sides.
finish the process
by moving the hands
from the bottom
of the toes,
up the front of
the body,
over the head,
and down the back
of the body to the floor.
repeat this movement
fully, 3 times.

give your partner
a chance to experience
the results.
if you wish,
exchange verbally what the
two of you experienced
during this interaction.
then, if desired,
have your partner
do the same for you.

opening to gravity

stand facing your partner
and close your eyes.
allow each other
time to center
and then take your
partner's hands.

without moving
become aware of their
size, shape, and temperature.
then concentrate on the
energy flow between you.

next get in touch
with the energy pull
called gravity;
the energy that comes from
the center of the earth
which keeps you grounded,
from flying off the planet.
feel the force, its weight
and then
rather than resisting it
let it come into you.
open the bottom of your feet
and allow it to enter you.
see/feel it
as a golden energy
flowing through your feet,
melting all your
muscles, bones, nerves.
then open your ankles
and as it melts that area
let it move up
into your lower legs.
feel it flood your knees
and gently flow up
into your thighs.
let this flowing energy
wash into your hips,
through your hips
and into your lower
belly and back,
moving up into your
chest and upper back,
through your shoulders.

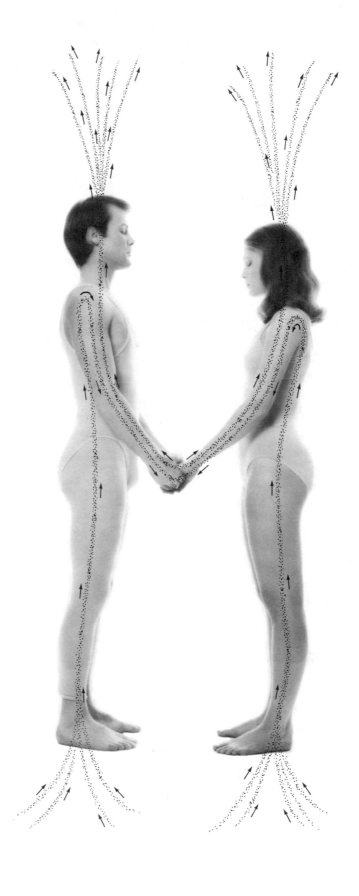

experience this energy
within you.

then let it move
down your arms,
elbows, forearms,
wrists and hands
into your partner's hands.

feel this stream
of golden energy
moving from the floor
through you,
up your body and
out your arms
into your partner's
hands, arms and body.
at the same time
experience energy
coming from your partner
into your hands and arms,
up through your shoulders
up into your neck,
jaw, cheeks, eyes, forehead,
back of the head and
out the top of your skull.
feel the energy
streaming through
and into you
from your partner
and from the ground.
hold this feeling/image
as long as you want to,
then when you feel
it's enough, let go
of your partners hands.
experience how you feel
and open your eyes.

exchange verbally
with your partner
what happened for you
during the exercise.

most of us
treat gravity
as an enemy.
in this exercise we
open to gravity
so that rather than
it being heavy,
we become light.

center touches
_____

with eyes closed,
the person to be touched
creates a 6-inch sun
6 inches above
the top of his head.
next, he arches that sun
in front of his body
to the level of
the base of the spine.

the touching partner
visualizes a sun
6 inches above his head
and imagines that
this sun comes down
between his hands.
the person to be touched
now brings his sun
from the front of his body
into the base chakra
just in front of the spine
and sees it glow there.
the person doing the touching
brings his hands
to the level of
his partner's base center,
the right hand in front
of the body,
the left hand in back
of the base of the spine.
as the hands make contact
with the body,
the toucher's sun
fuses with the sun of
the person being touched.
both partners
see their combined suns
blazing within
the first center.

after 30 to 60 seconds,
the toucher presses his hands
gently but firmly inward
and moves his hands and sun away.
the person who has
been touched feels the
effects and then moves his
sun to the spleen center
and repeats the procedure.

continue this same
balancing, energizing contact
with your hands over
the solar plexus
and both your suns
blazing there.
repeat this process
over the heart center,
the throat center,
the brow center,
and over the crown center.
when working on the crown,
stand behind your partner
and put both hands
on the top
of his head.

when you finish,
both partners
return their suns
to the point
6 inches above
the top of the head
and allow each other time
to experience
the results.

it is desirable
to follow this procedure
with a brushdown.

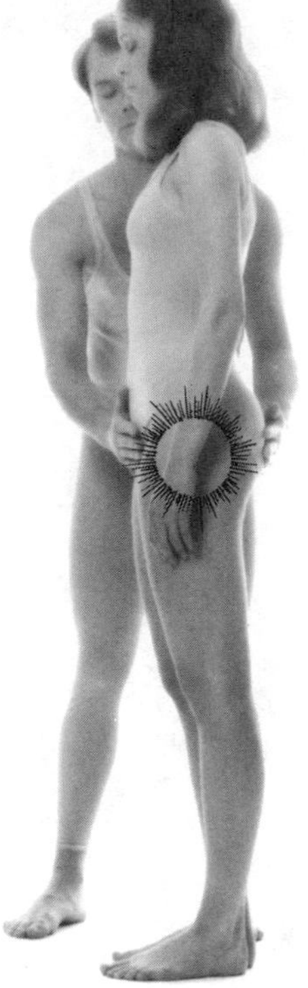

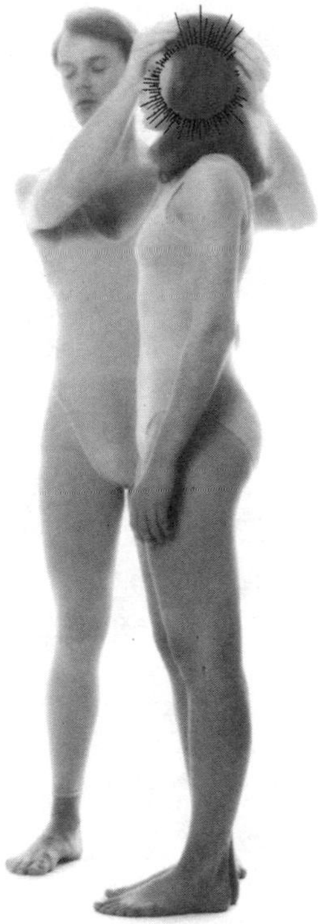

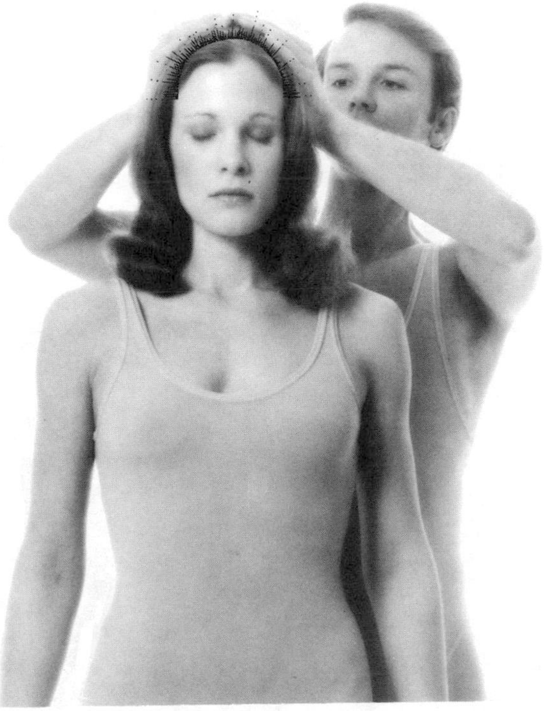

brushdown

stand behind your partner.
he closes his eyes.
put your hand on top
of his head and
stroke down the back
of his head and neck,
down the middle of the back
over the center
of the buttocks and off.

then place your hands
on top of the head again.
bring your hands
down over the outer
back of the head and neck,
down over the outer
shoulders and down the
outer back,
over the outer buttocks
and off.

place hands on the side
of the head.
gently move down over the ears
and side neck,
over the shoulders,
down the arms and hands,
over the fingers and off.

now raise your partner's arms
so they are straight out
to the side
even with his shoulders,
palms down.
place your hands underneath
his fingertips,
brush across his fingers and palms,
under his arms to the armpits
and down the side of the body
over the hips
and off.

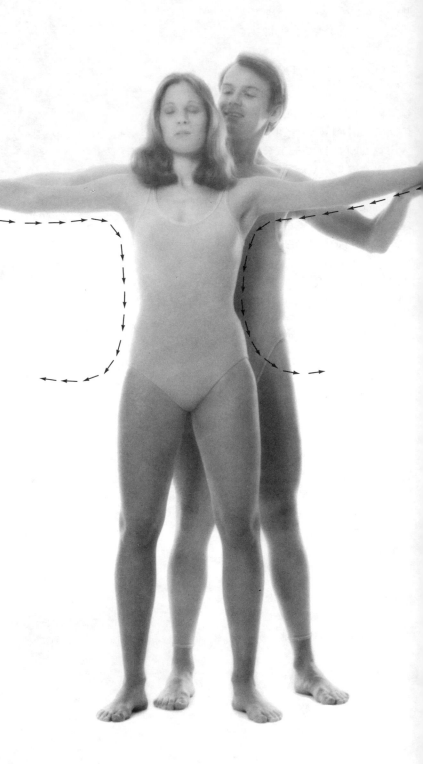

move around
to face your partner.
put your hands on top
of his head.
bring your hands
extra gently
over his face,
down over the neck,
down the center front
of the torso
to the upper pubis
and off.

place hands on top
of the outer shoulder.
bring them down
over the outer front
of the torso
to the upper pubis
and off.

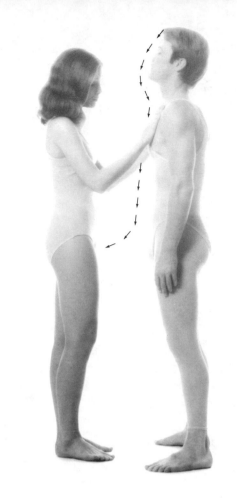

raise your partner's arms
so they are straight out to the side
even with his shoulders,
palms down.
place your hands underneath
his fingertips.
brush across his fingers
and palms,
under his arms to the armpits
and down the side of the body
over the hips and off.

move to the side of your partner.
place one hand over the center
of the upper chest
and the other hand on his back
directly behind your front hand.
bring your hands over the
upper chest to the outer shoulder
down the arms, over the fingers
and off.
do this 3 times on the left
and 3 times on the right side
of your partner's body.

next place one hand over
your partner's front left hip,
the other hand over the buttocks
directly behind your front hand.
brush straight down
over the thigh,
the lower leg,
down over the top of the foot
and off.
after repeating this motion
3 times, do the other leg.

after, give your partner
time to experience
how he feels.

repeat each
of the strokes
3 times.
don't be heavy-handed;
use a medium gentle
wisp-like stroke
with the hand flat
over the body.
let your hand take
the shape of the place
being worked on.

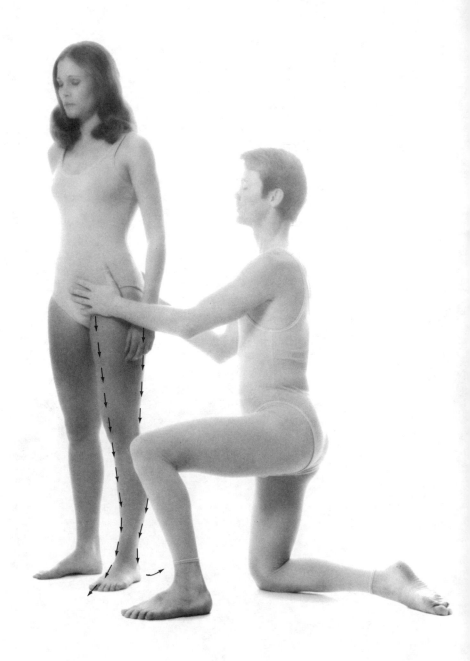

touch polarity
_____

the person
to be worked on
lies on his/her back.
the person who
will do the touching
sits in a comfortable position
at the side of the person
lying down.

first, place your right hand
in the center of the chest
of your supine partner.
let it remain there
until you feel good contact,
the energy flowing.
next place your thumbs
on your partner's temples
at the side of the head.
the fingers of your hands
touch the ridge
on the back of the skull
where the neck joins the head.
keep a good steady pressure.
after about 30 to 60 seconds
(you can sense when it is enough)
take your hands away
and give your partner a chance
to absorb the effects
of the touch.

repeat this same time sequence
after each of the following touches.

in the next application
place your right hand
over the solar plexus
and your left hand
over the forehead,
your left thumb is on
the bridge of the nose.

after following the time procedure,
move down to
one of your partner's legs.
let the top hand
rest on the upper middle
of the thigh.
the thumb and third finger
of the lower hand
touches the center of the ankle
just below the ankle bone.
after the allotted time,
repeat this process
over the other leg.

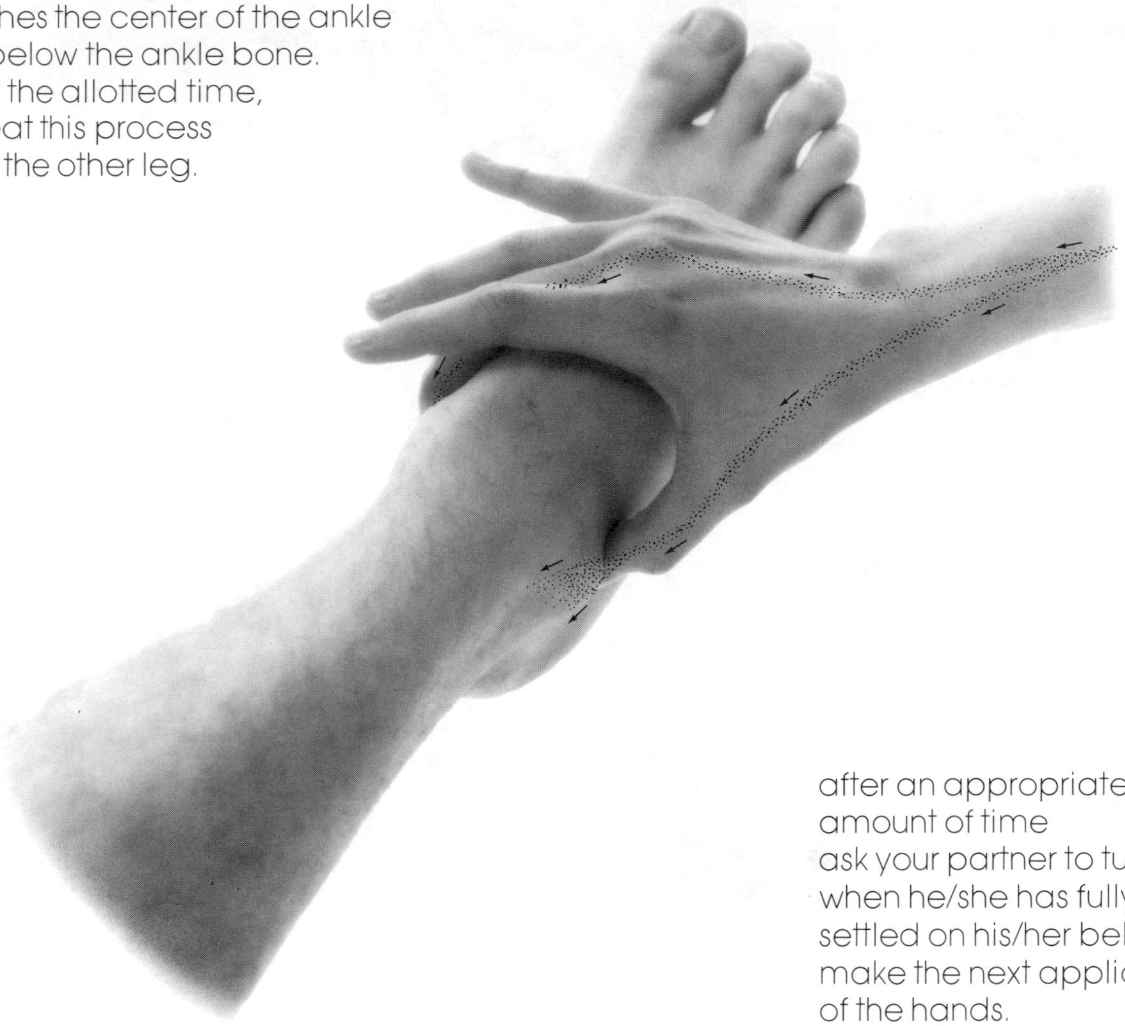

after an appropriate
amount of time
ask your partner to turn over.
when he/she has fully
settled on his/her belly,
make the next application
of the hands.
place your left hand
on the back top of the head
with your thumb gently pressed
into the opening
for the spine
in the skull (occiput).
the thumb and third finger
of your right hand
rest over two points
on the sacrum,
subtle indentations
to be found
approximately 4 inches
above the coccyx.

on the next touch
return the thumb and
third finger
of the right hand
to the two points
of the sacrum.
the left thumb and third finger
of the left hand
move to two points
on either side of the spine
just between the shoulder blades.

next move back to the legs.
let the upper hand
rest on the upper middle
of the thigh.
the thumb and third finger
of the lower hand
touch the center of the ankle
just below the ankle bone.
after the allotted time
repeat this process
on the other leg.

then bend the right leg
at the knee.
put the
ball of the foot
under your left armpit,
to stretch
the achilles tendon
and with your left arm,
massage the right calf.
with the right hand
gently press
all the areas of the gluteus.
repeat this process
over the opposite leg.
finally place the left hand
over the crown of the head,
the right hand
at the peritoneum
between the anus
and the genitals.

after, allow your partner
as much time as he/she needs
to digest this experience.
then if you desire,
you can discuss the experience
and/ or exchange roles

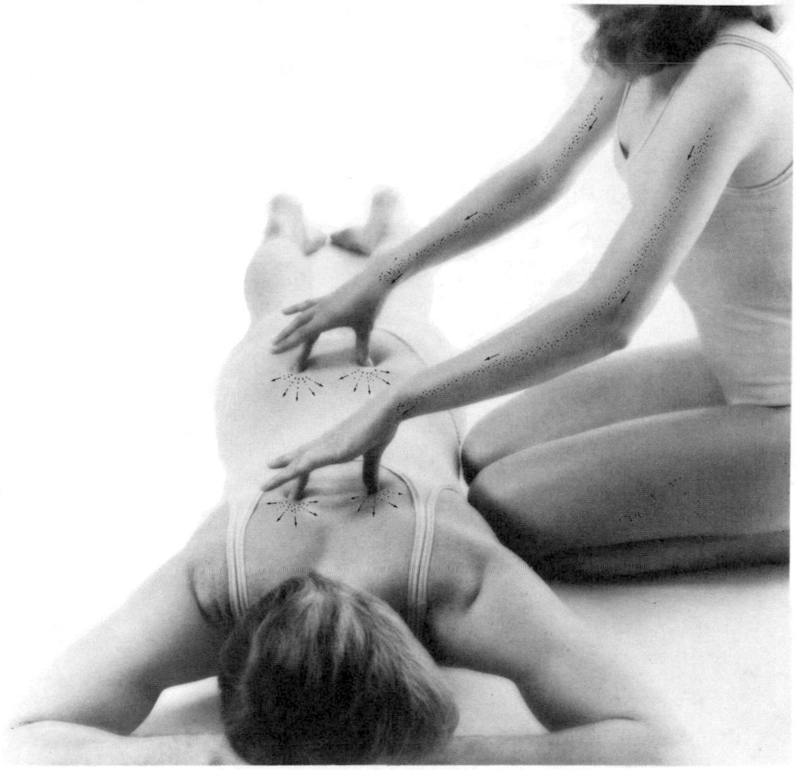

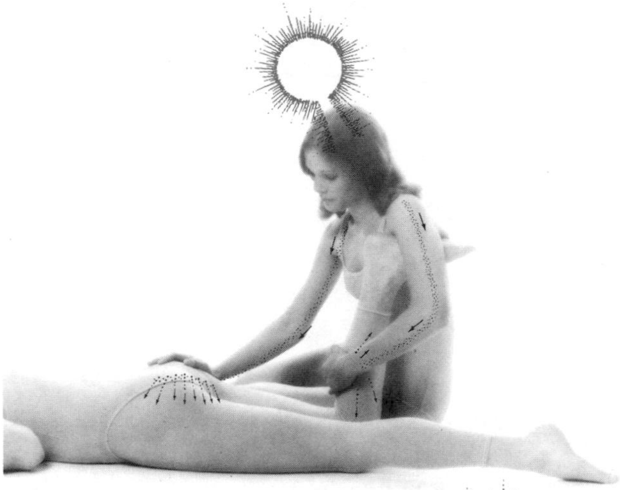

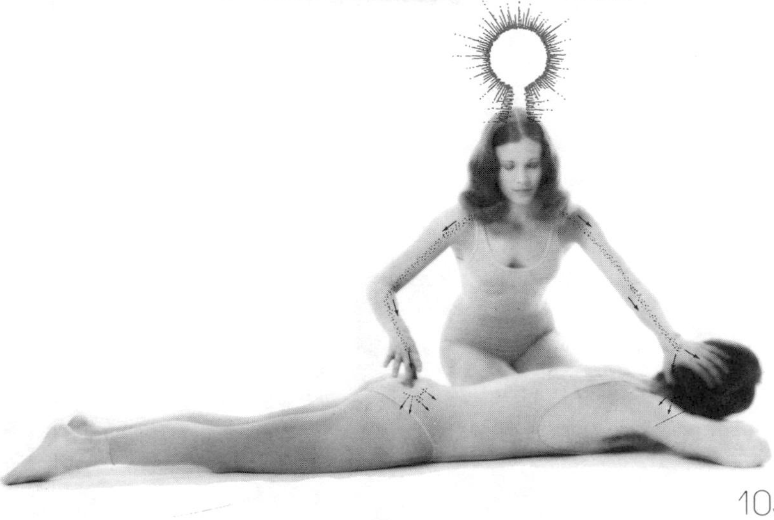

polarity chakras

have your partner
lie face down.

after allowing time to settle,
place your left hand
on the crown of his head.
this hand remains there
throughout the exercise.
put your right hand over
the base of his spine.
leave that hand there
for 30 to 60 seconds,
longer if necessary or desirable.

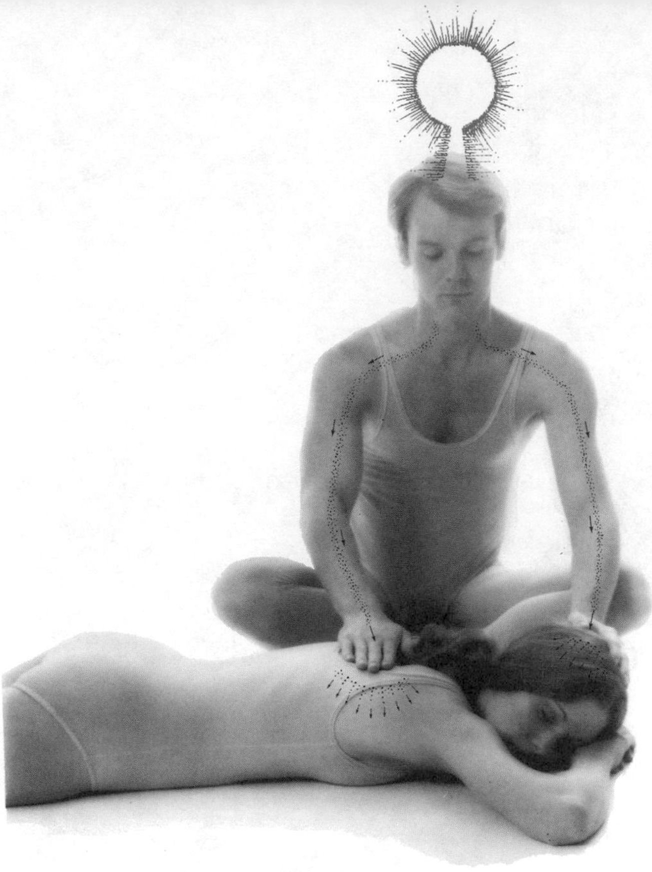

then move your right hand
over the spleen center
halfway between the pubis and navel.
after the allotted time
move sequentially to the solar plexus
just above the navel;
the heart center
in the middle of the upper back;
the throat center
at the back of the neck;
the brow center
in the middle back of the head.

now move your right hand
under the buttocks
below the base of the spine and
feel/visualize the energy
flowing freely up the spine
out all the centers
and the top of the head.

feeling/visualizing white light
on the part of the giver
and the receiver will
increase the effectiveness
of this exercise.

try combining
the exercise with
the simple polarity experience.

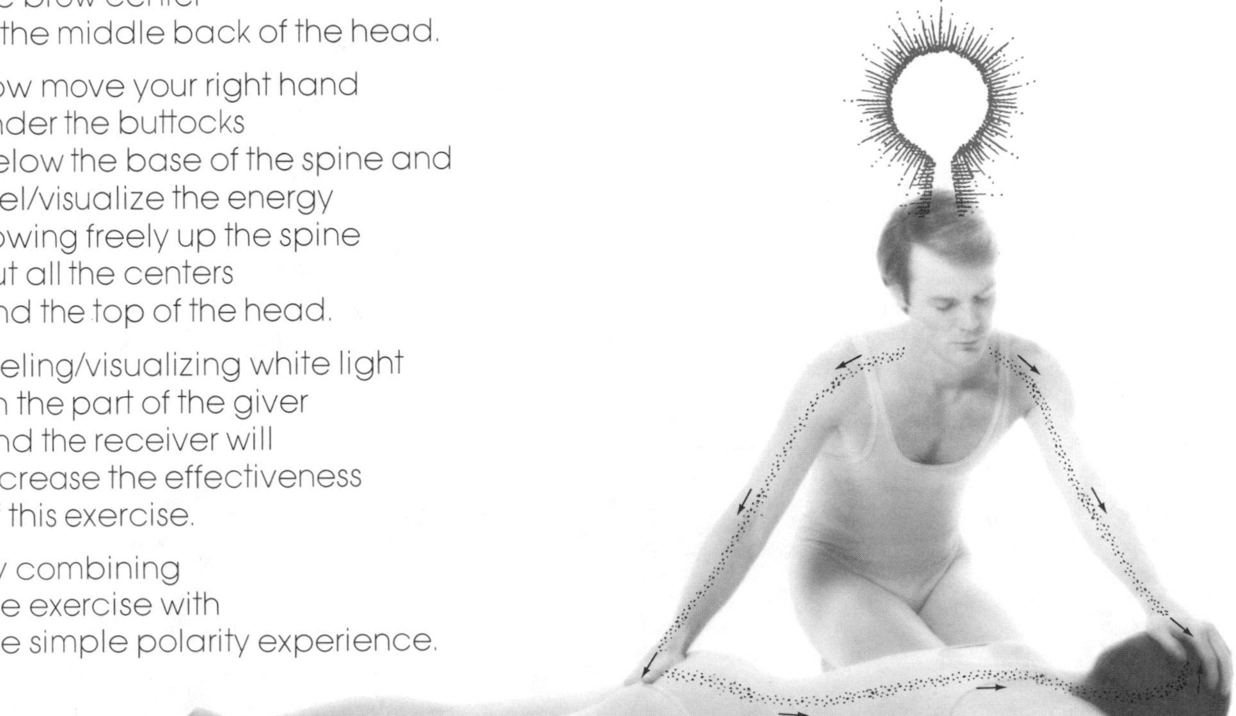

connecting chakras

sit knee to knee
facing your partner.

close your eyes and
after taking time
to settle,
imagine a white light sun
in your base center,
your partner does the same.
when this sun is
shining brightly within you,
visualize it beaming out
toward your partner;
your partner does the same.
as you continue to
shine out toward your partner
imagine/feel his/her energy
emanating toward you.

after about 30 seconds,
let this energy contact
remain on its own,
and move up to and repeat
this process in the spleen chakra.
in time move up each center
one by one,
until you are connected
in all of the chakras.
see/feel this contact,
all the centers
connected and beaming,
for 30 to 60 seconds.
then let the image fade,
experience how you feel
and open your eyes.

this procedure
can be done
laying on your side
next to your partner
in bed.

107

there's no
you or me
there's just
we
        e
          e
            e
              e
                e
                  e
                    e
                      e
                        e
                          e
                            e
                              e
                                e
                                  e
                                    e
                                      e
                                        e
                                          e
                                            e
                                              e
                                                e

chapter 7
ENERGY HEALING

health is bliss,
wholesomeness,
flowing energy,
in harmony
with totality.

a well
organized organism
works with
integrated integrity
as each part relates
and operates
with the whole.

a continuously
rebalancing,
connecting,
exchanging,
overlapping
interrelationship
with all/
every aspect of
environment/other/
mind/body/soul,
a complete whole.

healing
is the process
of un-dam-ing,
rebalancing,
and/or boosting
of the energy
throughout
the organism.

a transfer,
transformation,
or removal of energy
from one force field
or a series of
force fields
to another,
be it magnetic,
chemical, physical,
electrical, surgical,
emotional, or psychic.

for ultimately
most all dis/ease
is caused
by a blockage
or imbalance
in the core/energy body.

usually this is
brought about
because one part
of the system
tries to dominate
the organism
at the expense
of other parts
or the whole.

symptoms are then
usually the expression
of a subordinate part
or parts
that are in conflict—
that don't accept
the dominant direction,
the life style
that is
generally being pursued.

in gestalt therapy terms,
it is the classical
top dog/under dog conflict,
one part of you
is saying to
another part of you:
"you're holding me too tight,"
"you're putting me under
too much pressure,"
"stop trying to control me,"
"let me be."

a great deal of physical
and psychological distress
is the result
of these
seemingly weaker aspects
not being allowed
to really express themselves.

left with no outlet,
they use their power
to communicate
through discomfort.

at first they speak softly
through minor
aches and slight symptoms.
but not being heard,
they increase the volume
of their voice
through greater pain
and intermittent
malfunction.

if they continue
to be ignored,
they will cause
serious breakdown
or illness,
and eventually
if you refuse to
listen to them,
they will kill you.

once again,
balance
is a primary factor;
for if you either do
too much
or express too little,
and the body
or various parts,
nerves, glands,
muscles become
chronically tense,
frozen under overstress,
the flow of energy
is blocked,
and the result
is that some symptom
or malfunction appears
in a structurally weak
or symbolic area.

healing, then,
is a transformation,
a return to balance
and flow,
a continuing to
appropriately
open and grow,
to know,
to experience
your process/being.

ideally,
healing will be done
in a feeling, compassionate,
nonpersonal, objective way
where the healer
and the person
to be healed
move out of the way
and allow
the wisdom current
of the universe
to flow through them.

not acting
but having the
knowledge and faith
to allow the energy
to move through;
not creating limitations
but becoming receptive,
open channels
through which
infinite energy
is allowed to move,
to improve,
because ultimately
there's nothing to do
except to assist,
direct, and allow,
to lend a helping hand,
aiding your being
to heal itself.

now understand
all forms of healing
or therapy,
regardless of the system
or orientation, have
three basic ingredients:
suggestion, belief, and
energy transformation.

in every healing situation,
there is,
implicit or explicit,
the suggestion,
be it through
training, uniforms,
degrees, or ritual,
that the person
or practitioner
has the power
and the ability
to create a change.

second, there must be
a conscious
or unconscious belief
on the part
of the participants
that the patient
will get better.

finally, and most important,
there must be
a transfer or exchange
of energy.

if any of these elements
are missing
in any form of therapy,
usually there will be
little or no results.

in the following chapter,
we will be
primarily concerned
with self healing.
it is important
to realize,
as you do
these exercises,
that excessive skepticism
or expectations
will create minimal
results.

if you can be
open and receptive,
you will find
these different methods
for wholeness,
synthesis,
self regulation,
cleansing,
rebalancing,
and deconditioning
simple, effective
ways to erase old tapes,
to equalize the
energy organism,
to keep it clear,
in a constant state
of flowing,
harmonious wholeness
that is health
and holiness.

earth air fire water

with your eyes closed,
relax and visualize
an image of yourself
moving toward a
body of water.
have that image stop,
turn and face you.
take a good look at it.
now have the image turn
toward the body of water
and become identified
with the image.
as you move
toward the body of water
notice that
there is a large
pile of clay
as well as a
pile of wood nearby.
take some clay
and using the water
to soften
and smooth the clay,
build a statue of yourself.
it can be any size
and in any style you wish.
as you construct it,
it may change
or take on a shape
different than
what you intended to build.
allow this
unconscious process
to take over.

when you feel
you are finished
stop and take a look
at the work.
then with the water
smooth it out and
add any details or
final touches.
when you have finished,
again look at the whole statue.
now go to the wood
and begin to pile it
under and around
the statue.

then, light the wood
and watch the statue
burn in the flames.

out of the smoke,
or from the cracking statue
something desirable
will emerge
and circle above in the air.
if it is something
acceptable to you,
allow it to enter
and become
part of the image.
now see the image
walking toward you.
when it is a few feet away,
ask it to stop
and take a look at it.
observe how it looks.
see if it is different
than before,
then allow it to merge
with you.
take time to experience
how you feel.
open your eyes.

this visualization
may be done
every day.
it is a way
to integrate and balance
the 4 basic elements,
to purify your self,
to not get stuck
in any image,
to allow latent
constructive forces
to emerge.

after experiencing it
a few times
it can be done
very quickly,
without diminishing
the results.

tantrum meditation

for 5 or 10 minutes
breathe randomly in and out
through the nostrils
while walking around the room.

for 5 to 10 minutes
move around the room
in whatever manner
you are moved to.
allow your arms and legs
the freedom to take over.
allow the sounds within you
to do the same.
move as fast or as slow
as you need to,
make as much or as little
noise in whatever way
you need to.

for 5 or 10 minutes
with your arms raised,
elbows even with your head,
jump up and down,
landing on your heels.
each time you come down,
make the sound WOO.

after, take some time
to allow this experience
to settle within you.
it may bring out
suppressed feeling aspects
of chaos which
need to be let out
so that your energy
can flow free.

a way to release/relieve
tension/pent-up emotion
and deep chronic
nagging discord.

lost treasure

find a comfortable place
to sit or lie down.
close your eyes and
allow yourself time
to deeply relax.

visualize yourself standing
at the edge of a
clear, calm lake
on a warm, sunny day.
feel the peace
of the location
and the warmth of the sun.

just in front of you
there is an open boat
in the water
full of big, soft pillows.
see yourself lying down
in the boat
as it drifts toward the
center of the lake.
like the boat floating
on the water
experience yourself floating
on the pillows,
and completely relax.
when you reach the
center of the lake
imagine yourself
sitting up in the boat
and finding
a magic diamond pendant
which you put
around your neck.
it will protect you
from any harm and
give you magical powers
like the ability to
swim easily,
breathe under water
and have great strength.

now, dive into the water
and swim down to the bottom.
(remember the diamond
if you should need it.)

after a short search
you will find
an old treasure chest
containing something valuable,
a positive attribute
that you possess
but are not in touch with.
bring the chest
to the surface.
if it is heavy
use your magic diamond.
swim to the shore and
open the treasure chest.
if it is locked,
use the diamond
to open it.
if you don't understand
what emerges
from the chest,
it will speak to you
and your diamond
can help you understand.

after you have determined
what the aspect represents,
decide if you
would like to again have
this treasure as a
conscious aspect of yourself.
if this is what you wish,
stand up and face the sun.
either embrace the aspect
or hold it up to the sun.
see the part melt into you.
after you experience this union
hold the magic diamond
up to the sun
and let it merge and
become a conscious part of you.
finally, see the sun
enter and merge with you.
after, take time to
absorb this entire experience
and then open your eyes.

this can be done
over and over again
to re/establish contact
with hidden or disowned
aspects of your self.

erasing doors
_____

find a quiet place
to sit or lie down.
close your eyes
and allow yourself
to relax completely.

now, see an image of yourself
walking into a house
and down a long corridor.
you will pass 3 doors
on your right
and 3 doors
on your left.
notice there is a label
on each door to your left,
a word or two
that describes
what is behind it.
take note of each
as you walk by.
these labels are not
created by your conscious mind
but rather they are
meaningful areas your
unconscious wishes you
to explore.
now return to stand
in front of the door
which is most intriguing
or meaningful to you.
before opening the door
surround yourself
from head to toe in
a circle of white light
for protection and
then go into the room.
see/feel and be aware
of what you find
in the room
from a dis/identified
point of view.
you may find past feelings,
events, old relationships
or associations.

experience whatever is there,
no matter how undesirable
or painful
but from an unattached perspective.
watch as you allow
any emotional reactions
to take place.
stay with the experience
until all excessive feelings
have been discharged.
now bring in a bright light
to illuminate the room
allowing you to see
details that did not show up
under ordinary light.
observe/experience and allow
these situations to discharge.
when nothing new seems to emerge,
flood the entire area
with cleansing white light
erasing everything in the room.
come out of the room
and explore
the other 2 rooms
or walk over to the right
side of the corridor.
this time consciously
put a label on each
of the 3 doors,
subjects like sex, anger, fear,
love, work or relationships.
choose the one
you most wish to explore.
first envelop yourself
in a circle of white light
for protection,
and enter the room.
as you did on the other side,
see/experience what is there
from a dis/identified space,
then bring in more light
so that you can see
with clarity
all the details.

when you feel
nothing new is emerging,
flood the room
with white light
erasing everything that is there.
then walk out of the room.
(you can experience each
of the doors in turn
if you wish.)
when you feel finished
return down the corridor
and out of the house
through the door
by which you entered.
after, take some time
to digest your experience
and then open your eyes.

often during this exercise
you will see
pictures of the past,
remember old feelings
or associations.
by letting these situations
discharge without
being attached
you will finish them.

this process
can be used
to clear karma
at the end of each day
by taking your problems
or upsets
through the rooms
in the above way.

heal thyself
———————

if you have an illness,
symptom or problem
you do not understand,
find a quiet place
and lie down on your back.
close your eyes.
for 5 to 10 minutes
imagine you are lying
at the edge of the seashore.
your feet are facing
the water.
as you inhale each breath
imagine the water from the ocean
washing over and through
your body
relaxing, cleansing and
re-energizing you.
as you exhale
the water washes down
and out the back
of your body
removing all toxins,
waste and fatigue.

when you are
deeply relaxed
visualize yourself
in a clearing
surrounded by a forest.
experience the color, smell,
and feeling of the area
as intensely as possible.
then, from the trees
that surround the clearing
a figure of a person,
animal or being will emerge.
it represents
the symptom or problem.
have a dialogue with this image:
ask who it is, what it wants,
and what it can tell you
about your difficulty.

it may be mad or shy at first
and refuse to speak.
it is your task
to convince it
that you are genuinely
interested in learning
its needs.
(see if you can really listen
to what this aspect of yourself
is trying to communicate.)

ask any questions you wish
and be really open
to hearing the answers.
usually this being
is talking for a part of you
that you have ignored.
often it will tell you something
you don't want to know
but need to hear.
many times it will represent
your childlike nature
wanting you to relax, play
and enjoy life more.

whatever its needs are
see if you can accept them.
if you are willing
to do what is asked,
let the being know that.
ask if it is willing
to meet you the following day
for 10 minutes
or perhaps every day for a week.
if you make any appointments
with the figure
be sure to keep them,
or you will destroy
the relationship/communication
you have established.

when you feel finished,
thank the being for coming
and watch it disappear
into the forest.
then, when you are ready,
let all the images fade
and open your eyes.

this interaction may
not only dis/solve
your symptom
but provide you
with a friend/guide
who will assist you
in various other aspects
of your existence.

healing inside/out

_____

close your eyes
and become comfortable.

slowly scan your body
for points of pain
or excessive tension.
when you find an area
that needs some attention,
place your hand there.
experience how that
place feels.
let your hand rest there
as you begin to visualize
the color, texture,
and quality of that area.
next see an image of yourself
getting smaller and smaller
until it is the right size
to walk around inside your body.
now see that image
moving through your body
to the place
that is to be investigated.
explore that area;
find out what it needs,
what you as that image
can do to create more ease
and harmony there.
stay as long as you need to
and then open your eyes.

repeat this process
as many times as necessary,
and then if desired,
move to other areas.

visual healing

in bed at night
just before you
go to sleep
or any time
during the day,
close your eyes
and relax.

see the number 5.
let it fade
and create it
two more times.
do this same process
with the numbers
4-3-2-1 and 0.
after you have
made the 0 three times,
see yourself standing
in the center of the 0
in perfect health.
experience yourself
with as much detail as possible.
then imagine yourself
doing all of the things
you would be able to do
in perfect health.
see yourself doing
all these things as completely
as possible, see yourself
successfully and joyously
doing each task until
you go to sleep.

do not see the injury
getting better,
this gives energy
to the problem.
rather, see the healing
as already having
taken place.

you are
perfect
at this
very moment
you are perfect
and you
have always
been so
yet you go on
seeking
for perfection
because your mind
tells you that
you are incomplete.
you define yourself
as incomplete
as a seeker
and because
of this definition
you never
really experience
your real
buddha nature
buddha is
one who finds
who is enlightened
who attains
who is total
while you
live in
the constant hope
that this book
this seminar
this guru
will be the answer

there is no answer
because ultimately
there is no question
questions and answers
are the mind's game
so that you
cannot attain
it is the game
of postponement
some day
in the future
my enlightenment
will come

and so you go on
pursuing goals
desires happiness
but when
you finally get
what you think you want
that is not it
or you don't want it
anymore

here and now
in this very moment
you are one
with the sun
air ground sky sea
free
totally
completely
utterly

only you
don't believe that
you don't think
this is true
and that very you
is what keeps you
from realizing

for realization
is giving up
and down
in and out
any mental knowing
of what it's
all about

letting go
becoming the flow
becomes the glow
completely being
the son/daughter
of cosmic life
here to know
beyond knowing

it's your
forever now
perfect
self

perfection is
your very core

but you
seldom realize it
anymore

don't identify
with the changing
rearranging
outer duality

you are bliss

consciousness

love's
everlasting
reality

so breathe deep
and open
the rainbow door

enter the bright diamond
that is the other shore

dance to the inner lights
soar to the inner heights
bask in the inner delights
warm sun days without nights

in the peace within
the outer war

for perfection is
your very core

you
god
it

BIBLIOGRAPHY

Assagioli, Roberto, M.D., *The Act of Will,*
Viking Press, 1973.

Assagioli, Roberto, M.D., *Psychosynthesis: A Manual of Principle and Techniques,*
Psychosynthesis Research Foundation, 1965.

Atkinson, William W., *Thoughts Are Things,*
L.A. Fowler & Co., 1912.

Bailey, Alice A., *Esoteric Psychology: A Treatise of the Seven Rays* (Vols. 1 and 2),
Lucis Publishing Co., 1942.

Campbell, Joseph, *The Mythic Image,*
Princeton University Press, 1974.

Garrison, Omar, *Tantra,* Academy Editions,
1972.

Harding, D.E., *A Contribution to Zen in the West,* Harper & Row, 1972.

Huxley, Aldous, *The Perennial Philosophy,*
Harper & Bros., 1945.

Iohari, Harish, *Leela,* Coward,
McCann & Geoghegan, Inc. 1975.

Keges, Ken, Jr., *Handbook to Higher Consciousness,* Living Love Center, 1972.

Krishnamurti, Jiddu, *Freedom From the Known,* Harper & Row, 1969.

Leadbeater, C.W., *The Chakras,* Theophysical
Publishing House, 1968.

Metzner, Ralph, *Maps of Consciousness,*
MacMillan Co., 1971.

Mishra, Rammurti S., *Fundamentals of Yoga,*
Julian Press, Inc., 1959.

Oyle, Irving, *The Healing Mind,* Celestial Arts,
1975.

Rajneesh, Bhagwan Shree, *The Book of Secrets,* Harper & Row, 1974.

Rajneesh, Bhagwan Shree, *Only One Sky,*
Dutton, 1975.

Ramacharaka, Yogi, *Science of Breath,* The
Yogi Publication Society, 1905.

Rawson, Phillip S., *Tantra, The Indian Cult of Ecstasy,* Avon, 1973.

Rendel, Peter, *Introduction to the Chakras,*
Samuel Weiser, 1974.

"Three Initiates," *The Kybalion,* The Yogi
Publication Society, 1908.

Watts, Alan W., *The Wisdom of Insecurity,* Pantheon, 1951.